Dark Thoughts

Race and the Eclipse of Society

Charles Lemert

Routledge
New York London

For my children,

Anna Julia, Noah, and Matthew—

but especially, in this time, Noah,
who holds the middle ground

An eclipse brightening the dark sky—
Their times bent
To embrace tenderly,
Then part.

We remain,
In the spark
Of times like these.

Published in 2002 by
Routledge
29 West 35th Street
New York, NY 10001

Published in Great Britain by
Routledge
11 New Fetter Lane
London EC4P 4EE

Routledge is an imprint of the Taylor & Francis Group.

10 9 8 7 6 5 4 3 2 1

Library of Congress Cataloging-in-Publication Data

Lemert, Charles C., 1937–
Dark thoughts : race and the eclipse of society / by Charles Lemert.
    p.cm.
Includes bibliographical references and index.
ISBN 0-415-93444-3 (hc.) — ISBN 0-415-93445-1 (pbk.)
1. United States — Race relations. 2. United States — Race relations—Psychological
aspects. 3. Racism — United States. 4. United States — Social conditions — 1890–
I. Title.

E184.A1 L444 2002
305.8'00973—dc21 2002016561

Contents

Part III. Between, Before, and Beyond, 1873–2020

Dark Days, September 11, 2001

...April 15, 1865...September 24, 1869...May 18, 1896...
June 28, 1914...October 23, 1929...December 7, 1941...
February 21, 1965...December 25, 1979...
September 11, 2001...

The eclipse had been long coming. No one knew when or where the sleeping forces began their slow, certain awakenings across the face of modern hope. To a world long accustomed to the light of future things, the prospect of its loss was the Unthinkable itself. In the realm of natural things, everyone knows that according to ordained schedule the moon crosses the sun, darkening the world for a time. But no one, save those who devoutly prayed for it, was prepared for *this* dark day—a day when the most foreign of social things would slide into place, cut off the light, then remain as the uncertain order of unknown days to come.

The day itself was bright as only a freshly chilled autumn sky can be. Trees in the city parks and along the rivers winked of colors to come. What clouds there were only sharpened the glisten. From the highest towers, the westerly reaches beyond the motorways, shopping malls, and suburbs teased the inner eye. Some of those near the top were logging on to a new day. Monday's fog may have lifted before Tuesday's dawning of the days ahead before another weekend. Some may have dreamed of fresh romance in the Delaware Water Gap.

But this most American of urban vistas came, they knew, with a risk—one they could not have known was already hurtling toward them. Who among those who daily rode up to the top of the world could not have thought (at least once) of the terror the towers invited by their very arrogance? Seconds—minutes at most—remained before all reveries would be shattered beyond repair—before this improbable oak of modern vanity quaked and swayed.

The inferno rose to meet the brilliantly open sky. Some sent their parting words. Some—fewer still, but many enough to chill the bones of those who survived—measured the absurd...whether to plunge into the wounded sky or to hope against hope that man's mighty structure would hold firm against the flames.

What passed through, or over, the minds of those who leapt? Might they have seen, in the seconds before falling shuts down the last conscious thought, visions of the dark days leading up to this one that would be forever theirs?

When passing through time's sparse remains does the mind flash upon stories of fates previously escaped? Or does it embrace the blind chards of sensation? If the former, some may have seen in the past the long unfolding of this day. If the latter, they might have seen nothing more than the unspeakable glare of sunlight unfiltered except for the flames—flames that were in fact the sun's distant refraction across light years of vegetable heat upon the oily nether regions from which the fire now sprang. Light and heat embracing each other across times and distances too great to measure. Whichever it was, their day ended well before high noon.

Those who survived to live another fate were forced to face a world eclipsed by thoughts of a long-dreaded darkness no one truly believed possible. They sat, those who could spare the time from their daily round of hungry babies, in whichever corner of the globe, watching, again and again, the impossible ending—the empty skyline still bright blue, filled with a sickening dark smoke from a hole too deep to fathom.

The hole in time's space was at long last open for all to see—the slow motion aperture in the dark insides of history's camera obscura. There have been many dark days in the lives of those joined each to the others through the unfolding of the imperial modern.

April 15, 1865—When Lilacs Last Bloom'd

> When lilacs last in the dooryard bloom'd,
> And the great star early droop'd in the western sky in the night
> I mourn'd, and yet shall mourn with ever-returning spring.
> —Walt Whitman

Even when the poet is not the one falling, even when the drooping stars at night are local gods, the whole world suffers. The darkest days, it would seem, are linked to each other by a vast network of underground caves in which the very absence of light binds each to the other, day after day.

The death of Abraham Lincoln on April 15, 1865, at the moment of his triumph over disunion and human injustice, would remain as a ghostly presence in the days that followed. The American Civil War had been one of the last, and most bloody, of conflicts between the broken remains of the feudal past and the grimy wealth of the new industrial order. Just two years after Lincoln's assassination, Marx would publish his magnificent story of the origins of the capitalist mode of production in the factory system. The first book of *Capital* appeared after two decades of work that, its brilliance notwithstanding, left unanswered the most obvious historical question. *How* exactly did the feudal, with its several forms of economic servitude, give way to the false schemes of formally free but materially bonded labor markets? The *why* is easier told than the *how*. In retrospect it is obvious that the efficiencies of mass production demanded a factory system populated by pitiful laborers paid at the limit of animal survival. The *how* is a more difficult question, one readily left to the imagination.

The answer suggested by the American Civil War is too seldom considered. The old order died harshly, by wars that rent asunder the worlds as they were. The death of any enduring social structure is always, and necessarily, a figure of speech meant to soften the bloody truth. Whenever a large structuring social thing recedes into morbid injustice, thousands upon thousands of bodies, social and particular, suffer the pain upon which the new builds its beautiful towers to a future that can never be. The American Civil War was the revolution that defied the vulgar theory of revolutions. The black peasant class of agriculture workers were freed, according to the theory, but only to languish as an unattached reserve of economic misery in the South until, half a century later, war in Europe called them north to the industrial world. The Civil War itself was even odds for the greater part of its four years. In the end the industrial North finally destroyed the agrarian South—and destroyed it not because it had the stronger will or the better military genius, but because it had factories able to supply its bleeding armies.

The dark thought of human progress presents itself as the light of day. In truth, such as it is, historical time always moves through the blood soaked battlefields and the monotonously still graveyards. Social change is itself an analytic cut—a severing of a once-was in order to clear the way for a presumed-to-be. As in all such social things, race is never far behind. The terrible ambiguity of the American Civil War is whether it was, or was not, a war for the liberation of the black slaves. To say it was is to put the best possible face on the underlying history of which this war was but one instance. The modern world system was, from the first in the long sixteenth century, a death machine for those who labor in its dark exclusions. The capitalist mode of production could be said, thus, to be a system for the production of formally legitimate deaths.

Did Lincoln have to die as he did? Perhaps not. But surely he could not have endured what came after. He had lived through his own dark days in order, perhaps, to give the world the tragic figure few could ever forget—the saintly leader lost; such a one inspired not so much by the gods as by his own brooding thoughts of the needs of his precious union and the frailty of his species.

In the northern climes, where seasons change, and the dogwood and magnolia bloom late, if at all, the lilac is among the first full-blossoming bushes to follow the timid crocus and the scrawny forsythia. Whitman's metaphor for the drooping star of human hope cuts into his otherwise boisterous celebration of the new America. And that is how dark days are. Many are sun-filled, whatever their season. The gleaming light draws the eye and stirs the heart toward the realization that as the lilac fades in time, so too do the heroes for which they stand.

Dark days are something else. They may slip from conscious attention. But they are always there, waiting to spring forth, to set the brilliance in its place.

September 24, 1869—Black Friday

At first, when any of them is liberated and compelled suddenly to stand up and turn his neck round and walk and look towards the light, he will suffer sharp pains; and the glare will distress him, and he will be unable to see the realities of which in his former state he had seen the shadows.

—Plato, The Republic

The masses live in the tiresome regularity of dark days. They beg and poach what scraps of food and fuel can be had. The fortunate few, who live in the light of relative luxury, are the ones more inclined to identify this or that day as "black." For them, the blackest days are those when the money markets crash. Black Friday, September 24, 1869, was the day the price of gold collapsed, leaving those with a stake in its market ruined.

Truth be told, Black Friday was far from the worst to come. It would not be until 1873 that the panic would spread to all corners of the economy, to set off the spiral of the long depression of the 1880s. As with every depression since, America's troubles partook of the global. Though on the surface, Black Friday was unrelated to the economic dislocations caused by the collapse of the South's economy, the connection is plain enough to see. America was largely preoccupied by Reconstruction for a good decade after Lincoln's death. At the very least, Black Friday led to the panic of 1873 which, in turn, led to the collapse of the Freedman's Bank in 1874—thus ruining the economic chances of the nearly four million freed men and women. By the election of 1876, when political compromise entailed the withdrawal of Federal support for the emancipated millions in the South, Reconstruction itself collapsed. And thus began the restoration of the feudal ghost of the American South that would be the specter of what would come a century later for all colonized peoples around the world whose own languid ghosts would haunt their false freedoms from white rule. When the colonizer offers the hand of generosity, the other hand is still in his pocket, counting the costs. When Black Friday fell, late in the 1860s, it was merely a question of time before America's white colonizers would, for all intents and purposes, abandon the black freed people to a fate no better than their West African cousins after Belgium and England and France were forced aside in the decolonizing struggles of the 1960s.

Still it is the white bankrollers of the colonial system who declaim their economic misery as *black* days—as, that is, a darkening of accounts wherein they deposit their moral responsibility for the grief upon which capital wealth is extracted. The truly darkest day then was not September 24, 1869, but March 2, 1877, when political compromise handed over the South, once again, to the now broken, but determined, heirs of the plantation system. The gold market would recover in time, but the market in human labor would languish for the most desperate for a century and more. Thus, one could say, as did W. E. B. Du Bois, the first honest historian of Reconstruction, that this truly was, more even than 1848, the beginning of the global struggles between the capital class and the mass of industrial workers. Blacks from the American South would gain some measure of economic dignity only two generations later when the Great War of 1914 would end the flow of European labor to the American North, thus to open the pathway north for the grandchildren of the first freed men and women to the passing glories of the Harlem Renaissance, made possible by their integration into the industrial order.

Whites of means, with all our well-bleached moral priorities, think of threats to our markets as the darkest days. The colonized people in their several colors—apart from not having been in a position to name any day black or any other shade—are not known to have thought of March 2, 1877, as one of their dark days. It was a day dark in its consequences, but otherwise a day marked by little more than white folks doing what they had always done. Whatever their political allegiances, generically liberal whites tend to express their faith in humankind only when their market positions are secure. The political economy of European Diaspora morality may be said, therefore, to be a willingness to help the poor on the remains of capital gains. Trickle-down is at the essence of liberal morality. It is, no other word will do, a *niggardly* sort of generosity—a morality founded in the white projection onto the other of the shadows that cheapen its inner soul. No one enslaves, by whatever means, without *feeling* the moral effects of their actions. This is why a mere analytic approach to social history and theory will never get at the truth of social things like these.

Is it not apt, therefore, that one of the earliest systematic meditations on the nature of intellect referred to the metaphor of the cave? Quite possibly better than anyone since, Plato described the first dawning of thought itself as peeking out from the shadowy cave. The light of thinking the eternal truths, he said, was at first painful to those who had only known the shadows. The liberation of the mind is *always* painful. The tragedy of the culture of the West is that thought itself came to think of thinking as painless—as the easy course to progressive truth that trashes the harsh realities to the Unthought. A Buddhist will tell you otherwise. Sitting for days and months waiting for the light to dawn is as painful as bowing five times daily to Mecca. When, in Plato's words, the seeker stands up, stretches his neck, turns to the light, "he will suffer a sharp pain, and the glare will distress him." Whites, whatever their allegiances, are surely distressed by what they see when those enslaved according to their alleged races come out into the light of their freedoms. They suffer to be sure, but the harsher pains may be in the legs and backs of the colonizers who must, as Aimé Césaire has said, rethink the entire colonial system—that is: rethink a world that was itself based on light thoughts and now, at the moment of the passing of the old order, turns out to be dark as hell.

No wonder they would enforce, or at least abide, the system that was ordained from Black Friday on—the system that would replace the legal slave with the virtual slave in the comic name of Jim Crow.

May 18, 1896—The Colored Race

> *I've known rivers:*
> *Ancient, dusky rivers.*
> *My soul has grown deep like rivers.*
> *   —Langston Hughes*

When, on May 18, 1896, *Plessy v. Ferguson* was handed down by the Supreme Court of the United States, the system that had prevailed in fact since 1877 was given the full approval of law. Separate but equal (where the separateness was discerned in a single drop of blood) was nothing more than the glare of white law upon the reality of black suffering. Just as the European laws doing away with slavery established the artificially free market in human labor at the beginning of the industrial order, so *Plessy v. Ferguson* had the effect of legalizing the system under which freed men and women were bound over to an economic system that was free in name only.

In his dissent, Justice John Marshall Harlan said of the Supreme Court's majority opinion: "Everyone knows that the statute in question had its origin in the purpose, not so much to exclude white persons from railroad cars occupied by blacks, as to exclude colored people from coaches occupied by or assigned to white persons." *Everyone knows* is among the more powerful of locutions. It makes its appeal, not just to common sense, but to the hard truths that *everyone* pretends not to know. Justice Harlan spoke to the essential dishonesty of much more than the opinion of his colleagues on the bench. He spoke of the dishonesty of the system itself, beginning with its willful violation of the expressed purposes of the Constitution of the United States. The very system Lincoln glorified as having been conceived in liberty was called out as the bastard it was and would remain.

We peek out from our caves, endure the pain of the glare, and then so accustom ourselves to the light that we forget from whence we came. Is there any person born of woman who did not come from the comforting warmth of the dark amniotic seas? Plato's figure of the cave is, of course, a displacement of the truth of the human origins. We come kicking and screaming into the light of day, which, for the longest while, is both painful, and to be avoided at all costs. The newly born sleep on, when they are not sucking and pissing, to hold on to as much of the maternal cave as they can. If this then is the originating desire, is it not obvious that we all continue to look back to the warm comforts of the shadows?

The differences among us—differences described by the plentitude of racial theories—are differences not in the primal desire but in the ways society sorts us according to the analytic truth of our relations to the shadows. Some, thus, are said to be creatures of the womb—or if not elemental and fetal in their natures, at least more like lower mammalian critters than the truly human. Others, thereby, say of themselves that they are critters of the light, thus of a higher order of being for having stood up, turned their necks, and left the cave that no one ever leaves behind. The grave is the womb to which we return, as the pyre is the warm heat of the maternal bodies in which we first experienced any human sensation at all.

It is said that human blood, like the amniotic fluids, has nearly the same proportion of salt as do the seas from which all creatures crawled in the days before the light was cast upon the surface of the earth. Human being, as it came to be supposed in the modern era, is thus the very essence of the analytic divide upon which thinking itself is founded. Everyone knows, of course, that enlightenment is a metaphor. But for what? For the shear brilliance of the clear and distinct idea? For the gods whose spirits are customarily represented by fire? Or, more probably, for the human urge to escape the origins of our bodily natures? If the last of these, then the strange logic would be that the human is never fully human until it defines for itself the social space of its own consciousness, which is, in effect, the space of light analytically cut off from the eternal darkness that now and ever will be everywhere at once. Death, like the shadows, is (as everyone knows) the final return of all to the One. We in the privileged strata of the European Diaspora ward off death's inevitability by producing a worldly home of pure light built on a foundation that hides all the dirty secrets in the hellish subsoil. Race, then, is the analytic cut by which the purportedly special humanoids assign the inferior social positions to those who must become the bearers of the secrets they hide in their own dirty basements. We are all black. Every birthday is a dark day on which one is reminded of the uterine comforts lost until the final return. Everyone knows this to be so, which is precisely why whites among us invent social compositions like *Plessy v. Ferguson* as ways of saying it isn't so.

We all swim in the seas and rivers. We all have known rivers. But those who have been assigned to this-worldly caves are the ones who know them best. The rivers ancestors drowned in trying to cross over to freedoms are the ones that compel a soul to run deep. We humans can only get deep in the soul if we swim in our own blood. Those whose blood was spilled to make the modern world know this best. Those who had it built, and prospered because it was, are the more shallow as a matter of course. No one who is not from those who had to swim in the bloody rivers could possibly know the truth of social things so well. They thus remember their Black Fridays while forgetting the days their class darkens for others—days like May 18, 1896, when they invented "colored people" as legal beings cut off from the law by the law itself.

June 28, 1914—Black Hands and the Great War

> *The offing was barred by a black bank of clouds, and the tranquil waterway leading to the uttermost ends of the earth flowed somber under an overcast sky—seemed to lead into the heart of an immense darkness.*
> —*Joseph Conrad*

I never knew why, sometime after 1910, my mother's mother left some far Balkan outpost of the Austro-Hungarian Empire. It may have been because of the trouble brewing in Serbia. As today in the same region, political unity was a fragile thing. Trouble rode on the wings of death—literally in the case of the Black Hand separatist cause that fought for Serbia's unification with Bosnia-Herzegovina. Black Hand stood for unity or death.

Sunday morning, September 28, 1914, the Black Hand assassinated Archduke Franz Ferdinand and his wife soon after they arrived in Sarajevo by train. Thus began the First World War in Europe, the war still known as the Great War because with it the violent twentieth century began in earnest. From 1914 on, the world would enjoy no more than occasional relief from war or the promise of war. In effect, though surely the Great War would have been incited by some other incident, one can say that September 28, 1914 was the dark day on which the black hand of death visited the most terrible of human centuries.

Hence the irony that the century when modernity blossomed with its scientific, artistic, cultural, and technological promise would be also the most violent—the brightest flower of human progress brought forth by the black hand of death. Literalists will quibble that centuries do not begin in off-years like 1914. But even they, when they are serious about history, would have to admit that, as the hopeful 1890s that followed the end of the long depression gave way to the twentieth century, it was already clear that deep in the soul of the modern world there was a darkness that led nowhere.

Some have called Joseph Conrad's *Heart of Darkness* the prophetic novel of the century to come. It could also be said to be the European counterpart to an American classic that appeared in 1903, the year after Conrad's novel. Both took the dark veil of race as their theme, though each looked in a different direction. Where W. E. B. Du Bois's *Souls of Black Folk* remained notoriously optimistic about the future of black people in America, Conrad's *Heart of Darkness*, a story of the setting sun of European grandeur, was a stark look into the darkness of the white soul.

Heart of Darkness begins with Marlow telling his tale aboard a yawl anchored on the Thames at London, then the greatest by far of the world's cities. Conrad begins much as he ends,

> In the offing the sea and the sky were welded together without a joint, and in the luminous space the tanned sails of the barges drifting up with the tide seemed to stand still in red clusters of canvas sharply peaked, with gleams of varnished spirit. A haze rested on the low shores that ran out to sea in vanishing flatness. The air was dark above Gravesend, and farther back still seemed condensed into a mournful gloom, brooding motionless over the biggest, and the greatest, town on earth.

Such was Europe before its Great War—a luminous space, peaked with varnished spirit—a haze of vanishing flatness—a mournful gloom, brooding.

Where Du Bois in *Souls* pronounced the problem of the twentieth century the problem of the color line, Conrad wrote the recurring story of the century as the problem of the dark heart of the white world. This surely is why his story of Mr. Kurtz deep in the dark of the Congo is retold so often, mostly notably in Francis Ford Coppola's *Apocalypse Now*—where Vietnam takes the place of the Congo, and the arrogance of American military prowess is crippled as was the capital avarice of European greed for the Congo's natural wealth. Du Bois, the American Negro, wrote from black to white and ended his book with a seldom-read benediction, a sort of mock prayer:

> Hear my cry, O God the Reader; vouchsafe that this my book fall not stillborn into the world wilderness. Let there spring, Gentle One, from out its leaves vigor of thought and thoughtful deed to reap the harvest wonderful. Let the ears of a guilty people tingle with truth, and seventy millions sigh for the righteousness which exalteth nations, in this dreary day when human brotherhood is mockery and a snare. Thus in thy good time may infinite reason turn the tangle straight, and these crooked marks on a fragile leaf be not indeed.

They are words not exactly upbeat, but they look to the future and appeal to the better soul of the white world. Conrad, the European white, looked into the dark where, in the end, Mr. Kurtz's last words bless the terrors to come, "The horror! The horror!" He ends the book, much as be began it. He is back on the Thames, his story over. In the time of its telling, the sun has set, all light gone from the sky: "The offing was barred by a black bank of clouds, and the tranquil waterway leading to the uttermost ends of the earth flowed somber under an overcast sky—seemed to lead into the heart of an immense darkness."

The difference between white Europe on the eve of its Great War and black America on the eve of its migrations north is all the difference in the world. What, again, was "great" about that war, which by contrast to wars to come, was anything but a *world* war? It was the magnitude of its effect on the exuberant hopes of nineteenth-century industrial capitalism. Though many great and affluent moments would come again, most immediately in the roaring twenties, never again would the spirit of capitalism be able ever to deny what "everyone knows"—that the evil in the jungles has to do with a darkness covered over by the world's greatest towns. It was a darkness that would fall again, and again.

October 23, 1929—Black Thursday

> *In the middle of life's journey, I found myself in the darkest forest.*
> *I had lost my way. Oh, how impossible it was to understand.*
> *The wood was rugged, wild, and terrible.*
> *Even now, I tremble with fear at the very thought.*
> *Is is so terrible that even death is not worse.*
>   —Dante, *The Inferno*

Recovery from the war of 1914 was strong, especially in America. The Treaty of Versailles in 1919 was, however, a fragile accord that would not hold the peace in Europe even for the decade of the Jazz Age. For centuries, poets like Conrad and Dante had dreamt of dark times amid life's journey—times when death was all about, ever to return.

Just after the Great War, in 1921, William Butler Yeats lamented the darkness that would drop again, the beast as dark as death that was slouching toward Bethlehem. The next year T. S. Eliot's *The Waste Land* opened with the eerily familiar line, "April is the cruelest month, breeding/ Lilacs out of the dead land. . . ." Eliot's lines are so well known as to be trite, save for their curious quotation of Walt Whitman's allusion to April's dark day when the lilacs last bloomed. To this American in London, Europe must have seemed especially wasted by the war, and particularly so by one fleeing the vulgarities of the new America. But to Yeats, a descendant of Ireland—that is, of black Europe—the dark war was not a question of Aprils past, but of the brooding cloud over the heart of a darkness covered by twenty centuries of stony sleep. Such a terror does not pass lightly away.

The dark day of the crash of 1929, Black Thursday, came a decade after the end of the war. Jazz suited the twenties. Like no classical form, not even the requiem, jazz plays lightly upon its own fugue lines. No other musical form, save perhaps hip-hop at the end of the century, would be quite like it—measured fragments, borrowed from folk rhymes. The twenties, in the European Diaspora, were an age that prospered on the thinly veiled prohibitions against the underlying river of darkness.

Jazz, with its roots in the African-American South, traveled north in the teens with the new industrial workers. In the twenties in New York, whites traveled uptown to Harlem to enjoy their first open tastes of black culture.

The formal prohibitions on hard drink sent whites in America underground where, out of the glare of moral rule, they found profit and pleasure. In their slumming in the dark world, they enjoyed a brief descent in an exotic world, where, like jazz, the individual must improvise against the common score.

Thus it is remarkable that so few of those ruined on Black Thursday were able to learn from their visits to the colored world any of what might have allowed them to improvise a deeper social form suitable for depression and war. Instead, throughout the European Disapora, they reverted to the heroic ideas of modern culture—escaping the effects of Black Thursday only, and again, on the wings of war and death—wings that fluttered as never before over the whole wide world.

December 7, 1941—The Day That Will Live in Infamy

The Buddha has no doctrine to convey.
The truth is ungraspable and inexpressible.
It neither is nor is not.
                    —*The Diamond Sutra*

Franklin Delano Roosevelt's denunciation of the Japanese attack on Pearl Harbor was, hard to deny, just and inspiring. Still one wonders to what degree it occurred that this was the first—and would be, for the longest while, the only—direct attack on America by a people outside the European Diaspora.

"The date that will live in infamy" began President Roosevelt's address to the Congress of the United States the day after the attack on December 7, 1941. That evening he would address the world by radio beginning with a recitation of the history of international aggression since 1931, when Japan invaded Manchuria. "It is all one pattern," he said, referring equally to Italy's and Germany's aggressions in Africa and Europe, as well as Japan's in Asia and the Pacific. War was declared on Japan on December 8th. Three days later Hitler and Mussolini declared war on the United States. Then began the first, truly world war of the twentieth or any other century.

Roosevelt's radio address on December 8, 1941, ended with the speech's only, and oblique, reference to the evident racial differences at work in the pattern of evil against which he declared war: *"And in the dark hours of this day-and through dark days that may be yet to come-we will know that the vast majority of the human race are on our side."* On that dark day, "race" was still commonly used in its now archaic sense as a generic for "the human." This was still a time when *the human* was itself as much a construal of the universal merits of the European man as a narrow biological classification. To refer to the human race in those days was to refer to a universal principle that applied in fact only to the super-ficies of all humanoids—to, that is, the enfranchised ideal white man. All others were understood to be copies of the original. Even white women of the European capitals were thought to be in drag, their votes and minds considered the mere imitation of the rights and convictions of their men.

The war against the global pattern of evil would yield more than one unintended consequence. One, of course, was that it was the motive force that led to recovery in time from the collapse of 1929. Another was that America's reliance on women and blacks in the war effort began an unraveling of the social basis of the European ideal that would come, slowly at first, after the war and the search for the normal. Hence the curiosity that the lagged time recovery of America, first, and Europe, after, settled into a largely fabricated and short-run fiction of the normal life as heterosexually coupled, well housed and convenienced, prosperous in all things mechanical and electronic. The truth of the post war normal proved to be ungraspable and inexpressible, neither real nor false. Hence it happened that the normal that sought to send women back home from the factories and the resistance movements was, ever after, a cover for the experiences of the previous quarter-century. Likewise, what was remarkable about the first victory of colonized people over the white colonizers is that it would come in 1947, so soon after the end of the world war, and with such relative ease. In India, Britain simply gave it up with a grace that showed it had taken to heart Gandhi's famous retort of years before that "Western civilization would be a good idea."

There would indeed be dark days a-plenty after the day that would live in infamy. India's peace with Europe would be purchased at the cost of perpetual war. The condition for peace in South Asia was the creation of Pakistan with its perilous borders on Afghanistan and the Islamic world. And, in 1941, few would have anticipated the series of decolonizing adventures that would alter, for better or worse, the global pattern between the white and colored peoples—and not the least in America where Gandhi's principle led to racial confrontations.

February 21, 1965—The Bullet It Was

And among the signs of God
Is showing you lightning,
Occasion for fear and hope . . .
              —Qur'an Surah 30

One day late in the 1980s, I was looking for an apartment to rent in Cambridge, Massachusetts. One of the many I looked at seemed familiar somehow, as though it were haunted. I was shown through the entire place. I didn't know why I knew I didn't want to live there. Then, upon leaving, as I stepped from the porch, the ghost rose up. This was exactly where I had stood when I heard the news that John F. Kennedy had been assassinated in

Dallas—November 22, 1963, a good quarter century before. The house had changed hands and was much the better for it. Though I had suffered fits of loneliness there during my graduate school days, what came back to me was the ghost of a dead president.

Why is it that we remember where we were on our darkest days—or, suppose that we remember? Perhaps by bringing them into the frame of ordinary life we aim to dull the pain.

The selectivity of human memory is itself the strongest case for the arbitrariness of dark days. None of the dark days that had preceded this one in the near full century since Lincoln's assassination would prove to be dark in and of themselves. What we remember is always a secondary revision, not so much of the objective reality of this or that day, but of its emotional value to us and our kind. For many, a far darker day in objective fact would be February 21, 1965—two years after the president was murdered, and three years before his brother and Martin Luther King, Jr. would die by the same sort of black hands.

On February 21, 1965, Malcolm X was gunned down by agents of the Nation of Islam, from which he had been exiled since his remark on the murder of President Kennedy. He had said, late in 1963, no more than what he had been saying all along—that the white world is violent, that the murder was, thus, no more than the chickens coming home to roost. If anything, the remark was tame when compared to his most famous speech in Cleveland in April 1964. In "The Ballot or the Bullet" he had declared the American dream a nightmare. But, more terrifying yet to whites was his rejection of the then already fading non-violence of the black civil rights movement. "I am not an American." Hence, the ballot was meaningless. Though he did not himself urge violence as the principal means, he did promise that should whites not change their ways racial violence would likely be the bitter fruit of their violent system. Malcolm's speech ended with a challenge to President Lyndon Johnson:

> Tell him, don't wait until election time. If he waits too long, brothers and sisters, he will be responsible for letting a condition develop in this country which will create a climate that will bring seeds up out of the ground with vegetation on the end of them looking like something these people never dreamed of. In 1964, it's the ballot or the bullet.

In February 1965, Malcolm died by the bullet. No one had really expected President Johnson to heed the warning. He was already too preoccupied with the war in Vietnam. Just two weeks before, the president had ordered the bombing of North Vietnam that would require the troops on the ground, and the burning of the jungle—the war that would be Coppola's *Apocalypse, now and then.*

In what remained of the fabled 1960s, Americans at home and abroad would die in urban turmoil as well as the war. Yet, even today, no one knows, or will ever know, the final tally of the Vietnamese who died just as senselessly as the Americans. February 1965 would be the dark days when death by the bullet would become the norm that for years to come would truly make the American dream a nightmare, and nowhere more so than for the poorest, consigned to life in its impoverished cities.

Ironically, Malcolm's fate at the hands of the Nation of Islam was sealed by his own visit in 1964 to Mecca. There he experienced Islam firsthand and, to his astonishment, realized that the Muslim world came in all colors, including white. In the few months that remained to his life he became, if not exactly a man of racial peace, a man who grew to reject the race hatred of the American Nation of Islam in the name of the racial harmony of the more worldly Islam.

He who had been for American whites a lightning, an occasion for fear, has since become, as much or more than the others killed as he was, a symbol of hope. Islam is based on a God so true that fear and hope are no more susceptible to distinction that are being and non-being to the Buddhist.

December 25, 1979—Slouching Toward Kandahar

I am death, shatterer of worlds
Annihilating all things.
With or without you, these warriors
In their facing armies will die.
                    —Bhagavad Gita

William Butler Yeats' *Slouching Toward Bethlehem* (1921) became the title of Joan Didion's stunning political and cultural exposé of the underbelly of the American Sixties. The figure of Bethlehem as the birthplace not of hope but of the deadly beast was never more apt than in 1968, when America's war in Vietnam collapsed upon the racial troubles everywhere at home. While the war of 1914 was the first of two in which America would begin to think of herself as the savior of the European Diaspora, the war of 1965 in Vietnam would be the first in which the Americans would be mercilessly beaten back. It was a defeat that would deepen the darkest broodings of the Western World.

Just as the Americans did not take the lesson of the French defeat in Vietnam, so the Soviets ignored the lesson the American defeat might have taught them. On Christmas Day, 1979, Soviet troops entered Afghanistan to fight a war they would lose in more ways than one. After ten years searching for a mythical beast in the Afghan caves and mountains, they withdrew, and with their admission of defeat, so too fell the Soviet Union. By 1991, only the Americans stood as the king of the cold war mountain.

Then, and a decade later still, in 2001, just weeks after the fall of the World Trade Center towers in New York City, the Americans entered Afghanistan. Everyone knew—or at least thought they knew—that this would be another Vietnam, that the Americans would be frustrated, as had all previous invaders of this land on the edge of Pakistan. Then, against all popular wisdom, by December 7, 2001, the American Marines were poised to enter the Taliban stronghold at Kandahar—exactly sixty years to the day after Pearl Harbor. They sought the source of terror, who escaped a while longer to live another day in still darker caves above the plains of southern Afghanistan or who knows where?

The eclipse—of which the fall of, and from, the New York towers—had become a sign, if not a symbol, was widely taken as a call to arms in a war against terror. What it started, however it turns out, was a search for a beast that will never be born to daylight until the dark thoughts within the white soul are embraced for what they are.

Part I

The Beginnings of a Millennium, 1990s

One

The Coming of My Last Born, April 8, 1998

We arrived just too late. The drive to the hospital in far, rural New York State took five hours. She took but four hours and fifteen minutes after the first signals. When we came to the viewing window we immediately saw the most newly born. It had to be her. She was freshly bathed and wrapped, ready to meet her parents. Or, so we thought. Something was not right. The nurses were a little too preoccupied with the particular knots of professional care, not enough with the bond waiting to be tied.

What could be wrong?—every parent's first worry. Through the glass veiling the space between our all too well attended child and us, the light began to dawn. I said it first, "Geri, she's black!" She said, "Charles, get over it. She couldn't be." I said (or now think I said), "I know black when I see black." We both laughed, as much to bridge the distance the nurses were keeping, as to replay a family joke. In that instant we found our child, and each other as never before.

What was wrong, of course, had nothing to do with our baby's health. What was wrong was wrong in the hearts of those good nurses. In the sheltering recoil of this newborn, they felt the pressure of the world's confusions. They were frightened for the unnamed baby they held through her first moments in this world's time. They feared we would turn our backs and run. Such a fear is not easily passed over in this world. They did not know us, but we all in this mixed company of black and white strangers knew the facts perfectly well. They are facts white couples seeking to adopt must consider. They are facts neither right nor just. In the political economy of adoption white babies are harder to find, while babies of color often do not find a home. Our struggle was, however, even more complicated than normal. The family joke is that, against the one-drop rule of American race relations, I think of myself as black.

It is not easy living in whiteface. While some whites still get off on blackface, *no* one respects my kind of minstrel. Still, I am what I am; or, I should say, I am what I have come to understand myself to be. On the surface I am the whitest of white boys. Inside, where few others can see, I am the grown son of a black mother who, important to say, was the grown daughter of a white woman. Florence, my black mother of the spirit, was the spiritual daughter of Sarah, a white lady of the South. I was Florence's by adoption of a kind, as she had been Sarah's. We both had genes and biological parents reasonably suited to our complexions. Florence, of course, had less choice in the matter. Because of this she understood me as no one else did. I was the only one in my immediate family who had the least inkling of these strange facts. My now long dead bio-parents were not ever alive to the possibility. My brother does not to this day feel as I do. Though he too loved Florence, he does not think of her as mother. We cannot, therefore, talk openly about the play of race in our "family of origin," as the demographers say.

My family, such as it was, was not all that exceptional, except perhaps in the way Florence and I came to understand what we felt but for years could never talk about. Why her teachings affected me one way and my brother another is, I suppose, part of the unsolved mystery of these relations. In my day, and still now, these truths are everywhere guarded by a code of silence. I claim no credit and deserve none. Perhaps I talk too much.

Without a conscious effort, it is impossible to be an American—to be, I imagine, any sort of Diaspora-European—and not know black. The world of all our fathers, over the last twenty or so generations, was black from the first. Black was our economic, if not our genetic, family of origin. In the New World it became, against every prohibition, the strongest chord of our family songs. Still, few sing along. That so few whites do does not mean they cannot, or should not. Never mind that we all do it badly. We can do it because, however we present our racial selves, we whites could not talk or walk as we do without the centuries-long ministries of colored people. The European-Diaspora began in the search for China; but it was built on the shores of West Africa. We white folks would not have been who we chose to be without our own quest for and conquest of brothers and sisters whose differences we alone came to insist upon.

For us, the adoption struggle came to an end like a flash of lightning in a storm-darkened sky. We were safe before we understood the dangers. On a spring vacation trip to Maine, the cell phone rang. "If you can be in Elmira, New York, next Tuesday at 12 noon, I may have a birth mother for you. She is due in a few weeks. She wants to meet you at her doctor's office." We had just crossed over into Bath, Maine—the town where I had spent my summers. Just off its northern shore, in the Kennebec River, there had been a wonderful island summer camp. In my day it had served the well-off. Today it is broken down, grown over. Still, I loved those summers before the dawn of differences. They had given me a sense of myself apart. Their only fault was this impossible-(then)-to-define feeling that something or someone was missing from the fun. You might say, I was born again in the very town where, more than half a century later, Anna Julia was born to Geri and me.

At first, Anna's birth mother wanted no more than a single visit with us. We were formally invited to the last sonogram before delivery, and nothing more. On these sparse terms, we came. It was, of course, awkward at first. None of us would have been there had there not been secrets to keep. Still, in the surround of photographs of hundreds of babies, a warm society grew by the kind indifference of the office staff. They accepted us for what we three so obviously were. In the practice of obstetrics, adoptions are the normal accidents. When our turn came to enter the darkened chamber, we were silent in the glow of the screens. The technician traced Cathy's very white belly. The pictures made no sense to me. We looked for a sign.

In the silent breech, Cathy said, "I can't say why it is, but for the past two weeks the names Julius or Julia has been coming to me." Geri and I froze for a second, only we understood. We had long since decided that our baby, if a girl, would be named "Anna Julia." When we explained this to Cathy, our deal was sealed. Her religion was of a more fervent, evangelical kind than our well-practiced Episcopalianism. Still, no tongue in that room had to confess that we all thought some spirit was moving events along beyond our control. Religious people mean something quite definite when they talk about their holy spirits. But, anyone can believe, as we did, that when things get out of hand some other unseen force is at work.

Only then did the technician say, "I think I see a vulva . . . there, right there. I think you are going to have a girl." She did not qualify the "you." We were all proud parents in waiting.

And so we were committed to the events that led us to a hospital far away where the nurses would shrink before the world reality they held in their arms. They could not have known that the single feature they feared would cause us to bolt was nothing to speak of against the mysteries of life that had led Florence to Sarah and me to Florence; then to Matthew and Noah and their mother; then, at time's remove, me to Geri; then us to Anna—the fourth generation of an improbable line. We were the white parents of, as the rule allows, a black daughter. She was two weeks late, not two weeks early. It took a while for us to relieve the dark thoughts of the hospital staff. We left for home the next day. The papers signed. The bills paid. The contract fulfilled with fresh affection.

Never after would I think of the "social contract" as Rousseau's abstract dream. We had made a deal that gave birth to a whole new social order. It was a very small order, but one as well sealed as any world could be. It was not until then, so late in the reading life, that I truly understood a philosopher's desire to trace everything back to its social origins. The social contract never works when people think of themselves as the analytic agents of its origin. It only works when, and rarely, all those party to it realize that they, like their children, are all, and necessarily, adopted.

The darkest thought in the modern world is that its vaunted solitary souls would lose their rights before the collective agreements that allow the company to move ahead. The deeper truth of the social contract is that the Anna Julias of the world remind us who we are. Whenever we live well with others, we do by affirming the first fact of human society. In the best sense of the word, a good society is one in which all who come to it, by whatever means, accept the social whole as their adoptive mother.

The Eclipse of Society, 1901–2001

Times change. A century passes. People think the turning of a calendar means something. They are optimistic. They are not entirely wrong. For one thing, at the end of the times just passed, there was reason to hope that people were willing to give up at least one bad habit. Some did. Others did not.

The bad habit is that of cutting living things into their supposedly elemental parts. This habit is practiced in many different fields, some quite basic to ordinary life. Anna Julia, when she was just shy of two years, played with blocks. She stacked them to compose surprisingly complex structures. Once built, she delighted in smashing her structures apart. So far as I could tell, she enjoyed the tearing apart as much as the building up. The parts and the wholes were to her objects of equal interest. What makes you think is that she took so much pleasure from breaking up her funny little structures.

Building things, including human relationships, not to mention tall buildings, is a well-considered good; destroying them is anything but. Most people share this basic value. Just the same, you will find a number of educated people who never question the idea that tearing things apart can be a good thing when it comes to a practice they call "analysis." Analysis is not necessarily evil, of course. Many who do it, do it to do good. What they don't seem to understand is that breaking things down into parts is risky business. Analysis is, at best, a destructive act taken on the gamble that the breaking apart is a necessary means to an ultimate good. It wasn't always that way.

Once upon a time, the word "analysis" had a better meaning than the one it came to have at the end of the twentieth century. Before analysis became a habit of thought, "to analyze" meant, oddly, "to unloosen." It is one thing to unloosen a complex structure in order to examine its parts; quite another to smash it to pieces. Unloosening, like dissecting, occurs in the most ordinary of circumstances. Anna Julia, again, but well before she played with blocks, enjoyed the contrasting shapes and shades of a mobile that hung above her crib. This was before she could build or smash apart anything. She would stare for good long stretches at the slowly turning black and white triangles, squares, and trapezoids slowly floating above her. She wiggled and giggled at them, as if to enjoy their naturally unloosened configurations. I supposed that the structure of her world was so impossibly complex that its shapes and colors were beyond her. Yet, she studied her little world's parts as the surprising whole they were—loose, dangling, and just out of reach. It is comforting to think that taking pleasure at the unloosened parts of an impossible world might be more basic than tearing it to pieces.

Still, one must wonder how it happened that analysis came to be a tearing apart rather than a gentle unloosening? How did this habit of mind and science, as of ordinary living, come to assume its now primary dictionary meaning:

> **To analyze:** to dissect . . . to examine minutely, so as to determine the essential constitution, nature and form apart from extraneous or accidental surroundings.[1]

The word is anything but innocent. To be an analyst of any kind, to analyze in any of a number of possible ways, to dissect the parts of some essential constitution, whether scientific or practical—is to cut wholes into parts. The assumption is that the solution to a problem is found in the pieces not in the situation as it lies. How can it be that so violent an act as cutting things up is the way to truth or progress?

It is very well known that the twentieth century was the most violent in human history. From its beginning around 1914 until the beginning of its end around 1989, the twentieth century suffered wars and civil violence without relief. With rare exception all this violence grew out of struggles over presumed rights of various kinds—rights to lands, to religious shrines, to territorial prerogatives, to shipping channels, to oil fields and drug markets, and the like. The wars were fought, for the most part, in the name of national, ethnic, class, or racial honor. Whether global or civil, whether between nations or clans or street gangs, they were over who had what right to which part of some whole. They were, like all wars, analytic struggles. Those who fought them were willing to die in order to claim some material or moral part of a global whole.

As Walter Benjamin once observed, art and war serve each other's purposes whenever a regime seeks to inspire the masses to service that preserves the societal status quo. The same has been said of science and war (and was said most urgently by those who suffered under Hitler, as did Benjamin).[2] Science simply cuts more sharply than does art. Whatever good it does, analytic science makes progress by the steady cutting up of complex things into their simpler parts. It is not that science is false, or wrong, or necessarily evil; but that, when applied to some objects, analytic science can do considerable harm. In this, as those who suffered in the holocausts of the century knew very well, scientific analysis has conspired with the violence of everyday life. It may even be, more strongly put, that whenever analysis is turned upon human and social wholes it will, more times than not, inspire a public violence. To shred wholes into pieces in order to extract the truth of social things can be—and has been—a most enervating spectacle. It is not that normal sciences knowingly serve political evil, though God knows that the abnormal ones do. As is so often the case, it is the unwitting violence done in the name of good that matters. And we can be sure that when people are broken up and stuffed into cells, they cease to be what once they were—which, in brief, is the meaning of social violence.

Just the same, this habit of analytic violence may be losing its grip. It is hard to say for sure. Certainly there is violence to spare in the world at large. Still, somehow it would seem that the terrors visited by and against the remains of the modern world incline tragically toward the ruins—burning rubble at the heart of the city, decaying armaments strewn upon the deserts and mountains, refuse left by humans who embrace violence as a refusal of the terrors of impoverished cities. Still, the terrifying waste of it all, including the outright evil alongside the plain old misery, does seem to arise from a global giving up on the old ideals of violence done in the name of good purposes. It has long been understood, if not readily accepted, that postmodern warfare does little to liberate and a lot to debilitate the remains of the social in the weak world. When, on the other hand, the strong world suffers violence, its fallen buildings and lost lives inspire renewed hope for a return of the old militant spirit of modern toughness. But the days of our fathers—who were, in the word of the day, the last great generation—are in the past. We who remain must look deeper than they. Evil in their time was itself incapable of pity, so it was not pitied. We—if there is a *we* of any reach to be had—are owed less sympathy because, having seen the eclipse of their world order, we cannot claim immunity from the analytic cuts that made the modern world what it is, or was. When the towers fall, we remember equally those crushed in their construction as by their destruction.

It may well be, as some think, that we can no longer speak of human *society* as people did during the violent twentieth century.

Even before the literal crash from the modernist high, three very big social things—a weirdly uneven millennium, the sneaky half-millennium of the modern age, and its violent last century—came to a figurative end all at once, as if to prepare the way for things to come. That figurative moment appeared as three grand stars of the universe fell into a line of considerable, if uncertain, magnetic potential—an eclipse along one axis generating a force perfectly capable of pulling events moving along another axis off their course.

To turn a page in time is nothing in itself. But to turn such huge chunks of human time all at once can excite the imagination. In calendrical fact, we who live in the early years of the new millennium can look back to the events of the last century, there to see the long undetected irregularity in its arch—a sort of reflex of the millenarian arc it ended. Those who taught us (or taught our teachers) taught that time moved steadily ahead, always westward on the forward purpose of dawn, carrying all in its light. This may not be so.

In the twilight of the twentieth century, it became apparent just how unnecessarily so this doctrine may be. Whether a New World Order is born any time soon we shall see. What is there for the heartier souls to know is that the high hopes of the twentieth century's dividend of peace and prosperity paid out little more than new and different aggravations among the world's separated parts. In the new millennium a unique capacity for deception is required by those who still believe that the curve of human reason is toward universal truths or common dreams. Some find this prospect abhorrent. Some celebrate it. But few among those who lived through the last decades of the twentieth century trusted the future as their grandparent's parents had trusted theirs at the previous *fin de siècle*.

In just one short century the ringing hope that prevailed at the end of the nineteenth century had turned to caution for most, to despair for many. Even though the markets boomed for the better off, it was plain for those who would see that the future was not inclined toward good for the masses of men and women. For a while it was thought that the twenty-first century would grow up in ways that might be less terrible than the one from which it came. Still, even before ghost of evil past rose up from nowhere and everywhere all at once, even the most optimistic no longer thought of the social order as the protective cocoon it was supposed to be.

The good and evil of social arrangements are, of course, and always, entirely up to the times. This may be why, when the times change, even when they change by calendrical whim, people have a harder time judging the arrangements themselves. At the very least, when so grand an eclipse occurs, the fog is sucked off the land just long enough that, looking back, one beholds the truth. In that moment, just before the light returns, the picture is seldom pretty.

Quite apart from the terrible violence bred against the hope of modern peace, the modern era had not lived up to expectations. Instead of stable democracies in Europe, there were wars. Instead of a healing union in the United States, there were the aftereffects of a bitter apartheid. Instead of a rising standard of living worldwide, economic development was so grotesquely uneven as to shock all but those whose faith in progress was blind. Instead of the triumph of the Enlightenment values of the European Diaspora, the land is strewn with moral wreckage. Instead of plenty for the many, there is wealth for the few—and no end in sight to the uneven spiral.

Had the half-millennium of the modern era been successfully true to itself, the talk of its end would not be so seriously inflected. It is one thing for professional postmodernists like Jean Baudrillard to speak of the hyperreality of a world of simulations without an original. It is still another for men and women like Václav Havel and Toni Morrison, and others like them who speak in plain language to and for the mass of humankind, to plead for an end to the analytic violence. Havel speaks with the authority of those who suffered Communist rule. He knows very well the violence wrought when a grand idea turns into a weapon of political destruction.

> Things must once more be given a chance to present themselves as they are, to be perceived in their individuality. We must see the pluralism of the world and not bind it by seeking common denominators reducing everything to a single common equation.[3]

For those who fear the loss of modernity's dream of a universal humanity, Havel would say that the truth of the human is in the particulars. He speaks for beings who are self-consciously real in their own right; for those who require no analytic removal from the dreamt Whole.

Toni Morrison speaks from another quarter of particular human frustration with the ideal of the Whole:

> The conventional wisdom of the Tower of Babel story is that the collapse was a misfortune. That it was the distraction or weight of many languages that precipitated the tower's failed architecture. That one monolithic language would have expedited the building, and heaven would have been reached. Whose heaven, she wonders? And what kind? Perhaps the achievement of Paradise was premature, a little hasty if no one could take the time to understand other languages, other views, other narratives. Had they, the heaven they imagined might have been found at their feet. Complicated, demanding, yes; but a view of heaven as life; not heaven as post-life.[4]

Havel and Morrison, as different as their human experiences are, strike the same chord. Whatever unites the world, its mundane reality is differences. The cardinal One that subsumes an infinity of subsequent numbers is now eclipsed by an ordinal First, defined relatively by the relations of its members. The integrity of social things is now in their many parts.

The terrifying, final effect of the twentieth century was to flush away the illusion of universal truth. This one effect accounts for the moral force of the eclipse of millennial time across the shorter arcs of modernity's half-millennium and the millennium's last, all-too-earnestly good century. From the first, this now passed millennium slithered out from under a murky phantasmagoria. The millennium that came to be Reason itself devolved, by fits and starts, from an unreasonable fear of ignorance. Fear of the dark was the cultural invention of the European millennium's invention of itself in the Renaissance under the illusion of the lights extinguished when Rome fell.

The play of light on dark is the foundational trope of modern culture. Modernity's millennium came into its own brilliant light in the fifteenth century. It thus took, *mutatis mutandis*, a good ten centuries to bridge the two millennia of the Christian era. The first was itself punctuated by the shadows that fell when Alaric (370–410 CE), king of the Visigoths, sacked Rome. The world's then most proud global empire fell to the dark savages who, ever since, have come to stand for the deadly outer limits of human society. We remember Alaric, if at all, through comic books translated from the French. We speak of the Goths he led, if at all, under the trope of darkness and evil. Was Alaric any less the young, conquering hero than Alexander (356–323 BCE)? Was he more cruel? Less brilliant? The questions are seldom asked. When the modern era revived the principles of classical culture, it did so to scare away the dark ages for which the West unreasonably holds Alaric and the Goths responsible.

According to legend, it was the Frankish King, Charles the Great (742–814 CE), who broke the savage spell when Leo III ordained him the Holy Roman Emperor in 800 CE. But like so many of the legends out of which modern Europe imagined herself, the Carolingian Renaissance was, at best, a false start. It was no more than a sacred map without geographic coordinates—an ideal in service to the political interests of the Roman church. The Holy Roman Empire shed no more light than that sufficient to encourage the great university at Paris in the thirteenth century, from which came the medieval synthesis—which, in turn, was resource and foil for the rebirth of Europe in the fifteenth century. Then, and then only, could it be said that the new culture was beginning to dispel ten centuries of dark thoughts. Europe was reborn first in fifteenth century Italy where classical form was ingeniously applied to the subjects of Christian piety. The form, of course, overwhelmed the subjects, thus dooming the medieval otherworldly synthesis. It was no accident that the patrons of Florentine art in the fifteenth century were spiritual kin to the Genoan adventurers and Iberian patrons of the world exploration which began the fabulously long sixteenth. Nor, was it coincidence that the first blossomings of religious and scientific rationality in the first decades of the sixteenth century were broadcast upon the waves of New World exploration.

The cruel work of analysis can have its effects at a considerable remove—and no more bitterly than in the bureaucratic organization of Renaissance studies. The modern university, a brainchild of the late nineteenth century, divided the foundations of modern beginnings into separate analytic departments. The research university came into its own modern form to serve, among other interests, Europe's evident need to codify its self-understanding as an invention of world importance. As necessary result, the universities officially cut off the economic history of the New World explorations from the bright shining light of Italian and Dutch art or the bracing poetry of the English theater (not to mention the separation of these two in turn from the social history of Calvinist rationality).

Such were the lasting effects of Europe's foundational dark thought. How could the Universal Europe be reborn in the contradiction between the bright lights of its art and philosophy and the crass search for gold in the sacred lands of peoples who were, without exception, dark? Had not Europe just been resurrected from the shadows cast over the land by the Visigoths? Why then would its so-called rebirth depend so completely on the economic success of the explorations of the lands of mythic savages? Why, indeed? And, how? Hence, the violence of the disciplinary letter. If only the arts and letters could be kept at tolerable analytic distance from social and economic history, then perhaps European learning could sustain the myth of its enlightened reason against the dark facts of its economic avarice.

Analytic work was, thus, at the heart of modern culture. Divide and separate was the tactic by which modernity pursued the strategy of proclaiming its culture as the universal truth, while at the same time, with much the same terrible swift sword, its economic system plundered the very lands and cultures that defied the global ideals. In point of fact, Europe was never Europe apart from its Diaspora. This is why the several Americas, Australia, both Indies, Siberia, and Africa figure so unevenly in the social imagination of European culture. Before they were colonies in the nineteenth century, they were aboriginal opportunities for early capitalist gain. Whether rich in timber, fur, or minerals, as were some, or excellent prison stations or slave trading posts, as were others, the outposts of the European Diaspora were there from the beginning of the European ideal itself.

These, then, were the contradictory groundworks of the millennium just passed. At dirt level they turned on two impossible figures of speech which together conveyed the dream of a rebirth of light.

The "Renaissance" of the sixteenth century was, of course, not a rebirth of an original lost in the darkness. It was an original all of its own making—a culture unlike any that had ever been before. Though other cultures were as cruel in their treatment of vassals and slaves, none denied its cruelty with such aplomb. In this fabricated renaissance, modernity invented itself *ex nihilo*—out of the dark nothing of the wilderness it sought to conquer in the West while covering its ambition with legends of its supposed renewal of debt to the East—to Greece, to Palestine, to the far corners of Rome. This is why the second figure was necessary.

Enlightenment was the organizing trope of a culture that wanted more than anything to believe that no savage Goth would ever again darken its lands. Is it possible that this dark fear explains why the settlers in the European Diaspora, including the North Americans, and other Creoles, and Boers, and European colonizers elsewhere, were so vicious in their assaults on the cultures and people native to the lands they conquered? Why else, if not to transpose the contradiction between their overt culture of Light and their not-all-that-covert political economy of enslavement?

Modern culture in the West always renewed itself by resort to the myth of historical Progress. The ideal of a continual forward movement toward the Good Society necessarily turned on the outrageous lie that these good Enlightenment people were establishing the Universal Good of Humanity itself. The truth, of course, was—whatever was good, whatever was true, whatever was of universal value—that the European Diaspora was different in its culture only in one significant aspect. Its science and technology, including its techniques of corporate administration, were marvels of efficient, productive, ameliorating genius. This is beyond doubt. But, if honesty counts for anything, it must be said that these triumphs were gained not by the march of ever more enlightened Progress, but on the backs and wombs of those whose rape was their original condition. Some cultures may be better on this score than others. Some delude themselves more elegantly. But there is no evidence that the acclaimed superiority of modern culture was ever good enough to be the universal One—except of course in the sense that today the world must speak American English as the only valid passport to the global markets.

In the late twentieth century, these lies and distortions, innocent though some were, came out of the blinding light into their true darkness. These are the dark thoughts that haunted the world's moralists at the end of the century that ended the millennium that was supposed to have cast out the deadly ghosts once and for all. But why, just then? It will be a good long while before we know the answers, before we know if these are even the proper questions. Still, one answer comes fresh to mind.

That last century of the millennium was not just any old century. None began with so much hope. No previous century, if one may speak this way, had dared against all reason to trust its own values so completely as did the last century of Europe's modernity.

From its roots in the gilded last years of the nineteenth century, and even from its true beginning in the Great War, the twentieth century was filled with a preternatural confidence—not just among the dominant classes but also for many of the long oppressed. In Europe and the United States, and their Diaspora, women and the children of the colonized and enslaved joined in the expectations already held by the white working classes. Their actual conditions were as miserably deprived as before. Still, they too hoped to ride the wave of the new times. For Europeans who migrated to the Americas, for Southern blacks a generation later who looked to the American North for work, for women who began to see some prospect of enfranchisement—the new century that would prove so dangerous began with a defiant hope that, even when crushed, rose again. Only at time's remove can this century be seen for what it was.

But the force of the twentieth century's end was no mere reflex of relative disappointment. High hopes brought low do not lead to social change. They may, however, so distract the collective mind as to allow the change. The wars and economic failure, the nasty inward turn of politics, the abiding racism, among other social evils, were terrible enough to encourage challenges to the idea that Progress was near at hand. But, more important was the well-organized stupidity. It is not that war and racism are not stupid. They are; but social evil of these kinds is always rooted in collective feelings far out of the reach of conscious thought. Stupidity has more to do with ideas and values patently at odds with the beholder's interests. War and social hatred may arise from blind rage. But collective stupidity is more the dulling of the conscious senses. People cease to hear and see, or feel and taste. In a stupor, they wander off down paths that lead nowhere in particular. The stupidities of the twentieth century were, therefore, not so much world wars and social violence as the Cold War and the two small hot ones it inspired.

Though, at the time, they knew little of what would soon come, at and just after the calendrical end of the twentieth century, people looked back on the Cold War in embarrassed astonishment. For all but the most stupid, it was hard to find the pulse of that long era of global politics born of culpable mis-recognitions. The Americans thought the Soviets were emotionally unstable. "At the bottom of the Kremlin's neurotic view of world affairs is the traditional and instinctive Russian sense of insecurity." This was how George Kennan put it in 1946 in the famous telegram that fixed American cold war thinking.[5] Soviets were aggressors because they were neurotic. The Soviets countered this American armchair psychology with their own well distilled dogma that, in Lenin's phrase, imperialism was the inevitable highest stage of capitalism. Americans, being obviously the most highly evolved capitalists, were, by that fact alone, imperialist aggressors. Neither was quite wrong; nor did either consider the vast subterranean beliefs their people, on both sides, held in common.[6] The Cold War was, thus, stupid in the sense of being a foolish distraction from the more basic facts of life in their powerful countries. American people truly wanted nothing more in 1946 than to enjoy the spoils of victory— life in the suburbs. People living under Soviet rule wanted nothing more than to repair the damage of war and find some semblance of American prosperity. By 1990 the people on both sides won out over the politicians. Enough Cold War. Thus by the end of the century the Russian people were free to demonstrate that they were as capable of greed and corruption as the Americans.

Hence, the stupidity of a four-decade-long preoccupation with a struggle that amounted to nothing at all. Of course, there were real threats. No one who lived through the Cuban missile crisis in 1962 could say there were not. But, more often than not, the threats were artifacts of the stupidity and not the other way around. The grand and willful foolishness of the Cold War led, ultimately, to the final stupidities of the so-called great powers. Just a decade after the French were humiliated in 1954 in Vietnam, the Americans embarked on the same path and were humiliated in the same place. Then just after the Americans were chased from Vietnam, the Soviets tried to prove in Afghanistan that they could succeed against a technologically inferior colonial people where the Americans had failed, as had the French before them. Then, as time passed, the Russian successors to the Soviets replayed their old tape in Chechnya, just as, not much later, the American son was true to his father's

World War Two convictions. Whether in the long run the Bush family crusade turns out well or poorly, by whichever standards may apply, will be seen. But, at the least, it is evident that, contrary to the father's hopes, the Vietnam syndrome endures, for it is as much a pain in the side of the colonized as of the frustrated colonizer.

A good case can be made that these were the conclusive wars of colonial liberation. The struggle of former colonial people for economic and social justice continues into the new millennium. But the great powers, such as they are, recoil ever more subtly, but evidently, from what the Americans still call "the Vietnam syndrome." Though the phrase was put forth to insist that Americans were no longer afraid to fail at war, the 1991 Gulf War that inspired the phrase proved only what Vietnam and Afghanistan had already shown. When powerful members of the European Diaspora use their might to force their way, they reveal only how little they have learned from their own histories. The militant pursuit of evil ghosts, even of vampires—in the dark heart of the Mekong, or the poisoned deserts of Iraq, or the furtive caves of Afghanistan, or wherever—they repeat, as if by compulsion, the characterological flaw of their values. Such signs of victory as there may be are taken as a blessing of the gods, rather than as the deceptive work of the devil within.

Prior less-conscious motives may well drive collective acts of repetitive stupidity. The powers of the European Diaspora in the second half of the twentieth century were acting on centuries-old impulses. It may be that the Cold War and its *sequelae* were little more than an exasperated last effort to cover the contradictions of the modern age. Such self-righteous thinking, cast against the plain facts of human needs and wants, would be little more than a pitiful stupidity were it not that so many suffered.

In any case, the distractions of the Western mind were the opportunity others were looking for. As the great powers were trying to outsmart each other, people colonized by the West took back step by step the reins of local power. In so doing, they gave voice to the doubts they had formerly kept to themselves. The embarrassments in Vietnam and Afghanistan were already in waiting, long before the fateful twentieth century began. The renewed nation states of Central Asia, of the Balkans, of Southeast Asia, of sub-Saharan Africa, of Latin and Caribbean America, of the indigenous reserves of North America still suffered the effects of colonial rule. As the modernizing millennium ended, the one enduring monument to Western genius, apart from its technological brilliance, is the costly devastation its progress visited upon the regions stripped for capital gain.

The twentieth century ended with contradictions of another kind. Vast wealth and comfort prevailed in the centers of capital administration. Desperate poverty overwhelmed the rest of global space. The world was globalizing in both uncomfortable senses of the word. Light and dark were, somewhere along this way, transposed into wealth and poverty. Wealth moved precariously with lightning speed between global markets without market-places. Frankfurt, London, Wall Street, Nikkei, Seoul, NASDAQ—these oddly disembodied metonyms were the centers of economic power. None, not even Wall Street, is truly a market*place*. The goods of such disembodied global markets of the twenty-first century circulate outside the modes of their production. What productive labor is still required is extracted on the backs of the temporarily employed of the world's most poor. Meanwhile in parts of Rwanda, of El Salvador, of Uzbekistan, of the Sudan the very idea of dignified work for livable wage is little more than a vague rumor driving people to vast but empty centers of population that could be called cities only in the most analytic senses of the word. Mogadishu, Lagos, parts of São Paulo, and Tijuana are among these depots of despair. There the trails and trains of migration from nowhere to nowhere unload victims of an economic system not even Marx could have imagined. Like the wealth, the poverty is global. Like the rich, the poor see what is going on. They know where the food and medical care, the jobs and shelters, they do not have are going; just as the global capitalists know, or think they know, where the dollar and the yen are going on this or that Monday morning.

When, at the end of the last century, the eclipse of cultural times passed over the skies people rubbed their eyes to see again. What those who were willing to see saw was that some monuments to the past had begun to wither in the momentary darkness. Others went to great lengths to say it was not so.[7] But then, not long into the times, on the day the sun shone brightly, the tried and true monuments to economic power came down. In the space of these dark times, both fictive and real, it seemed that society itself was passing from the scene.

No one could have predicted just how dependent the idea of the Good Society was on the establishment of tough-minded nation states ready to do necessary evil in service of the Good. By the same token, not even the most perspicacious student of modernity's global economic system was quite prepared for the vulnerability in that system so evident at century's end.[8] The powerful nation states that had ruled the modern world system from the sixteenth to the late twentieth centuries were, it turns out, utterly dependent on the global arrangements they ruled for so long.

If the *nation state* is the analytic space of *society*, then the *world system* is the analytic home of the nation. From Portugal and Holland to Great Britain and the United States—the geopolitical cores were, for the times allowed them, powers abroad in the world because they were coherent societies at home. The cultures they sent into diaspora aboard the sailing vessels of colonization were epiphanies of their territorially local variations on the general theme. But they were important to the integrity of the separate societal states. The very idea of nationhood was, of course, a global idea. It presupposed a global system that yielded before economic power. All that began to change with the eclipse.

In a global space of markets without visible marketplaces—where the cost of goods and services is set by young men and women in shirtsleeves and unpressed pants who consume only at the margins of their long, caffeine-juiced days—there is no assured place for the nation state; hence none for society.

For a long time, people lived—or aspired to live—under the sway of faith in an embracing society. Their belief drew upon ancient traditions and under-standings. In English, for example, the word "society" first meant an intimate association of men of like kind. Though gradually the term allowed for such associations among men *and* women, the term was rooted in the idea of a cer-tain intimacy of human contact. But somewhere in the course of the long mil-lennium the idea of society took on a different, heavier, analytic weight. When people speak today of British "society," for example, they no longer refer to any sort of intimate association of persons, not even among those of that class which still sends its heirs to the best schools. By society, they more likely mean, in the words of the *Oxford English Dictionary*, "a collection of individuals composing a community or living under the same organization or govern-ment." John Locke may have opened the door to such a meaning in 1690 when he wrote of "political society." But, even he meant by "society" something lively and concrete. Sometime near the end of the nineteenth century, the new social sciences got hold of the term and squeezed from it the juice of human life.

The analytic squeeze, like the culture that gives it muscle, is disarmingly gentle. It does not feel like a stranglehold until all life is gone. The word "society" can only mean life—direct, compelling, demanding, vital. When "society" referred to vital connections in Locke's political society, or even to the stuffy ones of high society, it referred to a living, local arrangement of some kind. When it came to refer to an analytic abstraction, society began to die.

In the last decades of the nineteenth century, social thinkers quite rightly felt they had to say something about the differences between the smaller, usu-ally agrarian, communities of the past and the new, more complicated urban societies that characterized the new industrial order. It was then that society lost its connection with intimate associations. One of the most famous essays in that day was Ferdinand Toennies's *Gemeinschaft und Gesellschaft* (1887), which began:

> Human wills stand in manifold relations to one another. Every such relationship is
> a mutual action, inasmuch as one party is active, or gives, while the other party is
> passive, or receives. These actions are of such a nature that they will tend toward
> preservation or destruction of the other will or life; that is, they are either positive
> or negative.[9]

Like nearly everyone else at the time, this author felt that the new social rela-tionships were potentially destructive of human life. He then drew the analytic line between *Gemeinschaft*, the positive form of association, and *Gesellschaft*, the negative one. The former is real, intimate, private, and organic (or living). The latter is imaginary, public, and mechanical. Who could deny the difference between local associations with people we know first hand and those with people who do not, never will, and don't care to, know anything personal about us? The problem, rather, is in the terms, and how they came to be understood and translated.

Gemeinschaft came into English as "community," while *Gesellschaft* came as "society." Of course, terms can mean whatever a language community decides. There is no reason that the signifier "society" cannot legitimately stand for the abstract, mechanical bureaucracies of the business world. But why was it necessary abruptly to deprive the word "society" of its original semantic rights, and to hand them over to "community"? The answer, I suppose, is that the early social analysts had need of a term to characterize the larger whole of associations; hence, "society" was pressed to this alien, lifeless service. This left the rest for "community," which, ever since, has stood by implication as the weak sister among associations in the "modern" world. But this is not a question of semantics.

Strange—is it not?—how the term "society" took on this powerful, if lifeless, meaning just when the then powerful nation states were huffing and puffing their ways to world rule. The modern world was intent, thereby, on redistributing social meanings, thus to cover the shameful cruelties it had to execute. This is the way with analysis. In the name of reasonable science, all kinds of human meanings and values can be broken down and shoved around as though they had no rights of their own. Thus it happened that, for the course of the twentieth century more or less, "society" came to stand for the big and powerful, but mechanical, whole of social things no one quite knew what to make of.

This is the kind of thinking many people grew tired of in the last decades of the millennium. Many—increasingly many—felt they could say what they felt because the politicians and governors of the big societies were not quite able to administer these unruly and abstract things. When the analytic managers wanted to bomb some chieftain or mullah, their bad guys seemed always to get away. When they wanted to add more jobs to their societal economies, the jobs they added soon disappeared to some other acronymic place. NAFTA, ASEAN, EEC, IMF, GATS, MERCOSUR, OECD, OPEC, WTO—whatever. People in the communities back home were left to work in hamburger joints and check-out lines. Whenever the governors of these societal states tried to do some good, like protect or beef up their systems of health insurance, someone always came along to catch them with their pants down, hence to change the subject. Not long ago I jumped into a taxi in Utrecht only to be asked if I thought my president really did *it*? I no longer remember which *it* it was. Still, in a world where local gossip circulates along the same paths as local jobs and incomes, it hardly makes sense any longer to speak of "society" as this deadly, mechanical social abstraction. Unless, you want to talk about a "global society," which makes even less sense than the semantic game that came into play about a century ago.

"Human society"—perhaps; in any case, the society of humans when and where it occurs is, and must be, about intimate associations among men and women and children. One thing the analysts seem to overlook is that living beings seldom care much about big stuff like analytic "societies." Perhaps they should. In fact, C. Wright Mills has helped us understand that their lives depend on it. But it seems pretty clear that the worst way to get people to understand the effect of big things on their little lives is to talk to them in analytic language. Mills tried to avoid this kind of talk when he said the problem individuals have is in confusing personal troubles with public issues. He was on the right track. Even so, many, including his admirers, still talk in analytic ways.

Worse still is the habit of cutting an already mechanical big thing, society, into a bunch of very little things called "individuals." The analytic claim is that societies are big and well structured; individuals are small and well motivated. Society is supposed to keep individuals in line; individuals are supposed to provide the moral and intellectual energy that keeps society going. Ever since this idea came into use near the end of the nineteenth century, people have been trying to figure out how this is possible. For the longest while it was assumed that there were only two analytic possibilities: Either societies run things and tell the individuals how to behave; or individuals run things and help make the societies better than ordinarily they would be. This is a very appealing distinction. Until recently, I too believed it was useful.[10] I'm less sure as the years go by.

The problem is, as I say, that this way of thinking about how things work in societies boils down to trying to solve a problem that did not exist before Society became an analytic thing in its own right. The idea that individuals are agents of whatever good action and change there can be is, in effect, an attempt to get around the idea that societies—with which individual human beings (sometimes known as "persons") used to be intimately associated—had come to be thought of as big and impersonal. I know very few people who enjoy thinking about themselves as "individuals." This is because most people, left to themselves alone, tend to be lonely. They enjoy intimate associations. They may say they are real individuals, but the very claim requires an audience of others. Most people, their beliefs aside, intuitively understand that individuals alone hardly ever get anything done—especially when they want to change big things like "societies."

By the end of the twentieth century, many people—usually those whose parents and grandparents had been poor, enslaved, or otherwise badly treated—were coming to the conclusion that analysis was one of the reasons they or members of their families had suffered. In the larger scheme of things what analysis is about is the kind of breaking down of complex things into elemental parts such that those thought to be the most elemental "individuals" can be assigned the jobs at hamburger joints or, if that won't do, put in prisons or other cells that have the effect of keeping them in line. Under such a system it can take almost nothing to get put in the wrong cell—one drop of a certain kind of blood, one too many of a certain kind of chromosome, one too many desires for persons with the same kind of chromosomes. The most elementary analytic principles are usually very hard to see with the naked eye. This makes the analysis all the more powerful because it allows the analysts to resort to science, a good bit of it false. Only scientists can tell us what blood and genes are really all about. We may or may not be able to tell whether they are telling the truth.

This is why at the end of the twentieth century people who had had it with analysis were also skeptical about science. It was not that they felt science did nothing good. They were willing, much of the time, to take their pills when prescribed. What they began to suspect was that science is not all that different from other analytic enterprises—some good, some not. This upsets real scientists, who feel that those who think this way ought to go jump off a building and see what happens. In fact, near the end of the twentieth century such a scientist, one of unknown and uncertain scientific respectability, notoriously said just that.[11] It is not known whether anyone ever did.

In any case, near the end of the twentieth century a good many of those born of parents who'd done hard time in colonies or bread lines or slave camps had had enough of analysis. Their weariness with analytic cells fueled a kind of disgust with science—and especially with something called "social science." The sciences fell on hard times. Still sciences of various kinds are done and, still again, many of them do good. But their word is no longer taken on faith. So far, the world seems to be doing reasonably well—at least not worse—with sciences that suffer a public reputation somewhat less than that of the gods they once were. Even so, scientists are still thought better of than are governors and other politicians. That's not nothing.

So, as the new millennium began, things were different from what they had been—a century before, at the beginning of the modern age; not to mention a millennium before, as time approached the end of what was said to be the dark age. The difference at the recent end of the times was that the people who were traditionally stuffed into cells not of their own choosing were less likely to stay put. They were not necessarily better off economically. But at least they were having their say. Their say sometimes had its effect. One effect was that, since they did not like being told they were "individuals" who belonged in certain cells, many of them came up with the idea that the trouble was with the analytic method. Why should anyone be put in a cell without due process? Why should we think of ourselves as individuals? What is this thing "society" that once was so local and common? Why should our passports be assigned by our societies and their national administrators when we also belong to groups that are the more important intimate associations? And, most telling of all, they asked and still ask, What's wrong with our figuring out who we are without the bother of that dreadful choice between individual and society? Why can't we, as individuals, also be members of the intimate associations we are accustomed to, and not the ones imposed by law? And so on.

One of the surprising consequences of all these questions and differences is that, to an increasing extent, analytic sciences are beginning to pass away and take with them the fulsome authority of "society" itself. This did not mean that people no longer worried about their personal troubles and public issues. It meant only that they began to think in different ways, with different results. One of the remarkable discoveries of this new thinking is that, lo and behold, some people had thought this way before, long before. In fact, it turns out that there were writers at the end of the nineteenth century and since who thought without benefit of analysis. They did quite well without it. What they used in its place was what has since come to be called "social theory."

Social theory has come to be known as the means by which people talk (or write) in public about their intimate associations—that is, their societies in the older sense of the word. Social theorists are accordingly less infatuated with analysis. Some do it quite well. But, even when they do it, they do it less as true believers than in order to simply get by. In truth, social theory had become so popular toward the end of the twentieth century that people who previously would not have been caught dead using the words, found it useful to advertise their particular brand of analytic science by calling it social theory.[12] Still, social theory came to mean something uniquely non-analytic— more an unloosening of thought which entails a lack of respect for official party platforms, disciplinary protocols, and academic orthodoxies.

One thing about social theory (as distinct from social science) is that, having unloosened the idea of analysis, social theorists tend to be willing to think and write with less regard for the scientific correctness of their ways. As a result of their willingness to unloosen rather than cut up the things they talk about, social theorists are just as curious about the practical and mundane side of their social worlds as about their analytic or professional aspects. Hence, the thinking of social theorists is more vulnerable to the impinging murk of events near at hand or, better said, underfoot. Social theorists, in addition to being unresponsive to officialdoms of various kinds, are analytically sloppy. They refuse to pick up the dirty underwear all data leave behind. In any case, they reject analytic closets like "society."

It is nearly impossible today to think of the worlds in which one lives as a society of one kind or another. It may have been possible in the days of Alaric or Charles the Great if only because societies only changed once every four or five hundred years. In any case those societies (if that is what they were) were very small, hence intimate—probably too intimate. But, by the end of the twentieth century the world, or "globe," was changing quite a bit. So social theorists have come to talk of the worlds as though they were likely to change at any minute—changes to which they were sympathetic even when it could not be known how much better, if at all, social things might be in the possible new. It is easy to understand why, by contrast, those with administrative charge over such people have grown suspicious of them.

One of the unqualified virtues of social theories is that they are never indifferent to endings—that is, to the unravelings at the end of grand historical rugs. People say the most urgent and critical things just when the worlds of which they speak start to come apart. Whether by permission or necessity (or both), endings require fresh accounts. The only difference between social theories at the end of the twentieth century and those at the end of the nineteenth is that the later ones were more in evidence and greater in number.

But the late nineteenth century was anything but slack. There were plenty of social theorists who, in that day, were more than ready to think outside their cells. One might even say that all the earlier ones would have been surprised at what was made of their ideas in subsequent generations. Take, for an example, one of the reputedly more stodgy ones, the great French sociologist Emile Durkheim. No one was more intent on making sociology into a science. He fought the first fight for sociology as an analytic science with strict and methodical rules. Yet, amid all his ambition, Durkheim seemed to realize that analytic science had its limits. For one thing, as famous as he became as a sociologist, he was more famous for his public philosophy and his contributions to the French national system of public education. His still classic work, *Suicide* (1897), is today considered by many to be the first great work of empirical sociological analysis. But his last great work, *Elementary Forms of the Religious Life* (1912), has come to be considered one of the first great works of rebellious social theory. Durkheim was as much a social theorist, and a public intellectual, as a scientist. In this he was typical of the superficially correct but latently unruly character of sociology and social science at the end of the last century.[13] He was not alone.

Max Weber too was devoted to science, yet it was a science that encouraged the play of subjective meanings. In later years, he gave up his university career, and continued his work amid a group of freethinking, independent scholars that included Georg Simmel, one of the fiercest of them all. Others, like Freud, invented whole new fields outside or on the margins of academic science. Psychoanalysis certainly has had its flirtations with science, but its brand of analysis was, with rare exception, an unloosening of the parts of the psyche, not a cutting apart. Some, to be sure, were university men. William James, George Herbert Mead, Charles Horton Cooley—the great founders of codifiers of modern social psychology—were if anything even less analytic than Freud and Weber. James, like his more famous brother, was as much a writer as an analyst. George Herbert Mead's oddball attempt to wed analytic behaviorism to a semiotic theory of the self was founded on a neverending interior dialogue that could never be exactly contained in the brilliantly sloppy thoughts he himself would never make into a book. It was left to his students to publish notes of Mead's lectures as *Mind, Self, and Society* (1934), much as two brilliant students of Ferdinand de Saussure edited his founding work of structural linguistics as *Course in General Linguistics* (1916). There is a reason why these two latter-day giants refused to pin themselves down.

Odd, is it not, that the beginnings of social science were set so loosely upon habits of mind so markedly less cruel than the analysis that came to be. These great turn-of-the-next-to-last century social thinkers are still respected today. Each wrote serious works of analytic social science. Yet, each was different from the others in ways one does not today often find among analytic social scientists, even among formalists in fields that decline the science suffix.

In the new millennium we live in the eclipse of certitutde. *Some things we know for sure. Some things not. All things are open to inspection.*[14] Words such as these could well have stood as the elaboration of Immanuel Kant's famous slogan for Enlightenment: *Dare to know.* Yet, the same three statements, turned on their side, could just as well stand for the situation today when Enlightenment faith has been cast into doubt. When certitude is the normal expectation of investigation then the difference between what is known and not known, like that between the good achieved and not yet achieved, is merely a matter of time. Enlightenment faith, with all its competing contradictions, resolved on historical Progress. Its faith was that what was not yet known, or achieved, would be, one day. But, today, after time has been swept up in the eclipse, the same formula means differently. In the new millennium, some things are known for sure (just as some are good). But among those that are not, there is no "yet." It is not just that the idea of Progress has slipped away. It is more that the political and social will to make it has been lost in the dark passing of time.

At the beginning of the twenty-first century many people lived well. Unemployment was down in many neighborhoods. Money was being paid. Buildings and homes were being built. Cars and cell phones, webs and nets, and all the rest—there were more new objects of commercial desire than even the deepest of pockets could consume. Yet, all this shrank before the misery of the world's many for whom, at century's end, there was no Progress, and no hope of Progress. World grain stocks were down to two months' reserve. Global warming was racing toward danger levels. Grain producing land per person was half of what it was in 1950. Diagnosed HIV infections were at forty-seven million and growing among the poorest populations with no end in sight (up from zero in 1980). Worldwide, thirty-five percent of the labor force was un- or underemployed. They live without economic hope. Their number is growing. Then, still, there are those no one bothers to count. And on it goes.[15]

The differences are not, however, in the numbers, as terrible as they may be. From the turn of the last century to the more recent one, the terrible difference is in the loss of a living connection, however loose, between those With and those Without the means to decent life. Progress, at least, was a means by which the whole of human society—however unloosened its several parts may have been—maintained connections among the parts. But, in the new century, the final analytic cruelty has become the cutting off of the many poor from the thin echelons of the few well off.

This, quite literally, is where social theory comes in. By any reasonable measure of social and economic justice, there is no justice and no apparent will to secure it. As the powerful well-off give up on the impoverished powerless, they are exposed. The analytic trick of liberal progress is laid out to dry. In times past, it was taught that all things worked together for good. In the new times, all things are cut asunder, each from the other.

Even before the sound of terror began to roar, the new unruly voices were not bashful. Their music blasts away in the subways. They have always understood where social things go wrong, always understood exactly how perverse analytic thinking could be. Frantz Fanon—for one example among those who was born among, worked with, and spoke for the poor of the colonial world—could see very well through the *camera obscura* of the world economic system:

> The settler and the native are old acquaintances. In fact, the settler is right when he speaks of knowing "them" well. For it is the settler who has brought the native into existence and perpetuates his existence. The settler owes the fact of his very existence, that is to say, his property, to the colonial system.[16]

Thus it is that the decolonizers of modern thought understand the inversions of modern thought. Progress is backward. The colonizer from the modern world is the one who wants to hold things back. The colonized is the one with the stake in moving ahead. Progress is the opposite of what it claims, another of the myths of liberal history by which the European Diaspora covered its analytic dirty work.

> The colonial world is a world cut in two. The dividing line, the frontiers are shown by barracks and police stations. In the colonies it is the policeman and the soldier who are the official, instituted go-betweens, the spokesmen of the settler and of his rule of oppression. In capitalist societies the educational system, whether lay or clerical, the structure of moral reflexes handed down from father to son, the exemplary honesty of workers who are given a medal after fifty years of good and loyal service, and the affection which springs from harmonious relations and good behavior—all these aesthetic expressions of respect for the established order serve to create around the exploited person an atmosphere of submission and of inhibition which lightens the task of policing considerably. In the capitalist countries a multitude of moral teachers, counselors and "bewilderers" separate the exploited from those in power.[17]

This was 1961. Fanon would be dead before the year was out. He had lived both in the colonies of his birth and death, and in the metropole. He, therefore, knew the world better than it knew itself. It is no accident that the policeman rules the colonized while the teacher rules the colonizers. Analytic work cuts by whatever means is necessary—and efficient.

The modern world, including its economic system, was always suscepti-ble to internal rebellion. In some ways, it may well be that the new social theories are a continuation of the Romantic resistance to Enlightenment truth-seeking and analysis.[18] Indigenous, local, rooted in folk traditions, unwilling to grant the Whole its claim to universalizing rule; hence: dark, in the several senses of the word—these in various combinations are the roots of romantic rebellion. Romanticism can be trouble, and an evil of its own kind. Still, from the beginning, and from within, Romanticism has always chipped away at the analytic mind. Montesquieu's ode to social differences. Kant's starry skies above. Rousseau's sexual innocence. Voltaire's fantasies of Candide's other America. Marx's odd attachment to Hegel. Freud's dark continent. Durkheim's fascination with primitive knowledge. Weber's gloom, and his wish for the charismatic leader. Few of the great Enlightenment thinkers failed to allow for the unruly differences of indigenous people, many of whom were, in fact, dark. Though the thinkers were, to a man, willfully ignorant of the global divide between colonizer and colonized, none could have thought as he did outside of an evident dependence on the dark others of the new worlds. For them it was the unacknowledged, ever-present aboriginal people who secured the ideas of local variations, of capitalism's tragic superiority, of the original social contract, of the elementary labor process, of the social truth of knowledge itself. There are no exceptions to this rule. Even the greatest of classical social thinkers—those whose work advanced the analytic divide even as they themselves resisted it—knew in their deepest souls that the world upon which they cast their mediations was dark, savage, different, divided. Without this analytic principle they could not have thought.

Yet, even in their day, there were social theorists more willing than these to investigate the analytically loose parts of the global Whole. They paid a price for their differences. Though each was notable in that earlier day in his or her cut off, indigenous society, none was recognized more than diffidently by the colonizers of the global mind. Their day would come—after their deaths; in some cases, a full century after their most brilliant moments. Anna Julia Cooper, Charlotte Perkins Gilman, and W. E. B. Du Bois were all Americans, but all lived in the world. They were far from alone in their times and they had their counterparts throughout the world. All three were social theorists in the sense I have been using the term. All three resisted analysis in order to speak of their world as it was and not as it was supposed to be. Understanding how they thought, and lived, goes a long way toward lifting the shadows cast by a too long day in the Light.

This grand, illusory world of the modern era was, in effect, a global closet. Its brilliance was ever a play of light upon shadows. Modernity, for better or worse, was, as many have noted, a show of positive Progress against a reality of destructiveness. Modernity might have been better off had it not tried to pass. The Goths, the Romans, the Ottomans, even the Hellenizing Greeks, made no bones about their imperial drives. That the powers-that-were of the European Diaspora did may have wrecked their chances for a longer life. Still, a half-millennium is not bad. We who have survived it have only to learn the lessons it taught.

One such lesson is that taught by the loose sociologist, Erving Goffman. Whether we are among the normal or the deviant—the favored or unfavored—of our social worlds, passing is a near universal and necessary stratagem for human life with others. Passing is about kept secrets—especially those the revelation of which can cause us harm. Some secrets must be kept forever; some are meant to be told when the time is right. This, said Goffman,[19] is the difference between dark and strategic secrets. When it comes to social worlds, the dark secrets are those with the potential to wreck the show; the strategic ones are those able, with proper timing, to enhance it. When it comes to the face of a world culture like that of the European Diaspora, this is a difference between evil and failure. When a culture presents the world with a face that turns out to be ordinarily evil, its bright face is lost. Its dark secret has been outed. When, by contrast, such a culture allows it to be known that it is, after all, a failure in some things, the confession has the effect of humanizing the confessor. This is the strategy of unkeeping the secrets of liberal Progress. "Well, yes, we have failed so far. We feel terrible about that. But we will keep on trying. We feel your pain." And so on.

Even analytic societies, even cultures of global ambition, live in a neces-sary closet. Thus, they must manage their faces. How touching it is when those in charge of a nation's self-presentation confess their failure to achieve the progress they "sincerely" desire. They touch us by preaching in our churches, by visiting our neighborhoods, by speaking with real feeling. They talk our talk. These little moves have the effect of keeping the dark secret that there is no real prospect of change. In a world, such as the recently passed liberal mod-ern one, where hope was promised on the assurance of Progress, evil was the discovery that there is no hope because there is no Will to Progress. When such a dark secret is not kept, the word is out that Leviathan is what Hobbes feared from the start.

The eclipse of which I speak was in effect a double passing. The dark secret of modernity was revealed in the passing of light from the daytime surface of things. Among the first to understand the ubiquity of passings, behind which the truths of modern life are hidden, is the Harlem Renaissance writer, Nella Larsen. Her two novellas of the 1920s told the secrets of the twentieth century as well as any before or since. Though others more famous, perhaps, told such a truth, Larsen's writings have lately drawn considerable attention.[20] This may be because she so mysteriously passed out of the shadow of her own past, came to public light for a wonderful moment in the late 1920s, then disappeared once again as though she had never existed. She herself passed as an eclipse, or a flicker of the one coming. In the wake of the events in America she wrote of, there were the first suspicions that all the analytic categories that had served the liberal world so well might collapse one upon the other. She thus gave notice in the late 1920s of secrets told in the late 1980s when, among others, Judith Butler let it be known that once the closet door is opened no one is safe—all secrets will be told, and the truth of analytic things will be known.

The Harlem Renaissance in the 1920s in the United States was just such an outing of the truth. It was one of global importance. In Europe, where the Great War had just been concluded, there were too many unsolved despairs, and too short a moment in which to reflect. The United States, as later, had been spared land war and the intimacy of association with enemy nations—thus to prevent intimate associations with their indigenous neighbors. This often is the advantage the Creole settler has over the financiers and politicians in the metropole. Thus it was that the colonized mind of the white American Creoles were subjected to ideas they could hardly believe. Some of them traveled uptown to the cotton clubs. They saw things they never thought could be true. People mixing changed the way people mixed. Though this Renaissance was soon crushed in the Depression and World War II, the Harlem moment had put an end to the secret. It was hard ever after to pass over the dark secret of liberal modernity's evil. Hence, some forty years after, in the 1960s, the dark secret was broadcast as never before—and this time, worldwide. It was then that the social ethics of good men became known for what they truly were; and then that society and other such analytic things began to pass away.

Is it coincidence that the proud ideals of liberal culture were outed just as the centuries and millennium passed over? Passing cuts both ways. When the culture of Light is subjected to its own darkest thoughts, then its claim to be the final Good is brought into the dark it had tried for so long to extinguish. It is one thing to out those weak and vulnerable. It is another to out the arrogant who take the Good as the closet of their necessary evil. As I say, an eclipse along the axis of time can, when the conditions are right, pull events on the axis of social things out of line—the uprooting of the deep-rooted towers being the material exclamation on the silent truth of social things. Why this happened when it did is far from clear. That it happened, as it seems, is still open to resistance. That *something* happened between the pull of changing times and the weary push of liberal morality upon the world's surface seems nearly certain. At the least, it is open to inspection as never before.

Two

Blood and Skin, 1999

The trouble with being white, or being taken as white, is that it gets under your skin. Whatever they may say about race being a social construction, it turns out that skin is awfully important, if only because it can be gotten under. Take, for example, my current household, which in more ways than one has recently had some experiences on account of our skins.

The birth of Anna Julia has changed everything, including how we feel about how others feel about our skins. White people in intimate public associations with people of darker skin may react in different ways. Some of them, for instance, just love the idea of interracial associations. They feel no qualm in saying so. One of the ways they say so is by running their hands through Annie's hair. Annie has wonderful hair. I love it too. We all do. But I am speaking here of perfect strangers. They don't ask. They just run their hands through her hair. We don't necessarily object. It is well meant. Annie feels good about it, so far as we can tell. But that is not all. What seems even more exotic to me is how white people comment on how "adorable" Annie is. She is adorable. But after a while you have to stop and think about what they have in mind (and what, were the roles reversed, I might have in mind). They sometimes do all this uninvited petting and cooing over our beautiful child while holding their own children in their arms. White babies are cute too. I know first hand. My phenotypically white sons were beautiful babies. But, these days I wonder what the white kids are feeling when they see their mothers get so excited about this darker kid. We live in a very white place. The people around here are, shall I say, liberals, more or less. So this kind of thing happens a lot. I understand very well why they are charmed and surprised by their mixed race encounters. As I say, before Annie, I might have done the same. (Truth is, I know I did.) Now I realize it is just one of the little ways that dark thoughts worm their way into people's heads. This kind of thing is not necessarily bad. But it can be, and sometimes is.

Our extended household includes one of Anna Julia's godmothers. Like Annie, Marilyn is not white. Mona (Annie's name for Marilyn) is a very impressive, and formidable, woman. She moved out here with her family many years ago. Off and on, she has lived in this very white place for thirty years. For much of that time she and her kids were the only, or nearly the only, black people around. She knows the routine very well.

These days, she and Annie regularly venture into the world from playground to playground, to all the libraries, many of the churches, most of the parks and beaches all around here. They are inseparable, as a result of which they have become quite famous in some quarters. Often, when there is a public happening, they are the ones whose pictures end up in the local papers. In these precincts they make a very noticeable couple. A few years ago, when city people chopped down a huge tree up the street for the Christmas tree at Rockefeller Center in New York, camera crews swarmed the place. Annie and Mona were among the first they shot and interviewed. To tell the truth I don't blame them. I would have too.

Still, you can imagine the stories Mona tells about encounters she has had over the years around here. She has been an active member of the Episcopal Church for most of her adult life, and belonged to a number of them. Just the same, she can enter a church she's been in countless times and, often as not, be told in the most ingratiating manner how to find the right page in the prayer book, and such like. Or, when she is invited to attend special events of various kinds, her pleasure often turns sour when, on arrival, some well-meaning liberal tells her where the kitchen is. Once, she was even asked to come early to help out "if she can." This was 1999, mind you.

The worst story is one Mona brought home from our church one day. For thirty years, she worked for a company that manufactures, among other products, high-end skin creams and lotions. She can purchase these products from the company store at discount. We always love it when Mona brings us a box of "product." She enjoys giving product as gifts. On one occasion, at church, she gave a gift of lotion to a friend. Another church lady—a woman, I dare say, who is well known for her liberal values and ideas—observed the exchange. After Mona stepped away from her friend, but before she was out of earshot, this all-too-good liberal woman was overheard to say to the gift recipient, "You better not take it. She might have stolen it." This, as I say, was nearly the twenty-first century. I told Mona I was going to tell this story. She told me not to bother. "It's an old story. It happens all the time."

Well, it's not an old story for me, and will not be for Anna Julia. I know what's coming for her. We already see it when the four of us walk about in public. When Geri and I are out with Mona and Annie, people usually stop and think before petting and cooing. Some just move on. A few even stare. I realize they may only be trying to figure out who's the parent in this mix—or is he a grandparent, or is she, or what? You can't blame people for their confusion. But, then, who do you blame? It gets under your skin.

Now what really gets under your skin is the assumption some people make about the connection between skin and something they call "blood." They don't always say what they mean, of course. For a long while, I never understood the connection. Truth is, I still don't. But when I was a kid I would hear stories about "blood" from people who would never talk about "skin."

My father, the biological one (I was fatherless on the nonbiological side), often spoke to us about what he called "Lemert blood." He thought it was a good thing to have. But what kind of a thing was it? Since father was a physician by trade, for the longest while I thought he knew what he was talking about. Eventually, I figured out that by "Lemert blood" he meant something other than the nourishing fluid that courses the body. He meant, in some peculiar sense, "race"—as if to say, "We Lemerts are a strong and good race." Though my father was not by any means a liberal, he never mentioned skin in connection with the blood of which we biological Lemerts were supposed to be proud.

As it turns out, we Lemerts have a little book on our family tree. I have no idea who put the thing together, or why they did. Different versions of it kept appearing in the mail. Then, one day, I don't remember when exactly, it stopped coming. The last copy I have of "The Lemert Family in America" is way out of date. It makes no mention, for example, of Anna Julia, born in 1998. It still lists me as married to the mother of Annie's brothers. This is fine. Geri doesn't seem to mind. Bonnie has become a friend again. But I have wondered why the genealogical Lemerts stopped working on this book. As best I can figure out they may have stopped some time just after the 1960s. Could it be that the eclipse was too much for them?

Or could it be that the biological Lemerts stopped looking into their family history because someone found a genetic surprise somewhere in the past? You hear stories all the time of people who forever believed that they were of a justifiably proud "race" only to find out that their family "blood" was out of whack with their "skin." I have no evidence that this was true of all the long dead Lemerts listed in this book. Still, it's an interesting question—one that enjoys a kind of surface plausibility. For one thing most of these Lemerts were from the South or the Border States like southern Ohio. For another, it seems that the older ones were a very sour lot. What made them so?

The booklet, it happens, includes a few ink drawings and an occasional photograph (some apparently from the days of Louis Daguerre himself). One in particular is of a Lewis Lemert (1802–1882). When I was a kid, I'd pause on this page to study the image of this very scary man. I still do. Other pictures are just as frightening. These were not happy people. It is entirely possible that there was some bad blood—plain old human meanness. This occurs to me because, even as late as my day, I had seen evidence of bad blood in the family tree. My father, for example, could be terrifyingly angry and on occasion cruel—so much so that his little brother, on his deathbed, is reported to have risen up out of a coma and said, "My brother was a son-of-a-bitch." My uncle was eighty-four at the time. His brother had been dead nearly thirty years. Still, I knew what he meant.

There definitely was bad blood among the biological Lemerts. But what kind was it? As it turns out my father's second-to-last words on his deathbed were gracious words of gratitude to Florence for taking care of "our family." So far as I know it never occurred to my father to insist that Florence's name be entered at the proper place into "The Lemert Family in America." Nor did he give any hint that he thought he was living in whiteface. Nor did he or anyone else I knew from this tree ever consider the possibility that, whatever our family ties to whichever unnamed nonbiological Lemerts, there might have been some other-than-white biological ones. It happens. I was always touched by my father's deathbed words to Florence. She was, too. We told the story again and again in the years that followed. It made me cry. It made her proud. Is it possible that my father, in his heart of hearts, truly recognized Florence for who she really was—to me, to my brother, to him and to Helen, my birth mother; and for what she, in her local way, was to the world that had given him so much? The only reason I think he might have is that he was a man who could say and do the meanest things to people, but I never once heard him utter a word that was what we used to call prejudiced.

Could my father have known, as his deathbed recognition of Florence's place in the family might imply, that the vaunted Lemert blood was really bad *racial* blood after all? Or, was his brother's deathbed declamation the better one? That the bad blood in the family tree was nothing more than hardbitten meanness? Or, is it possible that both told the final, dark truth? That when there is bad racial blood among white people they can turn ugly on each other because they cannot quite abide the dark truth?

Like I say, your blood can get under your skin.

Whose We?—Dark Thoughts of the Universal Self, 1998

As the sun set on that odd millennium, the world was faced with dark thoughts long denied. Something particularly strange was happening. It was more and more difficult to tell who was who—or, more precisely, who belonged to whom. People were claiming rights and memberships, not to mention actual relations, with brash imagination. It was then that the old skin and blood game took on new meaning. Not even the most revered were exempt.

Late in 1998, the same year Anna Julia was born, DNA tests confirmed with reasonable "certainty," that Easton Hemings, the fifth child of Sally Hemings, was fathered by Thomas Jefferson. This kind of thing had long been rumored. As time passed, the Founding Father was best known in the popular imagination for three things: author of the Declaration of Independence, slave-holder, and father of a child or children by one of his slaves, Sally Hemings.[1] Plainly, two of the three were dark thoughts in more ways that one. The three together were darker still.

Why these thoughts were as dark as they were was never entirely clear. Everyone supposed, or should have, that Thomas Jefferson had had sexual relations with Sally Hemings. For years people had heard tell of his leaving her early of a morning. Plus which, why would he be different from any other slaveholder? The darker thought was that the man of liberty was unable to get himself out of the slaveholding system, much less get the nation he declared and led out of it. Still, even this can be explained. Jefferson was dependent, emotionally as well as financially, on his beloved Monticello. So much so that Joseph Ellis describes his elegant, original, cerebral home on a mountaintop as a perfect expression of his character. His domestic haven worked much like his mind to segregate the treasured ideals from the terrible realities. In any case, over time, Jefferson's debts were such that he could not free his slaves without ruining himself (and them). He took on more debt to maintain the plantation he required for his mental wellbeing; hence his financial insecurity. No won-der Jefferson was unable to persuade fellow revolutionaries, legislators, and planters to do what he could not. The system was too deeply entrenched. Over the years, people have generally been able to forgive Jefferson. To a remarkable degree, the people who loved him did as he did—segregated the ideal from the reality. This had been a habit of long standing among the freedom loving people of the West.[2]

Still, it shook the habit to know, for *certain*, that Jefferson really had fathered his country in more ways than one. The mental habit of denial was very strong until then. White people could look into the skins of African-American people, see the varieties of color, and ignore the only possible explanation. Yet, in the late years of the twentieth century, the denials were hard to maintain. Not only were there many more "facts" of the DNA kind, but many more people were willing to claim relations long denied.[3] Even in the absence of facts, the oral histories of the relations were enough for more and more people to play the skin and blood game in new and original ways. The differences were palpable.

Some words tell truths people don't want to admit. I don't mean big analytic words like "society," "self," "race," and the like. Words like these tend to tell lies of various kinds. The words I have in mind are both commonplace and simple. Because they are common, they are used regularly in public company. Because they are simple, they resist being twisted around into analytic meanings. Take for particular example words like "we."

As the twenty-first century was beginning, the word "we" suddenly became a troublemaker when used in public. Before the eclipse, one could say "we"—as in, "We the people, in order to establish a more perfect . . . [whatever]"—and expect everyone to know exactly who was included in the "we" and who was not. In those days, if anyone thought about it, they seldom said so. After the eclipse, those who used "we" unthinkingly may have had to explain themselves. Someone was likely to jump out of her seat to object to a speaker's assumptions about who was included in his "we." This came to be known as the *Whose We?* problem. It was, and still is, much more than a semantic problem.

All first-person plural pronouns, and their variants, can be trouble under certain conditions. What made the *Whose We?* problem so interesting was that it arose with such suddenness. One day a person who had used "we" all his life would say some local version of "We the people" and one of the people in hearing range would ask *Whose We?* He might have only meant to say something like, "Well, shouldn't *we* have this meeting at breakfast? How 'bout seven tomorrow morning?" And she may have only meant, "Right, and *who's* going to get my kids to school?" Still whenever and wherever *Whose We?* is said, it has come to mean: "Wait one minute. What makes you think I share your experiences, assumptions, beliefs, and feelings?" It is not that those who ask this question don't have their own experiences, assumptions, beliefs, and feelings. They do. That is just their point. They mean to change the way people talk and think about them. They usually begin in the smallest of ways, even when they intend to change something big about their local worlds. One of the better effects of the *Whose We?* problem is that it brought a little sociology into common conversations.

Words are not neutral. They convey much more than their agreed upon semantic value. They are, like it or not, almost always sociological when they are used for public consumption. When words are used in public (as opposed to, say, in the bedroom), they have a fungible market value. Their meanings are being offered for sale or barter if the cost can be borne. When the consumers of public rhetoric, or even of plain ordinary talk in public, are uncertain of themselves (or made to feel that way) they may buy a word's meaning without complaint. When, under other social circumstances, they feel they can complain about the cost, they may not buy at all. Hence, "Whose We?"

Whenever a speaker uses the word "we" out-of-doors, he may be taking the risk of including those who do not want to be included, not to mention those who might want to be included but realize perfectly well that they are not wanted. Speakers should know better. But, until recently, many didn't. The consumers of their talk did, of course, because they were the ones who paid for it. There is, I think, no better illustration of the uneven distribution of sociological competence. Those who pay usually are the better sociologists of whatever value is being sold.

In point of fact, everyone ought to be, or potentially can be, competent to judge when they ought, or ought not, to use a word like "we." This is so because anyone who really pays attention to the prevailing social arrangements on their street, will see for himself who belongs and who does not. Except for a few of the more notable secret societies like Sigma Chi or the KKK or the CIA, belonging is the most basic of practical sociological works. Belonging, and the right to belong, is where all "society," whether intimate or not, begins. Whenever and wherever there might be a social contract, its terms have to do with belonging, and not much else. Social contracts ought to be more social than they normally are.

Still, most people have a good bit of commonsense competence about belonging. Nearly everyone knows, almost by instinct, if he or she belongs at a party that may be forming in the neighborhood. You may decide to crash it, but at a risk. The reason there is always a risk in crashing social parties is that those throwing the party are almost always of one of two states of mind, neither of which disposes them kindly toward party crashers. *Either*, they are throwing the party precisely because they only want to associate with their kind. *Or*, they throw parties all the time and never stop to think about the invitation list. Of course, it is often the case that people with the second attitude are no more than naive instances of the first. But they who think in the first way are anything but naive. Still, they, in turn, fall into two subcategories. *Either*, they want to exclude people who, they fear, might want to crash their party. *Or*, they are sick and tired of not being invited and want to have parties of their own.

It might be said that one of the more devastatingly subtle effects of the eclipse just passed is that of breaking up many of the traditional parties. Ever since people started showing up at parties to which they were not invited it became much more difficult for everyone to figure out who were the included and who the excluded. *Whose We?* is the problem of not being certain which party to go to. Those who were, until then, accustomed to sending out the same old invitation list (and suffering, I might add, the same old characters showing up), are more likely to brood over the dark thought that their membership credentials are not in self-evident order. This is not a new brooding. The only thing new about it today is that it is now done in public. This is because *Whose We?* is, by its very nature, always a public question. Just the same, even before people started asking it, the dark thought was there, lurking in some corner of the social mind.

Take, for example, the most famous sentence of the most famous American Creole[4] of the early European Diaspora, Thomas Jefferson, who wrote in June of 1776:

> We hold these truths to be self-evident: that all men are created equal; that they are endowed by their creator with inherent and inalienable rights; that among these are life, liberty, & the pursuit of happiness: that to secure these rights, governments are instituted among men, deriving their just powers from the consent of the governed.

Hardly anyone, anywhere, has not read or heard these words. They are among the most quoted, copied, and beloved words in modern culture. Yet, the careful reader of them, as they appear above, might notice an error. In the second line where one expects to find "certain inalienable rights" there appears, "inherent and inalienable rights." Actually, there is no error. These are the words as Jefferson wrote them. His revolutionary colleagues revised them, in less revolutionary ways. Jefferson himself felt so strongly about his words that he included them along with his autobiography written many years later.[5] In this case, his fellow revolutionaries weren't willing to go so far as to say that the inalienable rights of the people are also "inherent." Even for them, Jefferson's was too strong a We-statement. They preferred the indefinite form—"certain inalienable rights."

One of the reasons "we" is such a potent little word is that its value is necessarily derived from the sociology of any situation in which it is used. When someone says "we" in public, he or she is claiming a membership of the included. In bedrooms, people use "we" all the time to claim a membership of sorts; but only the inexperienced take it all that seriously. But today, in public, "we" is serious business. It is frequently necessary to back up we-claims with a declaration of one's own right to belong or, under other conditions, of one's right to declare independence from the traditional membership rules.

Whichever form they may take, since the eclipse, declarations of rights to belongings of various kinds are ever so much more carefully scrutinized than before. This is because they have become ever more complicated. For starters, when you live in a society, or social world, where *Whose We?* might be asked, you have to have an answer at the ready. Curiously, such an answer is no longer simple. Not that it ever was. The difference is that, most places, in the new millennium the answer necessarily involves a claim about one's "self" (as it is said) as well as about one's group affiliation. There is a reason for this. Claims about group membership today require some certification of one's personal right to make the claim.

When the group into which one claims membership is no longer assumed to be the nation immediately at hand—or some other such universally recognizable group (such as whichever social class prevails in the neighborhood)—those who claim the membership have to have their immigration papers in order. These papers are always very personal. When, for example, a member of a persecuted group flees his native "nation" for safety in, say, the United States, he may properly claim the right to stay in the host country if and only if he can certify that his group back home is in fact persecuted. As it turns out, one does not prove this sort of thing merely by documenting the group's political situation. One must also demonstrate that he actually belongs to that group and this proof *always* entails excruciating details of his personal life. That is to say, the right to enter a new group from a previous one is necessarily a test of having a proper *self*. Selves are always and only documented by facts of a very personal and painful nature. In the example, it may take years of waiting (perhaps in refugee camps) before it is determined whether one's *self* is in order. If it is, the person is allowed to remain in the United States, usually as a member of the official group known as "aliens." "Alien" is a more generous analytic tag than you might suppose. When affixed, it serves to identify, thus to hold, immigrant peoples safe from harm elsewhere as it holds others for work in the host country. Though, as a rule, neither status pays well, both are sought after, hence desirable.

What is true of political refugees and immigrant workers is usually true of anyone who claims a right to belong not previously taken for granted. One of the more interesting of these claims is one made by those who have every reason to assume they are proper members of a group, often a national group, but who, after years of bitter experience, know very well that rights self-evident to them are not self-evident to others. This, very probably, is why Thomas Jefferson's revolutionary colleagues got rid of the word "inherent." It is one thing to say that rights to belong are "self-evident" *and* "inalienable"; quite another to concede rights to those for whom they were "inherent" to begin with. To admit the clerical error of exclusion of those whose rights, it turns out, were also "self-evident" is to hold oneself up for trials of all kinds.

In Jefferson's day, those who shared in his declaration of independence were, by and large, members of a relatively small, powerful class of men, all of them white. They were among the minority whose education and social standing would have been sufficient for them to use the expression "self-evident." You can see that the expression involves a prefix that would eventually become an important analytic category.

"Self" is one of those words that stands between little, but tricky, words like "we" and robust, but analytic, ones like Society. Still today, *self* is used as a common prefix or suffix, as when one says without regard to grammar, "I myself did it." This is said to be a reflexive expression pointing back to the one speaking. Eventually, about the time other big analytic terms were coming into their own, the reflexive *self* was broken off from common language and turned into the very large categorical thing. By the end of the nineteenth century, analytic social scientists were already talking about *The* Self, as in "Self and Society." In Jefferson's day, this practice was less common. The reason it was is that almost no one ever asked *Whose We?*

So when men said, "We hold these truths to be self-evident," they were, to be sure, speaking for "themselves." They were also speaking as a class of powerful men who already had the right to use words like "self-evident." Any We that uses such an expression without qualification, no matter how well intended, is arrogating to itself a certain degree of secret knowledge—declaring, thereby, truths the evidence of which is known, if not only, at least obviously, to themselves. Whenever anyone asserts the self-evidence of his or her truth, it is time to hold on to your pocketbook. There is fine print somewhere.

This may be why these men got rid of Jefferson's word "inherent," which then, as today, meant something like "natural or essential." It is one thing to say, "We assert our own self-evident rights to life, liberty, and the pursuit of happiness, and we won't let anyone take them away." It is another to concede that such rights are "inherent" in the sense of being an essential *human* right. People who are already claiming a relatively Gnostic principle of evidence may have very good reason to put a limit on the extent to which the rights they profess might be thought of as universal. They may like the idea, in principle, but have completely sound social reasons for holding back. Why else would they not want to give the evidence for the rights they were willing to declare? It is well known today that they did have a good reason to hedge their bets.

From the first, Americans overplayed their strong hand. Few national cultures make louder, more moralistic, Strong-We claims equating their local rights with those of all human society. American righteousness was trouble from the very beginning—as in the deletion of Jefferson's "inherent." But that was not the only revealing slip of the eraser. Jefferson's co-conspirators also deleted another telling passage he had left with them, one that might seem to have been as agreeable a complaint against the British throne as colonial rebels could make:

> He has waged cruel war against human nature itself, violating its most sacred rights of life and liberty in the persons of a distant people who never offended him, cap-

tivating and carrying them into slavery in another hemisphere, or to incur miserable death in their transportation hither.[6]

This passage was immediately deleted. But why? The line is delicately phrased as denunciations go. Is not Jefferson making reference to the enslavement of the colonial people? No, of course not. Had he been, then it would not have been necessary to drop the line to appease Georgia and South Carolina. Jefferson was being coy with his colleagues and his own situation. He had to have meant "slavery," not metaphorically, but in the definite sense. Yet, he phrases the passage as if to join the denunication with the same inherent human rights he wanted in the first lines. Everyone knew exactly what he had in mind. How could they not have? The slave system was the most distinctive feature of the colonial economy, and the one that flew in the face of revolutionary righteousness.

This second deletion, like the first, was about much more than politics pure and simple. It concerned what Alexis de Tocqueville would later call "America's most formidable evil threatening its future." But the revolutionary generation did not need instruction from an alien. They knew. Later, Jefferson admitted that the slavery system was as much the responsibility of the colonists as of the British and that he was attempting to slip the abolitionist line past his Southern colleagues.[7] The American revolutionaries knew the limits of their righteous claims. They, like Jefferson, had interests and other inconveniences that kept their values in check. The Americans were, in this, no different from others of strong cultural position who seek to extend their rights to the whole of humanity. Since the giving of rights always carries with it membership costs, and benefits, rights are seldom given away incautiously. Hence, Jefferson's duplicity was America's, and that, *mutatis mutandis*, of all rights givers.

The extent of the dilemma of rights givers everywhere can be seen by comparing the American declaration with, for prime example, the grand charter of English rights. The Magna Carta of the early thirteenth century began, as you might expect, with a very long list of names. John, the king declaiming the rights, had very good reason to implicate all the others in church and court who were signing on to this charter of independence. So it begins, "John, by the grace of God, king of England, lord of Ireland, duke of Normandy and Aquitaine, and count of Anjou." Like today's refugees from El Salvador, John felt he too was required to give a personal history, hence to show that he was a *self* proper to the edict he was announcing. It turns out that in 1215, when the great charter was first given, King John was in fact at some risk of being, if not a refugee, at least a king without a land. He was not, him*self*, completely happy to be giving away these liberties (which, later, he renounced).

This is one reason (the other being the protocol of the day) that John's declaration of rights begins with a long list of those whom he consulted—clergy, experts, nobles, and the like. This list has the effect of saying what the

Americans felt they did not have to say. John did not believe that the liberties were "self-evident." As a result, by the time the Magna Carta gets to "We have also granted to all freemen of our kingdom, for us and our heirs forever, all the underwritten liberties," everyone knows whose liberties are being granted. They were not bad liberties at all; anything but. Still, you see what is going on. This ancient declaration of rights, handed down by one who was only exceptionally exposed to the *Whose We?* problem, nonetheless gives more detail than needed about *Whose We* will have the rights.

It is a very long step in time to the French Declaration of the Rights of Man in 1789. The French had benefited not only from the English but even more so from the American declaration. As a result the French were willing to declare the rights of the French citizen "human rights." Even if, at the time, they were not self-evidently more freedom-loving than the Americans, the French declaration was much more clear on the crucial point. In Article VI, borrowing from Jean-Jacques Rousseau, for example, they said, "The law is an expression of the will of the community." This would seem to be a hedge against the universality of the rights to belong. But these were professed earlier, in Article IV, which said: "The exercise of the natural rights of every man has no *other* limits than those which are necessary to secure to every other man the free exercise of the same rights." This still does not go as far as the "inherent," or essential, rights Jefferson wanted to include. In any case, he was not in Philadelphia when his colleagues excised this and other of his words. He had already gone home to his Virginia plantation in the company of his personal slaves who were constantly at his side.[8] He was so disgusted by the deletions that he called attention to them in the years to come.

Any declaration of rights of belonging, and its benefits, is a tricky business. Those who declaim in the name of a We must be careful either to explain which We precisely (as did King John in 1215 at Runnymede) or, if they mean it, to say "everybody" as the French nearly did in 1789. The very worst thing is to be ambiguous, as the Americans were in 1776 after Jefferson left town. Self-evidence is never evident unless the selves declaiming it mean to include all those who are inherently "human" (which they did not). Alternatively, they may mean to follow King John's example and give the full and explicit list of those selves to whom the rights extended are being precisely restricted. Anything in between creates problems. The Americans, in particular, took a long time to solve them. It was not until the election of Andrew Jackson in 1828 that democrats definitively limited the rights that previously had been narrowly extended in republican fashion to America's ersatz patrician class. It took until 1863 for black slaves to be declared free, and another good century for those rights to become effective. It was not until 1920 that women, whatever their color, could vote. And, oddly, as the century ended there were people in California and Texas and other places who wanted to remove whole groups of immigrant workers from the membership roles that made them eligible for health and education benefits. This was the kind of problem that the

French, among others, avoided in the first place by not meaning what they said. They never permitted more than a relatively few of their colonial subjects to become full members. The rest may be evicted at any time. This, I suppose, is much like Thanksgiving or New Year's suppers at various plantations or households. The help are invited for a meal, allowed to clean up, then sent on their way at dusk.

The *Whose We?* problem, we can see, is particularly acute for people in the lineage of men like King John, Rousseau, and Jefferson. Though some are, most are not necessarily bad people. Many of them, like at least two of the three I mention, were among the best men one could find in their days. They were, very often, fair, brilliant, and powerful. If they were powerful, as Jefferson came to be, they were because they were first fair and brilliant. If they were never to hold powerful offices, as Rousseau never did, their ideas had a power of their own. But even if they were ruthless and held what power they had by accident of birth, they occasionally submitted to the demands of the people. King John, also known somewhat ironically as John Lackland (1167–1216), actually signed off on the Magna Carta in 1215 at Runnymede under the insistence of many of the We whose liberties were thereby secured. Men such as these were either good or bad. If good, they had ordinary human impulses (as Jefferson and Rousseau did for sex), just as John Lackland (not so good) had a healthy appetite for power. Good or bad, they were, in effect, men.

Still, what is most striking about people in comparable positions in present times is that they are so excessively disturbed when asked, *Whose We?* There are two reasons for this. First, the question identifies them as the problem at hand. Second, the problem others have with them is personal as well as political. *Whose We?* is two questions at once: Who the hell do you think you are? Who elected you to decide who belongs?

It might be said, therefore, that those who, as a class, bear the brunt of this rudeness are members of a loose analytic group that might be called the Strong-We. Their situation is, thus, homologous (but not analogous) to the situation of those who ask *Whose We?* The question that shocks the Strong-We arises in the same or similar circumstances from which it is asked by a Weaker-We. Same origins; different effects. The effect on the Strong-We is to threaten, without necessarily weakening, their social position. They shake because they know their position is no longer taken for granted—because, put otherwise, their *Self*-understanding is being called into question. Generally, but not always, the Strong-We, being strong, recoup their losses and hold the line. Like I say, none of this is ever simply a matter of semantics; nor, most pointedly, is it in the effects of the query on those who pose it.

Hence, the other side of the story. Those who demand *Whose We?* might be called—though deceptively so—the Weak-We. They are the ones whose strength lies in the anything-but-semantic weakness of their social circumstances. They may not always be actually weak at the time of asking the question, but they know weakness in the social, economic, and political senses. This is why they create trouble. Hence, again, the homology.

So far as anyone I know knows, the various social worlds on the planet have always been divided between those who were stronger and those weaker, socially speaking (where, for simplicity's sake, "socially" is meant to embrace all aspects of social life, including the political and the economic). How those divisions are imposed and enforced is subject to many variations. They are not always permanent. Give a "certain" unequal distribution of human rights and benefits four or five hundred years, and the arrangement is likely to change. Sometimes it may even turn topsy-turvy—though topsy-turvy reversals, like the one in 1848 in Europe, seldom last more than a few months. More often, the changes are readjustments in the inequalities at hand. Some, but not all, who were weak under the previous regime become stronger; and vice versa.

One of the remarkable things about the present situation, however, is that, though things are changing quite a lot, and some of the formerly weak are stronger than they had been, on the whole the weak are getting weaker; and the strong, while a bit shaken (and fewer in relative number), are getting stronger. With one exception: The weak are better organized than once they were; and they speak out.

Hence the Weak-We are those who today are more acutely aware of them*selves* in relation to the Strong-We. Their strength is in their history of social weakness, which allows them to demand *Whose We?* Which, in turn, has the effect of shaking the Strong-We.[9] This makes the latter more defiant, which may explain why the Weak-We, and those spoken for in Weak-We utterances, generally find themselves in a less equal social position. Like bears in the woods, the Strong-We are more dangerous when attacked. This is when they are most likely to piss on you, or worse.

There are numbers of many kinds that illustrate this peculiar arrangement of worldly things. One set of data has been circulating for years among the Weak-We. Believe it or not, just a minute ago I received a copy of these data from, not coincidentally, a Brazilian sociologist who currently lives in the United States without having given up his concern for the poor in his native country:[10]

If the Earth's population were a village of 100 people, with all the current ratios as they are today, then that village would look like this:

Asians: 57
Europeans: 21
Western Hemisphere: 14
Africans: 8

Women: 52
Men: 48

Nonwhite: 70
White: 30

Heterosexual: 89
Homosexual: 11

Number possessing 59% of the wealth: 6
Those living in substandard housing: 80
Those unable to read: 70
Number starving: 50
Number with college education: 1

Some Strong-We types may well dispute these numbers. But even if they are off in minor details, the picture is clear. Most people, by a long shot, are poor, illiterate, and starving. Most are not white. By contrast those able to read this page are, by a large number, likely to be white, wealthy, and members of the European Diaspora. Those not able to read this page are likely to be directly or indirectly related to people who are, or once were, poor, illiterate, non-white, starving, and born in the former (or current) colonies of the European Diaspora. This is the world of the Weak-We, or the world they represent, when they say, "Whose We?"

Numbers, like words, can lie. But these numbers are too big to lie too much. Plus which, whoever looks out on the world as it is is unlikely to be all that surprised by them. The numbers are shocking only because they are pretty much what one feared they might be. By the same token, this is why, also, Strong-We people are no longer very surprised when confronted by the Weak-We. This is why the Strong-We very often live in gated communities.

Though, as a rule, the Strong-We are not self-consciously cruel, it does turn out that they, or their agents, are known to have thrown up barriers of various kinds—fences around refugee camps, gated walls around clusters of fancy homes, and reinforced perimeters on borders with regions where there is an unusual number of Weak-We people.

As a result, the Weak-We very well understand borders, fences, gates, border guards, tunnels, guard dogs, surveillance towers, metal detectors, passports, lock downs, unemployment lines, work-fare offices, green cards, detention slips—and all the other paraphernalia used in border maintenance. As often as not, the lives of today's Weak-We, like the lives of their ancestors, are organized around lines drawn in the sand between them and Strong-We people, who tend to have the bigger homes and the better lands.

Again, these are not semantic lines. But they do determine how people talk. One of the themes repeated by the Weak-We is of the reversal of fortunes between them and the border guarding Strong-We. For example, a contemporary of Thomas Jefferson, the Seneca chief, Sagaoyeatha, in 1805, addressed some Christian missionaries: "Brother, our seats were once large and yours small. You have now become a great people, and we have scarcely a place left to spread our blankets."[11] Again and again, the Weak-We speak of reversals, including more complicated ones like that made famous by Sojourner Truth in 1851:

> I can't read, but I can hear. I have heard the Bible and have learned that Eve caused man to sin. Well, if woman upset the world, do give her a chance to set it right side up again. . . . Man, where is your part? But the women are coming up blessed be God and a few of the men are coming up with them. But man is in a tight place, the poor slave is on him, woman is coming on him, he is surely between a hawk and a buzzard.[12]

The Weak-We, in all times and places, are very often people descended from ancestors from whom rights were taken. They know the stories of the original conditions from which what was theirs was stolen. This is part of their power, when they can and do speak up.

When, today, the Weak-We ask their upsetting question, they do from their side of borders fixed in place, over many years, by the Strong-We:

> The world is not a safe place to live in. We shiver in separate cells in enclosed cities, shoulders hunched, barely keeping the panic below the surface of the skin, daily drinking shock along with our morning coffee, fearing the torches being set to our buildings, the attacks in the streets. Shutting down. Woman does not feel safe when her own culture and white culture are critical to her; when the males of all faces hunt her as prey.
>
> Alienated from her mother culture, "alien" in the dominant culture, the woman of color does not feel safe within the inner life of her Self. Petrified, she can't respond, her face caught between *los intersticios*, the spaces between the different worlds she inhabits.[13]

This, many will recognize, is Gloria Anzaldúa. She speaks of her*self* as Chicana, *tejana*, lesbian, and native to the dangerous economic and territorial borderland between Mexico and the American Southwest.

One of the ways the Weak-We surprise the Strong-We is that they know who they are and they recognize each other. When they are asked who they think they are, the Weak-We have an answer. They very often are those who, as Anzaldúa says, do "not feel safe within the inner life of her Self." They live, in a fashion, outside themselves because, among other reasons, they know the stories of the border guards. They, therefore, recognize others who are similarly on guard, and recognize them even when they do not speak the same language.

Chicanos of the American Southwest have lived in the United States since they were trapped by the diplomatic theft of the homelands of 100,000 of their Mexican ancestors in the 1848 Treaty of Guadelupe Hidalgo.[14] Yet, they understand, needless to say, the experience of Mexican and other Latino workers in the United States today because they understand borders and their dangers.

And, in turn, they understand early immigrant workers—contemporaries of their great-great-grandparents—who were the first waves of many Asian peoples to come to the United States to build the land, the water system, the railroads. The early generations of Asian workers were subjected to a growing body of race-based immigration law, which had the effect of restricting rights in order to control and segregate these workers. Thus, though strangers to each other, the Weak-We of many different histories recognize each other in the marks of the legal and physical barriers imposed by the Strong-We.

Lisa Lowe gives one account of this odd fact of life that forms the kinship between Asian workers in the nineteenth century and Latino workers in the early twenty-first:

> The state, and the law as its repressive apparatus, takes up the role of "resolving" the contradictions of capitalism with political democracy. The historical racial formation of Asian immigrants before [the 1965 change in immigration laws] has mediated the attempt to resolve the imperatives of capital and the state around the policing of the Asian. In the period since 1965, legal regulations on immigration include Asians among a broad segment of racialized immigrants, while the policy has refocused particularly on "alien" and "illegal" Mexican and Latino workers. Asian Americans, with the history of being constituted as "aliens," have the collective 'memory" to be critical of the notion of citizenship and the liberal democracy it upholds; Asian American culture is the site of "remembering," in which the recognition of Asian immigrant history in the present predicament of Mexican and Latino immigrants is possible.[15]

Anzaldúa is a poet. Lowe is not. Anzaldúa writes more directly out of her life in a Weak-We world. Lowe knows that world very well, but writes in and for the language of analytic peoples. Still, they know each other in more ways than one.

To speak of large membership groups as the Strong-We and the Weak-We is a loose analytic way of getting around the deadly effects of putting people in cells or otherwise on the other side of borders of various kinds. Analytic terms are not, as I say, evil in themselves. They are used, in the name of science, for good purposes. Sometimes they achieve a considerable good. The question is, do they do enough good to cover the damages?

Take this analytic term "Self" which, as I say, has a foot in both camps. As a mere reflexive, *self* allows people to speak emphatically for themselves, to make clear who is saying what, even to insist on the right to say or do whatever is at hand. But, as an analytic notion, *Self* does quite a lot of violence of another kind. The violence done by the *Whose We?* defiance is of another order from the violence done by cutting things up and off. Still, in the case of middling words like "self," the potential for damage in both can be found.

Even in its small reflexive sense, "self" has always, from its beginnings in Gothic and Scandinavian, not to mention Old English, borne a potential for a very big idea, "identity"—as in the 1175 *Pater Noster*: "*He fondede god solf mid his wrenche.*" When a god enjoys intimate society of any kind, he remains a god. It is in the nature of a god to be capable of being identical to himself, without respect for any analytic cut, including gender. Such a meaning was always in the background even, years later, in a later English translation (ca. 1400) of *The Rule of St. Benedict* (original Latin version, ca.[16] 525 CE). Here the subject was not so much a god, as a god's effects on his subject. Still, the identarian principle is at work: "*Oure awn self we sal deny, And folow oure lord god almyghty.*" Still, even here, it is plain that "self" is midway between the common reflexive (formerly used by the gods) and the analytic thing it was soon to become.

Even, however, in the seventeenth century, when the modern analytic form first peeked out from behind the cover of common human ideas of identity, "Self" retained its ties to the past. In his *Treatise on Human Understanding* (1690), John Locke said, for very notable example: "Since consciousness always accompanies thinking, and 'tis that, that makes every one be, what he calls self." Self is that what makes us ourselves. You see the effects of René Descartes who is thought, by many, to be the very first to lay the groundwork for the modern idea of Self. It is said, also, that Jefferson's most important philosophical principles came from Locke's psychology.[17]

In 1690, near the end of the century in which Descartes got the analytic ball rolling, Locke used the term "self" consistently. He meant, clearly, to speak of *self* as a way of speaking about the "consciousness" that had been groping its way toward becoming *the* "inherent" and essential feature of the human. Any being capable of entering a social contract was, necessarily, a very delicate invention. He had to have been like a god (hence, possessed of a conscious self by which he knew himself to be himself). But, also, this human had to have been a being whose self-consciousness—his awareness of himself—transcended the stupidity of animals and other natural creatures who were (and are) considered incapable of identarian thought (which is to say, incapable of using the reflexive competently).

Hence, the foundational anxiety over the beastly savage in human "nature." There could be no finer proof of the tardiness of nineteenth century claims that the culture of the European Diaspora was a rebirth of ancient Greek culture. The English *self* that arose on the back of the Latinate *ipse* was, in a sense, homage to the original dread of a return of Roman impotence before the savages. Had Descartes and Locke and Kant, not to mention Jefferson, been working directly from the Greek, they might have come to a different conclusion about a whole variety of subjects—from self-evidence, to individual rights, to the human consciousness of self, to the moral space between the gods and the animals, to even the *ego* that was behind Descartes' *Cogito, ergo sum.*

Instead, the early modern philosophy of human thought, which came into its own in the seventeenth century out of a virtual Roman culture, served to define the terrain of the modernist utopia. By the nineteenth century that fictional social space came to be known as "history." But in the seventeenth century it was the far more psychological principle of self-consciousness. Without the self-conscious mind, able to think itself first and foremost, there could have been no principle of human action so elegant as Kant's categorical imperative. "Act only on a maxim by which you can will that it, at the same time, should become a general law."[18] This was, not surprisingly, 1785—just shy of a decade after the Americans invented practical history; just a few years before the French Revolution interrupted Kant's walk about town. Kant, famous for his regularity, was stopped in his tracks only one other time—after reading Rousseau's *Emile*. Hence, differences and disputes notwithstanding, the common will among the greatest thinkers of the English, American, French, and German Enlightenments. The Human was nothing less, and not much more, than the possibility of self-conscious action predicated upon self-consciousness itself. One can hardly act so as to anticipate the general will without first being capable of consciousness of self which must be the predicate in any reasonable maxim. If it is true that Jefferson preferred Locke's psychology to his politics this is further evidence of his shrewdness. In the beginning, everything was psychology. *History requires moral action; which requires consciousness of the common will; which requires thinking; which requires consciousness of self.* This is how such a middling word as "self" came to be, by the end of the nineteenth century, such a big analytic one.

Still, one might wonder what the modern world would have been had it been Greek, rather than Latin, that was read through the dark ages? The Greeks very probably would have solved this little problem differently. Instead of "self" they would have stumbled upon "psyche," the term that has been carried over into late modern culture by *psycho*analysis (much as the Moors protected Aristotle during the dark ages). Among the Greeks, as among the Hebrews, "psyche" (as it came into the modern languages) referred to the life-giving "breath"; hence, "soul." Think how much less analytic moderns would have been had they taken their lead from the Greeks. It is one thing to transpose self-identity into the analytic Self. But quite another to cut up the very breath of human existence, the Soul.

As everyone knows, "soul" is susceptible to all manner of degradations when it is taken over by analytic preachers of all kinds. Still, we have the contradiction that the analytic science known as Psychology became, not the science of the Soul, but of the Self and its cognates. It is true that were psychologists to stop and think about what they are doing (which can be tricky business for analytic peoples), they would say that theirs is a science of "mind," or "mental life," but they would rarely be caught dead making the transposition of "mind" into "soul" or "spirit."

In a rare instance of parsimony the OED does just that. **Psyche.** *The soul, or spirit, as distinguished from body; the mind.*[19] It is plain that so parsimonious a definition has been able to maintain its integrity over many years because the *psyche* refers to the breath of life itself. The word is fungible only outside the marketplace of identities. It is metaphoric without being indefinitely substitutable. It is, pardon the expression, a *surd*—a necessary but irrational root that allows no final explanation beyond itself. It is, in short, that which reminds humans of the finitude they see and encounter every day in their differences with others who, against reason, are not exactly identical to themselves. This of course would not do when what one has in mind is modernity.

To speak of the human soul, or psyche, is therefore to resist, if not to block, the identarian impulse. The urge to replace the power of the gods with the power of the Self is a mighty one. Still, it would be a wonderful exercise in virtual history, to imagine what might have been had the late modern West imagined itself as that which was driven by a Soul, not a Self. Except when taken over for the purposes of fund-raising under the fear of condemnation to hell, the principle of Soul has to do more with that which simply *is*—and *is* without need of being identical to itself. To speak of a "soul mate," or a "soul brother or sister," is not to speak of one exactly the same as oneself. It is to speak of one who breathes the same air.

A soul, thus, is always something Other. It is that which is basic to life itself precisely because it comes from an Other not the same as oneself. This is why, it turns out, the old skin and blood game turns on an essential ignorance of the principle of Soul. In the strict sense, blood is that which carries the oxygenated breath of life to the various organs (including the skin) by which life, and action, are carried forth. To ignore this fact of life is to head down the path of modern analytic thinking.

To define history as the action of human selves self-consciously pursuing themselves is to set oneself up for analytic trouble. By contrast, had the moderns the courage to steal *soul* from the preachers of analytic doom, a lot of suffering might have been prevented. To have thus defined "history" as the course of life among breathing beings grateful for the spirit they cannot explain might have led to a little less cutting up. In principle at least, it would have settled the human down into more cooperative relations with all other living beings who, by a variety of means, are grateful for the clean air and light they exchange for energy. This, we now understand, was a virtual impossibility because, already by the seventeenth century (and decidedly by the nineteenth century), the analytic course of human thinking in the West turned on the dark thought of savages. Modernity, it might be said, is the fear of returning too innocently to life among the savage beasts. Hence, the self-preoccupation of so-called modern thought.

Descartes was thus the first to give eloquent expression to the moral principle that it is better for like kind to keep to themselves, even if it means throwing a line or two around the camp. *Cogito, ergo sum* was, in effect, the first analytic line of this kind. The Self is that which thinks itself in order to ward off the dark return of the savage Goths. This is why there is so little soul in so much of modern thought. It could not help itself. It was not possible, given the foundational dark thoughts, to think too precisely about the breath that enlivens the blood which courses alike among many beings.

The psyche, thus, is that sort of *mind* that is always, to some degree, other than itself. The psyche is the soul of differences. This is why it is possible to describe Freud and psychoanalysis as the Moors of modern thought. Until the eclipse darkened the Enlightenment sky, it was psychoanalysis, more than any literature other than literature itself, that preserved the dark thought as a necessary feature of human thinking. Though any number of poets and fiction makers did this in their way, Freud was the only one of the great end-of-the-nineteenth-century social thinkers to counter the analytic urge by an insistence on the impossibility of Self. Thus, for him, even in the earliest, most mechanical and structural of his phases, instead of the Self there stood, simply, the "I" or "ego." This Freudian "I" was, curiously, never an analytic thing, but always a breathing part of the soul by which the mind engaged in its never-ending struggle with the all-too-rational demands of the superego and the all-too-savage drives of the id. It is true of course that Freud himself, and most of his followers, failed to complete the Copernican revolution of removing the Self from the center of human life.[20] Freud himself had more than a few analytic moments between the early hydraulic theory of the psyche and the pysche's eventual resolution into drive theory. Still, from the first great work issued just weeks before the end of the last century, Freud allowed for the possibility of mental life as the work of a soul, not of a self.

In *The Interpretation of Dreams* (1899), Freud, a devoted reader of Sophocles and the Greeks, mapped the terrain of the Unconscious in mental life. Dreams are the ubiquitous language of this *terra incognita*. They are also, in the book's memorable opening line, "a psychical structure which has a meaning and which can be inserted at an assignable point in the mental activities of waking life." Dreams are always with us. They are the representations of that Other-within, which is always other-than-self (so to speak), yet assignably necessary to it. There is no consciousness without the Unconscious. In the central structure of mental life there are no identities. The self is not itself. In the place of the organizing Self of modern thought, psychoanalysis put the psyche—the *soul* that is always up against its necessary limits. This does not mean that psychoanalysis has been immune to the analytic impulse, some of it quite dreadful—as in Freud's own early cutting up of the sexualities based on what today we understand to have been a hasty reading of Sophocles. Still, like many of the social thinkers at the end of the last century, Freud and the movement he started resisted the analytic urge even as they were giving in to it. In Freud's case the resistance was never resolved. He thus was the Moor of modern thought who saved the Greek soul in the displacements of the psyche.

About the same time, another founder of twentieth-century psychology, worked the same terrain as Freud's. William James, however, worked it from the opposite border. His *Principles of Psychology* (1890) was one of academic psychology's early and enduring analytic textbooks. "Psychology is the Science of Mental Life."[21] This is James's first line, different in every important respect from Freud's opening words, just a decade later. James was on an analytic course. This required that he deal with the Soul. He wasted no time. In the same, first paragraph of the book, James dismisses the spiritualist idea of the personal *Soul* as the original source of the phenomena of psychology. Still, James did not go so far as to say there is no soul; only that it cannot be the foundation of psychological knowledge. When, later, James writes of cognition, he says that "the relation of knowing is the most mysterious thing in the world."[22] His fascination with religion in *Varieties of Religious Experience* reveals the full extent of his awareness of the limits of knowledge. For Freud, the Other was the Unconscious; for James, it was religion.

Yet, at the heart of his science of mind lay the Self wherein James reveals his own unwitting alliance with the Strong-We:

> The Empirical Self of each of us is all that he is tempted to call by the name of *me*. . . . We feel and act about certain things that are ours very much as we feel and act about ourselves. Our fame, our children, the work of our hands, may be as dear to us as our bodies are, arouse the same feelings and the same acts of reprisal if attacked. And our bodies themselves, are they simply ours, or are they *us*?[23]

There could hardly be a more gracious illustration of the struggles the better Strong-We put themselves through. James is speaking here of the old, old mind-body dilemma. Consciousness of Self is basic to mind. When that which is ours is called into question is it merely because we possess it, or because it is our Self itself? Is it that we are what is ours? Or that what is ours is us? You see the difficulty inherent to the idea of Self. In the same paragraph, James makes more trouble for himself:

> *In its widest possible sense*, however, *a man's Self is the sum of all that he CAN call his*, not only his body and his psychic powers, but his clothes and his house, his wife and children, his ancestors and friends, his reputation and works, his lands and horse, and yacht and bank-account.

You can hear the chorus, *Whose We?*

Thus began what is commonly known in the analytic world as Self-theory. And thus it began on the Strong-We assumption. Here, full-blown, is the universal self—the very Self who owns and works and thrives. He rides horses as did Jefferson till the last months of his life. But then there is the word James himself emphasized: "A man's self is all that he CAN call his own." No respecter of mysteries could possibly deny that ownership is always trouble, especially when what is owned is land and yachts and the like.

It is all too easy to sneer. James tried to think otherwise. In the section immediately following this very gentlemanly definition of the universal self, James attempted to enumerate the constituents of Self itself. Among the more interesting of these are the still provocative pair—the social self and what

James called the spiritual Self. The former gave rise to the unforgettable expression, "A man has as many social selves as there are individuals who recognize him." These others are the others within. But they were ultimately, if uncertainly, reconciled. Against the social, stood what he called the "Self of selves," which he labeled the spiritual Self. Then, quite outside his analytic cutting apart of the Self, James writes of "the sense of personal identity." Hence the other of the memorable lines from this section. "Am I the same self today as I was yesterday?"[24] This is the existential question of anyone who dares reflect on herself amid the societies to which she belongs, or from which he is excluded. It is, obviously, a very difficult question when asked analytically—when asked, that is, from within the terms of a Strong-We Self.

The reason not to be overly harsh with many of the early Strong-We social theorists is that they very often knew, as did James, that something is wrong in the analytic scheme. He could not put his finger on what was wrong. But he could, and did, acknowledge the difficulty. In *Varieties of Religious Experience*, he returned to the uncertainty at the heart of self theory in a chapter on the "Divided Self" where he described a man's interior life "as a battle-ground for what he feels to be two deadly hostile selves, one actual, the other ideal."[25] James's idea of the divided self was surely a, if not the, major source of W. E. B. Du Bois's double consciousness of the American Negro. Du Bois—one of the most distinguished of Weak-We social theorists—was James's student at Harvard, and long-time friend afterward. Just as James, on his side, suffered the division between analytic certainty and reality, so Du Bois, who knew Weak-We realities very well, for a long while felt that the solutions lay in the Strong-We culture of the European Diaspora. The divide between the Strong- and the Weak-We can be harsh, and usually is; but not always.

Still, it was with James, as much as anyone else, that "Self" crossed over from its past as a reflexive to take up its place in the analytic narrative. Subsequent self-theorists, from Charles Horton Cooley to George Herbert Mead to Norbert Wiley and Karl Scheibe, among others today,[26] faced the same dilemma that beset James. How is it possible for the human Self, with all its competing social pressures, to be the same today as it was yesterday? All along the way of this distinguished tradition, thinkers attempted to account for what James called the problem of personal identity in complex societies. None was able to outrun the analytical force of the concept itself.

Even so supple a formulation as George Herbert Mead's suffers the limitations of the analytic urge. "The self has the characteristic that it is an object to itself and that characteristic distinguishes it from other objects and from the body."[27] This may be Mead's most parsimonious summary of his idea of the Self. Yet, for all its freshness, it groans under the weight of the ages. Consciousness of self is, necessarily, the inherent human quality. It is that which locates the analytic Self between the world of inert objects and the body's animal passions. Mead's advance over the seventeenth-century psychologists, though considerable in the particulars, is superficial in the basics. The Self remains the organizing center of human variety, the presupposition of moral agency, the axis of cognition, the drive of history. For the several centuries of its coming out, the analytic Self was, always, the de facto Self of the Strong-We. It was the foundational principle of Universal Humanity. As such, it was always vulnerable to the reality of social differences. Its vulnerability lay in its ambition—in its self-claim to be the successor to the human Soul, in its willingness to serve as the zero signifier of all humanity. All that it took was for some wise guy to say *Whose We?* The self-evidence of the Self began to shake.

All Strong-We claims are ultimately moral; hence, political. Strong claims of this sort are, in fact, usually made quietly, as though the truth of them was perfectly self-evident. They are, even, made in silence. Thus, when someone breaks the code of silence, as Erving Goffman did in 1963, the reaction may be no more than a nervous twitter:

> Even where widely attained norms are involved, their multiplicity has the effect of disqualifying many persons. For example, in an important sense there is only one completely unblushing male in America: a young, married, white, urban, northern, heterosexual Protestant father of college education, fully employed, of good complexion, weight and height, and recent record in sports. Every American male tends to look out on the world from this perspective, constituting one sense in which one can speak of a common value system in America.[28]

The silence here broken is that covering the ludicrously over-strong idea that any complex society like the American one, even when it focuses its power on some global purpose, could possibly enjoy anything like a "common value system." It is one thing to believe, even to know that people in a Society share basic orientations to the grind of daily life. This is not hard to swallow. It would be hard to account for the grind otherwise. But, it is quite another thing to believe—as numerous politicians, preachers, social scientists, and other analytic types have from time to time—that it is possible for a society to enjoy a "common value system" in the sense of that which holds the Whole together. The difference is in the strength of the assertion. The stronger it is, the more moralizing is required to protect it. One might even say that faith in the Universal Self is the last analytic resort before the truth is out.

It is not, therefore, by accident that Goffman's smart-alecky call on the silliness of a strong common values scheme comes where it does. *Stigma* (1963), which ends with this coda on the unblushing male in America, is Goffman's most succinct statement of the deficiencies of Self-theory. By showing just how the stigmatized, in managing their spoiled identities, obey the same interaction rules as the normal, Goffman creates, in a word, the principle of the normal deviant.[29] If there is any universal among different human beings, it is not the content of their Self, but the common sense with which they obey the rules of interaction. There is no Self in the strong sense. There is, by contrast, a series of moves the weak Self can make to negotiate the delicate societal intimacies between social and personal identities. Social identifies are, in effect, the forms of social possibility handed over to the individual by the social group. Personal identity is, however, anything but the inner moral being appropriating the social unto its unique and highly spiritual sense of Self. With due irreverence, Goffman says:

> By *personal identity*, I have in mind only the . . . positive marks or identity pegs, and the unique combination of life history items that comes to be attached to the individual with the help of these pegs for his identity. Personal identity, then, has to do with the assumption that the individual can be differentiated from all others and that around this means of differentiation a single continuous record of social facts can be attached, entangled, like candy floss, becoming then the sticky substance to which still other biographical facts can be attached.[30]

Like candy floss! Like, even, the criminal with a record, the self is a sticky substance for the adherence of biographical facts. With Goffman, then, came the first use of the expression "politics of identity."[31] He effectively ridicules the Strong-We Self. Goffman, more than any unblushing white man of his time,[32] made it clear just how vulnerable the three-centuries-old Strong-We idea was.

Still, the idea was defended in the years that followed. Some of the defenses are empty and foolish. One in particular is compelling. In *Sources of the Self* (1989), Charles Taylor composes the history of the Self. He plainly diagnoses the vulnerability of the disengaged subject that stood behind both Descartes' and Locke's self-psychologies. He means to demonstrate the limits of the overly elegant punctual self by exposing its ludicrous doctrine that "we become constructors of our own character."[33] Taylor, in effect, understands the extent to which the Strong-We rely entirely on the myth of the pure subject, disengaged from moral space. His goal is to reconstruct a strong concept of Self on a sociological foundation. He begins:

> I want to defend the strong thesis that doing without frameworks is utterly impossible for us; otherwise put, that the horizons within which we live our lives and which make sense of them have to include these strong qualitative discriminations. Moreover, this is not meant just as a contingently true psychological fact about human beings which could perhaps turn out one day not to hold for some exceptional individual or new type, some superman of disengaged objectification. Rather, the claim is that living within such strongly qualified horizons is constitutive of human agency, that stepping outside these limits would be tantamount to stepping outside what we would recognize as integral, that is, undamaged human personhood.[34]

Here is a Strong-We statement with a difference. Taylor's "undamaged human personhood" is not lodged in universal properties of cognition, being, or practice. Rather, the Self is defined in relation to moral orientations that, in turn, are unavoidably social:

> My self-definition is understood as an answer to the question Who I am. And this question finds its original sense in the interchange of speakers. I define who I am by defining where I speak from, in the family tree, in social space, in the geography of social statuses and functions, in my intimate relations to the ones I love, and also crucially in the space of moral and spiritual orientation within which my most important defining relations are lived out.[35]

Self-definition, thus, is the narrative product of a pilgrimage within moral frameworks for the sense of the good in relations with others. Taylor uses the engaged but still Strong-We. "Because we cannot but orient ourselves to the good, and thus determine our place relative to it and hence determine the direction of our lives, we must inescapably understand our lives in narrative form, as a 'quest.'"[36]

The moral quest with others revives the Self as narrative. This is the bold leap beyond the disengaged Universal Self. Even so, Taylor cannot escape its gravity. What he must do to complete the idea is to speak of the concrete human differences against which any such quest must move. Taylor's position remains a Strong-We one because he assumes a social space and a geography of statuses that are wholly friendly to the questing Self. These are the social conditions, and the only social conditions, in which one could expect to find the "undamaged human personhood" for which the Self strives. Taylor moves well beyond even James. His social self is not a receptor of recognitions so much as a social force joined necessarily in framework with others.

Taylor requires a world relatively immune to the damaging force of social differences, which are not, in the end, polite questions of identity differences. Social differences, in the current situation, are about inequalities of such potency as to have the reality of death. Even Craig Calhoun, one of Taylor's most robust advocates, withdraws on this point. "The relationship of social change to change in persons and moral frameworks remains largely an enigma."[37] Calhoun then lists the changes in world order Taylor fails to address:

> The introduction of democratic politics, the rise of state bureaucracies, the shrinking size of the family, the transformation in numbers of people working away from their homes and/or among relative strangers, the growth of cities, the increased ease of travel, the conquest and loss of empires, and globalization of the economy, the change in living standards, the increase in capacity to kill in war, and so on.

Calhoun is right. Had Taylor not intended to lodge the modern, moral Self in concrete social life, he would not have had to account for the concreteness. He did. So he must. But he does not.

The bind Taylor put himself in is nothing more than the bind of the best Strong-We thinking. It is not enough to uncover the social nature of the Self; nor to embed it in a narrative quest with others. It turns out that these others with whom we are expected to quest can be extremely difficult—even when they are on our side (and most of them are not). This is the understanding that is second nature to the Weak-We.

When even so critical a modern liberal as Taylor fails to recompose the soul of the Western Self, it is clear that there is little good that can be done from within. The Strong-We cannot be other than it has been becoming through the centuries since at least Descartes, perhaps even Martin Luther, possibly Augustine. Strong-We is as Strong-We is. Its power always comes up against that which it cannot get around. The ideal of the strong Self as a universal property of human Being is simply not able to entertain the possibility of differences.

If there is any fact of world life it is that there are gross differences among the various membership groups of humans. These are differences too obvious to list. They arise from social arbitraries to be sure. The play among them is always uncertain. Is race really class? Is gender really sexuality? Or, again, class? Is class global or local?—and how does it play upon sex, skin, and gender? And so on. It is one thing to discover that many of these are social constructs—that there is nothing natural about the differences assigned to skin or blood; that the desire of others, like the desire for lucre, is plastic as much as it is given; that we are driven as much to destroy as to build; and so on. Social constructions are real. But in what sense? From whence do they come? Are they mankind's original nature?—or its original sin? After all these years, no one can even begin to answer.

When one day someone does, she will have to begin outside the culture of the Strong-We. For, if it is assumed from the start that social differences are either the accidents of failed progress or the necessities of nature, it is impossible to give those differences their due. Neither the left-liberal nor the right-conservative—the one affirming a vague progress, the other defending a just as vague naturalism—will ever convince the other. This is why both suffer the contempt of the Weak-We in roughly equal measure.

In the end, the question the varieties of liberal modernism—those of the right and the left—can never answer is the question they, together, pose. How is it possible to dream of the future while remaining true to the real present? Without the dream, the present is unbearable. Without present realities, the dream is a fantasy. The future of the present is—and always has been—the riddle of modern culture. This is where its left hand, bent back where it cannot see, touches ever so gently its right hand. This is where Marx meets the political economists he could never shake off.

Among the Weak-We this riddle is familiar. More than familiar, it is the most apparent necessity of their self-understanding. It is the social space of their souls. The Weak-We understand what, very probably, can never be truly understood by those who assume the upper hand. They understand, as Patricia Hill Collins puts it, "the necessity of linking caring, theoretical vision with informed, practical struggle."[38] Put this way, one sees the wisdom, but still may ask, Is not this no more than the familiar analytic question of the dialectic between theory and practice? In a sense it is. But the sense in which it is *not* lies in where the answer is sought. It is sought not in the analytic remove of technical elaborations that refine and comprise the theoretical vision to the empirical necessities of the practice. The analytic remove *always*, and necessarily, destroys the dialectic. This is its first cut—that by which Strong-We thinking is all too ready to squeeze the blood to fit the skin.

If the Strong-We were willing to look closely, they would see that just before the squeeze, the Weak-We stop, to make another move. They do it often, regularly. This move is always disturbing, upsetting, annoying, insistent. It is rude in its fashion. It is the move of story telling, as in Collins's prelude to her discussion of visionary pragmatism:

> As a child growing up in an African-American, working-class Philadelphia neighborhood, I wondered how my mother and all the other women on our block kept going. Early each workday they rode long distances on public transportation to jobs that left them unfulfilled, overworked, and underpaid. Periodically they complained, but more often they counseled practicality and patience. Stressing the importance of a good education as the route to a better life, they recognized that even if Black girls married, big houses, maids, and blended family bliss as idealized on the popular television show *The Brady Bunch* were not guaranteed for us. Their solution: we, their daughters, were to become self-reliant and independent.[39]

Then, she says, "The Black women on my block possessed a 'visionary pragmatism' that emphasized the necessity of linking caring, theoretical vision with informed, practical struggle." Collins then cites other black feminist women. But the citations, if one looks closely, are not the analytic move one might suppose. Everything Collins writes, even when she is writing to address the analytic terms of her disciplines, is always written in relation of the Weak-We others who know what she means.[40] At times, it is true, Weak-We academics like Patricia Hill Collins and Lisa Lowe, even Judith Butler, among others, write as though they were content with the analytic words of their professional fields. But, even when they are making careful, patient, practical moves against those fields, they begin with stories meant to affirm their ties—their Weak-We ties—to mothers, and to the other mothers, and others still.

As I say, stories of this kind are disturbing to the analytically strong. They violate the methodological rules. They are so very local, particular, variable—hence, unscientific.

The Weak-We are annoying, insistent, unrelenting because they are the better sociologists of the particulars. They begin with the experience of damaged personhood—if not their own, at least, that of those they know, or love, or heard tell of. They know very well that, whatever is common among human beings, there is a certain power to be had in recognizing the plain facts of life.

Their weakness, so to speak, is weak against the claims of those who insist on a universal Self, of whichever kind. The Weak-We assert their differences not to psychologize but to define moral and political frameworks just as Taylor would like. Their strength lies in the stronger grasp of societal relations—of the important bonds to which one must cling in a dangerous world. They, thus, remind the Strong-We of their limits, of the trouble at the heart of the analytic world, of the insufficiency of gentle sociologies of the moral quest. Their *Whose We?* is the darkest possible thought the Strong-We could imagine.

Three

A Call in the Morning, 1988

Wake up calls are disturbing. They come out of the blue, bringing news that changes life in important ways.

One came for me about nine on a late winter morning. I was still home. The night before I had hosted a small party honoring a colleague who had just been promoted. There was something not quite right about that party. At the time I brushed it off. Soon I would know what it was.

The call was from my school's academic vice president. "What are we going to do about that letter?" To which I could only say, "What letter?" I had no clue. It was, he explained, a letter from a man who had been a candidate for a job in one of my departments. I was a faculty dean at the time. Part of the work was to interview all the candidates for all the jobs in all the departments for which I was responsible. "Responsible," I should quickly say, is hardly the right word. In those days no one in particular was responsible for what went on. The then president was bored with his job, but still trying hard. This vice president loved his, for which reason he was not exactly happy that the president had introduced deans into the school's administrative structure. The result was administrative chaos.

Anyhow, the letter in question was from a man who had interviewed quite some time before, months before. He was upset, he said, with the treatment he received while on campus. He listed quite a number of things—all of them terrible, if true. But he named no names, except mine. He accused the named and unnamed of treating him in a way that was, in the phrase of that day, "racially insensitive." He was, you will now understand, black. As for me, he accused me of using the word "nigger" in a way he thought wrong. Had I in fact said what he claimed, he would have been right. The trouble is that I hadn't. Why exactly he said that I had I still do not know for sure, and never will. But I was more than able to understand that, had all (or any) of the things he listed happened, he would have excellent reason to protest. Why, exactly, I would be the only one named, however, was the puzzle. Yes, I know. "Why me?"— white man's blues.

I have long since forgiven him—this man whose name, at the time, I could barely recall; but which, from then on, I would never forget. Black people are treated badly all the time, and especially when they are seeking jobs. Whites willing to look, can see it every day in every way. So why blame him? And especially why blame him whom I considered a brother of sorts. And that, exactly, is where my troubles began.

The reason the party the night before had gone so badly is that "the letter" had been sent all over campus. Everyone, it seems, knew about it at least the day before. Why and how it had been passed around so far and wide you can very well imagine. I was the last to hear, but not the last to understand.

After the call, there began what we called in those days a "process." It seems that some colleagues on campus agreed that I "*could* have said" what this man said I said. When I met with the president to discuss what we should do, things did not go particularly well. He was, for good reason, scared. As one of my then accusers would later say, nothing strikes terror in the guts of white people like "racial incidents." The president knew, and so did I, that this incident would become public.

The call came at the beginning of the long spring recess. The students, who know dead meat when they see it, were away. So there was time—but for what? The process took time but to no important benefit for anyone. That is the trouble with liberal process. It seeks to "let everyone have a say" on the silly expectation that when they say what they feel their anger will go away. Such a process, it turns out, only results in forestalling the public expression of that anger. When people are angry for a good reason, even when they may not have the facts exactly right, they are not going to keep quiet—at least not about an incident of this kind.

The thing about the process was just as I say. It led nowhere. The people on campus who supposed that I "could" have said what the letter writer claimed refused to confront me directly. The president, a lawyer, thought they should, but felt he could not insist on it. For him, I was the trouble, whatever he may have thought about the facts. Quite reasonably he wanted the trouble to go away, which in the end could only mean that I should go away. Several times he suggested my resignation would be nice. One was the only time I recall getting mad at him. He told me he thought he was being very generous and that "a lot of guys in my position would demand your resignation." I replied, "That's true; and a lot of guys in your position would say to the accusers, 'He's my man; so you can get the hell out of here, unless you have some proof.'" He took my point, since the then President of the United States, Ronald Reagan (with whom neither of us was exactly enchanted), had recently said something of that sort to accusers of one of his men. Neither of us liked being put in the analytic category we suddenly found ourselves sharing—that of racially insensitive white folk. So, unhappy together, we tacitly decided to join hands and run the gauntlet together. We both knew, of course, that only I would also have to walk the plank, if it came to that, which it did.

The process included a long investigation of the facts. It went public very quickly after the students returned. What I feared was that this would be my fifteen minutes of worldly fame. For some reason, however, the news reports stopped at the borders of my state. Mentions of the incident in the national media (only two, so far as I know) omitted my name. The thing ended as these things often end. I resigned as dean but stayed on as a teacher. I was sent off, to the relief of all, for a year's sabbatical. I still work at this school, with great pleasure.

This little story is not a tragedy. Its point lies beyond the multicultural panic the incident fueled in the weeks following my disgrace. My wake up began upon the realization that many of those who came to my defense were less concerned about me than about "those people who would say such things to anyone." I was lonely, as you can imagine. I wanted support. But not this. They never said what they meant. But I knew. They knew I knew. It was creepy.

With time, I came to understand why colleagues (all of them, necessary to say, black) could join the letter writer in accusing me so. Their persuasive complaint was that I was "too familiar." Yes, exactly that. This was the word they used and meant. This particular "racial incident" had arisen upon nothing, but it attached itself to experiences colleagues had had with me. I had been too familiar with them. Finally, then, I knew what I had done wrong.

I have to say this carefully. I would be the last person in line to testify that I do no evil in the world. I have done plenty and regret it all. But this was not evil so much as stupidity. There is a difference. My stupidity was in assuming, without ever asking, that black people just plain understood that, though I was phenotypically white, I was in fact black. In trusting unreasonably that black people would appreciate how black I really was, I proved myself whiter than white.

I had reversed a white people's dogma to bizarre effect. When liberal whites want to signify their excellent racial attitudes they will often say they are "color blind," and just as often add something like, "I don't care whether you are white, black, or Polka-dot." They say this in the complete absence of any confirmation that any known black person in America, or anywhere else, has ever taken comfort in it. I would assume that they don't because all that the friendly white person is doing is talking about himself—how *he* sees, or *thinks* he sees, the others. Me, I had come to the same result, by a different route. By assuming that black people saw me seeing them as I saw myself seeing them, I was attributing color blindness to them.

Still today, I realize that one talks about this sort of thing with little likelihood of anyone, on either side of the color line, being much impressed. I just am what I am, for which—because of the color of my skin, not to mention the content of my character—I get no credit from anyone. The color line does cut both ways. At least in public, skin always trumps blood, not to mention (if I may be too familiar) soul, or self. To pretend this is not so is to be familiar in the worst way. I deserved what I got, and took it as well as I knew how.

When W. E. B. Du Bois spoke of the color line, and the Veil, he was not—as some think—proposing a nice little variant on the social psychology of racial personalities. A veil is a delicate thing—sewn of fine thread with painstaking care. The Veil of which he spoke is anything but this. That was his way. Du Bois often stole some figure from a refined parlor of European culture and turned it on its metaphoric ear. The Veil of which he wrote is always drawn to enforce the color line. Those on one side see things one way. Those on the other see them differently.

What we white liberals seldom accept is that the color line is a front that rarely allows for a no-fire zone. Those who cross over do so at their peril. I could never quite believe it when, in those old war movies, American soldiers dressed up like enemy soldiers to invade the enemy's camp. Is it really possible for any foreigner to speak another's language so perfectly as to go undetected? What I always liked about Clint Eastwood when he played those roles is that he usually kept silent or squinted as he does. Me, when I tried to play myself on the other side of the front, I talked too much. I should have kept my mouth shut and squinted more.

Those I offended were not my enemies, even if at the time I was theirs. Still, this is the kind of thing that happens when there are Veils and color lines. Everything gets confused. No one quite knows who's the friend and who's not. Life on the color line is anything but a movie.

The Rights and Justices of the Multicultural Panic, 1990s

One of the more telling definitions of the word "panic" is "groundless fear." Everyone I know agrees that to be grounded is good; to be groundless is frightful. The social being of such a good relies on its appeal to popular sentiment. In modern culture "being grounded" is just about as good as it gets.

This, of course, is a social habit especially pronounced after the eighteenth century, when Kant, among others, but especially Kant, demonstrated the appeal of a well-grounded good. In a single swipe he united the whole of modern morality. The well-grounded good, he said, was a duty so categorical as to compel the good person to act as the one whose action was necessary to the integrity of the societal whole. Duty, action, and universal humankind joined in the *ménage à trois* at the heart of modern culture. The genius of it all was in the grounding of moral thought in concrete duty, without stipulating the course of action required. Hereafter, deontological and teleological ethics swooned before the formidable beauty of an imperative that was neither contextual nor universal, but both at once. The true became the good. The key to "dare to know" was in the daring, not the knowing. The genius of the formula was that, for the duration of modern culture, the good served as so plausible a counsel to the lingering sentiment for the true. Beauty, by contrast, when not finally exposed to mass consumption, was confined to the better parlors— precious, when not degraded. Out of doors, on the street, only the good remained as an effective standard. And such a good it was.

No one put it better than Kant. To be modern is to live the good life, on practical grounds, always keeping the commonwealth well in mind. No overbearing natural laws. No bothering ultimate ends. Only the well-intentioned good—grounded in useful means; considerate of, but not obligated to, common ends. Permutations of the equation on the different sides of the Channel, or the Atlantic, tended to be washed away by an axial judgment so ferocious as to cleanse Being, Nature, and even Truth of their dusty pretenses.

Freud and Nietzsche were the first to recognize that modernity was, if essentially anything, essentially a culture of hysteria, the collective form of which is, simply, "panic"—the groundless fear that the ground of practical duty is falling away. Hence, the delicately sublime propriocentric function of modernity. It required some inexplicable inward center—a moral gyroscope—whereby its practitioners were expected simultaneously to keep one eye on the ground of specific duty and another on the general good of the community. It made little difference that few could pass the roadside test for moral sobriety. It is almost impossible for a human being to walk a straight line while regarding a finger upon the nose. But those not drunk with privilege understood the rule's extravagant foolishness very well. They did not have to read Kant or anyone else of his kind to appreciate the truth of pure practical goodness. Those who understood were not the ones to panic. It was the crowd of true believers who had the most to lose.

Crowds panic under any number of social conditions—too little air; too few exits; screams of fire; rumors of enemies down the street. They do not panic when they know where they'd like to go, and believe they can get there (even when they cannot). Nor do they panic when the enemy, even if a fire-breathing dragon, is visible and known. Panic is the fear arising upon an uncertain footing. It is the inability to make traction against a rumored evil one cannot see. The moral gyroscope fails to tune the inner sentiment to any duty at hand. The terror spreads. The crowd rushes. People stomp all over each other in the rush to exit the theater of illusions.

In the 1990s, just as the eclipse first cast shadows over this moral universe, those with investments in its analytic culture panicked. They came to fear that the moral ground was shifting in ways that rendered their propriocentric values futile. What they feared most of all was that which had been there, under foot, from the first. They feared the cultures from which they had extracted their own universal values—those no longer silent, no longer respectful of their all-too-odd morality, and no longer willing to regard it as their duty to be considerate of the societal whole.

Though the panic took on the appearances of arguments over certain words—notably "multiculturalism"—the truth of the fear lay in the loss of an illusion. They had thought that the ground was bordered by clear and distinct choices between rights and justice. They believed, without truly confronting their illusion, that the moral universe was thoroughly joined below appearances. They actually trusted that such necessary members as rights and justices were but opposing buttresses unto the final, progressive end. By the end of the millennium, this was far from clear.

"Multiculturalism"—the term is among the most confusing and misused in the language of social theory. "Multiculturalism" confuses because it makes obstinate reference to two things at once—reality and a theory of reality. The same has been said of another troublemaker of this sort, "postmodernism," with which "multiculturalism" is often, usually incorrectly, taken as a cognate of some kind. [1]

Though there is a close lexical kinship, the two terms are separated by an important semantic space arising upon different conjunctions of attributes. "Postmodernism," when used naively, is thought to be "nothing more" than a theoretical term. It is true, of course, that the word may be used as the name for a kind of theory. But this is properly done only when the use embraces, with delicate care, plausible statements of fact about the "real world." Just the same, any number of wise guys (and, remarkably, a few wise gals) go about using the word "postmodernism" (or, worse yet, the appalling adjective "post-modernist") in reference to what in their own minds is "nothing more than a theoretical fad" of vaguely French provenance. (Near the end of the modern half-millennium, the most notable wise guy of this sort was someone who called himself "Alan Sokal," the improbability of whose linguistic trickery continues, even today, to astonish and amuse.)[2] That some people who ought to know better speak or write this way does not excuse the irresponsibility of their misuse—and abuse—of the word. In this connection, it is proper to note for future reference that the difficulty otherwise literate people have in getting these two terms in their proper semantic spaces is associated by custom with a studied confusion of other terms of notable ability to trouble—"theory," "fact," and "science" among other examples.[3]

The trouble with "multiculturalism" among all the troubling terms used in and about social theory is that its corruption requires an altogether inexcusable, even malicious, misunderstanding of the facts of the world.[4] It is relatively easy to forgive those so alarmed by the *possibility* that the modern world might be drawing to a close that they would use the word "postmodernism" pejoratively in the sense of "only a theory, and an obscure French one at that!" One can well understand why those in social positions well respected in a given cultural arrangement such as the modern one, might fear the loss of position that would follow a decline in the fortunes of the arrangement itself.

"Multiculturalism," on the other hand, if it is to be used at all, can *only* be used to characterize, at most, a generalized attitude toward actual and unforgiving facts so evidently accepted as to be beyond necessity of reference. Whereas "postmodernism," when properly used, refers to a factual *possibility*. Works written by those who would never, normally, be thought of as "multiculturalists"—Samuel Huntington's *The Clash of Civilization and the Remaking of World Order* or Nathan Glazer's *We Are All Multiculturalists* [sic] *Now*, for example, do not fit into this category.[5] Still, evident or not, the term "multiculturalism," when used indefinitely as a substantive, remains controversial against a growing accord over the facts of the matter.

The most general of those facts may, however, be adequately summarized in the following: *The world at large and the social worlds of most societies in it are affected by global (as distinct from nationalizing) forces that can be called "multicultural" in the sense that peoples of different and often incommensurable cultural affinities live in sufficiently real—or, at least televisual—proximity to each other as to be*

*well aware of each other, and their differences—often to the point of open civil or,
even, armed conflict.* It is possible, of course, to propose a theory here, but one
would hardly be well advised to present himself as, say, a "multiculturalist" in
the sense that persons who are thought to suppose the modern world is coming
to an end are referred to as "postmodernists." This may be why two of the
more ambitious theories of the end-of-millennium world are decidedly not
"postmodernist," even though both argue that with the end of the Cold War in
1990 the world itself changed decisively—either by a clearing of the decks so
that the true monoculture might thrive, or by the end of the West's cultural
dominance.[6]

Hence, the dilemma attendant upon any serious consideration of the word
"multiculturalism." It is a word so embedded in "facts" (in, that is, warrantable
presumptions about the "real world") that one might have a theory in its name
only when one's feet are planted on some factual ground similar to the kind
that would be required to support some other person's "postmodernism." The
two terms, and their factual subject matters, are empirically allied, which
accounts for the tendency to treat them as virtual cognates, thus to ignore that
their respective relations to fact are distinguishable by the kind of fact
entailed—certain and available in the one case ("multiculturalism"); possible
and presently unavailable in the other ("postmodernism"). Those who might
wish to use either term are well advised to use either or both cautiously (if only
because, in a multicultural world, the unglossed use of such terms exposes one
to the threat of being thought of as a "postmodernist").

Therefore, a premise: *Though the world may or may not be postmodern, it is
certainly multicultural.* This distinction, along with the troubles involved, does
not mean it is impossible to speak of such a practice as "multicultural theory"
(though, if one must, he should avoid at all costs the usage "multiculturalist
theory," which, apart from the inelegance, is a slur of sorts). It is possible,
however, to "have" or "hold" a "multicultural theory" in the sense of sharing an
empirically reliable, if not universally held, attitude with respect to the
world's current state of becoming. Still, even this expression requires great
care. Theories of the world as it is, whether professional or practical ones, are
always, at best, representations of the world. They are, thus, no better and no
worse than the facts upon which they rely.

Therefore: here, for once, the proper and classic sense of the world "theory" applies strictly. As is seldom noted, the original Greek *theoros* meant "one
who travels in order to see things." Hence, if one wants to use the term "theory" properly there is no better field of facts in respect to which it might be
used than this, present and (presumably) actual existing, multicultural world.
A theory of the multicultural word would be something that could only be
accomplished by traveling about in order to see the varieties of things practiced in the name of the world's multiple cultures. This is why one who speaks
of "multicultural theory" is always at risk of contradiction (if not downright
embarrassment). The use of the word "multicultural" requires a settled opin-

ion, based on reliable (if not incontrovertible) facts, as to the state of the real world. But, to be a "multiculturalist" [*sic*]—as Nathan Glazer uses the word—is to purport to be a proper member of "reality." This is plainly absurd. What is not either absurd or embarrassing is to believe that people, including oneself, are not wrong to have and hold theories of their world that would account for its many-cultured nature. Therefore, a theory may be "multicultural" only because it is agreed that "multicultural" is a proper word with which to modify the term "world."

It is true that, as in many things, modern times (even postmodern ones) have lost much of what was considered to be sensible and good. Today, sadly, theories claim to be able to analyze and organize vast reaches of observable social realities—a practice outlandishly alien to the original practices done in the name of theory. The Greeks, for instance, were never so much theorists, as they were philosophers—lovers of the wisdom of their own powerful, but local culture. "Theory," as we have come to use it today, has broken all relations with philosophy—as, indeed, if Richard Rorty is to be trusted, philosophy itself has long since broken off with its own foundational practices.[7]

So, to speak today of "multicultural theory" one must not speak any too modernishly, as if "theory" *only* referred to a certain high discourse associated with claims to general truth about very large categories like justices, recognitions, welfares, and the like. To attempt to speak, or write, of the varieties of cultures inhabiting the world today, even theoretically, would be imprudent for reason of the certainty that the behavior will redouble one's trouble by virtue of misusing "theory" as a substantive available for modification by the adjective "multicultural"—hence, to err twice in one move.

To allude to the Greeks in this way is not to trifle with meanings or common sense. It may very well be that it is impossible to use the word "theory" as it has descended into modern usages in reference to the subject immediately at hand. Hence, irony, once again: At the very moment when the world, being multicultural, presents itself ready for the original Greek sense of "theory," modernists (having lost their habit of studying the Greeks) no longer trust the ancient wisdom. Still, a person or persons we know as "Homer" taught a theory of what came to be a civilization by telling stories of travels he (or they) either undertook or heard reports of. Homer's stories were, in every respect, shocking, upsetting, and entertaining. We would not know these stories if the Greeks had not first loved them and incorporated them into their own surprisingly multicultural dramas.[8]

By contrast, against every shred of common sense, some moderns (or modernists, if you must) consider "multicultural" stories told by authors probably as multiple as those who told the Homeric fables to be of surprising, arbitrary, and of recent origin—and, thus, as intrusions upon their values. This is why, as any wide-awake reader of the newspapers of the last years of the second post-Hellenic millennium knew, those who used the words "multiculturalism" and "postmodernism" as invective meant also to attack those who think of themselves as doers of "theory" in other than the official Enlightenment sense (as, that is, the general organizing truth of a category of officially sanctioned facts).

Hence, one can hardly speak of "theory" in relation to the "multicultural" without examining the name, the multiplicities of which make for the shockingly aggressive noun "culture," which forms the basis for adjectival "multicultural theory."

Even the Greeks, and certainly the Romans, understood very well that their manners of worship were opposed by those of alien social and political groups. I use here the word "worship," because that indeed was the earliest, now obsolete, sense of our word "culture." It was only very late in the nineteenth century that the idea of "culture" as a sustained order of common intellectual habit came into use. Only a truly modernist cast of mind could pervert so lively a word as "culture" to such organizational purposes. Today's idea of "culture" (which came into its own about the same time as did today's idea of "theory") was taken, it seems, at close range in the late nineteenth century from the biologist's idea of a "culture" as a medium in which one can grow microbes and other sometimes dangerous organisms. The current meaning in use among social theorists, including various social scientists, fell out of the sky after a long semantic journey from the cultivation of crops to the cultivation of the minds of human individuals. What can be learned from this passing glance at the word's history in the *Oxford English Dictionary* (second edition) is that "culture" refers to very local stuff—as in, those idols worshipped in a given temple, the crops grown in a specific field, the mind (or at best a class of minds) educable in a given pedagogic practice, or the stuff that grows in this or that petri dish. To speak of "culture" in a global sense is to speak nonsense—particularly so when the culture in question is the purported totality of global cultures.

The problem here, of course, is with the term "world," which finally I get to after having, at the outset, said that a multicultural theory, if any, must be grounded upon the facts of the "real world." Is it by accident that this word derives from the Teutonic *weorld* (for which, just as curiously, there is no Gothic equivalent) that came into something like its current usage only after Charles the Great established the Holy Roman Empire? Then, and for most of its history through Old English, "world" meant something like "this life" as opposed to the "other"—or, in the OED meaning: "the earthly state of human existence." In other words, the very idea of "world"—whether multicultural or not—assumes some limiting condition in time, and perhaps space as well, on the human order. To speak of a "world" is to speak of limits, or finitude. Worlds recognize their borders with other worlds. In the beginning of semantic time, the recognition was of transcendent worlds (as in the distinction most social theorists learn from Max Weber's *Protestant Ethic and the Spirit of Capitalism* between "this worldly" and "other worldly" ascetic practices). Today, when some still want to argue about the meaning of the word "multicultural" as affixed to "world" (hence to suggest something real in itself), the distinctions implied are ironic. Since the high modern era, just before the word "culture" became necessary in the sociological sense in the nineteenth century, "world" took a perverse turn into its present confused state of meaning. As the colonizing regimes of Europe and America sought to organize the many "cultures" of the earth over which they were extending the arm of Enlightenment policing, the word "world" came to designate the idea that all things human were naturally subsumable under a term that (again Weber) referred not to the other world but to the varieties of this worldly ethical conduct. In the nineteenth century "world" came to carry a secularized sense of the "profane" or "mundane"—as in Mark Twain, *Life on the Mississippi* (1883): "The guests were often this-worldly, often profane."

About the same time, which was also when "culture" and "theory" came into their "modern" meanings, "world" took on the absurd meaning the modernizers meant it to have, something like: "the unifying state of all human cultures." At first, such a meaning was limited enough to allow that those colonized were different in some measurable degree from the colonizers. The main idea was that the missionaries, slave traders, and early anthropologists among others who traded for profit beyond the seas were offering a unifying "culture" in exchange for the goods and services extracted from the regions they overran with their marvelous horses and superior firepower. Hence, the modern, quasi-secularized idea of "*the* world" is at best a ruse covering the unholy motives of the colonial system—which are currently disguised in such forms as the vestigial modernization theory that continues to influence the lending policies of the World Bank.

To speak of *a* world, then, is to speak of some or another distinction or set of distinctions organizing the volume of presumed social spaces that might be said to be "real" in some sense. Here, more trouble still. If social theorists are honest with themselves, they will admit that they don't really know what they are talking about when they use the word "reality." Today, not even the philosophers can help very much on this score. But even if they could, social theorists who aim to satisfy an empirical impulse would ignore them. This is why, in the hallways and lecture rooms, sometimes even in books, one encounters the expression "real world." This is actually a very hip expression— one that serves simultaneously to let the auditors of professorial wisdom know that the professor means to "speak to them," even as they nod in the direction of whichever colleague may be within hearing, thus to suggest that the speaker holds himself to the high standard of certifiable truth giving—that is, "reality."

The problem here is that, though there may well be a reality out there beyond the apperceptive competencies in which normal human beings trust, there is no "world" in the sense the term is used. The world that is still to be distinguished as "this world" from "*the* other world" can only be considered a unity in relation to a possibly transcendent one. To use the word "world" as we so blithely do to imply some coherence in the sphere of social and other things that transpire around the earth is, as I said, to speak nonsense. This nonsense, however, has been a very powerful one. It is the nonsense of the modern which, until recently, operated without too much resistance under the illusion that its truth was Truth itself, from which there were but a few steps to the quasi-scientific idea that what grows in European or American petri dishes will and should grow in all petri dishes.

This is why, when all is said and done, one cannot even speak of a "multi-cultural theory" in the sense of a theory apt to a practical world in which all things therein are "multicultural." If the "world" is multicultural, then in the current common sense of the term, it is no longer a "world."

But, in turn-of-millennium usage, one *could* speak of the "multicultural" in relation to "the globe," which surprisingly early in the sixteenth century came into currency out of the prior and proper sense of "a globe," that is: "a body having (accurately or approximately) the form of a sphere"—for which the OED lists the first occurrence as 1551, two years before its first recorded use with the definite article: "*the* globe," or "the earth." It would be, however, some centuries yet, at the height of Enlightenment faith, before the explorations of the sixteenth century on a physical "globe" would come to produce "the globe" as a surface upon which "culture" ought be spread. Hence, in 1752, even so skeptical a party to Enlightenment as David Hume would say: "The same set of manners will follow a nation over *the* whole globe" (OED; emphasis added). It was, thus, during the eighteenth century that "world" and "globe" came to be united, as they are today, by sly first appearances of what, a century after, came to be known as "culture." The foundational principle of Enlightenment doctrine was, simply but honestly enough, that everything in the "world" is governed by intelligible laws the knowledge of which is, thus, the basis for reason, hence civilization. In Isaiah Berlin's succinct words, the "essence" of Enlightenment, indeed of the whole of Western rationality that became clear in the eiteenth century, "is that there is a body of facts to which we must submit. Science is submission, science is being guided by the nature of things, scrupulous regard for what there is, non-deviation from the facts, understanding, knowledge, adaptation."[9] Thus it became possible to speak confidently of "the globe" only when the political economy of the colonial system drew up over its brutish shoulders the mannered cloak of a one, and true, "culture" which was thought to be the scientific essence of the "real" world. Or, as Ralph Waldo Emerson would put it in *Nature*: "All science has but one aim, namely, to find a theory of nature."[10] This entailed, of course, the beginning of the end of "worship" as the desideratum of necessity for "culture," allowing "culture" to become the more rigorous term for the "manners" that would follow "a" nation across the globe, in Hume's word. Emerson, thus, had left the religious ministry eventually to become the acknowledged founder of the uniquely American "culture" he announced in *The American Scholar*, presented the same year as his remark on nature, which at the time referred to "nature" as we know it, but also to "life" as such.

The word "multiculturalism," therefore, leads the social theorist in many directions at once. Its connotative risks owe, curiously, to its denotative necessity. It may well be that those few who would prefer that the world were not "multicultural" win the day even as they are losing it. The word would not appear in conversation as it does were it not controversial in "fact." Part of that controversy is, of course, over the "facts"; but the other, and larger, part may be over the trouble caused by any term that confuses by leading one from the lexicon to the world, thence to considerations of that world's history, which is to say: to the story of the world's presumed "reality," such as it was at the end of the twentieth century.

Trouble associated with the history of the term is real trouble as much because of what "multiculturalism" entails about the facts of the world as for what the word means. To be sure, some—like Nathan Glazer—are famously upset by the way the word is sometimes used as a political weapon. Arthur Schlesinger, for another example, writes of the prevailing multiculturalism of ethnic groups that were freshly in evidence in America in the 1980s: "The ethnic revolt against the melting pot has reached the point, in rhetoric at least, though not I think in *reality*, of a *denial of the idea of a common culture* and a single society" (emphasis added).[11] Schlesinger bemoans the threats to his society's national identity by the rise of group loyalties to ethnic identities among African- , Asian- , Native- , Caribbean- , and other Latin-Americans, among numerous others. (But, for the other side, see, among many examples, JanMohamed and Lloyd,[12] Lowe).[13]

By extension, and in actual political practice, the sense of threat to national identity can be associated with others who swear an allegiance to some or several social groups not necessarily ethnic or racial, but also evidently not nationalist—notably: the varieties of what are sometimes called queer identities (especially gay and lesbian), feminisms of various kinds, and what may roughly be called "identities owing to a sense of post-colonial experience." For an admirably respectful objection to these kinds of identity movements, see Jean Bethke Elshtain's *Democracy on Trial*.[14]

Obviously, what is particularly unnerving to strong monoculturalists like Schlesinger and gentler ones like Elshtain is that multiculturalism, as it applies to groups of individuals, in a society is never simple. It is entirely possible that individuals may identify themselves with a considerable number of social and ethnic groups long before they come to think of themselves as "American" or, for that matter, Dutch or British, Russian or Congolese. An individual born and bred within the territories of the United States may—for example, Gloria Anzaldúa—think of herself as Chicana, lesbian, *mestiza*, and *tejana*, among other possibilities, without ever supposing that she is significantly "American."[15] The unnerving wrought by strong identity politics like Anzaldúa's arises upon the impression that identity choices are simply "choices" and, thus, are "merely personal" or even psychological—thus all the more a decline down the slippery slope from the monocultural ideal thought to hold a nation together.

Anyone who reads Anzaldúa, however, or *any* of those in the border-culture tradition, understands very well that, though she writes personally, she is writing of the politics of social exclusions.

By further extension, the logic of fear associated with multicultural reality is that the world as a whole is as subject to these new allegiances as is even so radically multicultural a society as the United States.[16] When the idea of a world culture of any kind is subjected to scrutiny, it becomes an uncertain possibility—at least relative to the world system to which it would presumably apply.[17] Still, the prospect of an unqualifiedly multicultural world calls into question the supposed unity of humankind, just as in a given society like the American it threatens, in Schlesinger's word, "the idea of common culture"[18]—which is to say: the idea that what grows in one's national petri dish is good once and for all, and probably good for all humankind.

"Common culture" has been, thus, the social ethical foundation of Western culture since, at least, the eighteenth century. It is, in short, that by which the goodness of a society, or of *the* society of all humans, is determined. But, ideals are always subject to argument, even among those who profess to share them. Those arguments may be said to be the principal topic of the gossip—or, in the word used at the end of the millennium, the "discourse"—of civil society. Those who enter the argument in their local coffee shops, cocktail parties, or taverns do so from the points of view of their actual concrete lives. As a result, local talk of the good society always turns toward other, more arguable, subjects: general principles, applicable values, and specific social policies.

Western culture in modern times has considered it important that there be universal principles on the basis of which the good society may be established. The literature on this subject is too vast, and in some respects too familiar, to permit, or require, elaboration.[19] Without going into the long history of this discussion, going back at least to Hobbes and Augustine, not to mention Aristotle and Plato, it is sufficient to say that, at the turn of the twentieth century, the wider argument about the multicultural turned on two general kinds of universal principles.

The one concerned the universality of *rights*; the other, universal principles of *justice*. Evidently, as much as some have tried, the two are inseparable. They are two sides of any argument over the principles at stake in the ethics of organized society, as in the familiar argument that good rights policies yield good justice outcomes.[20] Still, the two principles invite legitimate disagreement over emphasis, even when they are not used in mutual exclusion.

Those who emphasize *rights* tend to think of the political and economic individual as the moral force behind (hence as the effective, if not the original, source of) whatever may be good in the good society. Their politics tend toward the protection of the rights of the individual. "Rights" people are, therefore, typically associated with political opinions Americans think of as "conservative" and Europeans think of as "liberal" in the classic eighteenth- and nineteenth-century senses.

By contrast, those who emphasize *justice* generally believe that when many individuals are left to pursue their well-protected rights they will sort themselves into stronger and weaker groups; hence into a social arrangement wherein the stronger will deprive the latter of their rights. Justice people, therefore, are inclined to trust some larger social entity (in modern times, usually the well-managed state, whether socialist or social democratic, even liberal) as the guarantor of individual rights or, more robustly, of social outcomes in respect to many, if not all, of the goods thought to be necessary or desirable in the good society. An emphasis on justice, therefore, is typically associated with politics that Americans think of as "left-liberal" and Europeans think of as just plain "left" or "social democratic," occasionally still "socialist."

One of the not very well thought through consequences of the necessary, if variable, relationship of rights to justices is that, when the discussion attends to the specific goods, or social and economic outcomes assured by the general principles, distinctions are very much more clear, to the point of incommensurability. Hence, those who speak earnestly of *rights* almost always consider the primary good in any society to be *freedoms*. Freedom may seem to be an abstraction, but in practice it demands very specific policies with respect to privacy, speech, property, mobility. When freedoms are entertained in public, the freedom (for example) of a pregnant woman to pursue her right to bodily privacy can come up against rival claims on behalf of the right to life of her fetus (a freedom that becomes public because of the proven wisdom of seeking an abortion at the hands of a qualified physician).

Whereas rights people usually (though not exclusively) think of freedoms, those who speak of justice as the ultimate principle in a good society tend to think of *equality* as the more applicable value. Justice people would think of the good society as one that guarantees basic equalities with respect to outcomes, ranging from civil rights and certain social opportunities (such as education in the United States) to more comprehensive social and economic outcomes (as in certain Scandinavian societies). Obviously, though distinguishable, arguments emphasizing equalities can be used against strong freedoms arguments. One of the stronger arguments in support of a woman's right to terminate her pregnancy is framed against the specific history of *unequal* access to information, health care, and social supports available to women, especially poor women, most especially poor women of color, that may render them less able to protect the long-term right to life of a child (including the child's rights or alleged rights to health, education, safety, and other social goods). Injustices demand a correction in the unequal availability of social goods, including certain goods deemed to be actual or virtual rights.

Still, the argument gets even more harsh, when the principles that issue in applicable values come to entail local social policies. Though people may share a principled appreciation for rights *and* justices, and may sing the virtues of freedoms *and* equalities, they will seldom agree on specific policies governing the local administration of the social goods glorified in principles or hinted at in values. In practice—that is: in real arguments in coffee shops in Des Moines or bars in Palaiseau—it is seldom the case that a strong justice argument will trump a strong rights argument; or vice-versa. Opponents move to the barricades, or the picket lines, even the bricks or bullets, with frightful ease.

As a result, any theoretical argument over multiculturalism, if it is to stop short of violence, must move with dispatch to concrete cases. Ultimately, when people are ready to fight over the facts of the multicultural world they live in, they are in actual practice ready to fight over specific (even if imagined) assaults upon their freedoms, or specific (even if imagined) deprivations in their equal access to social goods (including freedoms). Arguments turn to fights when real or allegedly real freedoms and equalities are at stake. As a result, a clearheaded understanding of the specific social policies by which social goods are distributed in a multicultural society is doubly difficult. In an uncontestedly modern culture there is a *presumption* of agreement over the principles, values, and policies in question. In a multicultural society the modernist ideal of a stabilizing common culture is held in doubt. One might even say that a multicultural society (whether global or national; whether modern or postmodern) is one in which there is no presumption of prior accord over such questions as these: What are the social goods? Who should get which ones?—and in what proportions? As a result, multiculturalism makes less sense as a theory of societies (including purportedly global ones) than as a study of the applicable values governing specific social policies by which the goods of a good society are distributed.

Here is where the argument turns dirty. Struggles over freedoms and equalities, in addition to being struggles over social goods or necessities, are always also struggles over social life itself. Individuals never enter society clean and clear of inquiries into their right to belong. The right to belong may be distinguished from rights to the social goods normally associated with belonging. Membership (sometimes called "citizenship") is the first condition for rights-eligibility. Or, put cynically, the first recourse of those in a position of power sufficient to protect their freedoms and unequal advantages is to deny membership to evident or potential rivals for the goods they consider theirs—by right or otherwise. Liberals, in the broad and inclusive sense of the word, have done this by using citizenship as much to exclude as to include.[21] Hence, the first question put to all, whether implicitly or explicitly, is the question of one's right to identify herself as a claimant on fair shares of the goods available in the social entities to which she petitions for inclusion.

Here is where the debate turns from principles of rights or justices, even from the specific value of freedoms against equalities, even from this or that policy, to the downright ugly question of *identities*—as in "identity politics" (of which the first known use is Goffman).[22] Far from being as so many think, a matter of personal self-understanding, identity is always political because declarations of identity, when made, are always and necessarily made on the verge of demanding membership. The demand is freedom itself; the membership is *always* the demand for an equal share of whatever may be the social goods of value in a particlular locale.

When all is said and done the important questions associated with political discussions of *identity* are, first, How does the human individual understand herself in relation to which social things?—and second, What rights and claims are associated with her identity claims? What makes a world real is scarcity. In such a world, declarations and investigations of identities are *always*, immediately or ultimately, claims on goods that disturb prevailing social policies and practices. Questions of identity are of intense, often vicious, public interest. This because it is widely recognized (though seldom discussed) that members of established human groups require certifications from petitioners for inclusion by inquiries on the theme, "Who do they think they are?" This interrogation extends well beyond superficial spiritual values into the realm of real or potential demands for material, as well as social inclusion. When, for an example, those previously excluded from, say, a fair share of competent education demand an equal share of the goods associated with a so-called "educational opportunity," they are simultaneously saying: "I belong; therefore I am a rightful claimant, on my own terms." This is the point all too often overlooked by those, like Schlesinger and Glazer (not to mention Todd Gitlin)[23] when they complain about the identity demands of those previously dealt unequal access to social and economic goods for which a proper "education" is expected.

This is where those who object to identity politics as overly personal go wrong. Those who hate (or fear, or doubt) multiculturalism tend most of all to object to identity politics as a trivializing of real politics by a petulant insistence upon personal recognition, referring to queer identity politics, say, disapprovingly: "If politics is reducible to the 'eruption of radical feelings,' something as seemingly 'ordinary' as protest against an unjust war lacks radical panache. Personal authenticity becomes the test of political credibility."[24] It is true that identity politics involve radical feelings and questions of personal authenticity, but it is not true that they involve "nothing more" than a preoccupation with the personal. The problem arises in most cases by a misunderstanding of the essentially social and political nature of the identity question.

The *Who am I?* question is, of course, subject to abuses of all kinds. Still it must be answered because it cannot be gotten around. Were it the case that individuals were utterly and unqualifiedly self-sufficient, then there would be no question of their identity. Curiously, in the whole of Western literature only one being was ever considered utterly self-sufficient—and he is one whose precise status in being is open to doubt (in large part because of his claim to self-sufficiency). When Moses inquired (Exodus 3:14) as to the identity of the being by whom he was being addressed through the mediation of a burning bush, God answered "I am who I am." Except in comedies of various kinds, no ordinary human being would think to respond in this fashion because all humans recognize the need to "identify" themselves, especially upon presentation in foreign crowds where rights of membership are open to inspection.[25] It might, therefore, be said that the ability to recognize responsibility for answering this question—if only by providing a name, even an alias—is what makes us human. One might even say that a "human being" is *that creature sufficiently conscious of its individual limitations as to be capable of representing himself as a proper member of associations of other creatures of like kind—with all the duties and privileges appertaining thereto.*

"Identity," therefore, is one of the more abstract names humans may use in recognition that they are wittingly "who they are" by consequence of the choices they make (from among those available, *when* they are made available) to associate with other humans.[26] The types of choices vary over time.[27] In ancient Greece, among other traditional social orders, it was common to identify with one's kin group (or, family) and one's polis (or, societal community). In modern times, it was expected that one would identify with one's "nation state." In multicultural (whether modern or postmodern) times, it is said that people are inclined to identify with their ethnic, sexual-orientational, racial, religious, immigrant, or engendered social groups. The list of possibilities is, in principle, indefinitely long. For an individual to declare himself an Athenian, an American, a follower of Christ, a Lakota, a bisexual, a Jew, a feminist, and so on (not to mention several at once), is to acknowledge membership or memberships by which those interested are meant to derive an answer to the question "Who are you?" The "*Who am I?*" question, thus, always bears an ever ready (even if provisional) answer, poised in anticipation of the inevitable inquiry from another, "Who are you?" To be human is to have an answer at the ready.

Ultimately, identity politics are the politics that more sternly test principles, values, and policies. An individual's freedoms and equalities are made known in the first instance by entry into foreign company: Who possesses the right to inspect the candidate? How does she reply? And with what answer or answers? And, is she accredited (or not) to answer as she does? Is the answer acceptable? These are the proper first questions for a *sociological* investigation of just how freedoms and equalities are distributed in a society. They are often precisely the questions asked in the study of what academic sociologists call social stratification, for which the first empirical line is always the basic demographics: Name? Address? Class? Race? Ethnicity? Sex?—and so forth and so on!

If, then, the identity question is so essential (possibly the only completely essential human question), why then does "identity"—or more precisely, "identity politics"—drive some people nuts when they are confronted with the reality of a multicultural world? At first blush, the answer would seem to be simple, and may well be. The inspection of the identity cards of the newly immigrant, or the recently assertive, is a troubling political questions *only* when those groups are either palpably ignorant of (by virtue of their immigrant status) or morally resistant to (by virtue of their assertiveness) the prevailing rules of social order. In principle this is a problem for any social group of any size, but at the given moment near the beginning of a millennium it became an especially troubling problem for those with vested interests in the nation state as the principal unit of social membership (hence, of privilege and its attendant duties).

"Multicultural," to repeat (and to amplify), is a proper adjective in reference to any world in which there is widespread dissensus with respect to membership rules, which is to say: principles, values, policies—and, above all, proper identity confessions. That the United States, a good number of European nation states, and perhaps the cultures of the world taken as a global whole might be called "multicultural" is tribute to the indisputably *social and political* (as opposed to "personal") value of identity. There are no identity politics (at least not in visible public) in social arrangements (including nation states) when members of subordinate groups are sufficiently deprived of equal access to the social goods as to be unfree to claim their memberships as they see them.

Hence, the irony of identity politics at the end of the twentieth century. This was a time when, for a number reasons, confidence in universal principles of humankind fell into grave doubt. Since the long sixteenth century, the nation state regimes of the modern world system had proven themselves perfectly capable of atrocities equal to the worst of the premodern systems. Yet, they prided themselves in somehow being morally better than the others, which pride extended to the presumption that their principles were *truly* universal; hence of considered value to all humankind. These were, in effect, values of the sort that claimed to have reduced the identity question to its thinnest possible value. The expectation was that, in the liberal modern regime, all humans could gladly reply that their values were, of course, "simply human." The expectation and the reply (where given with a straight face) are on the face absurd. It is remarkable that until recently so few groups laughed out loud. They did not, of course, because the politically weaker among them were vulnerable to the protections and regulations of the nation state and its various economic, military, and judicial instrumentalities.

Or, to put the matter from the point of view of those in the weaker positions in such an arrangement, members of many social groups—ethnic, racial, gender, sexual, economic, and others—were in effect deprived of the right to answer the identity question freely. It is entirely reasonable to assume that they might have, in principle, honestly replied by affirming their identification with the democratic values of this or that nation state, if anything in their experience caused them to believe that the universal principles of either rights or justices of those states merited their loyalty. In fact, little in the actual experience of most immigrant groups, most minority ethnic groups, most minority racial groups, all gays and lesbians, most women (so on and so forth) would truly have inspired confidence in the democratic principles of *any* of the major democratic societies of the European Diaspora. On the contrary, the actual, practical experience of those whose migrations and assertions have created the multicultural world is one of injury—and most especially the injury of exclusion which, in effect, is the injury of nonrecognition.

Hence, the situation as it stood at the turn of the last millennium: "Multicultural," insofar as it then referred to a theoretical claim, referred in effect to an argument among loyalists to the centrist liberal state, which had already entered into its decline. The grounds for argument were complicated by the evidence, since the revolutions of 1968, of the precarious promise and unpredictability of liberal democracy.[28] Those who complain about the culture of complaint,[29] or the loss of a common vision, miss the fundamental fact of the world as it is. Even those most injured by injustice, even those most deprived of their rights, affirm the ideals of the democratic order—and do so with a courage that gives the lie to those who claim that, somehow, the principles of that order are in effect long proven, well-established, and true in practice.

Insofar as the multicultural world affects social theory, it does so by transposing social ethical questions of rights and justices into questions of the nature of social and political membership and participation. In so doing a multicultural social theory reveals the necessarily left-leaning nature of social theory itself. Though the expression "social theory" is sometimes used duplicitously by conservatives to claim membership in a conversational circle to which they have no natural affinity, conservative politics and social theory mix poorly. Social theory may be distinguished from any specific instance of theory in a social "science" (as in "sociological theory") by virtue of its willingness to abandon the favors of a strict scientific presentation for an analysis of social reality that permits, even welcomes, a frankly political and normative commitment.

This is why what passes for multicultural social theory is always entirely an argument between and among proponents of various left, or as some would say "progressive" social theorists (e.g., Roberto Unger and Cornel West)[30] or "radical" social theorists (e.g., Anthony Giddens).[31] Social theory, as it had come to be understood at the end of the twentieth century, devolved in some more or less direct fashion from the personal politics ideal of the 1960s. Why that social moment in particular led to such a dramatic transformation of the social and political debates of the previous two centuries is hard to say. The answer may lie in the exhaustion of the traditional categories of liberal culture[32]—of, that is, attempts to resolve questions of rights and justices by formal references to the preferences for individuals or societies as the rival causal sources for the origins of social life (not to mention of the longstanding tensions between Enlightenment and Romanticism).[33] Though the rivalries and tensions remain, the only truly informative social theoretical instances of multicultural theory take the form of arguments over the relative merits of a politics of recognition (or identity politics) and the politics of redistribution (or post-socialist socialism).

On the surface, this would appear to be "nothing more" than a rehash of the rights or justice debate. But, it is more. Proponents of the politics of recognition assert that identity politics entail a real political struggle to overcome the effects of injuries inflicted by well-structured social (as opposed to interpersonal) insults.[34] Though the injury is experienced qua individual and usually entails a deprivation of rights, it is understood to be a consequence of membership in a social group (such as African guest workers in France) subjected to injustices at the hand of the host society. On the other side, those who are fixed on a post-socialist politics of redistribution are justice people who recognize, however awkwardly, that the politics of recognition must be taken into any viable account of redistributive justice.[35]

Though, as the millennium ended, there was far from perfect resolution of the debates *among* multicultural social theorists—or *about* multiculturalism and the multicultural world—it did seem that within the proper domain of social theory there was an important, if incomplete, transformation in the way social things, and their ethical and political consequences, were thought. One (but only one) sign of that change was recognition of real human differences that appeared in the wake of a lessening of hard commitments to categorical differences—those *between* rights and justices, those *between* freedoms and equalities, and those *between* the individual and societal world.

However high the moral principle, however true the theoretical concept, the plain fact is that there are mothers whose babies cry for milk. And cry they do *because* those charged with feeding the hungry refuse to recognize the essential membership, even of the babies, in the community of humans. The mothers do not give a damn about principles, values, or concepts. They care about life, which in this world is never so much supported by animal instincts as by social memberships. The growing recognition of the multicultural nature of the world accompanies a declining commitment to categories of all kinds.

In the new times, it remained to be seen if the multiculturalism debate at the end of the old millennium truly led to more milk for all babies.

Part II

The Last New Century, 1890s

Four

Calling out Father by Calling up His Mother, 1947

Tuesday afternoons were the best. The wash had been done the day before. Tuesdays were ironing day. I would rush home from school. These were the days I loved—the days when I would grab a snack before descending to the basement laundry. Florence was usually already at the ironing board. My mother, Helen, the one I speak of as my birth mother, did work of her own—shopping, cooking, washing dishes, sewing. But in those days I never saw her iron. Florence did that. Now that Mike and I were regularly at school, I never saw, or thought about, what else Florence did. Nor did I think about the contract by which she did whatever she did. But I knew she ironed, and I loved those days.

I sat on my own cardboard box in a corner reserved between the folding table and the washer. Florence would tell me stories. I don't remember all of them. She would sing. The words I forget, but the music I recall. Later, much later, when I had become a preacher for a time in my youth, Florence was convinced it was because of those Tuesday afternoon services when she preached the words and sang the tunes of her Zion Baptist Church.

The truth is that she was the minister in the family. Me, I didn't last long as a preacher. I was good enough at it, but there was something wrong with the people. I liked Christianity well enough. It was Christians I couldn't get along with—nor they with me. I've tried since then. Nothing works. But Florence was different. She had many more reasons than I to hate Christians. Though, in later years she would complain about the preachers and, as she called them, the "old ladies" at Zion, she didn't hate Christians. Not even white ones. On her days off, she would often take the bus out to the suburbs to drag me to the local Evangelical & Reformed church that in the late 1940s we very innocently integrated. She had the call. It showed in other ways.

One story she told me many times was about my father. My father, the doctor, was given to temper tantrums. Most of the others at home would learn to look the other way when he exploded, usually over nothing important, like the lumpiness of mashed potatoes or the sogginess of bacon. He was a little nuts. The others, so far as I could tell, just accepted that and went on their ways. Once, during a birthday dinner for his mother, he actually threw his food around the room and stomped out. Grandmother's response was to ask, in all dignity, if anyone wanted more of the roast beef. Me, I couldn't look the other way. I hated this shit. I still do and most of all when a rage comes over me. Florence hated it too. The difference was that she knew how to do something about it.

Once, when father was having one of his fits, Florence calmly went to the phone and called up *his* mother, who lived across town. She demanded that she—my father's mother—come over immediately. Grandmother and grandfather (a passive in these affairs) arrived in short order. Father had settled down. Usually his tantrums passed quickly enough. Only much later did I come to realize that they arose from some terrible disorder he suffered. I never knew what it was. Florence didn't care why these things happened. She just had her limits.

When my father's mother arrived with grandfather in tow, Florence told Gertrude what had happened. Gertrude sat my father down in the presence of us all (or so I was told). She, father's mother, laid down the law. He was to obey whatever Florence said because, if he didn't, she would leave. He knew, of course, that, as they put it, the boys needed her. What Florence needed was an end to the bad language. The violent behavior hadn't bothered her as much. She knew violence. But the angry language was to her inexcusable. Verbal abuse was her limit. So far as I know, my father never swore in her presence after that calling out. And ever after, so I came to believe, Florence had only to threaten to call grandmother (which meant to quit altogether) to get her way.

As the years went by, and we grew older, I saw Florence less and less. She had stopped living with us during the war. By the time my adolescent juices began to flow, she came only a few days a week. I was too far-gone in those days to wonder why. Perhaps it was the great American dream machine that cut her time with us. The new synthetic fabrics and automatic dryers had made ironing virtually unnecessary. Anyway, I was too old and too big to sit on that tiny box. Many years would pass before, later in our lives, Florence and I took up the habit of telling stories to each other. These were the stories by which I began to learn who and what had been and could yet be. And we told these stories, thus making ourselves up as we went along, until the very end. She had a last stroke when I was in Korea. I rushed to Cincinnati as soon as I got back. She lived on for weeks in the hospital. We even told a few in those last days. Just before she lapsed into the final coma, she asked that I read aloud the twenty-seventh psalm. I did, over and over again. She recited it with me—the King James Version. Sixteenth-century prose drifted up through the morphine fog to bind the ties of our tellings.

Some stories from childhood we remember direct. Others we don't. These we come to *believe* we remember. When stories are told and retold they enter in and become a part of us. Tuesdays at the ironing board church I remember, or think I do, because I can picture so many of the details and hear the tunes if not the words. The story of Florence's calling out of my father by calling up his mother, I cannot picture. I probably wasn't there. Yet, it rings true. I knew, and still know, that Florence ruled that roost. It took me many years to know that the arrangements that brought her into our little white family romance were what they were. But in the 1940s I could not have understood them, just as in the 1990s, after Florence had passed away, I could not ignore them. They are why, to this day, I think of her as mother. Helen was a good woman, and more than a birth mother to me. But Florence told the stories I cannot forget, the ones that made me who I consider myself to be.

These stories being told, it's about time I confess something. I am guilty of plagiarism. Though I know that some people have suspected it, I have never come out with the truth, until now. I will have to suffer the consequences. Here is the plain truth. Several years ago I published a scholarly article in a book edited by one of my field's most respected scholars. In my contribution I committed the academic sin of misrepresenting data. In short, I told a story out of my own experience but misrepresented it as the experience of another person. The name I used for this false other was David. In that article I told both of the stories I've just told here under the guise of this fictitious research subject.

I realize that my plagiarism was not the worst. Writers very often use fictional names in order to protect the confidentiality of those who tell them their stories. But I did just the opposite. I created a fiction in order to disguise a personal truth in a publication where readers have every right to know that the one telling the stories is telling the truth even when he resorts to ethical fictions. My plagiarism, if it was a terrible thing, was the perversion of a convention. The fiction used to protect the innocent was, in my case, used to protect the guilty.

The only thing I can say in my defense is that the essay in question was under the guise of a scholarly presentation. Scholars, still today, believe that it is important to keep oneself out of such a presentation. The idea is, of course, that to remove oneself from academic writing is to enhance the objectivity of the presentation. Anyone who has ever thought about it knows this is mere convention; and a not very convincing one at that. Scholars are also subjects. They put themselves into their writing all the time. Still, the very idea disturbs some people, more than they can say.

As it turns out, the cheating I did is done not just by scholars. Just as the millennium ended, there was a most notorious case of a biographer who did something similar. In a long-awaited biography of the American president, Ronald Reagan, his biographer, Edmund Morris, violated the line between truth and fiction. In this book, *Dutch*, Morris (now famously) invented himself as a fictional character many years older than he could have been. His purpose was to retell the story of a popular political figure as memoir—to introduce himself frankly, if somewhat fictionally, into the factual account of the life of an American President. Morris was doing nothing that other biographers had not done before. The only difference was that he did it honestly and with considerable flair.

Since President Reagan, at the time of the publication of "his" story, was sadly incapacitated by an advanced case of Alzheimer's disease, he was not in a position to complain. This left the complaining to his former colleagues and admirers. They were angry because Morris had been given exceptional access to the President. Reagan's friends had invited Morris to be *their* president's official biographer because Morris had previously written a stirring (and prize-winning) biography of another American president, Theodore Roosevelt. Since President Reagan's admirers thought their man was every bit as heroic as Teddy Roosevelt, they trusted Morris to make of Reagan the same sort of giant he had made of the first Roosevelt. It did not occur to them that Morris did not do this because he could not. Reagan was a different subject from Roosevelt. In any case, Reagan's friends were furious. Their man was beyond retelling his own story. The story had been given away to a writer who, in their opinion, had perverted it.

But what was the perversion? It was that Morris, in inventing himself as a character in the life of another, had invited the idea that the telling of truths about other people may require the telling of falsehoods about oneself—or vice versa. This may be why it was not only the friends of the former president who were outraged. Even good liberals, including writers never known to have especially admired Reagan, were upset with Morris. They complained that he had violated the basic rules of their craft. Though they did not care so much about distorting the truth about Reagan, they did care that others would begin to realize that nonfiction writers often use fiction to tell true stories.

Most of them had forgotten that one of the greatest memoirs of all time—one that is said to be *the* classic memoir of the end of the nineteenth century—used almost exactly the same device. *The Education of Henry Adams* (1906) was the true story of the passing of the nineteenth century as told by Henry Adams but told through a fictional character he invented—himself. Adams wrote of himself entirely in the third person. What makes that book great is that Adams, who was indeed privy to many of the important diplomatic and political events of the nineteenth century, is that he misrepresented himself as a third party other than the author of the book itself. The effect was to downplay the extraordinary access this descendant of the great Adams family had had to the events he wrote about. If he had told the story straight, as if it were "his" story, it might have seemed less true than it was. I often wonder what the betrayed friends of Ronald Reagan would say about Henry Adams' literary deception—he having been, that is, the most faithful of all conservators of the nineteenth-century life.

Why is it such a terrible thing to misrepresent oneself when telling the truth of another (as did Edmund Morris) or of a century (as did Henry Adams)? The answer, of course, is that it isn't—at least not necessarily. What is disturbing to people of many different cultural tastes may not be that fictions sometimes enter into to truth telling, but that they *always and necessarily* enter in.

Most of what most people remember about their childhood is remembered through stories told them at weddings and funerals, often by slightly, or greatly, drunken relatives of uncertain family ties. We "remember" what we are told, and what we are told is told for all kinds of purposes and almost never with an official censor on the truth of the "recollections." The truth is that that truth is just that—a re-collection of fragments patched together under the influence of a desire to tell a good story.

I do not mean to suggest that the plagiarism I committed in that scholarly article was of the literary order of writings by Edmund Morris or Henry Adams. Rather, I mean to say that as a crime of sorts it was a very common deviation from standards people would like to believe are true. People believe in truth roughly in proportion to their need to resist the lies the truths disguise. One might suppose that whenever sensible people get excited about the truth of certain arrangements (such as the factual account of the life of their favorite president), they are hiding something. Thus it was that I was hiding something that I had no business hiding, when I told a falsehood about a truth in my life.

Why did I plagiarize the story about Florence's office in my life? Why do I tell the truth of it now? As nearly as I can say, there are two reasons.

One is plain enough. It is that it takes a long while for us all to tell and retell—to hear and rehear—the stories that make us who we are. We look for excuses not to remember what we know. Sometimes the excuses are elaborately tangled up with otherwise benign social conventions. When I misrepresented my stories as that of a fictitious David I was, I suppose, caving in to a convention I then considered more weighty. At the time, in my personal life I had made no secret of my relations with Florence. Many of the stories were well known to friends and loved ones. She was no stranger in my inner circle. What I must have thought at the time was that, in publishing a scholarly article, I had to make it seem that the "data" of those stories were suitably objective; hence, not stories of my own. Somewhere in the intervening few years, I came to think differently.

But there is, as I say, a second, more compelling, reason for my plagiarism of the truth of my own self. I had already known by the time of the telling of those stories that mine were far from unique. Sometime in the late twentieth century, there began to appear more and more stories of white boys or girls brought up by good colored women like Florence. These took their place alongside still other stories of race mixing and passing. Of whites who discovered they were black. Of whites and blacks who discovered they were cousins. Of blacks whose parents had passed, leaving them to think they were white. It became, in fact, a little ridiculous to use words like "white" and "black" to describe these relations, these passings, these fictions of difference. In those years one could read and hear tell of any number of people in one or another relation of this kind. I even heard other whites tell of their relations with *their* other-than-white mothers by adoption. In some cases they told their stories for the first time, emboldened in one or two cases by my telling mine for the first time.

There was in fact nothing all that unusual about my relation with my black adoptive mother. Only the words used—or not used—to describe it still seem offensive to some. I once told my story to a group of storytellers among whom there was one phenotypically colored woman who went absolutely berserk on me. Her mother had brought up white children who paid her no mind. I was claiming a relation that was, in her experience, beyond the pale of economic and social justice. She is correct of course in her politics. And right to be outraged that her mother was treated as she was. But was she right to hate me as in that moment she did? What did I stand for in her experience? What did the fictional David stand for in mine?

Where is the brotherhood and sisterhood of all of us brought up on the nether side of the Veil that requires a fictional silence about this one important break in the otherwise impermeable color line?

The Colored Woman's Office:
Anna Julia Cooper, 1892

Anna Julia Cooper is one of the most distinctly recognizable of those powerful and influential American black women whose lineage goes back, at least, to Sojourner Truth and Harriet Tubman in the nineteenth century, and Phyllis Wheatley in the eighteenth. Yet, in contrast to other notable women in the tradition, Anna Cooper's reputation as a foundational figure among black feminists in America is fraught with ambiguity. What is striking about her, both visually and personally, shines against the ambiguities without always illuminating them. She is venerated for her heroic life. But Cooper is also, and regularly, the subject of controversy among those who today look back to her as she was in her lifetime. As a result, both the striking and the ambiguous must be considered if we are to understand, and take with full seriousness, Anna Julia Cooper's exceptional place in American history.

The ready recognizability of Anna Julia Cooper owes at least partly to a beauty so commanding that she has become a virtual emblem of the black woman in America (to use Cooper's own distinctive phrase). A familiar photograph of Cooper in early mid-life was selected for the jacket of *Black Women of America*—the most important, and most comprehensive, encyclopedia of writings by and about black women in American history.[1] In the photograph, Cooper faces the light that shades her face and shoulders. The image is of her profile, and she is oriented so that the photographer's front-lighting accentuates enough of the physical reminders of her slaveholding father as to encourage among the innocent an illusion as to the subject's race. Cooper's dress is adorned by a generous but modestly delicate jabot that comes to her neck in a white lace collar neat to the throat. Anna Julia Cooper's eyes are fixed, firm and unwavering; her jaw set, but relaxed; her hair drawn up as if to add substance to the jabot's already discreet Victorian fringe. Her lighted visage is framed against a darkened background, as though she were the classic figure of a cameo. Mrs. Cooper is thus portrayed very much as she was—entirely ready for business, yet composed, dignified, and slightly superior.

I know from experience that some white people coming upon this image out of context, with no prior knowledge of Anna Julia Cooper, do not at first realize that she was black. At the same time, those already familiar with

Cooper's important contributions to American social thought might well be reminded by this famous photograph of several of her most elegant lines, appearing at the end of an essay "The Status of Woman in America":

> What a responsibility then to have the sole management of the primal lights and shadows! Such is the colored woman's office. She must stamp weal and woe on the coming history of this people. May she see her opportunity and vindicate her high prerogative.[2]

Even those wise to Anna Julia Cooper may well be puzzled by these words, if not by the photograph. To whom does she refer? Which is "this people" upon whom the colored women must stamp weal and woe? Is it "her people" (an expression she hated)?[3] Or, is it the whole of the American people whose "primal lights and shadows" are to be managed by the colored woman? On the one hand, the essay in which these lines appear makes it clear that Cooper was a race-woman who believed deeply in the unique vocation of black women, a vocation she defined, in part, by the black woman's moral superiority to white civilization with, as she put it, "that blasé world-weary look which characterizes the old washed out and worn out races which have already, so to speak, seen their best days."[4] On the other hand, elsewhere Cooper makes it clear that she did not believe any less seriously in the West and American civilization: "But there can be no doubt that here in America is the arena in which the next triumph of civilization is to be won; and here too we find promise abundant and possibilities infinite."[5] How could a *fin de siècle* schoolteacher who would serve the famous M Street (colloquially the "Colored," later officially changed to Dunbar) High School in the District of Columbia for more than forty years believe otherwise?

Anna Julia Cooper did, in fact, sustain all at once many different ideas, values, and commitments—not all of which settle into clarifying focus. To understand Cooper is to come face to face with a woman who lived with heroic dignity, while refusing all along to be exactly what others would have her be. As a result, even those who are drawn to the influential ideas of Cooper's most famous book, *A Voice From the South*, may well express certain reservations.

One of the most frequently held reservations toward Cooper is that she all too comfortably accepted the white pieties of the true womanhood ideal,[6] in particular those emphasizing a woman's duty to establish the domestic circle. And there are grounds for the suspicion in Cooper's own words, written late in life but recalling the beginnings of her enriching domestic life in Washington, D.C.:

> The very next year [1888] I had planted my little North Carolina Colony on Seventeenth street where I immediately began, like the proverbial beaver to build a home, not merely a house to shelter the body, but a home to sustain and refresh the mind, a home where friends foregather for interchange of ideas and agreeable association of sympathetic spirits.[7]

The life Anna Julia Cooper built and lived from her birth in North Carolina, probably in 1858, until her death in 1964 in Washington was one centered deeply in the virtues of home, religion, and proper public conduct. How, indeed, could a woman of such classically Southern virtues become one of the most widely recognized symbols of the new black woman?

Whatever is to be made of the ambiguities created by the image and writings of Anna Julia Cooper they are surely not confusions arising from an uncertain identity. It is impossible to read even a few paragraphs of any of Cooper's writings without knowing that this woman knew exactly who she was—a woman who kept nothing within her conscious grasp in the dark. In contrast to writings of a later, and culturally more complicated time and place, Cooper gave not the least thought to shading the public presentation of her racial or gender convictions.

The years of Cooper's most important productivity as a writer and scholar—roughly 1886 to 1930—were anything but uncomplicated. She began her work barely twenty years after Emancipation and a short decade upon the collapse of Reconstruction in 1877—and continued through the rise of Jim Crow, through the era of the northern and urban migrations of which she herself was a pioneer, through the struggles in the early years of the twentieth century between Booker T. Washington and W. E. B. Du Bois of which she was more or less an innocent victim, and through the Harlem Renaissance in respect to which she took a generally marginal, occasionally dim view. She died in 1964 just when the Civil Rights Movement was turning toward its final agonal transformation into the Black Power phase, of which she would have surely approved for its power while disapproving of its manners. Still, though Cooper, a woman of the South, lived through all this history, her views were, if not simple, at least uncomplicated by the troubles the urban North could invite. Quite by contrast to the culturally and politically more fractious movements that took shape with the Harlem Renaissance in the 1920s, Cooper saw the issues of race and culture in very straightforward terms. Unlike, for example, Harlem Renaissance writers like Nella Larsen,[8] Cooper gave not the least thought to passing—either as an option for herself, or for others in her circumstances. In this sense, but only in this sense, she remained true to the title of her great book. She was a black woman of the rural South, one who brought the gentle manners of her mother to the near North, from where she cultured a life's work that led her across the seas.

Cooper herself was anything but uncertain as to her own true nature and purposes in life. In this, as in other respects, she was like the formidable race-women who were her contemporaries and colleagues in the race politics of the day—Mary Church Terrell and Ida B. Wells-Barnett.[9] Save for her close friendship in the early years with Charlotte Forten Grimké,[10] Cooper was never personally close to the other race-women of her age and time with whom she shared so much—politically, morally, and personally. Though in many ways an isolated figure, Cooper was an uncommonly self-assured person, not one to be easily shaken by what others thought of her. As a consequence, her self-certainty issued in good works covering a breathtaking range and number of areas of professional and intellectual accomplishment.

She was, for one, a college and high school teacher of the classics, the modern and ancient languages, literature, mathematics, and the sciences. Her teaching career began, by some indications, when she was scarcely ten years old and continued until she was well into her eighties.[11] But, of all the subjects she mastered, it was in the languages and history that she made her reputation as a scholar. After more than thirty-five years as a high school teacher, Cooper's translation of *Le Pèlerinage de Charlemagne* from old to modern French won her professional recognition while advancing her graduate studies at Columbia University. And, at the age of no less than sixty-six years, she completed her doctoral thesis at the Sorbonne on the subject of French attitudes towards slavery during the French Revolution. Her thesis defense in Paris on March 23, 1925, offered one of the surest proofs of her strong and courageous character. A member of her examining committee was the prominent and notorious Celestin Bouglé—a leader of the post-Durkheimian sociologists and an academic force to be reckoned with. Bouglé had previously written a book Cooper considered not so subtly racist. Rather than evade the subject, Cooper firmly took Bouglé to task and won his approval.[12]

But these endeavors of the academic life were but a part of a long life of more than a century (more than a decade longer than Du Bois, her younger contemporary). Through much of her active life Cooper was a popular public speaker. One of her best-known public speeches was delivered in 1886, when she was just two years out of Oberlin College, and not yet thirty, to a meeting of the exclusively male black clergy of the Protestant Episcopal Church. The talk, "Womanhood, A Vital Element in the Regeneration of the Race" (later published as the first chapter of *A Voice From the South* must have stirred some considerable controversy. In it she uttered the most famous of all her lines, declaiming, in effect, the black woman's moral superiority to the black man.

> Only the BLACK WOMAN can say "when and where I enter, in the quiet, undisputed dignity of my womanhood, without violence and without suing or special patronage, then and there the whole Negro race enters with me."[13]

These words are a play on what Cooper took to be the vanity of one of the great race men of the mid-nineteenth century, Martin R. Delany, whom she characterizes as "an unadulterated black man." The gentlemen clergy addressed by this young woman must have taken her meaning with some discomfort. This was Cooper's way—direct, eloquent, ever dignified, never obsequious; thus disturbing, but convincing. Surely one of the reasons she could speak and write so powerfully was the moral force deep in her character that was usually evident in her public discourse, notably in an address delivered before the general conference of the Society of Friends in 1902 on "The Ethics of the Negro Question."[14]

A Voice From the South, Cooper's best-known book, arose from a moral and religious depth that moved her work as a public intellectual and activist.[15]

Yet, Anna Julia Cooper's activism was never as widely recognized as Mary Church Terrell's or Ida Wells-Barnett's. Nor were her writings as numerous or as well known as Du Bois'. Cooper was the more quiet leader of social programs and causes for the poor in her home city, the District of Columbia. She was active in establishing a local branch of the YWCA and was an early and life-long leader in the social settlement movement. She was also a leader in the founding of the black women's club movement, and a regular contributor of agitating letters and columns to newspapers like the *Washington Post* and magazines like *Crisis*.

Though Cooper's professional activities and public speaking took her around the country and the world, the force of her social activism was local. She was a woman who knew how to put down roots in the city of her adult life where, but for four years in the Midwest, she lived from 1887 until her death in 1964. Even after retiring from teaching in 1930, when she was in her seventies, Cooper took over the presidency of Frelinghuysen University, a school organized to provide educational opportunities to the working poor in Washington's black community. She held the last position until she was in her ninth decade of life. At one point she literally took the financially struggling school into her own home.

Everything she did seemed always to issue from or return to her homes. Nothing better expresses Cooper's sense of her life's work than the ways she used and effectively redefined her home. Her first home on 17th Street, N.W., from which she moved into local life as member of Washington's black cultural elite was a figurative as well as literal hearth from which, over time, she developed a cosmopolitan life of many accomplishments.[16] She was always ready to bring others into that home, and not just the poor students of her night school late in life. Over the years Mrs. Cooper reared seven children including two foster children when she was young, and five orphaned children she adopted just shy of her sixtieth year. The youngest of the five children was less than a year old. Yet, she cared for these babies and infants on a teacher's salary while, among so much else, commuting to New York City and Paris in pursuit of her doctoral degree.

The ambiguity of Cooper's public image, as well as the seeming contradictions of her writings, may owe as much to her personal character as to the conflicting demands of her times.[17] In her day, as in today's attempts to understand her, Cooper stood out among others for the way her personal character allowed her to speak to her complicated times with precisely the quiet, undisputed dignity of her womanhood. These qualities are evident in all of her writings and activities. But they were conveyed with striking poignancy on December 29, 1925, when she addressed the Washington Chapter of the Alpha Kappa Alpha Sorority as it honored her for the doctorate from the University of Paris. Cooper began with an affirmation of faith in human progress:

> The impulse of humanity toward social progress is like the movement of a great
> water system, from myriad sources and under myriad circumstances and condi-
> tions, beating onward, ever on course to its eternity, the Ocean.

Then, later in the speech, she referred more to herself in relation to the conditions of her race:

> And now if I may be pardoned a personal word on an occasion so provocative of
> pride and vainglory, I may say, honestly and truthfully, that my one aim is, and has
> always been, so far as I may to hold a torch for the children of a group too long
> exploited and too frequently disparaged in its struggling for light. I have not made
> capital of my race, have paid my own way and have never asked a concession or
> claimed a gratuity. Nor, on the other hand, have I ever denied identification in
> every handicap and every limitation that the checkered history of our native land
> imposes. In the simple words of the Master, spoken for another nameless one, my
> humble career may be summed to up date—"She hath done what she could."[18]

Then, some time after the speech in 1925, Cooper added, in her own steady,
teacher's handwriting, the following note, set in the third person:

> The most significant fact, perhaps, in Mrs. Cooper's contributions to Education in
> Washington & certainly the most directly provocative of the cause of her own seg-
> regated group is the courageous revolt she waged against a lower "colored" cur-
> riculum for M St school.[19]

The belated note has several meanings, one less obvious than the others. In one
sense, Cooper is referring to her life's work as a teacher in which she pursued a
strategy of racial uplift close to that of Du Bois's Talented Tenth principle.
Cooper was a brilliant teacher and an effective school leader who, while principal of M Street School from 1901 to 1906, so strengthened its curriculum in
classical subjects that a markedly greater number of its graduates were accepted
to places like Harvard and other elite colleges. But, in a deeper sense, there is a
distant, wistful air to Cooper's handwritten note—one that suggests that in
1925 she had in mind events from twenty years earlier, events so painful that,
even during her finest moment of academic triumph—she could not keep them
out of her private thoughts. It would not be far fetched to assume that her pursuit of the French doctorate, when she was already at normal retirement age,
was itself partly an attempt to redeem a public disgrace visited upon her in 1906
for having done nothing worse that succeed as a teacher and school leader.
    The reference Cooper makes to her "courageous revolt" is undoubtedly an
allusion to her stewardship of the curriculum at the M Street School which
ended in what was certainly the most decisive public moment in her younger
life. In 1906, after five years of distinguished service, Cooper was dismissed as
principal of the M Street School and forced, for want of work, into a five-year
exile at Lincoln University in Jefferson City, Missouri. The action taken

against her was clearly prompted by agents of one of the two unadulterated race-men of that day, Booker T. Washington. Washington was of course the founding principal of the Tuskegee Institute from which he reinforced his position as the leader if the industrial education strategy of racial uplift—a strategy that at the dawn of the twentieth century was appealing to the white politicians and philanthropists who controlled what remained of the dominant society's post-Reconstruction outreach to the nation's black population. Washington's Tuskegee Machine, as it was known by its opponents, worked hard to exercise its control wherever in the nation the industrial education strategy was opposed—in fact or in the imagination. Cooper was a prime target of the Tuskegee's hostility, notwithstanding her strong commitments to the industrial education program at M Street, because she was herself so obviously well educated and so effective a model to her pupils.

For a full year, beginning in 1905, the white members of the District of Columbia's Board of Education joined, actively or passively, in the conspiracy to ruin Cooper's reputation and force her from the principal's office. The false complaints against her did not, of course, show the hand of the Tuskegee forces. They complained not of her curricular philosophy but against her alleged failures as an administrator. When these carpings proved insufficient, they turned to the ultimate dirty trick—accusing Cooper of a sexual liaison with John Love, one of her (then young adult) foster children. The controversy was played out in public for a long year, often reported in detail in the *Washington Post*. It is not hard to imagine the mortification such preposterous charges must have caused in a woman of her work ethic and impeccable morals. In the end, she was dismissed in the fashion to which school administrators still resort. They simply did not renew her contract at the end of the 1905–1906 school year.[20]

In the M Street School controversy Cooper's life was drawn into the battle between Booker T. Washington and his archrival in American racial politics, W. E. B. Du Bois. The struggle between these two men had been gathering force for a number of years since Du Bois's first public attack on Washington in 1901.[21] Yet, even before their differences broke into the open, Du Bois himself had fallen victim to Booker T. Washington's power in an episode that, harbinger of things to come, also involved the colored schools in the District of Columbia. In 1900, Du Bois suffered the indignity of rejection for a post for which he was both overqualified and ill-suited. He had applied, with some encouragement from Washington, for the post of assistant superintendent of the colored schools in the nation's capitol. Upon seeing what was at stake in the earliest days of his rivalry with the younger Du Bois, Washington abruptly withdrew his support and the post was denied. Though Du Bois had been ambivalent about a position that would have left him less time for his scholarly pursuits, he was disappointed. But of course he went on to other things.[22]

Cooper, too, went on after her dismissal. From 1906 to 1911, she taught college courses in Missouri. Then, when her enemies in the Washington,

D.C., school administration had left office, she returned to the M Street School where she taught until her retirement in 1930. As in everything else, Cooper suffered the dismissal and its humiliations with tough moral fortitude. Even so, she was left to suffer for her convictions without the active support of those upon whom she might reasonably have counted. To be sure, she was now left utterly alone. During the year-long siege in 1905–06, Cooper was actively supported by many in the community, and especially by her friend the Reverend Francis Grimké.[23]

On the other hand, among those who were notably silent were her class-mate at Oberlin and colleague at M Street, Mary Church Terrell, and W. E. B. Du Bois. It is, perhaps, less remarkable that Du Bois, already a national and international figure, did not lift hand or voice in support of Cooper in 1905. But the Mary Church Terrell story is intriguing.

Why did Cooper not have a closer relation to Mary Church Terrell? Not only had they been college classmates at Oberlin, but, after graduation in 1884, they had both settled in Washington, D.C., where their lives were closely connected as teachers at the M Street School and colleagues in many causes such as the local social settlement movement. Yet, Terrell kept her dis-tance from Cooper during the M Street School controversy and, even harder to explain, for years after. Though Cooper refers often to Terrell, Terrell's 1940 autobiography, *Black Woman in a White World*, mentions Cooper not at all.[24] Perhaps the explanation of Terrell's silence in the 1905 affair is rather straightforward. She, and her husband, Robert H. Terrell (himself a former principal at M Street), were at the time beholden to Booker T. Washington for his appointment to the District of Columbia's judiciary. But Mary eventually broke with the Tuskegee group in 1910 when she joined in the founding of the NAACP. Why in 1940, so many years later, did Terrell still have nothing to say of Cooper with whom she had worked in such proximity for over sixty years?

And, why, also were Cooper and Du Bois not closer? Though there were differences of an obvious sort between the two, Cooper had nonetheless been in close contact with him from the earliest years. She had been with him at the 1900 Pan African Congress in London, and, over the years, had corresponded with him over several notable race matters.[25] But Du Bois, who had many good rela-tions with women, seemed never to pay Cooper more than passing acknowl-edgement. Cooper's isolation from Terrell and Du Bois, when considered alongside their respective involvements in the M Street School controversy, add to the mysterious impression of Cooper as a solitary woman in history.

The facts of Cooper's life as a solitary figure are consistent with her theo-retical views on the Black Woman in America, such as those in her essay "The Status of Woman in America":

> The colored woman of to-day occupies, one may say, a unique position in this country. In a period itself transitional and unsettled, her status seems one of the least ascertainable and definitive of all the forces which make for our civilization.[26]

This is one of the most assured statements in Cooper's black feminist theory. She means precisely to argue that in the "transitional and unsettled" times at the end of the nineteenth century, the black woman is "unique," but unique in a particular way. For she alone, being "least ascertainable," is the most "definitive of all the forces" then at play. The intended primary sense of "unique" here is political and historical. The statement comes just after an appreciative, but uninflected, commentary on what some interpreters see as the "feminine principle" at work in Cooper's thinking.[27] Just before this passage, Cooper had stated that "in the reign of moral ideas she [woman] is easily queen."[28] But, then, as she often does, Cooper sets in rhetorical motion an abrupt shift to a disjunctive point which in effect means: Though in prior times woman as such had a moral responsibility, now it is the black woman who has the unique responsibility. She alone, the black woman, is the sole manager of the primal lights and shadows. So, for Cooper to have been a black woman in her times was to be unique in the sense of being subject to a distinctive historical calling.

Yet, it is impossible to escape a second, entailed meaning of such vocation: unique in the sense of being solitary, alone in bearing one's moral obligations. Indeed, she was. Cooper had married while still a young woman teaching at St. Augustine's College in 1877. Her older husband, George Cooper, a priest in the Protestant Episcopal Church, was very well regarded. But the marriage ended with his death two years later. She never remarried. And, though sexual scandal was used against her by the forces seeking her dismissal from the M Street School, there is no evidence of any desire on her part to remarry. Nor is there even a hint of romantic or sexual involvement thereafter.[29] Cooper lived without a domestic partner from the age of 21 until her death nearly 85 years later. Though, in addition to her foster and adopted children, she enjoyed a rich social life, especially with the family of her older and dearest life friend, Charlotte Forten Grimké, Cooper lived all those years as a single, widowed woman.[30] Yet, there is no sign of complaint on her part; nor, importantly, of loneliness.

Cooper appropriated the solitary life as part of her vocation. The homes she built in houses at 1706 17th Street N.W. and later (after 1916) at 201 T Street N.W. were the foundations for a wide domestic circle into which she brought foster children, the Grimkés, and other friends, and late in life the working poor of her adult education school. When asked in 1930 to describe her vocation, she answered simply: "The education of neglected people."[31] In *A Voice From the South*, shortly after the statement on the unique position of the black woman, Cooper reiterates the idea now with a stronger hint of this second meaning of the term "unique":

> The colored woman, then, should not be ignored because her bark is resting in the silent waters of the sheltered cove. She is watching the movements of the contestants none the less and is all the better qualified, perhaps, to weigh and to judge and advise because not herself in the excitement of the race. Her voice, too, has

always been heard in clear, unfaltering tones, ringing the changes on those deeper interests which make for the permanent good.[32]

Thus, again, one thinks of the photographic image of this woman: solitary, though not alone; quiet, but not voiceless; dignified, but attentive to the permanent good.

What set Cooper apart from others of her day who were engaged in a similar sort of work was that she, virtually alone, gave precise and unflinching voice to a theoretical attitude that today is very well known.

Inasmuch as she was herself unexceptionably concrete, it may seem a bit formal to refer to work as "theoretical." Just the same, Cooper's ideas, though simply put, were an important link in the more than century-long evolution of black feminist social theory from Sojourner Truth's legendary "Ar'n't I a Woman?" speech in the mid-nineteenth century to the full expression of black feminist thought in the 1980s. In a language that was surely invented by reporters on the speech, Truth is said to have uttered the powerful idea in 1851: "I tink dat 'twixt de niggers of the Souf and the womin at the Norf, all talkin' 'bout rights, de white men will be in a fix pretty soon." Truth, even less theoretical than Cooper, was one of the first to speak about her position as a black woman as a reason for calling into question the assumption that race ("de niggers of the Souf") and, to use today's word, gender ("the womin of the Norf") can be held as though they were separable categories of social thought.[33]

Though today Sojourner Truth's idea is well understood, Cooper's *A Voice From the South* was the first systematic working out of the insistence that no one social category can capture the reality of the colored woman. In her words, in the sentence immediately following the passage describing the colored woman's unique position, Cooper adds that the colored woman "is confronted by both a woman question and a race problem."[34]

At first, one might be concerned about the precise meaning of the expression "colored woman." Generally, when Cooper used the expression, she mean it as an alternative to "Negro," and in preference to, say, Truth's alleged use of "nigger." But here it is possible that she also used "colored woman" in a sense closer to today's expression "women of color"—referring, that is, to all women whose racial and social situations set them off from generically universal, or white, women. This interpretation is encouraged because the passage referring to the colored woman's unique position occurs in a chapter Cooper placed strategically just after her most carefully worked-through statement of black feminist theory, the famous essay attacking white feminists. In "Woman Versus the Indian," a title taken from a talk given by a leading white feminist, the Reverend Anna Shaw, Cooper offers an early statement of what today would be recognized as a social theory of the woman of color. Though some would not agree,[35] it is hard to imagine what else Cooper might have had in mind when she asks, against Shaw's careless opposition of Woman to the

Indian, "Why should woman become plaintiff in a suit versus the Indian, or the Negro or any other race or class who have been crushed under the iron heel of Anglo-Saxon power and selfishness?"[36] At an earlier but crucial historical time, Cooper focused the terms of debates occurring today. Many of the concepts at issue in black feminist and women of color social theory can be found, even if obliquely, in Cooper's essays. In fact, one of the most urgent debates among feminists a century later, bears on the central point in Cooper's thinking in *A Voice From the South*. Cooper anticipated by nearly a century today's debates over the insufficiency of such categories as race or gender, even class, to capture, by themselves, the complexities of a woman's social experiences. Susan Bordo's gender skepticism, Donna Haraway's reformulation of Chela Sanddoval's fractured identities, Sandra Harding's idea of the instability of analytic categories, and Judith Butler's queer account of the necessary trouble arising upon doubts about gender as an analytic category—all concern the most difficult of questions, *How are we, if we are a we, to think about the varieties of social experiences that may affect many people, perhaps all, but most dramatically women of color?* [37]

In the critical literature on Cooper the uniqueness of her personal politics in the history of black feminist thought is widely recognized. In addition to the symbolic use of her portrait, Cooper's most famous line is used in the title of Paula Giddings' history of black women in America, *When and Where I Enter*, just as the most powerful phrase in that line, "In the Quiet, Undisputed Dignity of My Womanhood," serves as the title for Hazel Carby's important discussion of black feminism after Emancipation.[38] More importantly, beyond the symbolic value of Cooper's words and image, there is ample and sometimes extravagant praise for Cooper. In her own day, Gertrude Bustill Mossell, author of *The Work of the Afro-American Woman* (1894), recognized Cooper's *A Voice From the South*, "as one of the strongest pleas for the race and sex of the writer that has ever appeared."[39] Claudia Tate, in *Domestic Allegories of Political Desire: The Black Heroine's Text at the Turn of the Century*, considers both Mossell herself and Cooper so important as to have been to the ideal of black womanhood what their contemporaries, Booker T. Washington and W. E. B. Du Bois were to popular ideals of black manhood. Tate goes so far as to state, as though it were self-evident, that "it is important to remember . . . that Cooper and Mossell were probably real-life models for many of the exemplary heroines of black women's domestic novels."[40] In a similarly grand historical claim, Jacqueline Jones, in her prize-winning study, *Labor of Love, Labor of Sorrow*, puts Cooper on a short list of black feminist writers whose "critique of black womanhood marked the emergence of the 'black matriarchy thesis,' for they suggest that the main problem in Afro-American family was an 'irresponsible' father who took advantage of his 'faithful, hardworking womenfolks.'"[41]

Even critics who harbor reservations about Cooper's alleged inability to escape the true womanhood ideal, give strong testimony to her importance. Ann duCille identifies Cooper, along with Mary Church Terrell and Ida B.

Wells-Barnett, as among those women who knew the legacy of the black woman born to slavery, but in giving "voice to the unspoken," were in fact that legacy to subsequent generations.[42] Even Mary Helen Washington, the most prominent critic of Cooper's supposed adherence to true womanhood virtues, concludes in the end that *A Voice From the South* "is the most precise, forceful, well-argued statement of black feminist thought to come out of the nineteenth century."[43]

Yet, for all this recognition, Cooper remains an essentially isolated figure in the history of black feminist thought. To date, there are few studies devoted exclusively to Cooper's feminism. Both of the currently available biographies of Cooper tend to underexamine her ideas relative to the details of her life.[44] And, the most serious scholarly works on the emergence of black feminist thought and fiction at the turn of century tend to leave readers somewhat in the dark with respect to Cooper's specific contributions to black feminist theory.[45]

This relative neglect might be due in some part to the nature of the theoretical position Cooper defined so precisely but wrote up so episodically. Though she was clear as to her convictions, Cooper's main work of feminist theory, *Voice*, was a composition after the fact, drawing as it did on occasional essays and public lectures.

As Karen Baker-Fletcher points out, *A Voice From the South* is structured into two distinct parts—a first that gives voice to the solo voice of the black woman, and a second which is more broadly expressive of the concerns of the racial and cultural community.[46] Most of the critical discussion of Cooper's book is devoted to the first, black feminist essays in which are found Cooper's most familiar statements and ideas. The first part comprises four essays, all (one assumes) originally public lectures: (1) "Womanhood a Vital Element in the Regeneration and Progress of the Race" (the talk delivered before the clergymen in 1886), (2) "The Higher Education of Women" (an 1890 talk to the American Conference on Education), (3) "Woman Versus the 'Indian'" (the well-known reply to Anna Shaw), and finally, (4) "The Status of Woman in America" (an essay of unknown origins, perhaps written for *Voice*).

Of the four essays, the first and the third are the heart of the social theory for which Cooper is best known because it is in these two that Cooper most daringly challenges, first, the black man and then the white feminist. Yet, even though she is in places quite severe in her references to both, Cooper is much more intent on defining the unique position of the black woman in human history than in dismissing the men of her race and feminists not of her race—with both of whom she had something in common, politically as well as socially. Whatever is found elsewhere in her writings, Cooper's unique theoretical contribution rests largely on the delicacy with which she held the other two figures—and it was the social figures as much as the real individuals that interested her. Her respectful, if firm, critiques of the black man and the white woman served her primary purpose, to give voice to the black woman.

Cooper pursued her literary purposes in *Voice*, as she conducted her long life after 1892, with reference to an acutely self-conscious understanding of the importance of the black woman in American political and cultural life. One might say today that she had been intent upon inventing the discursive space of the black woman, and it may well be that the importance of her theory is underestimated because her language is so practical, so direct to a reading public that was not primarily academic. Still, long before anyone had formulated the notion that intellectual work ought to be an archaeological discovery of the unique in social life, Cooper did just that. When reading her elegant language, one must continually pause to ask, Who was this woman? How did her social circumstances affect her social ideas?

The brilliance of her academic accomplishments, and the polish of her culture, might all too easily blind the reader to the most fundamental economic fact of Cooper's life. Though she lived well, she lived frugally, and was never a woman of means. She chose and furnished her homes, traveled to Europe, and raised her foster children as a single woman whose annual income never much exceeded $1800. While in the 1930's this sum (her retirement benefit) would have put her in the modest middle class, it was hardly a substantial income. What is more, Cooper pursued her intellectual and teaching work throughout her life with none of the financial or domestic support a spouse (even then) would have provided. On the contrary, she was forced to fight against the continuous opposition of her school supervisors for the most meager pay increments or the right to pursue her academic work. Her doctoral studies were subject to mean-spirited interference by school administrators who continued to hound her more than twenty years after the M Street School dismissal.[47] To be sure, she enjoyed a certain class advantage, but one she earned, protected, and nurtured entirely on her own. Winning the advantages of class culture is an entirely different matter from the reality of economic uncertainty. Cooper was, after all, a black woman in a border city during the Jim Crow era, and she was a woman who devoted her life to, as she put it, "neglected people"—her pupils, the young women at the YWCA, the struggling families of the social settlement house.

Cooper was, in this sense, a very solitary voice. If not poor, at least constantly at economic risk; if cultured and learned, ever attentive to needs of the poor. Compared to others, even other black women in her day—like Mary Church Terrell who came from a family of means (and had a successful husband) or Ida B. Wells-Barnett who in spite of her birth in slavery was married during much of her anti-lynching work—Cooper earned for herself every penny she had, just as she alone designed, maintained, and decorated her lovely home on T Street. Cooper herself is somewhat responsible for the illusion that she lived a life of privilege. One of the effects of her deep religious belief was the conviction that her life was a calling to which she responded, and that even the suffering we endure is a matter of choice.[48]

The facts of Cooper's unique personal attitudes and position in life are of vital importance to the interpretation of her life and theory, in three respects: (1) the broader circumstances of her relative isolation in her day, (2) the confusions in the critical literature, in particular about her attitudes toward the true womanhood ideal, (3) the distinctive literary, as well as theoretical, voice she claimed. Each merits its own consideration.

Though Cooper enjoyed good friends and warm recognition, she also suffered severe embarrassments to her natural human desire for human companionship and cooperation. After the effects of her birth in slavery (and their enduring consequences for her mother and brothers), the loss of her husband was the next such blow, but not the last.

Four years after George Cooper's death in 1877, Anna pursued her education at Oberlin where, because she had no financial resources of her own, she lived at the home of Professor Charles H. Churchill. Though this was an entirely satisfying arrangement for all concerned, it nonetheless served, it seems, to widen the social distance between Cooper and her classmates, a distance already created by age and race differences.[49] Though Cooper kept up a life-long correspondence with members of the class of 1884, the puzzling absence of any lasting ties with her two black classmates, Mary Church and Ida Gibbs Hunt (who were roommates at Oberlin), was certainly due in part to the economic necessity of Cooper's off-campus housing. As we know, more than twenty years after their graduation, the separation from Mary Church Terrell would be a factor of some importance in the events leading up to Cooper's dismissal from M Street School in 1906.

At the most desperate moment in her life, a person whom a feminist in Cooper's position would normally have had every reason to count on, left her (or was forced to leave her) without help. It is true, of course, that Mary Terrell was not free to act, even if she had wanted to, because, at the time of the M Street drama, her husband was a Tuskegee-sponsored appointee to the district school board; and true, also, that Terrell eventually did break with Tuskegee upon becoming a founding member of the NAACP in 1910. Race politics surely played their role. But there was another more subtle but telling difference between the two Oberlin schoolmates, one likely to be the better explanation for Terrell's life-long social distance from Cooper.

They were of different social classes, both by birth and in adult life. Cooper was born in slavery; Terrell to a life of means. Cooper was a widow on a teacher's salary; Terrell was married to a Harvard graduate and a prominent lawyer in Washington. Neither was poor by any means. But this does not mean that differences in class between Cooper and Terrell might not have played the decisive role in the mysterious social distance the one kept from the other. Then, as now, class differences could wedge their way between people of otherwise similar social position. Clearly, it was Terrell, if anyone, who, especially in the early years in Washington, lived the life of devotion to the "cardi-nal virtues—piety, purity, submissiveness, and domesticity," as Barbara Welter defined the principles of nineteenth century true womanhood.[50] It was the young Mary Church whose heart fluttered upon seeing the handsome Robert Terrell (and who, later in life, was not embarrassed to recount the episode), and she who left her teaching post first to travel at her leisure, then to marry.[51] Most important to the life of Cooper, it was Terrell who was beholden, thus, "submissive," not just to her politically-obliged husband but, at the time of Cooper's trouble, directly to Booker T. Washington himself.

There is more than one cause of the uncertainties in Cooper's incomplete, nearly lifelong relationship with Terrell. Early differences of race politics were also differences of class politics. The local story of these two great women leaders was part of the national debate between the then increasingly divergent philosophies of the two great race-men of the twentieth century's first decade. Both involved subtle yet important connections between race and class. To be sure, Booker T. Washington's philosophy, whatever its merits, was nothing if it was not a race philosophy of submissiveness most famously expressed in his notorious 1895 Atlanta Compromise.[52] But, just as importantly, it was the power of this philosophy in the hands of Washington and his agents that aggra-vated class differences within black communities across the nation. Washington's dispute with Du Bois, which led eventually to the founding of the NAACP, was not, of course, simply about class differences. It involved, centrally, a fundamental divergence of opinion as to the importance of higher education to racial uplift, a difference that entailed differences of opinion on the question of class advantages that American blacks could hope to gain. In reality, at the turn of the century, the actual class gains from higher education (as opposed to industrial education) were meager in relative terms (as is evi-dent by the economic uncertainties that beset both Du Bois and Cooper through their active lives). Yet the unassumed advantages were evident.

The principals in the national debate as well as those in the M Street School controversy well illustrate this complex and counterintuitive play of class and race. It was Washington, and in our story, the Terrells who, though they openly or tacitly sponsored a philosophy of industrial education, nonetheless enjoyed the considerable blessing of class privilege. By contrast, Du Bois and Cooper, though they believed in what is usually considered an elitist philoso-phy, endured relative economic marginality. Though neither side was poor in fact, the relative differences of actual class position ran counter to the assump-tions of the ideals themselves in more than these few cases, if not as a general rule. Tuskegee did in fact serve the poor, and Du Bois, no less than Washington, enjoyed the support of wealthy men and women, many of them white. Whatever the contradictions in any of the several positions in the national debate and its effects on the school politics at the M Street School, the nasty web of class differences trapped Cooper in an impossible situation she could not control. Whatever the Terrells might have felt in 1905–06 at being forced to abandon their former teaching colleague, the more terrible contradictions were Cooper's.

Critics who would take Cooper's high moral values as a sign of indifference to the poor may be correct in asserting that she did not suffer poverty after the Oberlin years. But they would be wrong to assume that she did not suffer as the weak and poor most often do—by being unable to control one's own destiny in the face of attack. Again, relative to Mary Terrell and the others, white and black, who forced Cooper out of the position at M Street School, she was abused in 1906, not alone because of her race or gender, but just as much, if only indirectly, because of her economic and political marginality. Her values led her to the Du Bois side of the national debate, just as they inspired her teaching and leadership in the school. But, having chosen her side (as if she had a choice), Cooper was ultimately defenseless. And the reason she had no choice as to the values was that she never once relented in her identification with the neglected people from whose circles she, and her mother, had come. Neither Washington, nor Du Bois, not to mention the Terrells, lived and worked for so long in daily contact with the poor.

All the principals in the great and local struggles went on their way after 1906. Booker T. Washington slipped soon thereafter into decline and death in 1915. Du Bois, however, was just then coming into his own. In 1910 he joined Mary Terrell and others in the founding of the NAACP, which led to his establishing *Crisis* magazine, by which he solidified his position as the leading intellectual spokesman for black Americans in the period between Washington's decline and the Harlem Renaissance. The Terrells soon after joined the other side. And Cooper, after five years in Missouri, returned to the District of Columbia in 1911, thence to re-knit her family and domestic circle in Washington, and enjoy another half-century of success and life. Still, it is unlikely that the pain of the dismissal ever left her, as it is probable that she was driven to pursue the doctorate (which, after all, was not required to her work) in order to compensate for the loss of face the public controversy had caused her. If this is even remotely so, as the witness of Cooper's wistful note appended to the printed souvenir of her most proud moment in 1925 suggests, then it is also so that she was, at least in part, even more driven to direct her energies after 1911 to her work—with students and the poor, primarily, but also to the graduate degrees that set her even farther apart. Whichever direction she turned, and no matter how well she enjoyed the particulars of her social and intellectual life, Cooper's life turned more and more to isolation. If her successes raised her in some respects, they did as compensation for the falls in other moments of her life.

No one aspect of Cooper's experience explains her unique and solitary position. Not even the injuries of the 1906 dismissal are as important as the effective force of her moral and religious ideas which surely were the energizing source of her unusually focused personal life. Even a woman of "quiet undisputed dignity" can suffer injury and seek to heal by her own constructive means. The best interpretation is, I think, that Cooper was indeed forced into a position of relative isolation by all the circumstances of her life—her widowhood, the poverty of her young adult life, the economic and political uncertainties of her position in the Washington school system, and her desire to clear the public record of the stigma of 1906.

Cooper was an individual of such deep moral resources that she understood her own womanhood quite uniquely. If 1906 dismissal led to the scholarly life which accentuated an already isolated position, then it led by a route through the character of a person who was not defeated by bitterness, and who converted her pain into a significant intellectual accomplishment. Her 1925 doctoral thesis, while different in every way from the book of her youth, confirms the wisdom and intellectual acuity already apparent in 1892 in *A Voice From the South*. She was not just a good and unique woman, she was a superior intellect.

The facts of Cooper's personal life shed clarifying light on the critical confusions in the secondary interpretations of Cooper's ideas—especially as to her thinking with respect to womanhood and to men. The two, of course, are related. Too soft on the men is too true to pious womanhood. As I say, Cooper's avowed piety, her high-minded morals, and her evident devotion to home and hearth lend reason to the rumor that she was old-fashioned. But the critical rumor persists in spite of the evidence that she was just as much a tough-minded fighter who permitted no insult to her dignity to go unanswered. Even her affirmation of the colored woman's office has not satisfied her critics.

The strongest and most frequently made criticism of Cooper is, in the words of Mary Helen Washington, that she "is never able to discard totally the ethics of true womanhood, and except for the one passage about black laundry women, she does not imagine ordinary black working women as the basis of her feminist politics."[53] Karen Baker-Fletcher generally shares Washington's view: "What is problematic in Cooper's text is the lack of self-criticism regarding the degree to which the black middle class could speak on behalf of working and poor black people."[54] On the level of Cooper's language, her literary style and allusions, this, to be sure, is so. Though Washington overstates her case, on the matter of literary voice, she and Baker-Fletcher are not wrong. There was, to be sure, a considerable piety in Cooper's language, most notably in her address to the colored clergy:

> We need men and women who do not exhaust their genius splitting hairs on aristocratic distinctions and thanking God they are not as others; but earnest, unselfish souls, who can go into the highways and byways, lifting up and leading, advising and encouraging with the truly catholic benevolences of the Gospel of Christ.[55]

Cooper was at least a believer in the virtues of piety and purity and, as we have seen, domesticity. These values were basic to her nature and, thus, could not have but have influenced Cooper's social thought including, as bell hooks observes, those statements that seem to suggest a belief in a universal "feminine principle."[56] While it remains to be seen if hooks is right, it is incontestably true that Cooper's moral values affect her notably less harsh views toward men. Though Cooper could be biting in her criticism of men, including men in general, she does frequently display a striking reluctance to denounce them *tant mieux*.[57] On the contrary, she thought in the manner of the times, as the passage just quoted reveals. She believed that men and women, by their different complementary geniuses, could "lift and lead" together. Cooper's famous rebuke of Martin Delany for his use of the "when and where I enter" line was generally as harsh as her attacks on men ever got.

It is also true that the very language she used opens doubts as to her ability to see the black woman of the South as culturally and politically different from the pious white women to whom she was for so long subjected. In "The Status of Woman in America,"[58] for example, Cooper juxtaposes the great black women of the century—Sojourner Truth, Frances Watkins Harper, Charlotte Forten Grimké, among others—to the great white women to whom she had previously referred at the beginning of the essay—Dorthea Dix, Helen Hunt Jackson, Lucretia Mott. The comparison serves, no doubt, to shift the rhetorical advantage by asserting the equality of the former to the latter. Yet, Mary Helen Washington is not wrong to question Cooper's use of words like "pleasing," "sweet," "gentle," "charming," and "matchless and irresistible personality" to describe the black woman's special virtues.[59] But Washington does not press this point, perhaps because she understands that what is at work here is Cooper's use of the rhetorical device of contrasting by simple comparison. In the use of such a classically "feminine" vocabulary Cooper means to suggest not just that black women are equal to the whites, but that in their equivalency they are superior. This, remember, is the chapter that concludes with her affirmation of the colored woman's office. There is something to Washington's criticism, though perhaps not as much as it may seem.

Ann duCille takes a somewhat more nuanced view. She sees Cooper's position on the womanhood ideal as conflicted and contradictory. Though, on the one hand "Cooper's feminist vision may have roved beyond the immediate material conditions of her constituency"[60] in overestimating what was realistically possible for poor women. At the same time duCille thinks that Cooper developed a strong critique of the prevailing ideology on sex and marriage and was among those who "laid siege to womanhood."[61] Still, duCille maintains the reservation that, "While [Cooper] had a finely honed sense of the imperialist impulse and its power to colonize the female mind and body, she never quite managed to fully extricate her own mind from the tenets of true womanhood. . . ."[62]

Claudia Tate seems at first to take a view similar to duCille's, that Cooper was of two minds. On the one hand, Tate, like bell hooks, takes Cooper's version of a universal feminine principle seriously but by attributing to it the force of a double-edged sword—cutting one way against the domination of men, cutting another against the all too cautious reformism of white feminists, Tate's position seems to be that Cooper knew just what she was doing in the use of the language of true womanhood[63] to establish a point of communication with those to whom she spoke (white and black alike) in order to isolate and define the political position of the black woman. Tate understands Cooper's opening essay, "Womanhood as a Vital Element in the Regeneration of a Race," along with Mossell's introductory chapter in *The Work of the Afro-American Woman*, as strategic transformations of the true womanhood doctrine:

> In these chapters as well as throughout their words, we find the construction of black womanhood in an enlarged intraracial domesticity as the signifier for enlightened, politicized black self-authority, self-interest, and self development.[64]

The least ambivalent defender of Cooper on this score is Hazel Carby who sees Cooper's understanding of what duCille calls the "imperialist impulse" in clear and unqualified terms. Carby believes that Cooper held a structural theory of women's power which allowed her to criticize "the intimate link between internal and external colonialization, between domestic racial oppression and imperialism."[65] In contrast to others (even to duCille and Tate), Carby interprets Cooper as an explicit, knowing, and unambivalent critic of the true womanhood ideal:

> Black women, [Cooper] argued, could not retreat into an abstraction of womanhood dissociated from the oppression of their whole people; their everyday lives were a confrontation of the division between the inviolability of elitist conceptions of womanhood and that which it denied.[66]

Were these critical confusions simply a matter of the textual evidence, it would seem to me that Tate's position, though not fully developed, is the more compelling on the literary facts. While I believe that Carby is closer on Cooper's ultimate political attitude, Tate seems to have got her literary method exactly right.

As a writer, not to mention as an actor in a dangerous world, Cooper was perfectly capable of catching her readers, or opponents, off guard. She used seemingly gentle means to draw those she addressed into rhetorical traps of frequently harsh and challenging proportions.[67] At no place is this tactic more powerfully executed than in "Woman Versus the 'Indian'"[68] which happens to be the essay that lends strongest support to Carby's reading of Cooper as a social critic of imperialism.

"Woman Versus the 'Indian'" opens with a simple, uninflected mention of the speech of that title delivered by the Reverend Anna Shaw to the National Woman's Council in February, 1891. Cooper's readiness to deceive for good purpose is evident from her opening compliment that Shaw's paper was "among a number of thoughtful and suggestive papers read by eminent women." She continues in this vein: "That Miss Shaw is broad and just and liberal in principle is proved beyond contradiction." Cooper goes on to document the broad, just, and liberal spirit of Miss Shaw and of Susan B. Anthony by reference to an episode involving Wimodaughsis, a national white women's literary club.[69] Then Cooper tells a story, one so archetypical as to invite the impression that it comes from collective rather than personal experience. The story: A colored woman applies, in writing, for membership in the club. When the color of the applicant comes to light, a certain "Kentucky secretary, a lady zealous in the good works" denies admission for the now obvious reason. Miss Shaw and, by implication, Miss Anthony promptly overrule the lady's officious good work, admit the applicant, and dismiss the secretary. Cooper comments on the story and on the character of the Kentucky secretary with biting sarcasm:

> I can't help imagining [that she] belongs to that estimable class who daily thank the Lord that He made the earth that they may have the job of superintending its rotations, and who really would like to help "elevate" the colored people (in her own way of course and so long as they understand their places) and [that she] is filled with grief and horror that any persons of Negro extraction should aspire to learn type-writing or languages or to enjoy any other advantages offered by the sacred halls of Wimodaughsis.[70]

The tone of the essay changes. At the very least, these are not the words of a blind adherent to the pious submissiveness of the classic, true woman.

Cooper here makes a series of rhetorical moves by which the reader is abruptly brought into her way of thinking. The first of these is the establishment of a strategic uncertainty. Assuming the story is true in all its details, the reader is left to wonder: Was the rejected colored woman Cooper herself? Cooper suggests this possibility by the use of a direct narrative voice. But she withholds confirmation by assuming the third person: "Accordingly the Kentucky secretary took the cream-colored applicant aside, and, with emotions befitting such an epoch-making crisis, told her, 'as kindly as she could,' that colored people were not admitted to the classes...."[71] The text creates the impression of a first-hand account, but it is only an impression. Cooper might have been the applicant, but it is hard to say why she would have been interested in joining a whites only literary group. By 1892, she was long committed to a literary circle with the Grimkés, which met twice weekly; and was already deeply involved with black women's groups such as the Colored Women's League of Washington which she cofounded in 1894—not to mention her involvements in the Negro Women's Club Movement,[72] to say nothing of her habit of keeping distance from white people.[73] It is more than possible that Cooper is here retelling a story so frequently heard that she does not hesitate to use it, perhaps to fictionalize it, for her own purposes. Though it is impossible to know for certain, this probability is supported by the larger intent of the story itself.

Just after the recounting of this episode, Cooper again praises Shaw, and Anthony, but now with a slight but noticeable hint of the attitude she presents toward the Kentucky lady: "Susan B. Anthony and Anna Shaw are evidently too noble to be held in thrall by the provincialisms of women who seem never to have breathed the atmosphere beyond the confines of their grandfather's plantations."[74] She is clearly affirming the just liberality of the white feminists, but the use of "noble" seems to play uncertainly with the obnoxious noblesse oblige of the Kentucky secretary. Cooper used words with precision and care. Was the "noble" in contrast to the false nobility of the Southern lady, as if to affirm the good whites against the bad? Not likely. Cooper was far too subtle for such a move. It is more likely that she means to distinguish the white feminists neatly but not completely. This, as we shall see, is more than evident from the major point of the essay which she defers until much later in this, the longest of her published essays.

The overall structure of the essay evolves from this introduction. Here Cooper is teasing. She opens to her theme, but without developing it in so many words. She thus imposes another element of ambiguity. What does she think of Miss Shaw, really? And why is she interested at all in her talk "Woman Versus the 'Indian'?" The reader must wait for answers. The uncertainty in these opening pages is easily overlooked, inviting a hasty reading. Mary Helen Washington, for example, takes the description of the applicant to be further indication of Cooper's inability to escape the reaching force of the very cultural ideals she, Cooper, so openly despises in the Southern lady: "Although her sympathies were with the poor and uneducated, Cooper's images in *A Voice* are almost entirely of privileged women: the struggling, ambitious intellectual, those fatally beautiful Southern mulatto women, a 'cream-colored' aspirant to a white culture club. . . ."[75] Washington does not say that she takes Cooper as that aspirant, but she does believe that Cooper, if not fully identified with such a type, was at least unable to separate herself from it. Like Baker-Fletcher and others who remain skeptical of Cooper's rejection of the true womanhood ideal, Washington takes the author's verbal imagery as of greater interpretive importance than the substance of Cooper's actual argument as it unfolds, while ignoring altogether the testimony of her life.

How Cooper unfolds that argument is telling. Just after she returns to Miss Shaw's nobility, Cooper makes the all-important distinction that governs everything that follows in the essay: that between the black woman and the Southern woman (later transposed with all due sarcasm into Southern "lady"). Here she is making the self-conscious distinction that was already set up by the biting sarcasm directed at the Kentucky secretary. But, importantly, she is quick to say that, though the difference between the lady and the woman, is confusing, the black woman knows the difference:

The black woman and the southern woman, I imagine, often get them into the predicament of the befuddled man who had to take singly across a stream a bag of corn, a fox, and a goose. There was no one to help, and to leave the goose with the fox was death—with the corn, destruction. To re-christen the animals, the lion could not be induced to lie down with the lamb unless the lamb would take the inside berth. . . . The black woman appreciates the situation and can even sympathize with the actors in the serio-comic dilemma.[76]

Is it likely, therefore, that the black woman who is able to appreciate the confusion could lie down with such a lion? Cooper understands the trap of true womanhood and, though she uses its language, it seems to me improbable that she would take an inner berth with it without some broader purpose.[77]

The narrative line of "Woman Versus the 'Indian'" then moves to other subjects—principally to a complicated theory of race and sex caste in American society which Cooper states as a general theory of Western Civilization. She now shifts momentarily from the Southern lady to "the American woman . . . [who] is responsible for American manners," of whom she says:

With all her vaunted independence, the American woman of to-day is as fearful of losing caste as a Brahmin in India. This is the law under which she lives, . . . The queen of the drawing room is absolute ruler under this law.[78]

The Southern lady *and* the American woman? Why the shift in terms? Does she mean now to put the liberal feminist in the same ethical category with the Kentucky secretary? Again uncertainty is her method. She shifts to "American woman" but leaves her meaning open, nagging. Still there is no doubt she is attacking something very much like the womanhood ideal.

When Cooper turns back to the black woman she, again, shifts as if to emphasize the distinction. Now, suddenly, "black woman" becomes the "Black Woman"—capitalized, and personified: "It was the good fortune of the Black Woman of the South to spend some weeks, not long since, in a land over which floated the Union Jack." The reader of "Woman Versus the 'Indian'" again wonders, Is Cooper here speaking for herself even if she was not the creme-colored applicant? Again, the answer is as unsure as the question is interesting. What is likely is that now Cooper is speaking for herself but through the means of creating a new social figure, a character who is no one less than the pseudonymous author who, in effect, becomes the figurative personage of its subtitle: *A Voice From the South: By a Black Woman of the South*. Here, after four long chapters, Cooper returns to a theme that appeared briefly in the book's Preface, significantly titled: "*Our Raison d'Être*." In the Preface she had introduced the Black Woman (with unexplained capital letters) as the only figure of importance in American culture who has not been heard. Only she, the "Black Woman," can give voice to the "silent South." Neither "our Caucasian barristers" nor the "dark man" should be "wholly expected fully and adequately to reproduce the exact Voice of the Black Woman." Hence, the Preface which is set in the impersonal third person is recalled at a crucial juncture in the key chapter where Cooper herself becomes the personification of that Voice.

As Karen Baker-Fletcher, Claudia Tate, and Elizabeth Alexander have all said in different ways, Cooper possessed a very self-conscious theory of her voice. That theory is, in one respect, a literary device, but it is also what Baker-Fletcher calls Cooper's "theological anthropology."[79] If, by this, one can also mean a general social theory of voice, then I would agree with Baker-Fletcher. The surprising thing is that, in the end, Baker-Fletcher imposes an unnecessary limit on her own interpretation. She is among those with reservations about Cooper's continuing submissiveness to the ideal of true womanhood which supposedly interferes her ability to speak for the poor, black woman.[80] How, it might be asked, could a black woman of the South like Cooper have a theological anthropology, or any other kind of social theory, without speaking for the poor?

How does a voice become a representative Voice? How does a writer or speaker, to use the expression Baker-Fletcher takes from Cooper, become the "Singing Something" of a people?[81] In the broadest sense, this is the familiar problem of the representative intellectual which is at least as old as Marx. But, in the more immediate context, this is the question of the provocative limitedness of language. If one is to sing the voice of an oppressed people, must not the song come forth in the language of that people? Today much more is known about this; but we must take Cooper on her terms. As a teacher of languages, she surely understood the problems of the translatability of voice and language generally. She, after all, taught poor children for whom Latin and Greek were more than simply foreign and ancient. In the culture of the elite public education to which Cooper held her pupils, the mastery of Latin and Greek, while valuable in its own right, was also, and urgently, the price of admission to Harvard and Yale, and thus to the prospect of class advantage. She could hardly be expected to have appreciated today's debates over the cultural values of non-Standard English usages. Her own language, especially in *A Voice From the South*, has to be understood in this context.

Today, it is well understood that whenever voice is seized by a formerly silent people the terms of political representation in the social whole also change. Both liberal and left ideals of democratic participation have been severely challenged in the past quarter century and mostly by the emergence of formerly colonized peoples in an arena once controlled univocally by the Euro-American dominant classes. While Cooper could not have had access to our understandings, she was, at the end of the nineteenth century, attempting to do just what the decolonizing and related social movements have done in the last generations of the twentieth—and this is surely what Hazel Carby is driving at in her interpretation of Cooper as a virtual decolonizer before the fact. Cooper was, most self-consciously, seeking to give voice to black women in America by creating, then assuming, the representative position of the Black

Woman of the South. To be sure, in *A Voice From the South* she did not very often employ the language of the poor.[82] Still, there is no good reason to doubt the stated purpose of the Preface, much less the argument as it develops in "Woman Versus the 'Indian.'" She knew exactly what she was doing all along and what she was doing was what she always did. She was working for "neglected people."

In several previously unpublished writings, Cooper did in fact address the question of the language of the poor. Her much later essay, "Sketches from a Teacher's Notebook. Loss of Speech Through Isolation"[83] drew upon her experiences during and after World War I as director of War Camp community service programs. This quietly brilliant and touching essay is shorn of lofty ideals and fancy ideas. Here Cooper is speaking from the heart of life with the most poor. The essay tells the story of her encounter with the Berry family, a desperately poor, isolated, and broken rural family. Years before Cooper knew them, the father had been lynched. Though the locals realized that a mistake had been made, the family was irreparably damaged. The mother had chosen to keep herself, and particularly her child, Walter, in as complete as possible isolation from the cruelties of the wider world. As a result the boy spoke in a strange, near incoherent idiolect. Slowly Mrs. Cooper coaxed the boy into a tentative relationship.

> "Mith Coo' show—I make bick *too!*"
> "Why certainly, Walter," I said, with ready comprehension, "I'll be glad to show you how to make a bas-ket," speaking very distinctly and letting him observe the motion of my lips in pronouncing "bas-ket."[84]

Can there be any doubt from this that Mrs. Cooper (Mith Coo'), even though proud of her "ready comprehension," knew how to, and was committed to, giving voice to the poor in their language? Importantly, the story makes its point about the defeating effects of social isolation with simple reference to, exactly, the naivete of bourgeois ideals of home and family life:

> And I wondered what our brand of education, what our smug injunction that the home "is expected" to cooperate with the school will find or create for the help and guidance of such a home, a type as truly evolved from American environmental conditions as are the blind fish in the Mammoth Cave or the broncos of the western plains?[85]

If then she could speak and comprehend the language of the poor, why did she not do so in *A Voice From the South*? One answer, as I said, is that she was above all else a teacher. But a different one is found in another previously unpublished essay, "The Negro's Dialect."[86] Here, she takes up the question of public abuses of Negro dialect. Her purpose is to demonstrate that popular culture's caricatures of Negro dialect are, with rare exception, linguistically (that is, phonetically) impossible—a foolish mockery of colored people.

Cooper here applies her considerable skill as a linguist in order to demystify popular perversions of black language and culture in such media as the *Amos 'n Andy* radio program. This later essay suggests that, even much earlier when she wrote *A Voice From the South*, Cooper had not been the sort of person who was willing, even remotely, to give comfort to the worst white images of black culture. She understood her work to be the lifting of the culture and its language. Whatever else she was, Cooper was a leader among the first generation of black women in America struggling to make the cultural as well as social and economic transition from the rural South to the cosmopolitan and urban North.[87] Everything they had, such as it precariously was, they owed to their hard-won ability to work out from slavery—from the South into the middle-class life won by education and learning.

What choice is there but to understand Cooper's ideas in context—in the context of her times, and of her life? Whatever the lingering effects of the true womanhood doctrine, they are at best, as Claudia Tate implies, a kind of literary slate on which is written the voice of the black woman by a Black Woman of the South. The book is about nothing if it is not about voice in this sense, and this becomes overwhelmingly clear as the narrative in "Woman Versus the 'Indian'" moves toward its conclusion. After the introduction of herself as the Black Woman, Cooper presents a version of her implicit theory of oppression, as Carby refers to it. But Cooper does so, again, by an odd path. She cites a then popular book by the astronomer and writer Percival Lowell. In *Soul of the Far East*, Lowell proposed that "personality" and "sense of self" decline in inverse relation to "manners." In simple terms, the theory is that the West is more "personal" than the East. Accordingly, it has fewer manners. America, being the most Western, is "the least courteous nation on the globe." But, in Cooper's hands, Lowell's not very convincing claim becomes an implicit theory of Western culture with quite a different meaning from Lowell's.[88]

Just before these remarks, Cooper tells a story (to which I shall return) in which she, the Black Woman, while a passenger on a train in the South, was exposed to the worst sort of rude and crude abuse. She uses, here, the common language:

> "Here gurl," (I am past thirty) "you better git out 'n dis kyar 'f yer don't, I'll put yer out," my mental annotation is Here's an American citizen who has been badly trained. He is sadly lacking in the both "sweetness" and "light."[89]

At first, it would seem this is an instance in which Cooper is calling her racist tormentor to the account of true womanhood values by judging his inferior (typically American) manners. The impression is heightened when she adds:

> But since Mr. Lowell shows so conclusively that the entire Land of the West is a mannerless continent, I have determined to plead with our women, the mannerless sex on this *mannerless continent*, to institute a reform by placing immediately in our national curricula a department for teaching GOOD MANNERS.[90]

But read the text closely. The American woman is "the mannerless sex on this mannerless continent." Does Cooper mean to put her in the same category as the ill-mannered men—as Lowell's American? Not at all. She is toying with Lowell's odd idea that manners decline in inverse proportion to a "sense of self." Though she *seems* to be calling for greater courtesy, she is actually demanding a better sense of "self," of personhood—one might even say of womanhood. Cooper underscores and capitalizes GOOD MANNERS perhaps to be ironic, as if to say: Against the personless, sterile manners, can we not *at least* have good manners?

Though this is a tricky passage to understand, the interpretation is supported by Cooper's return to the distinction between the Southern lady and the Black Woman. The former, being the bearer of all virtue and "manners" (not necessary good ones), is again subjected to Cooper's own brand of verbal abuse, after which she carefully turns back to the white feminist movement:

> Lately a great national and international movement characteristic of this age and country, a movement based on the inherent right of every soul to its own highest development. I mean the movement making for Woman's full, free, and complete emancipation, has, after much courting, obtained the gracious smile of the Southern woman—I beg her pardon—the Southern *lady*.[91]

Earlier, under the metonymic guise of Miss Shaw, Cooper has rebuked the Kentucky secretary and chided her precisely for her figurative liaisons with the true Southern lady. Here, it seems, the muted praise of Susan B. Anthony and Shaw, with their liberal and noble virtues, takes on its true meaning. Cooper does not condemn the white feminists to mere equivalency with the Southern *lady*, even though she does rebuke them for their recent courtings of the original true woman. This is evident from what follows in Cooper's discussion.

The true woman, the Southern lady, does not care about manners. Her concern is with the terrifying prospect of social equality with Negroes who have a quite different sense of civility from hers. The Southern lady fears that, "civility to the Negro implies social equality."[92] But quickly Cooper distinguishes the Southern lady's fear of social equality as forced association between the races and the Black Woman's (her own) idea that it means nothing necessarily more than a simple, human identity of needs and interests—that is, the need to move in like manner through the public sphere and its accommodations, there to buy and sell according means and desires. The Black Woman of the South then disclaims any particular or necessary desire for enforced association with anyone, whether colored or white.[93]

This would seem to be a regressive statement, a recourse to what would become the Tuskegee idea of race relations—of the common economic hand with separate social fingers. The difference, however, is that Cooper is writing here from a position of avowed moral and cultural superiority—to the crude man on the train, to the Kentucky secretary, to the mannerless West and to the mannerless woman. Whereupon Cooper introduces her version of what bell hooks has called her "feminine principle":

> And this is why, as it appears to me, woman in her lately acquired vantage ground for speaking an earnest helpful word, can do this country no deeper and truer and more lasting good than by bending all her energies to thus broadening, humanizing, and civilizing her native land.[94]

But, as I have been suggesting, this is not quite what it seems. Cooper's standpoint feminist principle, such as it is, is always qualified, as it is here, most dramatically.

Two paragraphs after the above statement of this apparently seamless and universalistic gender principle, Cooper returns (at long last) to Miss Shaw and her paper "The Woman Versus the 'Indian.'" This occurs nearly thirty pages later, as the long essay draws to its conclusion, and its main point. Cooper, aware of what she had been doing, but sensitive to the likelihood that the reader could be lost in the studied uncertainty projected over such a long intervening space, lets Miss Shaw back in gently: "This, too, is why I conceive the subject to have been unfortunately worded which was chosen by Miss Shaw at the Women's Council and which stands at the head of this chapter."[95] Now Cooper speaks of Shaw's voice from which she draws her concern for the unfortunate title:

> Miss Shaw is one of the most powerful of our leaders, and we feel her voice should give no uncertain note. Woman should not, even by inference, or for the sake of argument, seem to disparage what is weak. For woman's cause is the cause of the weak; and when all the weak shall have received their due consideration, then woman will have her "rights," and the Indian will have his rights, and all the strong will have learned at last to deal justly, to love mercy, and to walk humbly; and our fair land will have been taught the secret of universal courtesy which is after all nothing but the art, the science, and the religion of regarding one's neighbor as one's self, and do for him as we would, were conditions swapped, that he do for us.[96]

The invocation of biblical language at the end[97] fulfills the uncertain meaning of "GOOD MANNERS." As Cooper puts it here, "the secret of universal courtesy" is a simple morality of public, reciprocal regard. Good manners, therefore, are something quite different from the false social virtues of the true Southern lady. "All prejudices, whether of race, sect or sex, class pride and caste distinctions are the belittling inheritance and badge of snobs and prigs".[98]

More to the point of the entire chapter, however, Cooper finally begins to make herself more explicit, less indefinite with respect to white feminists. Cooper does possess a sort of fractured principle of universal womanhood, but the Black Woman's relation to womanhood is certainly not through the Southern lady. Instead, Cooper's figure of the Black Woman claims its representative power by relation to another—the no less idealized American woman, who had been mentioned earlier and dropped, only to reappear ever so necessarily at the crucial moment in Cooper's unfolding idea. If the Black Woman is to have her voice in the construction of the American woman, she must be able to set straight the terms of her moral courtesy to the white feminist. We see now that Cooper's purpose in rebuking the feminist metonym, Miss Shaw, can only be that of encouraging her, the white feminist, toward a greater appreciation of the secret of universal courtesy, as Cooper defines it. This she pursues at the conclusion of the long essay by describing with notable precision the error of Shaw's title. That error is not, of course, bad manners, or political insensitivity, but that of ignoring woman's sense of unity and identification with the weak. The problem is that the white feminist, like the American Woman, is in the same social and economic position as are the poor and thus is the natural ally of those who are weak. The idea quoted in full:

> Why should woman become plaintiff in a suit versus the Indian, or the Negro or any other race or class who have been crushed under the iron heel of Anglo-Saxon power and selfishness? If the Indian has been wronged and cheated by the puissance of this American Government, it is woman's mission to plead with her country to cease to do evil and to pay its honest debts. If the Negro has been deceitfully cajoled or inhumanly cuffed according to selfish expediency or capricious antipathy, let it be woman's mission to plead that he be met as a man and honestly given half the road. If woman's own happiness has been ignored or misunderstood in our country's legislating for bread winners, for rum sellers, for property holders, for family relations, for any or all the interests that touch her vitally, let her rest her plea, not on Indian inferiority, nor on Negro depravity, but on the obligation of legislators to do for her as they would have others do for them were relations reversed.[99]

The golden rule of courtesy is, thus, the foundational principle of Cooper's feminist politics. Those, like bell hooks, who divine a universal principle of the feminine in Cooper are not wrong. And, to be sure, Cooper's feminist politics would not be considered revolutionary by today's standards. But neither is Cooper's feminism, even remotely, a knee-jerk version of the true womanhood ideal. Nor is Cooper politically naive, which is why Claudia Tate and, more tentatively, Ann duCille see in Cooper versions of Hazel Carby's strong intepretation of her as a self-conscious social critic of internal colonization. Some might be more cautious, but Carby is close to Cooper's thinking. Cooper may have grounded her feminism in moral and religious principles that seem remote today, but her politics were a far cry from the true womanhood manners of the Southern lady.

For Cooper, who lived a largely solitary life in service of the poor, the domestic ideal was anything but lady-like submissiveness. It was, quite to the contrary, the practical form of that service and the expression of the moral culture from which she believed it must issue.

In the story of her confrontation with ill-mannered whites, mentioned earlier, the reader comes upon another of Cooper's more memorable statements—one that brings all the more clarity to her theory of the Black Woman. Cooper continues the story of what transpired during her—that is, the Black Woman's— train trip in the South:

> And when a little farther on in the same section our train stops at a dilapidated station, rendered yet more unsightly by dozens of loafers with their hands in their pockets while a productive soil and inviting climate beckon in vain to industry; and when, looking a little more closely, I see two dingy little rooms with "FOR LADIES" swinging over one and "FOR COLORED PEOPLE" over the other; . . . [I wonder] under which head I come.[100]

Though understated, these few lines express most elegantly Anna Julia Cooper's unique position in the social theory of America and of American women at another time in history.

Just as Cooper's personal life was one of solitary—often isolated— purpose, her most impressive theoretical statements drew upon her personal experience in order to define the unique and univocal position of the Black Woman in those times. The 1890s in the urban North were an historical moment when, for the first time, black women in America were rising in significant numbers to positions of prominence and relative power.

In 1895, three years after *A Voice From the South* was published, Frederick Douglass died late in the evening after he had addressed a meeting of the National Council of Women convening just four years after Miss Shaw's address to the same group. Though his relations with feminists, and notably with Sojourner Truth, were not always easy, more than any black man of the nineteenth century, Douglass had tried somehow to align issues of the race with those of women's rights. He did not succeed, and no man after, including Du Bois, did better than he. These differences were, very probably, unbridgeable by any man, even if, in Cooper's view, the solution must not exclude men.

In an exact historical sense, the end of the nineteenth century was indeed an exceptional moment for the Black Woman. On the surface, the United States was in a time of change, hope, and progress. But under the surface of white, dominant, and male culture, there lay unsettled discontents. The failure of Reconstruction and the rise of Jim Crow turned the color line into a virtual wall of political regression against which, in particular, the new class of urban blacks would struggle, preparing the way for the transitions from the rural South to the urban North, from the culture of Southern folkways to the urban ways of the new middle classes—transitions that gathered force after World War I. At the same time, the end of the nineteenth century was the period of still significant feminist struggle which would achieve a definite, though incomplete, political success in the 1920s.

More generally, the 1890s were a period in American history when the new industrial order was coming into its own. The older feudal system of the South which had bred both the slave economy and the culture of true woman-hood lay in ruins. Since the Civil War it was clear that industrialization had meant that the economic future lay in the North. It would take the better part of the century following for the South to shed its past and enter this new order. In the retrospect of many years, we can see to just what extent the new economic arrangements changed the class system, and how these changes brought instabilities in the caste systems governing race and sex—instablities that, by shaking the South and North differently, made the central point of Cooper's thinking evident to any willing to see. Race and sex can never be reliably thought through apart from each other because neither, in turn, is ever free from the causes and effects of class relations.

Amid this larger social business, it was, at the time Cooper wrote *A Voice From the South*, impossible that either the white woman, however good her manners, or a man of any race, however close one might be tied to him, could resolve the underlying structural tensions. Structural instabilities never arise along any one fault line—not of race alone, nor of gender, nor of class. But insofar as the emerging economic order would come in a degree and kind of industrial growth never before experienced, it was already impossible that America's refusal to acknowledge its own moral contradictions with respect to the caste-like exclusions of blacks, and women, and (in Cooper's essay) Indians, would not begin to break into the yield.

As a result, only someone like Anna Julia Cooper could read the signs for what they meant. In a society in which the Black Woman had no place to go—where she encounters two signs, FOR LADIES and FOR COLORED PEOPLE, neither of which defines her properly—then that Black Woman is uniquely situated to understand the larger structural situation. Cooper was not, by any means, the only social critic to grasp the situation. But she may have put it with such simple integrity and clarity because of the unique position her life forced upon her. She knew where she did not belong. Just the same, she knew how to live and serve with moral purpose. Being able, perhaps more than others, to tolerate the solitary position, she could read the signs for what they meant.

Ironically, Cooper's ability to tolerate and draw upon the uniqueness of her social experience, may also account for her extreme faith in the American future—a surprising faith she expresses, at the conclusion of her four-chapter black feminist manifesto, in "The Status of Woman in America." There, remember, she had said:

> What a responsibility then to have the sole management of the primal lights and shadows! Such is the colored woman's office. She must stamp weal and woe on the coming history of this people.[101]

Who is "this people"? Evidently she did mean to embrace the American people, and to claim for the Black Woman of America the unique office of moral responsibility for the future of the society as a whole. Just before this benedictory conclusion, Cooper also said:

> But to be a woman of the Negro race in America, and to be able to grasp the deep significance of the possibilities of the crisis, is to have a heritage, it seems to me, unique in all the ages.[102]

Only she who can read the signs, could have understood the possibilities that then lay ahead.

If only others had read them so well.

Five

Get on Home, 1949

My mother was born poor, but she married well for an immigrant girl who came of age in the Depression. She had but twenty-five years when she married my father, a medical student.

Her mother had been a seamstress in a remote village in what, as best anyone ever knew, was probably Croatia. I never knew her father who was an indefinite object of curiosity on the horizon of family stories. He had been, we were told, a military man. I have an old picture of him in uniform. It was never clear to me which military had outfitted him. Perhaps some far provincial regiment of the Austrian-Hungarian Empire. He had been killed in the line of duty. As the years went by, this figment of family imagination narrowed into a subplot about his being run over by a train. Years more, and the line allowed for the possibility that drink was a factor in his death and that he may or may not have survived the family journey to America. However and whenever my grandfather met his end, it is certain that he left my grandmother, Adele, and seven children to miserable conditions.

Sometime in 1914, when the Great War brought an end to the long nineteenth century's hope for human progress, my mother's family left their village in southeastern Europe for the Middle West of America. Three of the seven children died as did their father on one or another edge of the family migration. In the beginning, none of them spoke English. Still they settled in Cincinnati, a city of inviting German culture. They did speak German. My mother's mother must have known someone or some agency well enough to risk little for the journey. Whoever it was had not come through on their promises. Within months of their arrival my mother, her sister Olga, and their two brothers, John and Tony, were left to the mercies of a religious orphanage. Adele simply could not provide for them.

Yet, this remnant family survived the poverty. Grandmother Adele learned the skills of a practical nurse, which led to employment with income sufficient to reunite her children until they grew to young adulthood. Olga, the oldest, married a carnival operator. Gilbert, in time, joined his brothers-in-law, John and Tony, to fight as Americans in the Second World War. In due course all three returned home as wounded and modestly decorated heroes.

John brought back an English war bride, who eventually left him somewhere in Arizona. Soon after his return from war, Tony married. He too was left after a while. Again, I don't know why exactly. Gilbert returned to his carnival work until he was electrocuted while saving a boy from a broken power line. He survived the shock, but left Olga upon his recovery to live in a *ménage a trois* with Mabel and Bill. The *ménage* provided Olga an adjoining apartment. Every Saturday afternoon, for some forty dutiful years, Gilbert sent Olga a weekly check. Olga grew deaf during her domestic travail. I never knew how, or even why. Deafness seemed to suit her. There was so much one need not hear. Her sons stopped speaking to her along the way. She died alone.

It was my mother who had married really well, once and forever—for better or worse. She met my father during the Depression when he was still a student. Their foundational attractions were not hard to guess. My father, nervous and nerdy, was drawn to my mother's classic Balkan beauty. My mother to his sad but handsome visage (not to mention the good fortune of his profession).

Though my father's family was comfortable, even in the worst of times, the family story had it that my mother was forced to give up her life to support the struggling medical student. Just exactly what life she gave up was never clear. When I grew old enough to inquire, she always said that she "could" have been a wonderful dancer. This information was usually delivered with a flourish of arm and leg plausible to the legend. I took these as claims on a reservoir of untapped talents thwarted as the condition for her life among the white bourgeoisie of our modest river town. Her claims to artistic merit were, however, justified at a remove by the delicate touch with which she decorated our houses, mostly with flowers cut and arranged by her own hand. She loved flowers and gardening. This much was clear.

My mother had married "the doctor." This was the indirect reference she used when fielding phone calls from his working-class patients who then could call their physicians at home. "The doctor cannot come to the phone at the moment." The expression served to document mother's acquired status which distinguished her by grace from the referent's patients who lived up and down the short hills of the urban bottoms to which Cincinnati consigned its white and black working classes—to the North and West Ends, respectively.

I was born to the doctor and his wife in 1937. Shortly after, they built a house high on a hill to the west above the bottoms. My father's practice had started well enough. Babies were part of the middle class deal, even for those, like my parents, who soon realized that they were not fully equipped to the care of small children. Thereupon they called Florence to the family to care for me and my brother who was born just as a second war was breaking out in Europe. Florence, when she was not living with us, lived first on Guest Street and later on York Street in the West End, which was then a strong black community. After the Second World War, on Christmas Eves, my parents entertained my mother's family with a party of bright lights and lavish meals. My brother and I would gaze upon this scene from the kitchen where Florence prepared and served the meal. Of the three of us, only Florence understood the one-night stands of family harmony we were observing.

These are the recollected childhood stories of one little white boy. Father was the breadwinner and commandant of the household. Mother passed his orders on to the rest of us. Florence made the material and emotional things work out for the best. My brother and I grew up into the deadly boredom of the middling postwar suburbs of America.

At some impossible to determine moment in all this the family that never was truly one began to fray at the seams. Somehow my father was not the same after his three years' wartime service in China. What "the same" might have been, I never quite knew. But that is how we came to think of him. He napped a lot. Got a late start on his days. Bought new Oldsmobiles each year. Nothing quite made him happy.

Mother, on the other hand, carried on in her way. She did what mothers of her racial and class kind were expected to do. Got us to and from school. Arranged piano lessons. Took us to an occasional cultural event at the zoo or at Cincinnati's once grand Music Hall on Central Parkway. For herself, she attended regular monthly social gatherings with a group of girlfriends from her youth. News, even bad news, of these women could lift the spirits of our desultory family table. One lost her husband to cancer. Another died herself, also of cancer. One was married to a local bandleader. Another was our family attorney. Mother's girlfriends were one of her two ties to the outer world, and to whatever it was she gave up to marry the doctor. The other was her membership in the Westwood Garden Club, which met for lunch and business once a month and always issued in a new floral arrangement at the dinner table.

Then something changed one day, in 1949 or so. I heard the story of the event that led to the decline in my mother's domestic verve only later in life. It was told me by Bonnie, the mother of my boys, who in her turn would ply *my* mother with questions about *her* boys. The local family story is very simple and, for its day, typical in form, if not detail.

Over the years my mother had risen in the status ladder of the Westwood Garden Club to become its president. This entailed a great deal of administrative work, of which the most demanding was planning and bringing about the club's display booth at the Cheviot Harvest Home Fair. This work required that she remain at the meeting some hours after the luncheon meetings.

On this one day, as the story goes, the doctor is said to have called my mother at the club while she was conducting business. He demanded to know what she was doing, and why she was not home with the boys. I do not know what she said. It may have been something cleverly hostile or defensive. At which, the doctor shouted at her over the phone, "Get on home. Take care of the boys." Never mind that at the dawn of adolescence in those street-safe days, we neither needed nor wanted taking care of—nor that Florence was everyone's preferred choice for these purposes. Mother felt the rebuke for which she had no proper retort. Embarrassed, I am quite certain, and without words to describe what she felt, she called the meeting to an end, gathered up her things, and hastened obediently home.

I cannot say for certain that this was the event that took the wind out of mother's sails. But I do know that Helen Lemert grew, thereafter, more distant from me. And I know that her marriage to the doctor was from then on more evidently at odds. She kept to her clubs and friends. Sometime about then the Christmas Eve celebrations ended, as did parental socializing of any kind—save for mother's annual turn at hosting the gathering of her girlfriends. My parents stayed together to the end, as people then did. The doctor died before his time, just twenty years after the Garden Club incident. Mother followed him a few years later. She gave it up but a few months after she had fulfilled her one remaining marital obligation—the burial of my father's mother.

Mother died in 1974. She was sixty-four. It had been a little more than sixty years since she came to America filled with her mother's hope. Sixty years, exactly, had passed since the Great War brought on the troubles of the twentieth century. Helen (whose maiden name I dare not reveal in this weird world for fear someone will use it to steal my identity) had come here, as a child, just as Charlotte Perkins Gilman, nearing old age, was giving up her life's work for retirement. Helen never knew anything at all about Gilman or the other early feminists. Nor had she, in the years of her disappointment with my father, read the popular writings of Betty Friedan that started the feminist movement in America in the 1960s. My mother never really had a name for the problems she had had with the doctor and "his" boys and Florence, the one who kept everything in order.

Bad Dreams of Big Business:
Charlotte Perkins Gilman, 1898

More than any sociologist of her day, perhaps more than any since, Charlotte Perkins Gilman fearlessly bridged the artificial divide between fact and fiction. Herein lies her abiding witness to all women and men who live their lives between doubt and hope wherein the disciplined practice of social theory begins. Without fiction, there is no imagination; without imagination, no dreams; without dreams, facts hardly matter. Theories are the ways people use their imagination to talk about the factual realities that hedge their social dreams.

Strictly speaking, a fiction is a fashioning, an imitating, of things the truth of which is not merely, or presently, factual. There would be no progress, not even scientific progress, without these imaginative fashionings after the real. Hence the disputatious role of theory in both practical and scientific life. Many people, ordinary ones and scientists alike, hate theory. Yet they could not live without it. When all is said and done, theory is the more or less disciplined talk by which people make what sense they can of their social worlds. Theory, thus, does its work in the always unsettled space between doubt and promise. Theory seeks, thereby, to describe the possible in order to capture the imagination of others. Whether it tells stories or explains data sets, theory is the work of telling others what one holds to be true about the world. Theory is the hope of convincing others to see things as one sees them, even to invite their participation. This is true, surely, of the most formal scientific theory. But it is pointedly true of theories, like social theories, which cannot help but depend on fiction to find and describe their facts.

Charlotte Perkins Gilman very well understood this perplexingly simple first condition of her craft, which ultimately is the craft of anyone who aims to be socially engaged. Gilman's social theories of the man-made world have endured over time because she seemed to understand without instruction on the subject that, in her day, the factual state of women in the world economy could only be described from some distant standpoint of the social imagination. The arrangements that consign many women to the bourgeois family and the commandments of men were as arbitrary then as they are now. But then there were no theoretical or sociological languages sufficient to their description. Far from being stranger than fiction, the strangeness of the factual is that, in many times and places, reality's finest expressions can only be rendered as fiction.

Among feminist social theorists at the turn of the nineteenth century, Charlotte Perkins Gilman had no peer because no one saw and spoke with such convincing imagination of the ways Gilded Age capitalism arrogantly structured the lives of women and men. Gilman's was the age when Big Business came to be the prevailing social fact of the modern world. And she, more than any other feminist before her, and long before Malcolm X terrified the white world with a similar idea, saw that the then-forming American dream of the good life promised by big business was, for women like herself, at least a bad dream, if not an outright nightmare.

She was one of the first to write of the bad dream of economic reality for women of her kind because, long before anyone ever heard of C. Wright Mills and the sociological imagination, she was a dreamer of social realities, as well as a disciplined thinker. She was not, however, an academic (though she did occasionally write for academic journals like *The American Journal of Sociology*). Her social theory took the form of social criticism of the prevailing foundations of bourgeois social life and its economic arrangements. In books like *Women and Economics*[1] and *The Home*[2]—just two of many essays, lectures, and books of this kind—she shook the gendered foundations of modern life. In her day, only W. E. B. Du Bois among social critics we read today rivaled Gilman's popularity as a writer. No academic sociologist in the United States came close.

Just the same, to have been a woman in that day, even an intellectual one, meant that if one were to move and shake the public sphere dominated by white males one had to discover some indirect path to the popular imagination. At the turn of the last century, one of the most popular forms of entertainment for women at home was the magazine that arrived weekly. This is why the art of fiction was so important to Gilman and other socially conscious women of the time, notably her older, distant relative, Harriet Beecher Stowe—both of whom published their best-known work in the periodic press. It is, in fact, not entirely implausible to suggest that Gilman's "The Yellow Wallpaper" (1892) did for the social criticism of gender relations what *Uncle Tom's Cabin* had done forty years earlier for race relations. Gilman's disturbing short story of a woman driven mad by the man-made world did not start a war as Abraham Lincoln famously said of Beecher's book in relation to the Civil War. But, for much of the century since its publication, "The Yellow Wallpaper"[3] did give vent to the outrage of women trapped in a system that exploited their domestic services. Gilman's short fiction was the opening shot of her war of words against the (to use her word) androcentric biases of the world capitalist system. For a quarter century from this opening blast to the surprising, otherworldly ideas in her feminist utopia, *Herland*,[4] in 1915,

Gilman wrote widely read works of fiction. Yet, Gilman's fiction always expressed the more studied values of her critical social theory. At every turn, her work gives off, still today, the sweet scent of the long-feared, always inviting, intercourse between the real and the imaginary.

It would be a long time after Gilman quit her public life and work during the First World War before C. Wright Mills, in 1959, would coin the phrase "the sociological imagination." But not even Mills understood what Gilman knew about the importance of imagination to social thought. For Mills, the sociological imagination was more a rhetorical hammer used to loosen the grip of academic sociology's empirically narrow and theoretically abstract methods. Mills, of course, urged upon us the notion that sociology always begins in the needs of ordinary people who suffer personal troubles for want of the ability to imagine the larger social structures that are, in most instances, the deeper cause of their sufferings. Mills was one of the first to plant the seeds of formal sociology in the concerns of practical life. But he was not *the* first. More than sixty years before Mills, Gilman saw that social thought was always the imaginative work of bringing into public view the force of social structures in the fate of the troubled individual. Granted, she did not put the idea as succinctly as did Mills. But he, by contrast, never came close to her in plumbing the depths of imagination itself. Gilman's "The Yellow Wallpaper" set a new standard for the use of fiction to expose the emotional consequences of social and economic structures, much as *Herland* opens possibilities for feminist social criticism that nonfiction writing can never achieve.

Imagine, if you will, an educated woman of the working or middle classes— any woman who comes to mind. She is, more often than not, white. She is educated, married with children, well sheltered with all the necessary provisions and many of the desirable unnecessary ones. Her duty in the social contract with her husband and his world is to care for the children and manage the household. In return, she is offered the honor of being considered a good woman, one who by her domestic labor and sound moral values fulfills the social ideal expected of such a woman. She receives no direct financial compensation. She is left in the home for long hours, sometimes days, with little or no help. The husband, by contrast, enjoys life at work in the wider world. She accompanies him rarely, but entertains his work acquaintances frequently. She is permitted no vocation of her own outside the family circle, save for activities that advance the good name of the householder himself. She feels confined. She very often falls into depression for which she takes to her room on doctor's orders.

Today, even though the circumstances of middle class women is much changed, it is relatively easy to imagine this woman of earlier times. Many of our mothers or grandmothers experienced just this and knew what it meant to be thus confined. Even though today's economy has put such a life well beyond the expectations of all but a small number of generally quite wealthy families, it is not too difficult for us today to imagine the suffering of the women for whom Charlotte Gilman wrote. They are the paradigm of what is wrong with the so-called traditional family. These are the women who suffered "the problem that has no name" that Betty Friedan would describe for a later generation of women in *The Feminine Mystique*.[5] Gilman was among the first to speak to and for these women. The woman in question was the subject of "The Yellow Wallpaper"—a woman driven to illness, not by the abuse of the man in her life, but by the man-made world. The yellow wallpaper is the nightmarish entanglements of a woman trapped in a system that demands her obedience and denies her participation.

In the 1880s Charlotte Perkins Gilman lived what Betty Friedan would describe in the 1960s for a later generation of women. She was herself a victim of the problem with no name. But Gilman (at the time, Charlotte Stetson) would not succumb to her personal troubles. She had married Walter Stetson, an artist, and a good man, in 1884. Their only child, Katherine, was born the following year. Neither brought wealth to the marriage. Walter respected Charlotte's creative gifts, but his career came first. He was the breadwinner. Her work had to be set aside. The first signs of her depression appeared soon after childbirth. Somehow, even as she lay ill in 1887, a young woman confined to her own room, Charlotte knew—she just knew—that her illness was not of her own doing. She understood very well that Walter and her physician (the same physician who a generation earlier had been called to the bedside of Harriet Beecher Stowe for the same "female" illness), were kindly men. The fault was not theirs any more than hers. They too were caught up in the structured relations of bourgeois life in early capitalist America. Though Charlotte Stetson would not find the formal language to describe the system until her first great work of social theory in 1898, *Women and Economics*, these were already the key words in her personal vocabulary. By courage and personal force, she exercised the sociological imagination to know that what was at stake in a bourgeois woman's life was ultimately an issue of economic structures. Gilman was the sort of person who trusted her feelings long enough to find the words that shaped the intellect that eventually described structured reality for others. Few social theorists live in such a way that the qualities of their personal lives lead to robust theories of worlds we all inhabit. Gilman did.

The circumstances of Gilman's family of birth were, almost certainly, the source of her feminist sensibilities. She was born on her father's side into one of the nineteenth century's most famously unconventional families. Charlotte's father, Frederick Beecher Perkins, was kin by marriage to the family of Lyman Beecher and his remarkable children, Henry Ward Beecher, the abolitionist; Catharine Beecher, the feminist; Isabella Beecher Hooker, the suffragist; and Harriet Beecher Stowe, the writer—who all carried forth their father's reformist values. From childhood, Charlotte witnessed firsthand the worldly work of the Beecher women. Yet, what influenced her more was not so much her proximity to the famous family as her painful distance from her father—to her, its most important member.

Frederick Perkins left his wife, Mary Prescott Perkins, and their two small children in 1869. Charlotte was but nine years old. His abandonment put her, her mother, and brother, at risk of financial ruin. Though Frederick clearly inherited the learning and independence of the Beechers, he utterly lacked the family's deeper sense of personal responsibility. Perkins attended Yale, but dropped out. He studied law, but never practiced it. Eventually, he settled into a stable career as a librarian—first at the Boston Public Library, then (from 1880) as Director of the San Francisco Public Library. He supported the family erratically. He sent money and affection as it pleased him. This economic disaster of the abandonment was severe enough. But its emotional consequences were far the worse. Through her adolescence, Charlotte seized every opportunity to maintain relations with her father who, true to form, resisted—most hurtfully on one occasion by cutting off her tender affections toward him in an abrupt and cruel letter of rejection.

Only a man damaged by some larger force could behave as harshly as Frederick Perkins did toward his wife and children. And the damage did not end with him. It seldom does in families. Charlotte, like many abandoned children, never stopped longing for her father's affections. It was no accident then that when she in her turn abandoned Walter in 1888, she moved with Katherine (then three) to California—first to Pasadena, then to Oakland, across the Bay from her father. Still, though he was nearby, he kept his distance. Most appalling of all, her father refused to visit his wife, Mary, as she was dying in the late winter of 1893. As she had before, Charlotte covered her pain at this insult added to injury. Her journal entry of Tuesday, March 7, 1898, was stark and false to the events of the day:

> Mother died this morning at 2.10. I lie down at 5.20 & rise at seven—I could not sleep. Get the breakfast and then go to the city, stopping at Dr. Kellogs, an undertakers, & the [San Francisco] Enquirer's Office. Go to father. To Mr. Worcester, lunch at Mrs. Morse's, father again, and home. . . . Father over in the afternoon.[6]

With rare exceptions, this was a typical journal entry—plain, strict to the facts, devoid of feeling. Though the author of "The Yellow Wallpaper" was a woman of powerful feelings when it came to literary expression, her private journal expunged the emotions she could not bear to embrace directly—and for good reason.

Charlotte had been emotionally starved by *both* parents, though for different reasons. Her mother, Mary, in part because of her husband's abandonment, forced herself never to embrace Charlotte. In her personal memoir, *The Living of Charlotte Perkins Gilman*, written late in life, Charlotte recalls her sad search as a child for her mother's love:

Having suffered so deeply in her own early love affairs, and still suffering for lack of a husband's love, [my mother] heroically determined that her baby daughter should not so suffer if she could help it. Her method was to deny the child all expression of affection. . . . She would not let me caress her, and would not caress, unless I was asleep. This I discovered at last, and then did my best to keep awake till she came to bed, even using pins to prevent dropping off, and sometimes succeeding. Then how rapturously I enjoyed being gathered into her arms, held close and kissed.[7]

Those who have never experienced the effects of emotional deprivation in childhood may find it difficult to believe that the loss of parental affections can have lifelong effects. But clinical records are filled with cases of children thus deprived who never truly give up the search for parental love lost in the earliest years. The brave ones are those who satisfy their desires through good work and positive relations in adult life. Charlotte was brave. Here were the feelings that gave rise to her ideas.

Still, it would be wrong to shrink the whole of Charlotte Gilman's life into the events of early childhood. Her life story turns on any number of contradictions that defy simple explanation. For one thing, "The Yellow Wallpaper" would never have been possible had not Charlotte trained herself, even in childhood, to look hard at the world about her. At the same time, the looking and longing could well have been the cause of the mental illness that struck her down in 1887 and continued to haunt her after. But, also, though Charlotte was intermittently depressed throughout life, she always managed to recoup her energies. Once she had fled her own room of the yellow wallpaper, she was rarely immobilized by the depression. She began her public career in 1888, shortly after leaving Walter for a new life in California. Until retirement she worked so productively she put her more canonical contemporaries, Max Weber and Emile Durkheim, to the test. (Weber, too, suffered a breakdown, but unlike Gilman, his kept him from work for a number of years.)

Over a full quarter century, Charlotte Gilman wrote seven substantial works of social theory, at least four novels, plus countless essays, poems, and short stories. At the height of her powers, Gilman singlehandedly wrote and published her own monthly magazine. From 1909 to 1916, *The Forerunner* was an exclusive forum for her ideas. She wrote *every* word of it—all the articles, including some of her best fiction and social criticism, and every jot of copy. For seven years it sold briskly, and helped make Gilman the literary force she was in the years before the First World War.

Yet, when she retired *Forerunner* in 1916, the year after she finished *Herland*, she too began to retire. Though she published a few books after, this was the effective end of her life's work. Perhaps something about the Great War depressed her own sense of hope as it had that of so many other moderns. The political collapse in Europe led to a train of debilitating events from which the world did not recover until well after the Second World War. The twentieth century is often said to have been the most violent in human history because war led to economic failure, which led again to war, then war again and again. Throughout the century that began in such high hopes for human progress, liberal political ideals were never able for more than a few years in the 1920s, then again in the 1950s, to sustain the peace upon which the good society depends. This is surely why the First World War dealt such a deadly blow to radical reformers in the United States.

Gilman's own ideals were clearly influenced, as was the thinking of most left liberals at the turn of the last century, by the reformist spirit of the socialist utopians, such as Edward Bellamy, whose *Looking Backward*[8] was by all odds the most important. (Gilman's own socialist utopia, *Herland*, bears Bellamy's influence.) But there were many other social visionaries, including the social gospel movement with which Anna Julia Cooper and other settlement workers were loosely affiliated. Even the W. E. B. Du Bois of *Souls of Black Folk*[9]— though true only to his own values—was under the sway of liberal hope that dominated in the first decade or so of the century. The war brought all this to an end. Gilman was far from alone in losing her way to the devastating effects of the Great War of 1914.

Still, as significant as world events were to Gilman's early retirement from public work, her ever-complicated story turns again back to the importance of the personal. For her, the personal and the social were never far from each other. So, it is also likely that she retired during the years of the First War in order to enjoy the pleasures of married life to George Houghton Gilman with whom she left New York after 1922 for the seclusion of his family home in Norwich, Connecticut. But the retirement came only after two decades of worldly success made possible by her second husband's financial and personal security.

Her long and successful marriage to Gilman gave Charlotte much more than the name by which she is known. The second marriage gave her the enduring domestic peace necessary for creative work. She had begun *Women and Economics* in the late summer days of 1897. These were the fresh early days of her romance with Houghton. She married this distant cousin in June, 1900. They settled in New York City, there to renew regular relations with her now teenaged daughter who had been living with her father. Ironically, she settled comfortably into the very sort of married life she had left in 1888 as a younger woman. In her memoir, Charlotte says of her second marriage, "We were married—and lived happily every after. If this were a novel now, here's a happy ending."[10]

Today, it is well understood that the living of a life necessarily includes the retelling of its story and that the retelling cannot be done without a healthy dose of fiction. Few of us, if any, have more than a passing direct recollection of the events of our pasts. If we are to have a life's story to tell our friends and lovers and children we must rely on the stories told us by others. All the stories that compose our life stories cannot help but take poetic liberties with facts no one truly remembers. Charlotte's own life story does indeed read like a novel, which is why her own *The Living of Charlotte Perkins Gilman* very nearly ends with the account of her marriage to Houghton. In a book of twenty-one chapters, she has very little to say of her life after the marriage in 1900. Only four scant chapters account for the thirty-five years she lived after 1900. Indeed all of the prodigious work of the New York years before the war are reduced to these few, haphazard chapters.

In Charlotte's artful fiction of her life, the drama is condensed into the deprivations of childhood, the depression and the first marriage, the flight for freedom in California, the years of growth and eventual fame. When Houghton enters at the end of the century, Charlotte's life comes to its "happy ending," as she put it—just more than halfway through her seventy-six years. It did not occur to her to finish *The Living of Charlotte Perkins Gilman* until 1935 on the eve of her death, nearly ten years after the first, incomplete draft was written. After Houghton died in 1934, Charlotte (well aware they she too was near death) moved back to California to be with her daughter Kate. Then, insisting on control of death as of her life's story, she took her life on August 17, 1935, preferring as she said, "chloroform to cancer."

She had found happiness with a man. This charming oddity of her life's story could only be because she found in Houghton what she had lost in childhood. He provided, one might suppose, the loving embraces her parents had withheld. But, the path to this man was anything but direct. In her love letters during their courtship, Charlotte's feelings of love for him are referred not to the losses of her childhood, but to the terrible loss of her young womanhood. Still, again, her story turns in a surprising direction. In a letter of Thursday, September 2, 1897, after a long day of work on *Women and Economics*, Charlotte wrote to Houghton: "I think I am taking more comfort with you than I have since the days of Martha Luther—my girl friend of '77–'81."[11]

Charlotte's friendship with Martha Luther during late adolescence in Providence, Rhode Island, was the first openly passionate relationship of her life. In *Charlotte Perkins Gilman: The Making of a Radical Feminist: 1860–1896*, Mary A. Hill, Gilman's most accomplished biographer, interprets Charlotte's passion for Martha as a significant passage from the disappointments of childhood to the boldness of her adult feminism:

> Defiance, anger, crying spells—all reflected the intensity of family battle. After all, her self-sacrificing, domestic, and emotionally dependent mother had clashed irreconcilably with her cool, ambitious, independent father. Now these mother-father conflicts erupted once again, this time in herself. To some extent, Martha provided a "lofty" isolated refuge, but the real peace-keeping maneuver, Charlotte decided, would be to strengthen her "self" and kill off the inclinations to remain "merely" a woman or to become a mother and a wife.[12]

Just how important was the youthful relationship? And how did it figure, if at all, in Charlotte's feminism, and especially in the striking platonic lesbianism of *Herland*?

It is not, of course, uncommon for a young woman to hold fast to other women in the developmental search for an independent self. But Charlotte clung to Martha ferociously. Not even Carroll Smith-Rosenberg's well-known argument that nineteenth century women often petted, kissed, and slept with each other without heteronormal embarrassment quite accounts for Charlotte's devotion to Martha Luther.

Charlotte's matter-of-fact journal entries for the last weeks of October, 1881, betray (as in the case of her mother's death) a studied attempt to control otherwise uncontrollable feelings. Late October, 1881, brought the end to Martha's passion for Charlotte. Martha accepted Charles Lane's proposal of marriage. Charlotte's dairy records the surface of daily life, thus signaling her deeper emotions. The entry for October 17, 1881, is poignant:

> Go to Miss Diman's. Miss Alden sick. I tell stories to Louise, who has an ulcerated throat. Home & get work. Go to Martha's all alone. Stay till almost 8. Nice talk. ("No!") Draw letter for guttersnipe. Sew.[13]

"Nice talk?"—("No!"). Of course not. And, who exactly is the guttersnipe? Martha? Her fiancé? Charlotte, distraught, relaxes her guard in these sharp contradictions to the facts of the day. Then, resorting to form, she takes up work, "Sew." Entries for the two weeks following the seventeenth make only passing references to her dear friend—with the pointed exception of Thursday, October 27: "Martha there. We take walks & converse. Verily I love the damsel." Then, on the Tuesday following, November 1st, Charlotte writes:

> No Abby owing to rain. Study and darn. Martha over. She hath a ring. I have a pain. Give her my blessing. Write to Sam and tell him all about it. Post the same. Note to Abigail. Sew.[14]

Martha hath a ring; Charlotte hath a pain! Though they would continue their now deeply altered friendship for many years, only Charlotte seems to have kept its special importance.

In the chapter of her memoir devoted to her first marriage in 1884, Charlotte begins with reference to the relationship with Martha:

> Looking back on my uncuddled childhood it seems to me a sad mistake of my heroic mother to withhold from me the petting I so craved, the sufficing comfort of maternal caresses. Denied that natural expression, my first memory of loving any one—not to mention [*she names several childhood friends; then continues*:—CL]. . . Immeasurably the dearest, was Martha. Martha stayed. We were closely together, increasingly happy together, four of those long years of girlhood. She was nearer and dearer than any one up to that time. This was love, but not sex.[15]

These words were written in 1925, thirty-four years after Martha left her. Still she adds: "This was love, but not sex." Though some speculate that Martha may have been a first lover, it is unlikely that we will ever know. But the speculation is encouraged by the evidence of the years after the break-up of her first marriage—the early California years.

In 1891 Charlotte met and by all reckoning fell in love with Delle Knapp, with whom she lived in Oakland in two rooms of a boarding house along with Kate and Mary Prescott who was gravely ill. Charlotte's journals are now filled with references like "Delle spent the night" and her memoir comments on the loss of still another love. "My last love proves even as others."[16] Clearly she loved Delle as she had Martha. But how, and to what effect?

Whether or not Charlotte Gilman enjoyed sexual relations with Martha and Delle, it is clear that they and other women were central to her efforts to establish an independent and feminist self-understanding. Late in life, in her memoir, Charlotte was notably defensive about the possibility of a sexual relationship with Martha and oddly silent about the affair with Delle. Why? Why would a woman who could be so shockingly honest about her mental illness, and so sharply disdainful of the marital conventions of the day, wish to cover the sexual feelings of those affairs? Just as the perverse matter-of-factness of her journals belies her true feelings, so the denial of sexual activity at a time in life when it would have made little difference to anyone (certainly not her husband) reveal something unsettled about Gilman's early attractions to women. What?

It may well be that nineteenth-century women, as Carroll Smith-Rosenberg explains, enjoyed physical contact with each not so much for sexual pleasure as for nurturing shelter from the androcentric world. But this alone does not fully account for the fact that, as in Charlotte's case, there could have been erotic passion in these relationships even when they were not consummated. Then as now, sexual pleasure is polymorphous. And sex is more than pleasure. Sex is a social thing regulated by the needs and purposes of the whole wide social world.

Social historians of sex and sexuality in the Victorian era—notably John D'Emilio, Michel Foucault, and Steven Seidman—explain how industrial capitalism intruded upon mundane patterns of sexuality in order to shape the bourgeois family as the social unit in which labor is reproduced. Control sex; control the family. As Seidman notes in *Romantic Longings* (1991),[17] in the Victorian era the contrast between normal heterosexuality and deviant homosexuality did not exist as we know it today. The control of sexuality was exercised according to a different social ideal of the productive, and reproductive, family. (This, not at all coincidentally, was precisely the defining moment for the bourgeois family Gilman worked to unmask and reform.) In the Victorian Age, says Seidman, sexualities were distinguished by a different social formula: between sex in the family and *all* other forms of sex. The perceived need was to regulate sexual practices in the service of industrial capitalism. Homosexuality was not talked about then as it is today. Homosexuality simply was not the issue. Disciplined families were. Thus, the very sexual practices that in our day would be viewed as homosexual were not, in Gilman's youth, fraught with social trouble as they are now. This may well explain why, when Gilman wrote in 1925 about her youthful affair in 1881, she *did* feel a need to explain the erotic away. Times had changed. Gilman lived on both sides of the historical divide after which homosexuality was born to American political consciousness.

This does not mean, however, that Charlotte's youthful desire for the love of women was any less significant to her feminist consciousness. Surely, as she says, the affair with Martha—like her love for Delle (and others about whom we know even less)—was a "refuge" (her word) that allowed her to work through the emotional deprivations of childhood which led to the fated marriage to Walter Stetson. Surely, in our day, we would think of them as lesbian or bisexual relations of one or another kind. But, whatever their sexual nature, these relations gave her courage to brave the losses of childhood and to live on her own in the California years, thus to prepare for the enduring refuge provided by her marriage to Houghton. Gilman's story is perfect proof of the wisdom of Adrienne Rich's famous 1980 essay, "Compulsory Heterosexuality and Lesbian Experience." Rich distinguished the *lesbian experience*, which includes the practice of homosexual relations, from the *lesbian continuum*, which includes all "woman identified experience" whether sexual or not.[18] Nearly a full century after Charlotte's painful break up with Martha, Adrienne Rich described the lesbian continuum as the encompassing possibility that it is (but for which the nineteenth century lacked a social vocabulary). The power available to women in their relations with each other, said Rich, "comprises both the breaking of a taboo and the rejection of a compulsory way of life."[19] For Charlotte, the lesbian continuum included both those relations that *might* have been sexual and those that clearly were not. Those of the latter kind were, if less acute at the time, more enduring over the years—most specially, her long friendships with Jane Addams, with whom she lived for a while at Hull House, and with Grace Channing, who after the divorce married Walter and helped raise Charlotte's daughter Kate. Without her relations along the lesbian continuum, Charlotte Gilman would not have become the most important feminist social theorist of her day.

In her public life, Gilman worked tirelessly, by writing and lecturing, to accomplish two social goals: get women out of the family into the economy; and restructure the bourgeois family itself. Both have come to pass in ways Gilman could not have anticipated. Contrary to Gilman's expectations, we know from writings like Arlie Hochschild's *Second Shift* that women who attempt simultaneously to maintain career and family suffer impossible burdens.[20] Today, the bourgeois family is much transformed by a rapacious global economy that has drawn most women out of the household to struggle, with or without a domestic partner, just to keep family life afloat. At the same time, as we know from works like Judith Stacey's *Brave New Families*, women are indeed restructuring the traditional family.[21] Women in families they choose (as Kath Weston has put it) are freer and more equal, though more burdened than in Gilman's time.

After the First World War, Gilman fell out of favor—so completely so that Connecticut College, a leading school for women but a few miles from her home in Norwich, ignored one of the century's most important feminists as though she had never existed. As feminism was reborn after the 1960s, Gilman regained the place of recognition she had earned. It is possible that this great visionary of the turn of the century also envisaged the renewal of her ideas. Near the end of her life, Gilman wrote:

> This is the woman's century, the first chance for the mother of the world to rise to her full place, her transcendent power to remake humanity, to rebuild the suffering world—and the world waits while she powders her nose. . .[22]

With a wink at the degrading expectations of the man-made world, Gilman leaves the future open, the sentence dangling on an ellipsis. In much the same way, her public life came to an open end. We know, if she did not, that her ideas anticipated the important outlines of feminist social theory at the end of the twentieth century.

It may be for fear of embarrassment that so few theorists comment on the original meaning of the word "theory." As I said, according to the OED, the word derives from the Greek, *theoros*—"one who travels in order to see things." Thus, another of the original meanings is, simply, "a spectacle." In our scientific age, these definitions of a very high-minded activity are surprising. They would not have been to Gilman. She was, if not a tourist, certainly a pilgrim who walked her way through her own inner space to get to a fresh view of the spectacle of industrial capitalism and its effects on women. It was not a pretty picture.

Today those with eyes to see can see what Gilman saw behind the debris of a family system crushed, in our time, by a capitalism more cruel than even in Gilman's time—or Marx's for that matter. For those more accustomed to a socialism from Marx's painstaking analysis of the evils of the capitalist mode of production, Gilman's progressive socialism might well seem a faint copy of the original. American socialists of the end of the nineteenth century—writers like Henry George, Edward Bellamy, and Gilman herself—understood something of European socialism after Marx. But, for the most part, they developed their ideas in quite independent ways. Perhaps it was the American pragmatism in them that caused these early radicals to attack the selfishness of the industrial bosses with a comparably positive, even evolutionary, principle of human progress. One of the ironies of the Gilded Age is that nearly everyone from the bosses of industry to their radical opponents was caught up in the innocent hopefulness of the new industrial world.

Thus it was that even those, like Gilman, who self-consciously represented social groups oppressed by the dominant social order, were alive with hope. W. E. B. Du Bois and Anna Julia Cooper are two of the more astonishing examples. They spoke for the American Negro oppressed by Jim Crow laws in the South and social segregation in the North. Still, in their writings of the last decade of the nineteenth century, both Du Bois and Cooper wrote with surprising confidence in the future of American society. Du Bois, in the most famous chapter of *Souls of Black Folk*, looked to a day when the Negro would be a "coworker in the kingdom of culture."[23] Similarly, Cooper, in *A Voice From the South*, ordained black women who experienced the cruel injustices of the American South as the moral leaders of the day—of a progressive era with "such new and alluring vistas . . . opening out before us."[24]

Gilman, likewise, concluded *Women and Economics* with a word of hope: "When the mother of the race is free, we shall have a better world, by the easy right of birth and by the calm, slow, friendly forces of social evolution."[25] This after 340 pages of relentless criticism of the evil she called the "sexuo-economic relation" at the heart of capitalism. Today readers will not be enchanted by the optimistic coda. Still, like other classic ideas, Gilman's basic feminist principles outlive the cocoon in which they developed.

One of the arguments among end-of-the-twentieth-century feminists is over the uncertain identity of women caught between family and the work place. Though the debate has taken many different turns in the last generation, it always returns to the dilemma Gilman tried to resolve by her social criticism of the sexuo-economic relation. She meant, in effect, to complicate the idea of sex—or, in our term, gender. A woman's gender circumstance is always, and necessarily, determined by, but not reducible to, her economic situation. Gilman never thought of Woman in the abstract. For the most part, she resisted the inviting danger of feminist essentialism.

Essentialism abstracts an important feature into a definition. Women are different from men. But their difference in fact may or may not be a difference in kind. Feminist essentialisms tend, one way or another, to claim that a woman's unique nature is a stable, immutable property of her gender. The allure of the essentialist move is the gain of a critical tool made powerful by isolating analytic qualities which may be turned back against arbitrary social arrangements that put those qualities at risk. While meant to sharpen racial, sexual, or gender differences, the problem with essentialisms of all kinds (even strategic ones) is that they don't speak very subtly to the lived reality of women's lives—or, for that matter, to the lives of those excluded because of their sexual orientation or their race. Essentialisms may be necessary to the polarizing purposes of certain political moments, or the analytic work of theorists, but they are not practical to the experience of real people they are meant to represent. In the vocabulary of our time, Gilman was more interested in the situated knowledge of women's lives. She was a writer and a social critic, a public speaker and an organizer. Her work was with those who do not tolerate abstractions well. In the one surprising instance toward the end of her career where she lapsed into a kind of inadvertent essentialism, she did so, almost by the accident of her political and literary purposes. Even then, there was no doctrinal conviction. Gilman wrote about women's lives, as lived.

People live in families, or the hope of families—or, at least, of other forms of intimate association. Yet, for their domestic arrangements to survive economically, they must work. Most women (and some men) who live in a world dominated by capitalist greed live with uncertainty doubled. For them the search for intimate association and viable work is hard work *and* neither can be had without the other. Gilman saw, early in the evolution of modern industrial society, that women had been assigned twice the responsibility for half the pay (if that). This is the sexuo-economic relation. Women must produce and reproduce the family association without which society would fail; and they must do so while held in servile relation to the man-made world.

"Economic progress is almost exclusively male."[26] This is Gilman's opening shot in *Women and Economics*. Among animals, she believed, only the human is so dominated by the male. There is some truth in this. "Queen bee" is a gender slur because it is a biological reality. In her day the continuing backwash of Social Darwinism encouraged the sociobiological gesture in Gilman's early writings. (Lester Ward, the academic sociologist who most influenced her thinking, encouraged Gilman along this line.) Still, Gilman's argument survives her questionable biological claims which, even today, retain a certain rhetorical force. Gilman equated the female human being with the workhorse. Both are servile to a master. "Their labor is the property of another: they work under another will; and what they receive depends not on their labor, but on the power and will of the other."[27]

True to her poetic gifts, Gilman uses a strong comparative figure while losing sight of her specific economic idea. She does not lose sight of the broader economic idea. She aims to show that the relations of men to women are entirely arbitrary to economic convenience.

> The labor of women in the house, certainly enables men to produce more wealth than they otherwise could; and in this way women are economic factors in society. But so are horses.[28]

The opening allusions to the human female as the workhorse of the species, sets up the argument that follows. Step by step, with compelling logic, Gilman dismantles each of the then prevailing moral sentiments that served once (and still do in many places) to justify the domestic confinement of bourgeois women. Does not the human female's sexual beauty gain her the natural happiness of marriage? Is it not her nature to sacrifice independence for the sake of home and children? Is she not paid in kind by the support of the breadwinner husband? Do not the children require her attentions? Is not the home the hearth of civilization? The book is a careful exposition of the stupidity of the assumptions that, in her day, would have tempted many to say, in reply to each question: Well, yes, of course. Gilman's sustained rebuttal of the true womanhood ideal is one of the earliest and still persuasive exposés of the naturalistic sex role theories that came to dominate social science after the Second World War.

Still, Gilman's thinking was itself a kind of crypto-functionalism. Though her biological figures of speech are a bit heavy handed for our day, her underlying social theory makes complete sense if we accept that, in the end, Gilman was more a social reformer than a devotee of the principle of social evolution. Her argument is that the fate of the female is necessarily bound to that of the male, as in turn his is to hers. It is not men who are selfish, but the system that makes them so. Greed is at the heart of the economy. "Social life tends to reduce this [selfishness], which is but a belated individualism; but the sexuo-economic relation fosters and develops it."[29] Here is the sociological imagination at its best. In the normal course of daily life, Gilman is saying, a woman may suffer but she does not actually see the selfishness of the world behind the men who make her the workhorse. The true nature of the relation between the sexes can only be seen in structural perspective. This steady attention to the economic realities is what saves Gilman's ideas from the more naïve functionalist thinking that, years later, Talcott Parsons made prominent in American sociology.

Gilman was first and foremost a socialist utopian. Her theories of social evolution served a political ethic more than a scientific concern. Had she been more the Marxist, she might have called for a reversal of the gender relations. But her radicalism was of another kind. She, like Du Bois and Bellamy, Cooper and George, looked to historical progress, not revolution, for a better society. At the end of the twentieth century very few people of certifiable common sense would trust the future for assurance of a better life. Hope, today, is all too realistically hedged by the stark economic realities that have so assaulted family life. Only the most fortunate few enjoy the security of breadwinning, productive labor. For most, the sexuo-economic relation persists, worse perhaps than even Gilman might have imagined.

Still, Gilman's ideas bear consideration because they navigate the waters between gender relations and economic reality with such a keen eye. She had lived at economic risk as a child, and had suffered firsthand the effects of the sexuo-economic relation on her family. Her ideas were always grounded in these experiences. As a result, she looked to a possible future more to understand the present than to predict a necessary outcome. And, just as she held out for the affections of her despicable father, so she could, at one and the same time, forcefully attack the men who made the androcentric world *and* feel compassion for them.

> So we may trace from the sexuo-economic relation of our species not only definite evils in psychic development, bred severally in men and women, and transmitted indifferently to their offspring, but the innate perversion of character resultant from the moral miscegenation of two so diverse souls,—the unfailing shadow and distortion which has darkened and twisted the spirit of man from the beginnings. We have been injured in body and in mind by the two dissimilar traits inherited from our widely separated parents, but nowhere is the injury more apparent than in its ill effects upon the moral nature of the race.[30]

She pulls no punches. Nor does she fail to understand that it is the structure of things that causes social evil. If women suffer more acutely, they do not suffer alone. Their men and their children are subject to the same ill moral effects.

When all is said and done, Gilman was a hardheaded realist about the practical consequences of the sexuo-economic relation. It is a curious thing that her phrase has not been reclaimed in this day when it would seem so apt to the debates over the relative merits of identity and socialist politics. Today, through the contributions of thinkers like Judith Butler and Nancy Fraser, we know that women are not alone in the struggle to find, on the one hand, a satisfactory recognition for their social identity and, on the other hand, to gain access to a fair share of economic wealth necessary for a decent life. Men as well as women, people of color as well as whites, heterosexuals as well as homosexuals, struggle with this dilemma. Far from being a postmodern oddity, this is, in many ways, the fundamental dilemma of modern life. Gilman, who lacked all the fancy terms we have today, understood this fundamental fact of life. Men as well as women would benefit from a wholesale transformation of the sexuo-economic relation. Even when she was writing her fiction, or concentrating on specific social issues like the quality of life in the bourgeois home, Gilman understood this. On this, in *Women and Economics*, she is refreshingly blunt: "A home life with a dependent mother, a servant-wife, is not an ennobling influence." When the woman is diminished, so is the man. A good decade before writing this, Charlotte grasped the principle perfectly well in her own life, even in the earliest of her fiction writings, well before she had worked out the theory.

"The Yellow Wallpaper," written six years before *Women and Economics*, remains today her most commanding, and disturbing, picture of the spectacle of the bourgeois family. The story begins innocently enough. The scene is a rented summer cottage, but it was a "cottage" in the grand bourgeois sense of turn of the century retreats that became the stock of wealthy suburbs like Newton, Massachusetts, or Greenwich, Connecticut. "Cottage" already signals just what sort of family story this is.

The man in the story condenses the two separate characters of Charlotte's own experience. John is made to be both husband and physician. The unnamed wife is attended by a woman, John's sister—a "perfect and enthusiastic housekeeper" who "hopes for no better profession." There are children. But it is the man—John, the physician husband—who figures as the looming object of the narrator's attentions.

Then, even as the idyllic scene is set, we are warned of something "queer" about the house itself.

> It is very seldom that ordinary people like John and myself secure ancestral halls for the summer.
>
> A colonial mansion, a hereditary estate, I would say a haunted house, and reach the height of romantic felicity—but that would be asking too much of fate!

> Still I would probably declare that there is something queer about it.
> Else, why should it be let so cheaply? And why have stood so long untenanted?
> John laughs at me, of course, but one expects that in marriage.[31]

Gilman, the author, is playing with the incongruity between the outside and inside of things. She uses the excess of the cottage, and its long vacancy, to invite the story's narrative line—that what is off is that this ideal little family will not achieve the felicity of a summer's retreat. The reader's eye is drawn to John by a gentle note of complaint. A woman expects a man to laugh at her. Is male dismissal of female sensibility the queer structure of the arrangement? Does Gilman ask us to think of the house as an icon for the whole of the bourgeois domestic scene?—even, perhaps, for the whole of the economic structure that is so delicately hinted by the pretense of the ironic "cottage"?

The poetic power of a short fiction is that it depends so mightily on the reader's imagination. So few words say so much. Here the reader is invited by the queer exterior of the cottage to imagine the impending trouble. It is a "beautiful place" with a "delicious garden . . . never such a garden."[32] But the central figure of the story is the room with ghastly yellow wallpaper:

> . . . dull enough to confuse the eye in following, pronounced enough to constantly irritate and provoke study and when you follow the lame uncertain curves for a little distance they suddenly commit suicide—plunge off at outrageous angles, destroy themselves in unheard of contradictions.[33]

On the exterior, all is delicious. Inside, all is confusing, suicidal, and contradictory.

The deadly interior of the house is, of course, the metonym of the bourgeois woman's confinement. Though the facts of Charlotte's own confinement in 1887 are absent in the fiction, the yellow wallpaper expresses the woman's nightmare. Her own physician, Dr. S. Weir Mitchell, was the leading medical specialist in women's illnesses, as they were called. His treatment was the same rest cure which he had earlier prescribed for Harriet Beecher Stowe. The treatment, intended as a relieving ministry, was in fact a harsh imposition the man cannot understand. The woman must refrain from all labor—bed rest, an occasional visit from the children, and, in Charlotte's case, no reading or writing. The rest cure, thus, by depriving her of what she needs most, is bound to fail for most—certainly so, for Charlotte.

The woman confined to this absurd contradiction is drawn into the wallpaper itself. The yellow wallpaper—"not arranged on any laws"[34]—comes alive as the emblem of the world's work on women.

> Behind that outside pattern the dim shapes get clear, clearer every day.
> It is always the same shape, only very numerous.
> And it is like a woman stooping down and creeping about behind that pattern.
> I don't like it one bit.[35]

The woman sees herself in the suicide patterns of the wall. She and contradiction become insanely one and the same. She is one with other women. "Sometimes I think there are a great many women behind [the moving patterns of the wallpaper], and sometimes only one. . . ."[36]

It would be easy to miss the importance of what happens next. The woman is driven mad—by the wallpaper; by the domestic arrangement; by the world. But she attacks in self-defense by stripping the paper away sheet by sheet.

This cannot be. The man, John, intervenes. But the woman overcomes. The story ends:

> "I've got to get out at last," said I, "in spite of you and Jane. And I've pulled off most of the paper, so you can't put me back!"
>
> Now why should that man have fainted? But he did, and across my path by the wall, so that I had to creep over him every time![37]

The man faints. The woman escapes. But who is Jane? She is never introduced. Could she be John's sister, the perfect housewife who aspires to nothing more—the true woman, that is, that Charlotte could never be? Or could Jane be the disturbed self of the woman who must always face her confinement? Is it possible that by this accidental woman Gilman is telling us that women, even when they escape the nightmarish world of the family, must in effect leave behind their very own selves—or, if not their selfhood, the ideal self that the world would impose? At the least, the woman who escapes must leave behind the true woman who remains with John.[38] And, in the image of the swooning husband (a reversal of the hysterical woman image), are we to think that even if she flees, then he is left in the garish room?

The queer house with its deadly room is the problem—not the woman, not even the man. Women, thus, are faced with an impossible choice. If they conform to the gentle absurdity of the man-made world, they are drawn into that world's selfish madness. If they rebel they must leave themselves behind as Charlotte did when she left Walter in order to reinvent herself. Fiction very often leaves the important questions unanswered. But in Gilman's case, Charlotte explains herself by what she became in real life, and by what she wrote in so many words in subsequent writings that made her social program completely obvious.

Woman alone cannot reform herself. Her freedom is freedom for all, even her man, especially her children. "The largest and most radical effect of restoring women to economic independence will be in its result in clarifying and harmonizing the human soul."[39] The human soul demands a structural change in the sexuo-economic relation.

Gilman would play this theme again and again. In *The Home* she wrote more bitterly of the "domestic mythology," attacking in plain language the pieties of the American home. As to the virtues of home cooking, for one example, she asks, in effect: But have you ever actually tasted it?

> "Home-cooking" is an alluring phrase, but lay aside the allurement . . . [and ask] whose home-cooking are we praising? Our own, of course. Which means nothing but that the stomach adapts itself to what it has to live on—unless it is too poisonous. . . . The long-suffering human system (perhaps toughened by ages of home-cooking)—will adapt itself even to slow death.[40]

Here is but a taste of Gilman's radical, practical socialism at its most cynical best. Why not, she asks, encourage a system in which those expert in tasteful, nutritious cooking prepare the food for the community? Would not all be healthier and happier under such a system?

The Home holds up very well today for its relentless practical sneering at the absurd practices of the bourgeois family. The book offers what might be called a countercultural course in home economics. After a brief history of the family, Gilman unmasks the domestic mythology just as, in *Women and Economics*, she attacked the ideal of true womanhood. "Let us begin," she says, starting with the highest of American values about the home, "with that fondly cherished popular idea—'the privacy of the home.' No one has privacy at home, least of all the mother. The mother—poor invaded soul—finds even the bathroom door no bar to hammering little hands."[41] The chapters following continue in this vein, exposing such myths as the home as the housewife's workshop, the lady of the house, domestic arts, as well as home cooking.

The more general analytic themes of *Women and Economics* are reconsidered in the closing chapters of *The Home*. As the woman suffers, so too do the boy and girl children—and the men! In passages that anticipate Nancy Chodorow's criticism of sex-role theory in *Reproduction of Mothering*,[42] Gilman unmasks the damage done by the sexuo-economic relation in the home:

> The home teaches the boy that women were made for service, domestic service, that the principal cares and labours of life are those which concern the boy, and that his own particular tastes and preferences are of enormous importance. As fast as he gets out of the home and into the school he learns quite other things, getting his exaggerated infant egotism knocked out of him very suddenly, and, as he gets out of school and into business, also into politics, he learns still further the conditions of life.[43]

Though bare of the theoretical sophistication of Chodorow's book (and perhaps a little too forgiving of the male ego), Gilman brings home the idea that gender differences are produced (and reproduced) in the arbitrary confines of the bourgeois home. Girls become wives and mothers after the example of the mother. Boys become men, full of their own importance, in reaction to the example of the servile mother.

Gilman never turned away from her socialist values. But neither did she come close to a systematic analysis of the capitalist mode of production. She was always clear that the problem at the heart of the sexuo-economic relation was that women were excluded from productive labor. Liberate women, therefore, and you will liberate the world, as she argued the point in a later work of social criticism, *The Man-Made World*:

> The scope of purpose of human life is entirely above and beyond the sex relationship. . . . To develop human life in its true powers we need full equal citizenship for women. . . . An economic democracy must rest on free womanhood; and a free womanhood inevitably leads to an economic democracy.[44]

Gilman's last major work of fiction, *Herland*, provides the graphic details of her dream of an economic democracy. Like Bellamy's *Looking Backward*, Gilman's utopia is set stark against the evils of capitalist individualism. Yet, unlike another socialist program of her day, unlike her own earlier writings, *Herland* takes a surprising step toward what amounts to a feminist essentialism. Only a world of women, from which all men from the outer world of economic competition are excluded, can be a true economic democracy.

Curiously, unlike "The Yellow Wallpaper," in which the narrator is the suffering woman, the *Herland* story is told in the voice of one Vandyck Jennings who, more curious still, is a sociologist. Jennings and two male companions from the real world come upon a lost colony of women. The women of Herland are descendants of a small band of female ancestors who, two thousand years before, survived a series of wars and natural disasters. Facing the destruction of the world as it was (by implication, as it still is!), the ancestral mothers rose up against the men who would have kept them slaves. These women were expressly "white,"[45] and otherwise, we are led to believe, remarkably endowed. In particular, they are able to reproduce themselves without benefit of the male sex. Over the centuries the saving remnant of women developed a most peaceful society with a prosperous economy. In *Herland* social control is exercised by force of personal will, not violence; the needs of all are produced in common, without competition; love (though a markedly sexless love) is shared out of respect, without domination. In a departure from her earlier concepts of sexual equality, Gilman seems to say that only women can bring about this socialist utopia.

The story itself is predictable. The three male visitors are discovered, overcome, and held. Their female captors possess a mystical power over the three men. It is clear that the ability of Herland women to control others by civilized force, not violence, is somehow key to the many virtues of their society. Child-care is shared and thoughtful, education is liberal to the individual's need, economics are practical to the requirements of all. Nothing is out of order in this world without evil.

Nothing, that is, until the men arrive. *Herland*'s dramatic interest is sustained by the tantalizing possibility that the men from outer society will reintroduce the long-lost sexuo-economic ethic. The men themselves are portrayed so as to represent the full range of appalling male habits—sexual appetite, competitiveness, boastful pride. Of the three, only the narrator-sociologist, Vandyck Jennings, in spite of his name (a caricature of bourgeois idiocy), turns out to be half-plausible as a mate for one of the Herland women. The story comes to its resolution just as Jennings is on the verge of enticing his love to leave Herland, to return with him to the outer world. Then tragic recognition dawns. The risk of discovery and pollution by the world's sexuo-economic values is too great. The relationship is forbidden. The men are expelled on the not entirely believable trust that they will never betray the way back to Herland. The novel ends, thus, on a tease. Will the corrupt world of poverty, war, and human greed find its way back to Herland where social evil has been overcome? Will the dream survive?

But, just as important as the novel's literary tease is its philosophical tease. Did Gilman change her mind in the end? Is it only women who can maintain an economic democracy? Was she, for all those years, really a closet essentialist? There is no way to know. It is possible that she was led to the appearance of an exaggerated feminist standpoint position by the demands of her genre. A feminist utopia does, after all, require a strong feminist socialism. The free rein of the literary imagination induces a more relaxed attitude toward theoretical principle. On the other hand, by the time Gilman published *Herland*, in 1915, she had devoted nearly a quarter century to life and work as a feminist social critic. She knew what she thought. There are few indications in her nonfiction social criticism that she was edging toward a change of heart. *The Man-Made World*, written just a few years before *Herland*, held firm to the practical feminism and socialist ideals that had governed Gilman's life work. It is possible she changed her mind; but unlikely. It makes most sense to leave the question open.

One of the considerable strengths of Gilman as a social critic is that she was willing to rethink just about everything. It is, therefore, entirely possible that toward the end she wanted to push her radical ideas to their extreme, not to make a point of principle, but in order to explore still another facet of the troubles women face in the sexuo-economic relation. She had lived as a woman who herself had struggled to escape the compulsory heterosexuality of that relation. Though she remained a woman who loved a man, she very well understood the need women have to escape the man-made world. Her final fiction was, perhaps, a final study of the prospects, if not the realities, of a woman's freedom from that world. *Herland* is not in the end an attack on men. Vanwyck Jennings was a plausible partner, just as Walter had been to Charlotte in her youth. The problem the novel, and Gilman's work as a whole, seeks to solve is that of the structured relationship between the genders designed by a coercive economic system. She had no settled judgment on this. Nor do we today.

In her day, Gilman's ideas were quite out of the ordinary. Where the bourgeois values of the Progressive Era coveted capital gain from the rising fortunes of industrial America, Gilman challenged the complicity of capitalist America. Where other white feminists of her own and earlier generations (including her

Beecher relatives), narrowed their struggle for women's rights to the right to vote, Gilman identified the suffering of women with the structured whole of societies shaped by the capitalist world system. Where many early feminists like Ellen Key and Margaret Sanger were willing to use the term "feminist" (which came into the culture first in 1910) to further the separate but equal status of women, Gilman challenged the very idea of the women's sphere and called for a complete transformation in gender relations. Where bourgeois people of all kinds held the family as a sacred sphere for women's work, Gilman attacked the bourgeois family as a ridiculous pretense and unmitigated disaster for everyone—men as well as women.

Though not by any means alone in her views, Charlotte Gilman was strikingly the odd woman out, even among radicals. Perhaps it was the sharpness of her views that made her the most influential feminist social theorist in the two decades on either side of the end of the nineteenth century. Nancy Cott, in *The Grounding of Modern Feminism*, has said:

> Since the 1890s, from California to the East Coast, as a soul stirring speaker and a prolific writer, Gilman had been conveying her critique of the "sexuo-economic" relation that she saw binding women to men, molding women to exaggerate sex-specific characteristics and to rely on men as economic providers. Gilman elevated into a theory of social evolution the changes that perspicacious women saw happening around them; she urged women to move in the direction already pointed out, by leaving their ancient unspecialized home occupation, following the path marked by modern industry and professions, and exercising their full human capabilities in useful work of all sorts.[46]

This was indeed the program that made her famous. Carl Degler thus began his 1956 essay, a foundational study in modern Gilman studies, with the following assessment:

> When Charlotte Perkins Gilman published *Women and Economics* in 1898, the feminist movement in American gained an advocate of uncommon intellectual power and insight. Quickly acclaimed on both sides of the Atlantic [by *Nation* magazine and *The London Chronicle*] for having written "the most significant utterance" on the women's question since Mill, she became the idol of radical feminists and was later judged [by Carrie Chapman Catt] "the most original and challenging mind which the woman movement produced."[47]

With more reserve, Mari Jo Buhle, in "Charlotte Perkins Gilman", assesses Gilman's place in history as that of "an analytic bridge between the views of the nineteenth century's woman's movement and the 'scientific' socialist conceptions of woman's advance common to the early twentieth century."[48] Gilman's thinking was, indeed, a bridge to twentieth-century feminism—but it was hardly a scientific socialism. When, after the 1960s, feminism emerged as a force in American, and world, politics, Gilman's ideas returned to favor but not because of their scientific value.

There are, of course, many ways in which Gilman's thinking is impossible for today's situation. The most prominent was her utter blindness to race; not to mention her relative innocence as to the difference made by poverty. She wrote for white, middle-class women—for those, like herself, who bore the brunt of the true womanhood ideal behind the late nineteenth-century bourgeois family. She did not, perhaps could not, see that African-American women, and their families, are differently situated in their domestic lives because the sexuo-economic relation affects them differently.[49] And, even with her impassioned hostility to the capitalist system, she does not seem to have recognized that poverty affects women and their families even more harshly than even bourgeois confinement. In these ways, Gilman's thinking is limited.

In other ways, Gilman was way ahead of her times and perfectly suited for today's thinking. Her idea of what later came to be called the sociological imagination still serves well because, as I said, it breaks down abstractions at every turn. She avoided essentialisms, where she did, because she was politically and ethically committed to resolving the troubles women experienced in a family arrangement defined by a false and arbitrary value system. She pursued her work open to all available methods and thus, today, instructs the academically cautious. Because she had lived what she thought, Gilman well understood the barriers with which social sciences protect themselves from the creative indefiniteness of the literary imagination. Few social critics have written as much good fiction as they have nonfiction and done so with such fine regard for the larger critical issues of the day.

Some may find her fiction too determined by her social values. Others may find her social ideas too indefinite for today's theoretical sophistication. And anyone sensitive to the realities of social differences will find her indifference to race a disturbing error of judgment. How could a daughter by marriage of one of the nation's great abolitionist families not imagine that women of color suffered the sexuo-economic relation differently and more severely than white women? Gilman's passions ran deep. Her socialist values were firm. She had a keen eye for political principle and for social theory. Yet, she could not see the difference that many, even in her day, realized was the difference at the heart of America's moral sickness. Gilman simply could not entertain thoughts as dark as these. The ones she could, however, were good enough for a lifetime's work, and good enough for us today to appreciate that, whatever the dangers, feminist promises are worth imagining and keeping.

All Kinds of People Gettin' On, 1954

Adolescent white boys in suburbs in the 1954 were a sight to behold. We wore our hair long and our pants pegged. We shopped our finery in the west edge of downtown Cincinnati. There some enterprising soul offered colored people's style to affluent white kids who were already listening closely to the music from Memphis. It would be another two years before Elvis would make his appearance on the *Ed Sullivan Show*. Another two years before our parents would get the first clue. Most of them, mine included, were too shocked by the sex to see the black in his act. We had little patience for them. Our blood was fresh. We listened to the radio on muggy summer nights before air conditioning.

I was sixteen years old in the summer of 1954—unsteadily ready to explore the far reaches of foreign bodies. We dreamed in white. To us, black girls were unthinkably outside immediate experience. It would be a long while before Elvis's black back-ups would dawn upon us. On a clear night, late, when all else failed, we could find Memphis on the dial. We understood little of what excited us about the music, just as little as do the kids in my all too white country village as they hip-hop on their skateboards. At that age, sex is everything. There was so little else on what minds we had. If we lapsed unconsciously into white prejudices about race and sex, it was mostly because nearly everything that passed before the dim eye of teenage consciousness was wet with desire. We were, after all, the world's first teenagers. We had a reputation to live up to.

That fall, the return of school was a blessing. It was the beginning of my senior year at Western Hills High School. I was a minor celebrity, if only because I was frequently seen in the vicinity of the real thing. I was persistent in my pursuit of the benefits of social proximity to the likes of Bud Herman, the senior school president and star of the basketball team. He and I were the co-managers of the school bookstore. Why he deigned to perform this service, I do not know. My reasons were plain. I would be seen with Bud. Just as importantly, by being the one who loaned books and sold sundries on the margins of the class day, I was regularly presented with girls who, for the several seconds of their business, were totally available to my flirtations. Bud may have sought this benefit as much as I, discounting it against the dreary after-school work and the negligible gain of association with me.

The bookstore work came with still other secondary gains and losses. On the one hand, we enjoyed normal access to the storage room in the basement. There we could nap from the fatigue of late night stirrings. There too, I fanta-sized that I might be able to score a sexual touch or two. No one ever visited the cave of dreams. I never had the nerve to ask. On the other hand, the stor-age room meant work. It was our job at various scholastic intervals to retrieve used books from the classrooms above so they might be stored in our retreat below. This involved pushing about an industrial hand cart. If we failed to man-age it well, the word would get out that these really cool guys were, in truth, engaged, not in the dignified work of commercial service, but in the grind of the hand labor everyone detested. We all had seen the men dragging them-selves home at 5:30 to the illusion of tiny homes in the tracts below.

One day, late in the afternoon, I was engaged in this low-end labor. I had planned my moves carefully—just long enough after classes to avoid the rush of observing crowds; just enough before the dismissal of the football players ready for trouble after their manly show. The only people in the halls were stray teachers doing whatever they did, kids in detention (who were of no social importance), and the staff of women who cleaned the classrooms. These women were the only black people to visit this entirely white school on the hill to the west of their homes. In those days, even the cafeteria staff was clean white.

This one afternoon, I was eager as ever to get my telling haul home before the jocks appeared. That elevator always responded slowly, mocking the bel-ligerence of the pupils it served. I was on the most visible first floor, sweaty from the heft of the books. When at last the elevator shook to the floor, its doors opened to three women of the cleaning staff. Each bore or dragged the tools of their labor—buckets, mops, cleaning rags, and a cart of their own. Their collective bulk was impressive. I had to await their move. Then I said it.

"All kinds of people getting off!" To which, one of them responded, more or less defiantly: "I guess so! And *all kinds* gettin' on!" I took the rebuke for what it was. I had not "meant" to refer to the racial difference between us. "All kinds of people" meant, so I thought, nothing more than "what a large number of people." In my crowd, that may have been its sufficient sense.

When that elevator settled to deliver the messengers of an unexpected embarrassment, there had been nothing more urgent in my head than avoiding the only embarrassment I could then imagine. I had not the least idea that there was in me a racial face to save—nor that my status was as white as it was. Even then, I did not fully grasp the dimensions of the scene. But I was, for the first time, aware that there was another line—a line that, if crossed, could change the world, as I believed it to be. I was hauling and lifting, as were they. We were all working in the darkening quiet of the day. The difference was that I had a choice. They had none. In the unquiet of what remained of my daily haul

I began, all too slowly, to see that hard hand labor descends to the mysterious dark of its necessity.

The meaning of words rests on an unspoken contract among those who employ them. Where the contract is fragile, words can mean almost anything. I did not then have a word for what I had learned. Still, it was then that it occurred that the line between the races could not be erased by furtive shopping ventures to the West End, or rapt devotion to the secrets we heard from the King's back-ups.

The Brown decision had been handed down that spring. Emmett Till was enjoying a final year of life before his fateful visit to Mississippi the summer of fifty-five. Somewhere in the back of her mind Rosa Parks, while sewing at work, was giving birth to thoughts of a sit-down to come. The summer of fifty-four I knew nothing about any of this. We white boys had that one last Christmas before the line of our foolishness would begin to appear. It would be a long time before I would come to terms with my remark at the elevator door.

I do not remember when I first finally touched a girl's naked breast, nor whose it was. But I remember exactly when it first touched me that there were differences not even Florence could scrub away.

The Color Line: W. E. B. Du Bois, 1903

Once, I dined alone in a hotel restaurant in provincial South Korea. After ordering, I left the dinning room for a moment. Upon returning, I thought it necessary to explain that I had already been seated. Before I could, the maître d' said, "Your meal is waiting for you, sir." How could he have known who I was amid so many in a very large restaurant? It took a while before I figured it out. The answer, of course, was that I was the one and only white person in the place. I was easy to spot, perhaps even interesting to follow, as I moved irregularly in violation of local prejudices.

When, just about a century ago, W. E. B. Du Bois wrote so memorably of the color line, he meant to evoke experiences of this kind, though ones very different in their occurrence and meaning. On my side of the color line, such a prejudice is a curiosity. On the side Du Bois had in mind, it is the fundamental fact of life. This is why Du Bois began his most famous book, *The Souls of Black Folk*, as he did:

> Herein lie buried many things which if read with patience may show the strange meaning of being black here at the dawning of the Twentieth Century. This meaning is not without interest to you, Gentle Reader, for the problem of the Twentieth Century is the problem of the color line. I pray you, then, receive my little book in all charity, studying my words with me, forgiving mistake and foible for sake of the faith and passion that is within me, seeking the grain of truth hidden there.[1]

Du Bois wrote in a voice attuned to his purpose. Whites were principal among the gentle readers to whom he had addressed his book, so lovingly composed yet far from gentle in its adventures across the color line. A few paragraphs beyond, he left no doubt which side he was on. "Need I add that I who speak here am bone of the bone and flesh of the flesh of them that live within the Veil?"[2] He may have supposed that this coming out was required by the book's declaration of purpose: "Leaving, then, the white world, I have stepped within the Veil, raising it that you may view faintly its deeper recess."[3]

Du Bois was thirty-five years old when *The Souls of Black Folk* astonished the world. His education at Fisk, Harvard, and Berlin was behind him. His Harvard doctoral thesis had created a stir of recognition among historians. His now classic urban ethnography, *The Philadelphia Negro*,[4] had also been well received. Du Bois had, thus, given public notice of his intention to write the scientific record of the Negro community in America. At the turn of the last century, most black Americans had been born to mothers and fathers who had been slaves. In those few years of emancipation, other leaders of the race had begun to set the record straight. But none was so supremely qualified as Du Bois to make the facts known. He was, then and ever, the sociologist using science in the service of his politics.

But he was much more than an engaged social scientist. Through the better part of the twentieth century, Du Bois was never far from the center of the politics that shaped the history of the American Negro. In 1998, a quarter century after Du Bois's death in 1963, Julian Bond was elected chairman of the board of the NAACP. As he took over the leadership of the organization Du Bois helped found in 1909, Bond recalled a family photograph showing him as a small boy holding the hand of the great man.

> I think for people of my age and generation, this was a normal experience—not to have Du Bois in your home, but to have his name in your home, to know about him in your home, to have grown up in this movement. This was table conversation for us.[5]

In the years after its publication in 1903, *The Souls of Black Folk* brought Du Bois's name into the homes of black people across the world. He passed quickly beyond mere fame to the higher status Bond describes. For many, he became an icon of racial possibility. There had been moral leaders, poets, race-men, political organizers, and intellectuals before him. But no one before had so perfectly combined all of these qualities.

For better or worse, Du Bois was well aware of his moral position among American Negroes (the name he fought to dignify by using the uppercase N). He was, perhaps, too insistent upon his moral position. He identified himself with the history of his race by the subtitle he chose for one of four memoirs, *Dusk of Dawn: An Essay toward an Autobiography of a Race Concept.*[6] Today Du Bois is honored as much by criticism of his shortcomings,[7] as by praise of his genius. In retrospect, it seems odd that anyone could be put forth, or put himself forth, as the embodiment of a people's hopes. That the idea was once entirely reasonable, and still plausible to many, is measure of the man's stature and accomplishments.

Du Bois must be on the short list of men and women of the twentieth century whose influence spread without ceasing as the many years of their lives passed by. Picasso and Borges might head such a list. Joyce just misses. He died relatively young, as did Franklin Roosevelt and Babe Ruth. The list is not long. Du Bois lived long, and worked hard. He was more famous at the end of life in 1963 than he was at the century's start. In the first decade of the century, Du Bois defied Booker T. Washington's concessions to white power. In the second decade, he became the NAACP's principal spokesman. In the 1920s, he was a leader of the Harlem Renaissance. In the 1930s, he wrote *Black Reconstruction*,[8] still another classic work of scholarship. In the 1940s, after forty years work in the Pan African movement, he was recognized as the spiritual leader of blacks the world over. In the 1950s, he defied the American government's indictment of communist conspiracy. In the early 1960s, he traveled the world, quit America altogether, and settled in Ghana to begin work on his life's dream of an Encyclopedia Africana. He was 95 when he died, still working. He died, as icons often do, at precisely the right moment—on the eve of the 1963 March on Washington. From the death of Frederick Douglass in 1895 to Martin Luther King, Jr.'s coronation the day after Du Bois's death, no other person of African descent was as conspicuous in the worldwide work of contesting the color line.

Du Bois may well have been a genius. But his accomplishments were born of his work ethic. Most days, for nearly eighty years, Du Bois began his work precisely on schedule at seven-thirty in the morning. Each hour, thereafter, was parsed for a specific task until bed around ten at night. He attributed his longevity to moderation in food and drink, daily exercise, and eight full hours of sleep. Personal discipline was the means to his many accomplishments. He wrote twenty-three books of fiction and non-fiction, of which many endure—three as classics. His articles, essays, and letters are too many to count. Still, his literary work never interfered with his politics. He founded the Niagara Movement, which led to the NAACP, not long after he began organizing the international Pan African movement. He established and edited three magazines, including *Phylon* and *The Crisis*. He traveled, lectured, while always, somehow, answering his mail. In the first six decades of the twentieth century, in the politics of race, there was no debate in which he did not figure.

But Du Bois's genius is evident less in the bulk of his work, than in its style. Though, in person he could be arrogant and difficult, in writing he was refined. It takes a while for some readers of *Souls of Black Folk* to realize the full meaning of the plural *Souls*. Even today, when the famous double consciousness passage trips from every tongue, the subtlety of its underlying idea is easy to miss.

> After the Egyptian and Indian, the Greek and the Roman, the Teuton and Mongolian, the Negro is a sort of seventh son, born within the veil, and gifted with second-sight in this American world—a world which yields him no true self-consciousness, but only lets him see himself through the revelation of the other world. It is a peculiar sensation, this double-consciousness, the sense of always looking at one's self through the eyes of others, of measuring one's soul by the tape of a world that looks on in amused contempt and pity. One ever feels his twoness,—an American, a Negro; two souls, two thoughts, two unreconciled strivings; two warring ideals in one dark body, whose dogged strength alone keeps it from being torn asunder.[9]

This is no mere social psychology of the racial double bind. The American Negro is caught, yes. But by "dogged strength" he overcomes what he "ever feels." He is two at once, always unreconciled. He is, yes, at war within because of the war without. But the struggle is his strength. The "peculiar sensation of always looking at one's self by the tape of the world that looks on in amused contempt and pity" gives the American Negro the "gift of second-sight."

And there is more to this gift than meets the analytic remove of the white eye. The Veil works mysteriously—one might even say, spiritually—on the two souls beyond it, as it does on the white soul before. This is why, in beginning the book, Du Bois offered to lift the Veil for whites, while warning that, if they go with him who is flesh of the flesh with them within, they will see what they cannot fully understand. The line and the Veil—Du Bois returned again and again to these figures. But he never allowed them to relax into analytic calm. Analysis is for the scientist that Du Bois was. But science moved just one of his souls. His spiritual being energized the other. The two souls, together, made him self-consciously who he was.

The color line is the stark exterior of the American Negro's experience. Though a figure of speech, the color line remains an analytic tool, a category serving to divide, classify, and segregate. By contrast, the Veil lends moral uncertainty to the analytic expression. In the early pages of *The Souls of Black Folk* the two figures of speech appear side by side as if to allow the Veil to unsettle the analytic police work of the color line. From behind the Veil, the Negro ridicules the white world that "looks on in amused contempt and pity"—those, that is, who deploy their pitiful powers to measure the souls of others. The measure taken is nothing beyond its cruel effects for which, ironically, whites are disadvantaged. They suffer in ignorance. Their color line segregates the terrifying object of white desire. But the line they draw turns out to be a Veil with the reciprocal effect of imposing the blindness upon which their civilization depends. In attempting to cover their eyes, whites are doubly crippled. They are mute as well as blind, even though, everyone knows, we talk all the time about that which we do not wish to see. Whether sexual or economic, white consciousness in the late nineteenth century was wide awake to the facts of life. Burgeoning industrial America could not live without the Negro's laboring powers—powers that exceed field and forge, thus locking imposer and imposed in a darkness only one understood. Thus, the unspeakable corollary to the Negro's gift of second sight—that moral consciousness encouraged by the secreting Veil—is the apartheid that organizes the singular soul of white folk.

Du Bois, the scientist, respected the mysteries of race. In 1940, nearly forty years after *Souls*, Du Bois wrote of the white world in *The Dusk of Dawn*. As he had done in *Souls*, he writes here of the mysteries of the color line:

> With the best will the factual outline of a life misses the essence of its spirit. Thus in my life the chief fact has been race—not so much scientific race, as that deep

conviction of myriads of men that congenital differences among the main masses of human beings absolutely condition the individual destiny of every member of a group.[10]

The doubling of consciousness works both ways—to obverse but comparable effect. In weakening the exterior, it strengthens the interior life of black folk. In protecting the fragile culture of white folks, it weakens their souls. On both sides, the Veil determines the destiny of all.

More than any of the great social thinkers who were on stage as the last century ended, Du Bois was a mover in global politics. As prominent as Durkheim was to Third Republic French politics, or Weber to late Weimar Germany, or Gilman to American socialism—none so stirred the history of his times as did Du Bois. Few of the others even survived the First World War which, in its way, killed Durkheim and Weber, while sending Gilman into retirement. Only Freud and Du Bois among this remarkable group survived to expand their work after the Great War.

The First World War changed everything for the hopeful bourgeois peoples who prevailed near the beginning of the twentieth century. In *All Quiet on the Western Front*, the greatest of all novels about that war, Erich Maria Remarque puts these words into the mouth of the generation that had suffered through it:

> We will become superfluous even to ourselves, we will grow older, a few will adapt themselves, some others will merely submit, and most will be bewildered;— the years will pass by and in the end we shall fall into ruin.[11]

And so, for many, it was. It would be a good quarter century before calm would settle in the West, then only if one ignores the wars throughout its decolonizing empire—Africa, Korea, Vietnam, and Afghanistan; then Africa again and still. Raymond Aron was not far wrong. The twentieth was the "century of total war." Among the rising middle classes, especially in America, the last glimmers of nineteenth-century optimism faded in the shadows. Not even the short run of the 1920s with its white flappers and New Black renaissance in the urban North could revive the simple innocence that had prevailed before the Great War.

Only those social thinkers attuned to the darker, less conscious forces of social evil were able to flourish after the War. Freud and Du Bois were chief among these few—Freud because he believed in the deeper drive toward evil; Du Bois because he knew just how the destiny of the American Negro was necessarily at odds with that of white folk. He knew very well that this war meant opportunity for blacks. It meant the end of the hordes of European immigrant workers coming to serve American industry, which nudged ajar the door of economic opportunity to blacks. Thus began the great wave of migrations to the industrial North. Thereafter, Negro politics and culture were decisively more urban and Northern than rural and Southern. Though the feudal relations of racial production would remain in force in the South until the 1960s, the urban and industrial migrations brought with them a new cultural awareness that would eventually destroy the racial caste system from which so many had fled. The renaissances in South Side Chicago and Harlem, in particular, marked the coming out of black culture into the consciousness of whites. As well, blacks came to further understand their side of the Veil better, and differently. Du Bois's own struggle with these social forces approximated what they meant to the millions who had already come to look to him for guidance.

In 1915, after the Great War had begun, but before the United States had entered it, W. E. B. Du Bois's "leadership position towered above all."[12] In *The Souls of Black Folk*, Du Bois had begun the move toward leadership with an essay, "Of Mr. Booker T. Washington and Others," a revision of an earlier, shorter comment on the Principal of the Tuskegee Institute and the leading race-man at the turn of the century. The essay was respectful but firm. Du Bois knew what he was doing by placing it third among the essays in *Souls*. Though his words would not immediately provoke his public rivalry with Washington, the battle began at that moment. The struggle between Du Bois and Washington in the first decade of the twentieth century was, in effect, the beginning of the transformation of a racial politics rooted in the traditions of the feudal South into a politics of the urban and urbane North.

Washington had been born in slavery and educated at the all-Negro Hampton Institute. He directed Tuskegee as the institutional emblem of his famous compromise with white power. Du Bois had been born free in the North and went to Harvard. He became the intellectual emblem of those devoted to the unique moral and cultural contributions of the Negro to American society. The rivalry between Washington and Du Bois is often viewed as one over principles. Indeed it was. But there would have been no philosophical differences had there not been, deeper still, economic realities by which the color line took on its urgency. The First World War changed things for whites in one way; for blacks in another. Washington's politics were rooted in the convenience of the whites who profited from the feudal traditions of the South. Du Bois's rose on the surge of industrialization in which feudal domination was refracted in the still cruel, but more rational, capitalist world system. Washington dominated Negro politics at the turn of the last century by force of his ability to control. He was as adroit at pulling the strings of black submission as Du Bois was at inspiring resistance to oppression. This difference was Washington's weak hand when faced with Du Bois's more spiritual challenges—and the Great War was the political and economic divide between the two.

To understand the importance of the War to Du Bois's leadership after 1915, one must compare his situation to the conditions of Washington's leadership some twenty years before. Booker T. Washington rose to prominence on the wings of Northern white relief at his 1895 Atlanta Compromise—"that in all things purely social we can be as separate as the fingers, yet one as the hand in all things essential to our mutual progress." Washington's memorable figure of the hand and fingers was for whites balm spread upon the sores of racial trouble. The year after, in 1896, *Plessy v. Ferguson* gave legal sanction to the restoration of racial apartheid in the American South. Washington's compromise was a double assurance to whites who feared the freedoms that permitted the social contact attendant upon the practical necessities of their economic contract with black labor. Washington's Tuskegee Institute was flush with white philanthropic payback for the Principal's singleminded devotion to the industrial education of blacks.

In "Of Mr. Booker T. Washington and Others," Du Bois summarized the political and social effects of Washington's 1895 speech:

> It startled the nation to hear a Negro advocating such a programme after many decades of bitter complaint; it startled and won the applause of the South, it interested and won the admiration of the North; and after a confused murmur of protest, it silenced if it did not convert the Negroes themselves.[13]

Then, on the point of his differences with Washington, Du Bois continued:

> Mr. Washington distinctly asks that black people give up, at least for the present, three things,—
>   First, political power,
>   Second, insistence on civil rights,
>   Third, higher education of Negro youth,—
> And concentrate all their energies on industrial education, and accumulation of wealth, and the conciliation of the South. The policy has been courageously and insistently advocated for over fifteen years, and has been triumphant for perhaps ten years. As a result of this tender palm-branch, what has been the return? In these years, there have occurred:
> 1. The disfranchisement of the Negro.
> 2. The legal creation of a distinct status of civil inferiority for the Negro.
> 3. The steady withdrawal of aid from institutions for the higher training of the Negro.[14]

Du Bois was still young when he wrote these words, green to the world of racial politics. Though respectful, he was tough—tough enough to reveal the lie in oversimplifying his doctrine of the talented tenth. Du Bois's commitment to higher education was far more than an elitist ideology of the supremacy of culture over economics. Though it is true that Du Bois felt that the poor must be led by the educated, it is not true that his politics were a mere culturalist reflex to Washington's crude economism.

When it came to racial politics Du Bois understood very well that the color line is always drawn in the factual sands of civil rights, political power, and false economic hopes. He spoke to the terrible misery visited upon the black poor, rejected forever from real economic progress—and rejected as much by Washington's smarmy compromise as by the feudal lords of Jim Crow. That he had staked his position in the cultural politics of racial difference (as Cornel West has put it) does not mean Du Bois had no feel for economic or political justice. Adolph Reed among others may think that culture is the realm of elite compromise. But those who share this tiresome view of politics may never have contemplated the contradiction between Du Bois and Washington. The latter was the proponent of the real politics of compromise and economic uplift, and it was Washington who lived the life of luxury as the private railway cars of Northern philanthropists eased onto the private rail link that led to his mansion at Tuskegee. It was Du Bois, the Northern freeman, who grew up poor (as had Washington); and Du Bois who remained, if not poor, always on the margins of economic security. He lived with the poor, in practice as in the imagination, in a way that the Washington of the Atlanta Compromise did not. Du Bois's talented tenth doctrine, so often the object of orthodox sneer, was a doctrine of cultural politics founded in fine awareness of the suffering brought down by the political economy of Negro life.

It is true that Booker T. Washington had been born of slavery and that his labor on behalf of poor Negroes in the South was based on his own firm principles. To build an institute like Tuskegee, as he did, is to set one's hands to the hard-hewn tools of field and factory. And it is also true that Du Bois, though he never enjoyed the resplendent comforts of Washington's later years, took advantage of a privileged education at Harvard and Berlin. His cultural advantage, more than once, gained him the generosity of white friends who protected him in trouble and sent him to travel abroad. Still, Du Bois never compromised. He died in Ghana and is buried alongside the continuing economic misery of sub-Saharan Africa. The one, Washington, aligned himself with the poor in a racial politics that served the interests of the white and well off. The other, Du Bois, walked and talked with the well-off; yet, in the end, it was his photograph that hung in the homes of the poorest blacks. Du Bois earned the respect of the poor because he spoke, and wrote, with feeling for their condition. In his personal style, he could indeed be a mannered snob. But his words, and actions, rang with feeling for the poor with whom he took his stand.

Du Bois's feeling for the poorest of those within the Veil was born less of his own childhood poverty than of the accident of years he spent in adolescence in Tennessee. At the end of high school in 1884, Du Bois had hoped to go straight to Harvard. But for a number of reasons, not excluding race, Du Bois was not admitted on first application. So, in 1885, he began three years of study in the South, at Fisk University in Nashville. Then, for the first time, he experienced life lived fully within the Veil:

> Consider how miraculous it all was to a boy of seventeen, just escaped from a narrow valley: I will and lo! my people come dancing about me,—riotous in color, gay in laughter, full of sympathy, need and pleading; darkly delicious girls—'col-

ored girls'—sat beside me and actually talked to me while I gazed in tongue-tied silence or babbled in boastful dreams.[15]

This is how Du Bois remembered those adolescent pleasures many years later. His feelings for those youthful years in black Nashville were undiminished when, even later, he was in his nineties: "Into this world I leapt with enthusiasm. A new loyalty and allegiance replaced my Americanism: hence forward I was a Negro."[16] To the end of life, he held the Tennessee years as the source of his racial pride—and as the antidote to the first rude, boyhood shock of racial difference.

More important even than the Negro world of Fisk and Nashville was a small village in the far eastern mountains of Tennessee where Du Bois spent the summers of 1886 and 1887 teaching school among the poorest of rural black folk. In his *Autobiography*, written some seventy years after those two college summers, he wrote of this impossibly remote village as though it were still his own:

> I have called my community a world, and so its isolation made it. There was among us a but half-awakened common consciousness, sprung from common joy and grief, at burial, birth or wedding; from a common hardship in poverty, poor land and low wages; and, above all, from the sight of the Veil that hung between us and Opportunity.[17]

These are virtually the same words he had used when he first wrote of this village in *The Souls of Black Folk*.[18] When he repeated them at the end of life, Du Bois had long been assured of his place in the wider world. The repetition was, thus, a way of giving account of his life's work—a way of saying that, though he had traveled the globe, his life remained in community with the most poor and forgotten.

From those summer days of college in 1886 and 1887, Alexandria, Tennessee, was his spiritual community. Thereafter, Du Bois kept Alexandria, forgotten by the world, dear among his most special memories of youth. As other stories of the early years faded, those of this one place seemed as special to him at the end of life as at the beginning. Alexandria was, perhaps, an antidote for the lingering poison from his earlier childhood in Massachusetts. Though Great Barrington gave him his start, and was relatively free of racial ugliness, it was also where the sad losses of his life returned. Great Barrington is where his mother endured the miseries of poverty, abandonment, and early death. There, too, he had lain to rest his dear son, Burghardt, dead in infancy because the white hospitals of Atlanta refused him treatment.

But, most of all, this Northern, free village was where a white girl's rude dismissal of his party card first taught him the truth of racial differences. It was there, or so he says at the beginning of *Souls*, "in the early days of rollicking boyhood that the revelation first bursts upon one, all in a day, as it were." He had done nothing more than join the fun and games of mixed company, when his ease with white children was broken by "one girl, a tall newcomer" unacquainted with local customs. "Then it dawned upon me with a certain suddenness that I was different from the others; or like, mayhap, in heart and life and longing, but shut out from their world by a vast veil." From that moment in childhood, he resolved to live, as he said, "beyond" the Veil. He disdained that little white girl's rejection, just as much as he relished the late adolescent reverie of the "darkly delicious girls" of Nashville.

Why the two types of girls—one white and removed; the others darkly delicious? Hazel Carby somewhat plausibly suggests that Du Bois may have been like other race men in imagining his adult masculinity as beyond, not just the Veil, but even the frivolity of girlish adolescence.[19] If so, Du Bois's fully adult recollection of the pleasures of the racial community (written more than thirty years after the first days in Nashville) was also a completely serious adult meditation on the origins of his life work. In his poetic imagination, the two types of girl were, assuredly, figures of the mysterious sexual play at work in racial differences. They were nameless. But a third would appear, fully named and human, as the one most dear to his understanding of the political situation.

The early chapters of *Souls* are, in effect, the manifesto of Du Bois's racial politics. Though *Souls* is a collection of essays, many previously published, they are ordered with purpose. The first four chapters, especially, declare the foundational principles of his vocation. In the first chapter, "Of Our Spiritual Strivings," he announces the double consciousness principle, stated lyrically against the historical fugue of Negro life in America. In the second, "Of the Dawn of Freedom," he scores the facts of life for the Negro American from the hope of Emancipation in 1865, through the rise of Reconstruction and the Freedman's Bureau, and their abandonment in the 1870s, to the beginnings of Jim Crow. In the third chapter, "Of Mr. Booker T. Washington and Others," he joins the philosophical to the political, against the facts of the previous chapter. His argument with Washington was not a matter of personal preference but of historical necessity. Then comes the story of his community. In the fourth chapter, "On the Meaning of Progress," Du Bois completes his manifesto. His criticism of Washington is framed by the historical record—the failure of Reconstruction, and the restoration of de facto apartheid in the South—by, as he puts it, "the barriers of caste" which Washington had so easily disregarded. Here is Du Bois resetting the clock of racial history in America. Washington's compromise would never do because the backward conditions of Negro life are insufficient by standards ever more rigorous than even those of the feudal South.

Of these opening chapters of *Souls*, none is more poignant, and important, than the fourth. "Of the Meaning of Progress" is surely one of Du Bois's most inventive literary moments. Here he means to call into question the most cherished value of the very Western culture that formed one of his two souls. Here is the "beyond" of the Veil addressed to his gentle white readers. Here is one of his most elegant theoretical claims posed, not as insistence, but in the surprise of simple stories told of his relationship to poor, isolated Alexandria.

"Of the Meaning of Progress" is irony that sneaks up on the reader. Here, he makes no mention of the easy frivolity of Fisk and Nashville. Du Bois leaps directly to the rural hills where he tells the story of Josie Dowell, the third of the figurative girls in his early life. When he first meets Josie, she is still a child, but "the centre of the family: always busy at service, or at home, or berry picking; a little nervous and inclined to scold, like her mother, yet faithful, too, like her father."[20] At first, Josie might seem to be poor kin to the darkly delicious girls he knew in Nashville—perhaps the more bracing antidote to the rejecting white girl of Great Barrington. Yet, Du Bois switches the figure of speech. "She had about her a certain fineness, the shadow of an unconscious moral heroism that would willingly give all of life to make life broader, deeper, and fuller for her and hers." Josie, the nervous scold, is in fact the "shadow" of moral heroism. She is double consciousness. She, and her family, "knew that it was a hard thing to dig a living out of a rocky side-hill." Their hardship "awakened common consciousness [of] the Veil that hung between us and Opportunity."

The story breaks off, abruptly. Then it is picked up again, ten years later when Du Bois returns to Alexandria. The Fisk years are long past. Harvard and Berlin are too. His life's work has begun. Every possibility lies ahead. He visits his community, his spiritual home where the gentle reader might reasonably expect some good word of Josie's progress in life. But, "Josie was dead, and the gray-haired mother said simply, 'We've had a heap of trouble since you've been away.'" Like Josie, his emblem of the Veil's terrible effects, the community Du Bois had taken as his own has disappeared. "My log schoolhouse was gone. In its place stood Progress; and Progress, I understand, is necessarily ugly." The third figurative girl of his childhood had become the measure of liberal culture. But was she, as Carby proposes,[21] the sign of its failure—that is, a play on feminine frailty? Or, was she the beyond in which lay the uncertain hope for racial progress? Carby is too sure of herself I think. It seems more probable that Du Bois left both possibilities open to the work that lay ahead.

In those ten years much had come to pass. The return visit to Alexandria may have been as early as 1896, the year after Washington's Atlanta Compromise and the year of *Plessy v. Ferguson*. If 1896, then it was also the year when Du Bois was formulating his theory of the double consciousness (which was first published in 1897). He had returned to "his" community when his own spiritual striving hung in the balance between the formidable possibilities gained by the highest education the world could offer and his moral commitment to those whose meager training was the condition of their suffering. The passage of the return is more, much more, than mere nostalgia for the terrible intrusion of Progress upon his community. As the coming urban culture advanced on the hillsides from which Josie's family dug out a living, Du Bois turns away from the feelings for those he had lost. He feels sorrow at Josie's death and Alexandria's passing. But he does not give in to sentiment. He asks instead the hard question of the very idea of Progress that lay at the heart of the European civilization that so enriched his other soul.

> My journey was done, and behind me lay hill and dale, and Life and Death. How shall man measure Progress there where the dark-faced Josie lies? How many heartfuls of sorrow shall balance a bushel of wheat? How hard a thing is life to the lowly, and yet how human and real! And all this life and love and strife and fail-ure,—is it the twilight of the nightfall or the flush of some faint-dawning day?
> Thus sadly musing, I rode to Nashville in the Jim Crow car.[22]

The train from the Cumberland Plateau down to Nashville heads West. In the late afternoon, riders may face the setting sun. Yet, as anyone who has lived in the humid summer heat of the American South knows, the afternoon light can be a deception and a relief. The midday heat lingers, but the thick air some-times stirs. The light can change tone, breaking bright through the branches. Hence the illusion of which Du Bois wrote. The light could just as well appear to be a dawning as a setting. "Is it," indeed, "the twilight of nightfall or the flush of some faint-dawning day?" The question rose on the beginning of a new cen-tury, double-sided and unsure like all else for those then within the Veil. What, then, is the meaning of liberal Progress when measured against the death of Josie—against the passing of the "shadow of moral heroism?"

Nearly forty years later, in *Dusk of Dawn*, Du Bois would return to this image of the uncertain meaning of the shadows. In the intervening four decades after his sad ride west in the Jim Crow car, Du Bois himself had trav-eled east to Atlanta, then to New York City, then again to Atlanta, and Europe, and Africa. In 1940 the light, while dusky still, promised a new day. The dusk had become a dawn.

> I have essayed in a half-century three sets of thought centering around the hurts and hesitancies that hem the black man in America. The first of these, "Souls of Black Folk," written thirty-seven years ago, was a cry at midnight thick within the veil, when none rightly knew the coming day. The second, "Darkwater," now twenty years old, was an exposition and militant challenge, defiant with dogged hope. This the third book started to record dimly but consciously that subtle sense of coming day which one feels of early mornings when mist and murk hang low.[23]

Why the switch from dusk to dawn? He wrote in 1940 as the cloud of another war hung over the world, a world still suffering the effects of the Great Depression. How could that have been a coming day? Again, the answer lies in the different consequences of the First World War which dashed the progres-sive innocence of whites, while opening—however slightly—industrial opportunity in the North to blacks.

In 1903, when Du Bois could not yet see the new day, the American Negro suffered the still feudal South and economic margins of the North.

Booker T. Washington was the man in charge. Jobs in the industrial North belonged to white immigrants from Europe. In 1914, a million and a quarter Europeans came to America; by 1917, barely a hundred thousand came.[24] In that necessary lapse arose an economic opportunity for millions of blacks in America—for, that is, the men and women who would have been the generation of Josie's unborn children. Though it would be years more until Franklin Roosevelt would begin truly to desegregate war mobilization industries during the Second World War, jobs were open to a whole generation as never before. Southern blacks rode the Jim Crows north to work in Chicago, Cincinnati, New York, Philadelphia. Booker T. Washington would die in the first full year of the great migration. His Tuskegee home lay in the lowland just south of the mountains. Tuskegee draws its water from the Tennessee hills of Josie's village as, no doubt, it drew its students from those few of Josie's generation who escaped the hills for the faint promise of a better life at skilled labor. Tuskegee is not far from Montgomery, Alabama, where, on a cold December day forty years after Mr. Washington's death, Rosa Parks would lead Martin Luther King, Jr., a still very young son of Atlanta's talented tenth, back from his Northern education into the rural south of the Civil Rights Movement.

The War of 1914 opened the way for Du Bois and those of his cultured advantages to measure both the facts and the spiritual truths of brothers and sisters like Josie. The valued life would be slow in coming, impossibly far off even today for millions, but the spiritual striving of which Du Bois wrote in 1903 would come to good effect. The color line would ride north on the migrations. When, in the first words of *Souls*, he proclaimed it the problem of the twentieth century, Du Bois was looking far ahead beyond the misery of Josie's sad death, beyond the dusk of his youth, beyond the regional effects of the Veil. He looked to the possible dawn, for him and millions of others—for those especially who gathered in Washington the day after his death in 1963 to dream, not just of interracial hand holding, but of the recognition that the color line was structured deep in the nation, and the world, as a whole. Josie, for him, was not so much a local failure, as the emblem of the realities and the promises known only to those with the gift of second sight.

All great thinkers come to their ideas in relation to those who went before. Weber makes no sense without Kant, nor Marx without Hegel, nor Durkheim without Montesquieu, nor Gilman without Bellamy. Yet, each is more than the sum of the borrowings. So it is with Du Bois—with one difference. He was, if not superior to his contemporaries, much more *sui generis*. He owed his debts, to be sure. But somehow, Du Bois always (perhaps even perversely on occasion) turned his borrowings to his own purposes.

When on rare occasion Du Bois encountered an intellectual peer at close hand, as he did Max Weber in the summer of 1904, it was the other who took the intellectual initiative. The following March, Weber wrote Du Bois, praising *Souls*, offering to take care of a German translation, and seeking his advice.[25] Du Bois, it seems, did not pursue the translation invitation, just as he seldom acknowledged the influence Weber must have had on him since his student days in Germany. This surely was in part due to Du Bois's isolation and his relative inability to broker comparable deals for those better established in the white world. But it was also his nature to think as he acted—in terms he alone would fashion.

Du Bois's three greatest works all bear the stamp of a thinker who turned the relative isolation of his working conditions to his advantage. His *Philadelphia Negro*, the first great work of American urban ethnography, is often said to be a methodological copy of Charles Booth's earlier classic, *Life and Labour of the People of London* (1889–91). But David Levering Lewis, reading behind the empirical mass of the work, observes that Du Bois thoroughly and remarkably "refined and applied what he borrowed."[26] Hence, Du Bois's most distinctive theoretical conviction—that race never stands alone, apart from the economic realities. *The Philadelphia Negro* appeared four years before *Souls*, which is itself the work of a man who, apart from the summers in Tennessee, had spent more than year living among the poor he interviewed in Philadelphia's all black Seventh Ward.

Even today some have trouble seeing what Du Bois saw pretty much on his own. Race makes little sense apart from class. Though, as time went by, Du Bois reformulated this thinking, race for him was always in part a class effect. Later in life, well after World War I had cleansed nearly everyone of unfettered faith in Progress, he became more the Marxist. To some, *Black Reconstruction*[27] might appear to be an exercise in class analysis. It was, to be sure, but it was more than that. *Black Reconstruction* endures because no other work of its day, and not many since, examine the facts of economic history in terms of the relations of racial production.[28]

Not only was he his own man in the way he thought, but Du Bois adapted his thinking to the changing facts of racial politics. At no point is this more evident than, as always, in the unusual use to which he put his most memorable concept. Where did he get the double consciousness idea at the start of *Souls*? To think about Du Bois is, eventually, to consider this question for which there is a long list of likely sources—Goethe, Emerson, Herder, Sojourner Truth, William James.[29] All are possible. Yet, in the end, it hardly makes a difference which might have been uppermost in Du Bois's mind. He thought, as few others did, of turning everything to his own ends.

Double consciousness is at once borrowed and invented to contain no fewer than three themes at once. As Paul Gilroy awkwardly puts it:

> Double consciousness emerges from the unhappy symbiosis between three modes of thinking, being, and seeing. The first is racially particularistic, the second nationalistic in that it derives from the nation state in which the ex-slaves but not-yet-citizens find themselves, rather than from their aspiration towards a nation state of their own. The third is diasporic or hemispheric, sometimes global and

occasionally univeralistic. This trio was woven into some unlikely but exquisite patterns in Du Bois's thinking. Things become still more complicated because he self-consciously incorporated his own journeying both inside and outside the veiled world of black America into a narrative structure of the text and the political and cultural critique of the West which it constructed through an extended survey of the post-Civil War history of the American South.[30]

Du Bois would have sooner not had Gilroy's compliment with all its unforgiving jargon had it not been for its basic truth. His thinking was "unlikely but exquisite"—and it was because Du Bois thought from the three points of view at once.

Race, nation, and Africa were always on his mind, from the earliest days. If Africa was not so explicit in the better known early writings, it was there in his 1896 Harvard doctoral thesis on the suppression of the African slave trade,[31] as it was in the meditations on Alexander Crummel and the sorrow songs at the end of *Souls*. It is all too easy to hear, in the double consciousness lyrics, nothing but the play of race and nation. But Africa too is there, behind the origins of the distinctive black soul, behind the economic hardships that gave voice to the sorrow songs.

It is a long journey, for Du Bois, from birth in 1868 in Great Barrington, Massachusetts, to death and burial in 1963 in Accra, Ghana. At his state funeral in Accra, President Kwame Nkrumah began, "We mourn the death of Dr. William Edward Burghardt Du Bois, a great son of Africa."[32] Just a few years before, during a world tour in the year of his ninetieth birthday, he had been celebrated in the capitals of Europe and the Soviet Union, and China. After which he quit all civil relations with the United States and went to Africa. He died a citizen of Ghana—truly a revered son of Africa. But, why had he traveled so far? In the answer lies the code to his life's work, and to his social theory.

In 1920, Du Bois published his second intellectual memoir, *Darkwater*. The Great War had ended, leaving the world uncertain. He was fifty-two, and in charge of his own destiny. In the years since *Souls*, Du Bois had helped found the NAACP. He became its most famous spokesman as editor of *Crisis* magazine, which he founded. In 1914, *Crisis* had 33, 000 subscribers[33]—not to mention the thousands more to whom the magazine was passed from hand to hand. The number of American Negroes who regularly read the editor's views on every important issue of the day is impossible to know. He was also much in demand as a speaker (and claims to have spoken to 18,000 "human souls" in 1913 alone). Du Bois wrote and spoke less as the scholar, more as the political actor. Mr. Washington was gone. If there was a spokesman in the war years, it was Dr. Du Bois—who, of course, offered the whites in charge none of the easy comforts of compromise.

But the war years were troubling to Du Bois's own early racial philosophy. By 1920 he and his many followers understood that the ideals of the double consciousness—"this longing to attain self-conscious manhood, to merge his double self into a better and truer self"[34]—would have to be reconsidered.

Though thousands of Negroes had joined Du Bois in supporting Woodrow Wilson in 1912, and, after 1914, millions more had served well in industrial work (and many later still in the war effort), little was returned that would promise an end to the longing for "manhood." Thus, as he would say in *Dusk of Dawn*,[35] the memoir of 1920, *Darkwater*, was a "militant challenge, defiant with dogged hope." He took the color line ever more seriously. This is when Africa begins to figure more urgently, if not yet saliently, in Du Bois's thinking. He had long worked with Africa in mind. In 1900 he had participated prominently in the first Pan African meetings held in Europe. By 1919, as the war was ending and the first truly international Pan African Congress was convened, Du Bois was a leader among those seeking to unite representatives of the African Diaspora. Thereafter, Du Bois thought more and more of Africa.

Gilroy is surely right to say that Du Bois continued to think from three angles at once. But, just as in *Souls* race and nation were the more prominent of his points of view, then, beginning with *Darkwater* in 1920, Africa came clear in his picture of the racial situation as his American nationalism began to fade.

> What, then, is this dark world thinking? It is thinking that as wild and awful as this shameful war was, *it is nothing to compare with that fight for freedom which black and brown and yellow men must and will make unless their oppression and humiliation and insult at the hands of the White World cease. The Dark World is going to submit to its present treatment just as long as it must and not one moment longer.*[36]

This defiance stands in a bitter essay, sarcastically titled "The Souls of White Folk." He is thinking of race now in relation to the colonized world, and Africa. He speaks less of the "American Negro."

Twenty years later still, in *Dusk of Dawn*, the most upbeat of his first three memoirs, all is clear. His thinking has changed. America is more an object of disappointment than of hope. Where race had been joined to nation, now race was joined to class and the world. Africa had become a way of thinking about the economic misery of blacks in global perspective. Between 1920 and 1940, there were three paths, each importantly connected to the others—culture, Africa, and economics:

> After the [First World War], with most Americans, I was seeking to return to normalcy. I tried three paths, one of which represented an old ideal and ambition, the development of literature and art among Negroes through my own writing and the encouragement of others. The second path was new and had arisen out of war; and that was the development of the idea back of the Pan African Congress. The third idea was quite new, and proved in a way of greater importance in my thinking than the other two; and that was the economic rehabilitation and defense of the American Negro after the change and dislocation of war.[37]

The defiance is more focused now. These words appear in an essay titled "Revolution."

Du Bois's first path was, of course, that of his important work in the Harlem Renaissance. As editor of *Crisis* he was able publish Claude McKay, Langston Hughes, Jean Toomer, Countee Cullen, Jessie Fauset, among others. Though the cultural works of the Renaissance would endure to advance the nation's debt to American Negro culture, both Harlem and *Crisis* would decline with the economic collapse of 1929. As subscriptions to *Crisis* fell below the break-even point, Du Bois lost his hold on power within the NAACP.[38] By 1934, after 24 years, he was terminated from the organization he helped found. At age 65, he returned to Atlanta University to resume a career as teacher and scholar. The following year, he published what may well be his most important work of empirical scholarship, *Black Reconstruction*, in which the theme was that Reconstruction had failed not because of the cultural unreadiness of the newly freed slaves, but because of economic realities. Black Reconstruction was a political economy of race relations. Du Bois's idea of culture, though European in content, was always bound politically to the cultural uplift of the American Negro (tied, that is, to his youthful nationalism). It is not surprising, therefore, that the other two of his inter-war years' paths converged upon each other. The turn to class and economic realities, encouraged surely by the bitter effects of the Depression upon his cultural work, led away from the nation to the world—and of course to Africa.

Dusk of Dawn is a continuing play of light against the darkness introduced in the story of Josie in *Souls*. Nowhere, however, does the figure play with such personal force as it does in his recollection, in *Dusk of Dawn*, of his first sight of Africa:

> When shall I forget the night I first set foot on African soil? I am the sixth generation in descent from forefathers who left this land. The moon was at the full and theaters of the Atlantic lay like a lake. All the long slow afternoon as the sun robed herself in her western scarlet with veils of misty cloud, I had seen Africa afar. Cape Mount—that mighty headland with its twin curves, northern sentinel of the realm of Liberia—gathered itself out of the cloud at half past three and then darkened and grew clear. On beyond flowed the dark low undulating land quaint with palm and breaking sea. The world grew black. Africa faded away, the stars stood forth curiously twisted—Orion in the zenith—the Little Bear asleep and the Southern Cross rising behind the horizon. Then afar, ahead, a lone light shone, straight at the ship's fore. Twinkling lights appear below, around, and rising shadows. "Monrovia," said the Captain.[39]

Light against the dark, from the beginning—the Veil, the blue sky above the color line, Josie's twilight, darkwater, the dusk of dawn, and now "the world grew black, . . . the twinkling lights appear below, around, and rising shadows." Here at long last is the true reversal of the figure. Here is the true dawn, found in the dusk of Africa which after 1940 became the measure of the light, white, colonizing world.

Africa dawned for Du Bois in the setting sun of what was left of his liberal nationalism. His faith in America, always drawn in against the color line, eventually disappeared. Neither the advantages of the Great War for the American Negro nor the successes of the Harlem Renaissance were enough to overcome the brutal reality of a world economic system that had dominated since the nineteenth century. He was, perhaps, a little chagrinned at his own naive hope that the system could work for good. "It was not until the twentieth century that the industrial situation called not only for understanding but action."[40] The action had already begun. Apart from his cultural work in the 1920s, Du Bois devoted more energy to the organizational work of four Pan African congresses—1919 in Paris; 1921 in London, Brussels, and Paris; 1923 in London, Paris, and Lisbon; and 1927 in New York. But in 1935, *Black Reconstruction* was to be his last great work of science. His turn to action meant Africa.

"I think it was in Africa that I came more clearly to see the close connection between race and wealth."[41] Race, nation, and Africa were, as Gilroy says, the three structural elements of his thinking—or his soul, really. But Gilroy's scheme[42] does not account for the growing force of Du Bois's spiritual journey to Africa. He gave up on nation, because, in the experience of his lifetime (which had nearly spanned the three-quarters of century since Emancipation), the nation had in effect given up on him, on his race.[43] To embrace Africa required him to let go of America, which had promised what it did not deliver.

Though Marx had figured in Du Bois's later thinking, it was just as clear that Marx's own limited ability to envisage the precise global terms of class struggle would in turn limit his appeal to Du Bois. Marx understood that capitalism was a world enterprise, and he understood something about the colonial situation, but he recognized little at all about the racial foundations of the colonial system. Though others would later describe these global relations of racial production, Du Bois was one of the first of the great decolonizing thinkers. When race is considered an economic, as well as a social, thing it must be thought also as a global thing. Hence Africa in the shifting balance of Du Bois's intellectual categories. His Marxism, such as it was, was always something more. That more was not so much Afrocentric as Pan African. He avoided all essentializing categories. He was thinking, now, of race as a global and economic problem that required action. He was, that is, already a harbinger of the decolonizing thinkers to come.

> Looking at this whole matter of the white race as it confronts the world today, what can be done to make its attitudes rational and consistent and calculated to advance the best interests of the whole world of men? The first point of attack is undoubtedly the economic. The progress of the white world must cease to rest upon the poverty and the ignorance of its own proletariat and of the colored world.[44]

How, then, did he journey from white New England to Africa? It is plain that he traveled spiritually through Alexandria, Tennessee. "How shall we measure Progress," he asked in his youth, "there where the dark-faced Josie lies?" He had no choice, it seems, but eventually to go to Africa. His own struggle against the color line led him, as it would lead others who came after him, through the dusk of America's oddly confused brand of raced-based colonialism to the world, where there where fewer moral deceptions. In Africa, a colony was just that, a colony where few could mistake the true intentions of the whites in charge. Josie came to be the measure of much more than the liberal idealism of Progress. She was, for him, the measure of the structured injustice of the world system itself. She was just that important because whatever else she meant to him in the summer of 1886, she grew, as mythic figures often do, into the archetype of racial suffering. Whatever dawn there would be, would be the dawn that rose on the dark-faced Josie. Though he first wrote of Josie at about the same time he wrote *Souls*, it can be said that the famous double-consciousness ideal was already up against the deeper economic realities that would surface over the years. This is why Du Bois repeated the story of Josie so many times, even in his last years of life. She had taught him, in the deeper workings of his spiritual life, that the American Negro could not for long measure his soul "by the tape of a world that looked on in amused contempt."[45] By the end, the hard realities of the world economy had made Africa, and the rest of the decolonizing world, the true measure of the failures of white world.

In the end, Du Bois was no longer an American Negro, any more than he was African-American except by spiritual kinship with his fathers and their fathers. He was African and socialist. He called for economic action, for a revolution in the colonial system. As ever, he expressed himself in the idiom of religion, now joined to revolutionary politics:

> Awake, awake, put on thy strength, O Zion; reject the meekness of missionaries who teach neither love nor brotherhood, but emphasize the virtues of private profit from capital, stolen from your land and labor. African awake, put on the beautiful robes of Pan-African socialism.
> You have nothing to lose but your chains!
> You have a continent to regain!
> You have human freedom and human dignity to attain![46]

When Du Bois died in 1963, the great, first wave of post-colonial poets and activists were already known around the world—Gandhi, Fanon, Memmi, Césaire. The wars of colonial liberation were well along. The once hard-sealed global grip of White Progress was slipping, never again to be what it once was.

Du Bois had his blind spots to be sure. Given his magnificent training in economic and social history, one might say that he was a bit slow in coming to recognize that race was at the foundations of the colonial system, hence at the heart of capitalism and class oppression. But how does one fault someone when he came to the issue well before others? Aimé Césaire's *Discourse on*

Colonialism and Albert Memmi's *The Colonizer and the Colonized* would not appear for a good fifteen years and more after Du Bois's first systematic meditations on the colonial system in *Dusk of Dawn*. It would be still another two decades before the first social scientific studies of the capitalist world system in works like Immanuel Wallerstein's *The Modern World-System*.[47]

It might be said, too, that Du Bois never touched upon the psychological effects of the colonial experience that so defined Frantz Fanon's *Black Skin, White Masks* and *The Wretched of the Earth*.[48] That the former student of William James who had proven himself such a fine intuitive psychologist in *Souls of Black Folk* never seems to have thought about Freud who conceived of the Unconscious as a dark continent is, simply, baffling. Still, criticisms of the sins of omission measure the work against an impossible standard. The fairer question is always, What endures as valuable, hence truly classical, in its own right? Here there can hardly be any question that, apart from the exceptional qualities and ambitions of his life and politics, Du Bois stands alone in two important respects. Better than any other work since, his *Black Reconstruction* uses empirical evidence to demonstrate that, insofar as race is a social construct, it is constructed of economic blocks. While works like David Roediger's *The Wages of Whiteness* begin to take up the empirical demonstration of Du Bois's line, none comes close to the systematic analysis of *Black Reconstruction*. And, though there are important and provocative theoretical discussions of race as a social and economic formation, not even such prominent works as Michael Omi and Howard Winant's *Racial Formation in the United States* match up against Du Bois's patient teasing of the theory from the historical record.[49]

It is one thing to say that race and class must always be thought in their relationship. It is another actually to do it. Today, we know very well from the important advances of, especially, queer theory and its affines that, in so far as analytic work demands an artificial setting apart of the empirical contents, analysis itself is a dubious, if necessary, activity. Du Bois, of course, had little patience for the fine points of metatheory. His politics required too much for that. But they also forced him to change his mind, which he did several times through the years.

Yet there is little reason to suppose that the younger Du Bois was of a markedly different intellectual disposition than Du Bois the elder, as (for example) the Durkheim of *Elementary Forms of the Religious Life* was so beyond himself as to be a virtual stranger to the Durkheim of *Suicide*. The outlines of the economic themes of *Black Reconstruction* were already present in his youth in *Philadelphia Negro* and *Souls*, not to mention his doctoral thesis (1898/1965). It was not just that he changed his mind over the years, which he did, but that he understood from the first, as Gilroy sees, that race, nation, and Africa (plus class, which Gilroy sees less sharply) were part and parcel. Those inclined to say that we today have begun to solve the problem of analytic categories and their relations have only to reflect on the furor attending each new book of

William Julius Wilson, since at least *The Declining Significance of Race*.[50] Wilson insists, as did Du Bois, that race can never stand on its own when the ravages of class disadvantage are as severe as they are today and were in Du Bois's lifetime. All of Du Bois's major works bear examination today—as models of just how courage and steadiness of purpose can produce, over a life's work, the careful explanation of just what the constant shifting of analytic categories against each other looks like.

Beyond the tributes that still can be paid him, the complaint that stands up to scrutiny is that Du Bois never even began to see that race and class, even Africa and the world, present themselves differently to men and women. Hazel Carby is absolutely right on this score. But, even she, usually the more astute social theorist, does not quite get to the heart of this problem (probably because she limits herself to *Souls*). Still, Carby gives good account of the way Du Bois used gender unconsciously "to mediate the relation between his concept of race and his concept of nation."[51] She has in mind, to be sure, the figure of Josie but also the grand way he spoke of racial uplift as the work of manhood. She shrewdly describes the way that, for Du Bois, racial manhood was the beyond of feminine sufferings and strivings—as in his subtextual references to Mr. Washington "as analogous to his anonymous black mother."[52]

It is true that Du Bois, who enjoyed respectful, if also lustful, relations with many women throughout his life, did not think of gender as one of the differentiating conditions of black experience. Yet he would hardly have survived the political wars in the NAACP without the ministrations of Mary White Ovington, to mention just one of the women with whom he enjoyed tender and respectful relations. There were others, of course: his own mother (anything but anonymous) and his dutiful first wife of fifty years, Nina—for whom, both, the gender difference meant confinement to the homes they provided for the boy and the great man. Yet, he was blind to gender. But why? Was it only because he was through and through the Victorian gentleman? Or was it that—unlike race and class, even Africa—it was much more difficult for him—for any man?—to think gender seriously in the absence of a feminist culture? To think with these powerful analytic terms is to live with them.

On the other hand, Du Bois might never have so fully thought through the experiences of race and class that made him the race-man of his times without the real and figurative effects of the experience with Josie. So, here again, one must pause before condemning. Feminist thought, from which has come today's understanding of gender, has itself been troubled, as Judith Butler puts it in *Gender Trouble* (1990). Among much else, gender is about sex, and sex is about the play of differences that no one of right mind—save those stuck in the missionary position—would think to categorize. One of the unexplored curiosities of Du Bois's spiritual infatuation with Josie is his confession late in life that his own first sexual experience was with not one of the darkly delicious girls of Fisk, but Josie's mother![53] Those sad words he took with him in the Jim Crow car back to Nashville and life itself were, thus, the words of innocence lost many times over.

It is possible, of course, to say, as Carby does, that Du Bois's all-too-male attitude toward gender was nothing more than the arrogance of *the* race-man. Or, it is possible to say that Josie had such power over him because she, and his experience with her and her family, so powerfully brought him home to all the realities of black experience. He had as little to say about the sexual as about gender differences. But are the silences the same? Or do they make a difference in how one thinks about these things? Here is a dusk, the dawn of which Du Bois did not think through. Yet, one supposes, since they were there below the surface of his recollections of Josie, had he lived in our time, he might have.

Part III

Between, Before, and Beyond, 1873–2020

When Good People Do Evil, 1989

Once, not that long ago, someone I barely know said he thought I was a "nice guy." It was sincerely meant so far as I can tell. There was a time when I would have enjoyed the thrill of such a comment. Now, I am not so sure. Nice people are not always very nice.

Why is it that those—nearly all of us, that is—who think of themselves as good are so often bad, sometimes downright evil? Or, if not evil, why are we so lax in lifting what we say and do to the standards of our best intentions? In one sense, this question invites the answer, "Well, we are only human." That we are. But I am not referring to human failure so much as to human evil—and to its surprising way of rising up where you least expect it. Think of all the ways.

One of the nicest guys I know, a quite generally well liked man in our town, has done some of the meanest things I've heard about. He has ruined people's lives with vicious lies. Spread ugly rumors about others. Attacked the people in his neighborhood least able to defend themselves. Yet he thinks of himself as a liberal in the American sense of the word, perhaps even as a radical. Were anyone to tell him what they really think about his behavior he would be amazed. Actually I once did just that. Not only was he amazed, but he went a little crazy with rage. The evil came out. Other people saw it, or heard about it. As a result, hardly anyone tells him the truth anymore. I certainly don't. Yet I can honestly say that, when he is not doing evil, I enjoy the man's company. He has a wonderful way of listening and smiling in conversations on subjects of no special value to him. He is a very nice man. I mean it.

Having cast the first stone, I should confess, as much as I hate to, that the same might be said of me. When, not long ago, I passed through a horrible personal tragedy, I came out with the idea that, as I said again and again, "Well at least this will make me a better person." Still a year or so after, I was up to my old tricks—trying to be a nice guy but making trouble, doing evil in the name of the good.

What kind of nature is it to be this kind of human?

I once had a friend who now hates me because I did something to him he thought was evil. What I did was get hurt and angry when I came upon evidence that he had been doing me in by double-dealing over something of unique value to him. I was right to be pissed. Perhaps I should have done something else with my anger.

In any case, his deception and my anger spoiled our friendship. We had grown together through a list of shared interests and, in the last years of our relations, we even worked together. When it came time for him to apply for a recognition he desired and, I thought, deserved, he sought my support. I offered it gladly until the day I found him out. His petition required a public defense of his work for which I needed all the facts. What I got from him were all but the one crucial fact on which everything else turned. He had put me in the false position of representing the not-yet-true as though it were already accomplished. The details of the deception are less interesting than the trouble it inspired.

In my anger, I grew righteous. One thing led to another as often happens. He deceived. I denounced. He was hurt, then just as angry as I. It was not, as they say, nice. Eventually, he realized that his prize was at risk. I realized that I had not been very nice. We tried to come together but, as it often is when relations turn sour, it was impossible for either to make things right. What started out as a good turn, turned instead to anger over the truth, which in turn inspired expressions of the right, which compounded the anger that spoiled the relation—which in funny ways changed our lives in greater or lesser ways. Somewhere along the way, truth done in the name of the good became an argument over the right, from which the evil grew.

He did not get the prize. He lost his job. He left. We no longer speak. There is not much to be said. So far as I can tell, he hates me. I hate, at least, what he did with his hate. After this episode, this otherwise very nice person spent quite a bit of time organizing people to his version of the story (conveniently leaving out the little detail about his deception—as, by the way, I am probably leaving out details of my evildoing). The list of people who came to join him in his feeling for me grew and grew. People I had known for many years—fellow travelers in various righteous causes, people of like political mind, at least one former lover (yes, I know, that is a story of its own), a former teacher, and on and on. For some reason a surprsing number of them live in or near New Jersey. What that has to do with it is hard do say. But I can say that it is a small world. It is not difficult to make trouble for someone—for oneself for that matter.

Not only is evil done by nice or good people, when it is done, it takes on a life of its own. Like the butterfly that caused a storm across the world, a slip between friends can, as this one did, grow into a bi-coastal affair—one that always seemed to speed through New Jersey. After a while, no one can remember who was the causal butterfly.

In a sense I was. Had I responded better to his deception, the story might have remained a very small social thing. His bad deed did not, after all, require mine. He may well be right about me. But the thing is that he got so mad that all the people he engaged against me ended up doing stupid things that had the effect not so much of injuring me (though it did that) as of making matters worse for him. In the end, as I say, he lost the prize while I lost friends.

It has now been years since. I occasionally think about the ghosts of this hatred, when I think of him. In my mind, he is as he was when I last saw him more than a decade ago—bent with anger, peering menacingly at the world from behind the shadowy rage cast over his soul. When righteousness comes over me, as it does, I even imagine that, were he willing to talk, we might repair the damage—thus to lift the shadow from his spirit and to annul the blight on mine. But, that won't happen—at least not in this world.

I know another person who is not the least bit nice. No one I know has any confusion about him. He is, truly, one of the most out-of-the-closet mean people I know. He reduces others to tears at the least whim. He writes letters to people filled with unspeakable condemnations of their work. He tells people, often with no good reason, how much he despises their behavior. Even when he is trying to be nice (you can tell), he has a genius for praising people in ways that injure. He is so mean that I once heard about his evil at a cocktail party in another city from a person I'd just met, who never met him, and whose name I can't remember. This guy is about as evil as evil gets in my well-polished world.

Still, while I cannot say I enjoy this not-so-nice person's company the way I do the nice guy's, I understand him much better. Oddly, I feel safer with him because I know exactly what to expect. Something about the devil you know. Plus which, when he does his evil deeds the circle of those injured is usually very small. The evil one knows does not seem to metastasize like the evil done in the name of the nice and the good. When you know you're at risk of a cancer you at least know what to do about it. When you think you're in the presence of someone really nice, and you're not, then you don't; and you may die. That's the problem with liberals and liberalism. They are so damned nice as to kill you.

Evil is not a mistake, though it may arise mistakenly. Evil is not mere human weakness, though weakness allows it in. In the old days, when most people were religious, evil was the personification of an elemental force of life. For many, sin was the work of a devil. Lately, the only people who talk about evil, besides those who are still religious in that way, are prison guards, substitute teachers, and psychoanalysts—people, that is, who see and hear the worst sorts of remorseless evil. But this is not the evil that spreads its deadly cells out from some modest site of good intention.

All or most people want to do, if not be, good. Yet no one is exempt from the rule of nature. The human invented good and evil as a way of separating our nature from the beasts. Then, when the natural beast within comes out we may despair as if our lapses back into our underlying natures cause the whole world to hurt—as indeed sometimes it does. Most of the allegedly great civilizations are as civilizations do—evil masking as the good, which, at the least, describes the spiritual ethic of today's sly remains of the system of global colonies and the slaveries they enforce. If, in the end, good people do evil, then what are we to make of the most precious of the modern world's analytic cuts?

When evil masquerades as something better than it is, or the good do the evil they despise, then we are faced with the one immutable fact of human life. Everything is related loosely to everything else, which in turn exposes the foolishness of all those very sincere analytic cuts meant to purify the good, the true, the right, and the beautiful of their naturally occurring complexities.

The Queer Passing of Analytic Things: Nella Larsen, 1929

When people are subjected to analytic cuts, they bleed. Sometimes they pour out the blood of their anger. James Baldwin had this experience more than once, and for more than one reason. Here is one of those, in 1965, as told by his friend and biographer David Leeming:[1]

> A well-known sociologist sat down on a chair directly across from the sofa on which Baldwin was sitting, with his brother David on one side of him and me on the other, and asked him how many "siblings" he had. After a long period of hesitation Baldwin asserted that he had no siblings. The voice was a whisper, but the signals of explosion were clear in the enlargement of his eyes. Not recognizing the signs, the sociologist assumed a vocabulary gap on Baldwin's part and explained that he had referred to the number of children in the Baldwin family. Baldwin, in the softest of voices, explained that he knew what "sibling" meant. He did have brothers and sisters, but no *siblings*. Refusing to accept Baldwin's rhetorical distinction, which he seemed to consider an attack on the vocabulary of his discipline, the sociologist became insistent. "Yes, but they are siblings," he said. "No," Baldwin now shouted, attracting the attention of the whole room, siblings were a category; you could not smell, touch, or love siblings. When the sociologist persisted, Baldwin raised both hands high in the air, and with his by now enormously enlarged eyes holding the sociologist's attention he brought the hands down with tremendous force on my right arm and David's left arm and literally screamed, still without taking his eyes off the sociologist. "These are my brothers; not my siblings, motherfucker."

You have to give that sociologist credit. In 1965, sociologists were among the very few academics who would be invited to sit down with James Baldwin. Still, this one was what he was—an analytic cutter so convinced of his powers that he could not look into the eyes of the man he was addressing.

You must also give Baldwin credit. One David was his blood brother, the other David was, at that moment, a brother of the soul. When one is with one's true brothers or sisters, touching them and feeling their skin next to yours, only a true motherfucker would pretend not to see what is plain to see. Baldwin's "motherfucker" was just the right epithet.

The very idea of mother fucking owes to the analytic line drawn by the scientists of the social. The incest taboo is said to be the one universal social rule because it is the rule that covers the analytic divide between nature and culture. The most unnatural *human* act is that of acting upon one's *natural* human desire for the ones from whom life came. Any parent, male or female, of a newly born child knows very well just how deeply erotic the feelings are in the months, and years, just before and after life begins. Why else would children separated from their mothers at birth long for them years later—and seek, very often, to find them? Why do we, who were not separated from our birth mothers, long for the proper touching they did not, or could not, give us? Why do we seek those caresses in the other mothers who sometimes become mothers to us? And why do they, the mothers and other mothers, return the pleasure? And why do those of normal relations with their mothers come to understand even the most normal of family romances is deviant in the particulars? And are these normal deviations inspired by the prohibition? If this, then what is normal?

When it comes to mother fucking one question always leads to another. All the world of analytic principle is called into the question. This was the primordial analytic cut into which the analytic sciences of the human *inserted themselves* (to use precisely the verb phrase used all too innocently by the analysts). For there to have been any such thing as society with a history there had to have been a deep, abiding cut between nature and being itself. That cut is where the human Being wishes to insert himself. It is the first mother of modern society, and the opening we bring from nature to society. We modernist humans do in truth seek to insert ourselves into the bodies of our mothers. That is the whole point of the nature that preceded the historical world of the human—is it not? The social and human sciences invented the analytic pretenses of which "society" is the mediating ideal in order to ward off this disturbing fact of human life. If there is anything universal among human Beings it is that we start with animal bodies. We are born as are other mammals. We suck as they do. We desire and need mother's milk as do they. And those mothers we everafter want to fuck want to be fucked by us. Mine did and that is why she turned me over to the only safe adult in our household, Mrs. Florence Brown Lyons. My birth mother had the same integrity as do all birth mothers who, in love, give away their infants for reason of their own limitations.

Baldwin was exactly right to call out that motherfucker. Insistent analysis of the relations of human feelings deserves to be called for what it is. The sociologist in 1965 and other analysts today very often get close to the others they would analyze. This, as I say, is to their credit. What is not is that they have no feeling. They do not see or hear. In getting close to others, the analysts of social relations need to cut away—to make them "siblings" even while they sit with their brothers and sisters. In this, they reveal themselves in all innocence. Their repressed desire to be the animals they are comes out from the closet. They remember the mothers they wanted to fuck. They protect themselves by crushing the sensitive feelings with an insistent vocabulary. To call them mother-fuckers is to call them out of the analytic shadows.

Passing cuts both ways. There is the passing of those who must, or feel they must, protect themselves from real social dangers. And there is the pass-ing of the kind Baldwin called out—the passing of those who have spent a life-time working hard to do good in order that they would never have to feel what they feel in the closet of their unconsciously held power. So far as anyone knows, the animals are not embarrassed by their animal nature, around which they do not try to pass. You might say, What about the chameleon? But is not the resort to camouflage in nature a tactic appropriate to real threats to sur-vival? Then you might say, Does not the person who passes in order to save her marriage or his job face just as real threats to survival? Yes, but with a crucial difference. That which they fear will be outed, while natural to them, is not so much *their* nature as the Nature imposed by a wicked Society. She who passes as white, he who passes as heterosexual, any who passes for whichever cause—they face real threats, but of a social kind. These are threats enjoined by the analytic cutting of Society with a capital S. They are threats, thus imposed, that resort to a claim about the naturalness of racial, sexual, or gen-der differences in order to maintain the artifice of a certain privileged idea of society. The chameleon that turns coat to save himself from the bigger lizard must hide himself against death. Those who feel they must pass to save their jobs, families, and other societal positions must hide to save their place in a societal arrangement that defines them as dead to the good and true. You might say, Is not this sort of social death just as mortal? No one can judge this for any other, of course. But it is not nature that cuts out people according to their skin, or blood, or any other of the innocent surfaces upon which society imposes differences in order to organize its prejudices.

Hence, the quandary: That which is analytically determined to be natural is, in fact, a denial of nature. It is, thus, a passing over, or getting around, the true facts of life. But, that which is natural in fact is, it seems, plastic before its mortal enemies. The chameleon turns his skin to save his skin. Humans who pass, whether from strength or weakenss, turn coat to protect their societal position. The Strong-We pass so as not to face the terrible things they must do to maintain their analytic privilege. The Weak-We pass, when they do (less often now than formerly), because they know very realistically where the social dangers lie and just how artificial a social death can be.

None of this, by the way, has anything at all to do with liberal tolerance, color blindness, equal opportunity, or any other of the good Strong-We pre-tenses by which they establish themselves as rightful members of the Good Society.

When it is a well-intended scientific practice, analysis can be just what one expects it to be. As in the classic definition of analytic realism:

These [theoretical] concepts correspond, not to concrete phenomena, but to elements in them which are analytically separable from other elements. There is no implication that the value of any one such element, or even of all those included in one logically coherent system, is completely descriptive of any particular concrete thing or event.[2]

These are the words of Talcott Parsons, the most famous of sociological analysts. Parsons wrote them in 1937 in *The Structure of Social Action*, the book he fully intended as the prolegomenon to a new analytic science of the systems of social life. He was a modest and good man, but an ambitious one. In the years after World War II, Parsons and a few others at Harvard and Columbia universities came very close to imposing their scheme on the already very academic human sciences.[3] Had the eclipse not begun its pass over the Western sky in the 1960s, the whole of academic social and human science in the world at large might have looked more as Parsons had wished. But that, of course, is virtual history. Parsons is less well read today. Still, there is no more enduring monument to the analytic urge in modern intellectual thought.

Just the same, today, to many, Parsons has become a kind of joke, most especially for the astonishing results of his analysis of the modern American family system. A very good bit of end of the twentieth century feminism began as an assault on the analytic idea of woman's role in the American family system. Parsons, it turns out, put into analytic language only what nearly everyone else in the 1950s, as before, thought, and felt, about women—that they are dependent sorts, best kept at work as housekeepers and caregivers to their public men and small children. The analytic idea was clean. Families are systems. Members live in roles. Roles are categories by which individuals obediently enter society. Roles tell individuals who they are and what they ought do. A family, thus, derives its status from the occupational role of its breadwinner. Men are breadwinners. This is their role. Women are mothers and wives. This is theirs. Everything else follows: Men have status. Women are dependent. Men work in the public sphere. Women take care of the private. It is just that simple.

Talk about fucking the mothers. You can imagine what James Baldwin might have said about this kind of talk. One does not, however, need to work too hard to figure out what the soon to arise feminisms thought. Scarcely a decade after Parsons, and other sociologists, encouraged the practical talk that cut women into homebodies, the new feminisms left little to imagination. At least white feminists of the middle and upper classes, and especially academic ones, minced no words in denouncing views such as those Parsons put into analytic words as the problem at the torn heart of family life. Parsons again, in 1954:

There is also, however, a good deal of direct evidence of tension in the feminine role. In the "glamour girl" pattern, use of specifically feminine devices as an instrument of compulsive search for power and exclusive attention are conspicuous. Many women succumb to their dependency cravings through such channels as

neurotic illness or compulsive domesticity and thereby abdicate both their responsibilities and their opportunities for genuine independence. Many of the attempts
to excel in approved channels of achievement are marred by garishness of taste, by
instability in response to fad and fashion, by seriousness in community or club
activities which is out of proportion to the intrinsic importance of the task.[4]

I knew Parsons. He was a nice man. He meant well. He was perfectly serious.
He did not have a clue. You can begin to see why he did not read Charlotte
Perkins Gilman alongside his Durkheim and Weber. He could not possibly
have read Gilman. She would have made no sense to him. For him, everything
about women was diagnostic. This was a result of his analytic work. Analysis
very often means well. It can be sincere. But this does not mean it does not
hurt people, as feminists ever since have shown time and time again.[5]

But if women are not role fillers, what are they? If they do not fit into a
prescribed analytic space in the social order of things, where do they fit? The
Woman Question, like other such analytic questions, always turns on how the
question is asked. If asked in order to dissect the subject from the societal
whole, the answer is as likely to sound like Parsons as any other, including a
goodly number of analytic feminisms. If the question is asked otherwise, then
other kinds of answers can be found.

The real question is, How is one to think about women, or gender; about
race, or sexuality; about class, and all the rest?

Though there are clearly good historical reasons for keeping "race" and "sexuality"
and "sexual difference" as separate analytic spheres, there are also quite pressing
and significant historical reasons for asking how and where we might read not only
their convergence, but the sites at which the one cannot be constituted save
through the other. This is something other than juxtaposing distinct spheres of
power, subordination, agency, historicity, and something other than a list of attributes separated by those proverbial commas (gender, sexuality, race, class), that
usually mean that *we have not yet figured out how to think the relations we seek to mark.*[6]

These are the words of Judith Butler in the early 1990s. She means to say that
even analytic words are fine. They have their place. But they also have their
limits. When the words refer to things that cannot be cut apart, then words
must be found that encourage thinking about their relations—about relations
too intimate to survive analysis. She may not have found the words. But she is
asking exactly the right question.

Butler's words, like those of the Weak-We generally, are deceptive. To
some they are analysis of another kind. In fact, some notoriously conservative
analysts thought so poorly of Butler's writing that in 1999 they awarded her a
tongue-in-cheek prize for bad writing. Undaunted, Butler responded: "We
have a disagreement about what kind of world we want to live in."[7] She
accused her accusers of glorifying what they suppose to be "common sense" in
order to attack writers who work on questions of race, sexualities, national-

ism, and capitalism—on (in my words, not hers) the subjects of living interest to the Weak-We. Those who seek to preserve the status quo will often, perhaps always, resort to a defense of ordinary language—to, that is, the language they consider clear, common, and (in the eighteenth-century sense of the word) "self-evident." They want language that keeps the cut-apart cut apart. Anything else is "bad writing" or, put more in the words of their true culture, "bad form." Bad form is dangerous. It keeps together that and those who, together, are trouble. Ultimately, analysts want to live in a world where the trouble is well organized. Butler wants to make trouble for them.[8]

I repeat too often. I know it. I shouldn't. But, I have too many friends who are analysts. I don't want to hurt their feelings. I realize I cannot make them happy. But still I long, as do good sons of the Strong-We, to experience their touch of love and friendship. But that is not the point. Analysts don't care a damn about it. That is their point. So I repeat: There are bad analysts and good ones. The bad ones are wise guys, or worse. They give prizes in the name of their good manners. The good ones seldom are wise guys. They truly believe they know how to make the world better. Parsons, and many who follow in his tradition, are good analysts. They make their own trouble, but it is not their fault. They are trying to do what cannot be done. This is what Butler, and others, mean to say. The trouble the Weak-We make is made because they want a world that is real and honest, even if it means giving up on such wonderful things as the good Self, clarity, progress—and all the rest. Some things are neither nice, nor convenient.

Analysis is as old as the hills. It is integral to modern thinking. Still, nice or not, it is convenient to say that 1937 is as good as any a turning point in the progress of analytic things. The Second World War was coming. The Western world had not recovered from the first. Its states could not keep the peace. Its economic markets could not make the progress. Some thought, as Parsons did, that the only way to keep peace and make progress was for science to apply itself to social worlds. Hence, his principle of analytic realism which was both the key to his great book, *The Structure of Social Action*, and to his dream of a unified social science in the years following the war then coming.

About the same time, in the middle of the 1930s, another turn was underway. The great Weak-We thinkers of the end the nineteenth century were either ending their lives, or completing them, or taking another step. Charlotte Gilman committed suicide in 1935. Her writings would languish unread, awaiting the new feminisms of the 1960s and after. Anna Julia Cooper was retired from public school teaching and in the middle of her tenure as president of a private school for the black working poor, many of them women. She wrote two short, but telling, notes in those years—one to a friend defending Gilman's decision to end her life; another to W. E. B. Du Bois encouraging him to oppose the prevailing white analysis of the racial failures of American blacks.[9] Du Bois did just that. *Black Reconstruction* was published in 1935.

Gilman, Cooper, and Du Bois were not alone among those willing and able to think things in their relations to each other. But they were among the pioneers. Gilman could not think of sexual differences apart from economic ones. Cooper could not think of woman without thinking of her several racial differences. Du Bois, in *Black Reconstruction*, thought of racial differences in their relations to the political economy, and he was beginning to think of them both in relation to the colonized world. None of the three ever quite thought through all the possible relations among gender, race, class, and the world colonial system. None of them dared, in those still Victorian times, to think of sex and sexuality—the most intimate of them all.

Only recently has *anyone* thought the intimate relations of social life in their actual and proper intimacies. No one could from within an analytic culture. Soon enough that culture realized that, far worse than a rock and a hard place, it was between a hawk and a buzzard, as long before Sojourner Truth said it would be. Rocks can be moved. Buzzards are another matter. Once analytic culture began to cede its grip to the weaker forces that were comin' on him, more and more people were able to look at, then speak of, the true and intimate realities of social life. And the strongest of these was sex.

Being the most unspeakable of intimate societies, sex troubles the analytic mind, and modern culture, most of all. Sex may not be *the* most important "problem." But, then, to speak of *the* anything on a list of problems is itself an analytic way of thinking. Whatever else can be said of sex, it is in the end that without which there is nothing human; hence nothing social. Without sex there are no societies, big or small. No life; no life together. If we were ever able to set aside the habit of thinking of things according to their numeric values, of assigning them a rank importance, we might see that all social things are very mixed up with each other. The racial or economic cuts might hurt more. For some, the exclusions according to gender hurt the most. Still, none hurts by itself alone. And, in its way, sexual injury may well be the deepest cut of all.

To grant sexual pleasure free rein in social life is, among other things, to look again at the blood and in it to find nature staring society in the face. Skin and blood are nature's way of containing while feeding the animal appetites. Their surface tensions can seem so various from the exterior view of the social analytic. But, underneath, sex is sex. Its variations—including its various solutions to mother fucking—are variations on the play of nature with and against the prohibitions of the social analytic.

This is why it was only after a long journey that social theory finally came to sex and sexualities. And why, when it did, it had to face up to what it had done, or had allowed to be done, in the name of perfectly good science. Sex touches human beings at the quick, at the root, at the core, at the heart of the most intimate feelings. This is why analytic cultures want so to organize it. It is too dangerous to be left on its own. Even more terrifying, sex always thrives in relation to other social discriminations. When we touch a body, or when ours is touched at the quick, we touch the skin that touches us. We experience its color, it roughness or softness, its way of moving slowly or precipitously toward the climax. And when we come finally to that point, which some call the little death, we come into the animal awareness that these differences we are taught to weigh so seriously mean nothing. All that matters in that moment, and in the ones that follow our coming back to life, is whether we were safe—whether we are *still* safe; or even whether we took our pleasure at the risk of death. All this is in the skin. His or her skin may be whatever color it is. His or her hands may be rough from hard labor or soft from a protected life. The other may move upon us in ways we are taught to suppose are female or male in their social nature. Others may come at us from behind, or from the front, in ways unique to their cultures and surprising to ours. However these events spill out in the experience, they are anything but analytic. Their social meaning is—for that one moment when all else stops—nothing whatsoever. We care only, if at all, about the death and its consequences. And when we fall into its arms deeply enough, usually without thinking, we may so long for its embrace that we cannot let go—until we die in fact; or until we overcome the social distinctions that blinded us.

Sex, as I say, may not be the most important thing. But it is, in its surprising fashion, the most honest social thing. Skin and blood, and the bodies they organize, do not lie. When we come at the hands of others, or at our own hands when the natural imagination is vivid enough, we come into a truth that will not go away. That truth is multiple. It is the many social realities we must, if Goffman is right, hide and manage if we are to compose a Self, if we are to have a face. Yet, no matter how many faces we may wish to present in public, the face of our soul is revealed in that instant when the eyes roll skyward, the lids shut down, the throat lets out its animal scream, and the body as a whole quivers under the ebbing waves—and we hit the salt bottom of an ocean we share with all mortal creatures.

This is why, as nearly as I can figure it out, sex and sexualities are so terrifying, which is why they are the last of analytic things we can talk about. Sex has the ability to queer the analytic urge like nothing else can. This is why *they* hate so those who will not hide their sexual natures. This is why they sloganeer for free speech and domestic privacy to cover their desire to invade bedrooms in order to police the normal perversions of those who will not, or cannot, toe the heteronormative line. The self righteous always know themselves. They know very well that moment when, coming, they came to themselves. Because they know it, they want to organize it. This is why even those Strong-We who get along very well, thank you, with the poor, the unwhite, the unmale can surprise you by their rage at the unstraight. We born of the body of the Strong-We may understand, perhaps even overcome in some ways, our racism, our sense of privilege, our guarded adherence to the masculinities and feminities of our culture. But we have the hardest time fondling bodies like, but not, our own.

Sex is not the most important thing. It may not be everything. It certainly does wipe away the evil done to bodies according to the colors, parts, well-worn calluses, and well-trained practices. But sex is the last relation social thought wishes to think because it so powerfully reminds us of the animal within that is free of the analytic rules and barriers of Society. Sex has this strange power to remind us that the Universal-We lives always at the margins modern society has sought to defend from the barbarian invaders.

Sooner or later, the Weak-We always talk about sex and sexualities; about bodies; about the way nature intrudes upon cultural convenience. In the 1930s the greatest of the social theorists from the margins were not all able to think what relations they thought in relation to sex. But some did. One in particular did just this in two astonishing novels published in 1928 and 1929. She had come from nowhere, and shortly after would disappear. To this day no one truly knows why she passed away from the social eye, as did the characters in her short fictions. She, perhaps more than anyone in her day, wrote about sex and sexualities in their intimate relations with the other social parts that can not be cut away.

Nella Larsen (1891–1964) passed so quickly from obscurity to fame, then back to obscurity, that she has become a near fictional figure.[10] She was, and remains, at least as mysterious in her coming and passing as Helga Crane and Clare Kendry—the fictional women of her two important novels. After the publication of *Quicksand* (1928) and *Passing* (1929), Larsen rose to literary prominence for a moment, won a Guggenheim (1930–31), divorced her husband (1933), and vanished from the literary world. Larsen wrote three other novels; none published, all lost. She was uncertainly accused of plagiarism. No one knows exactly what effect this had on her disappearance. She spent her remaining thirty-plus years working in New York City. She worked as a nurse, her original profession. She died alone. Her body was found in her apartment on March 30, 1964—a scant month after Anna Julia Cooper's death; less than a year after Du Bois's.

It means nothing, in itself, that three such brilliant stars would pass away just as a new movement for freedom was coming into its own. Coincidence, surely. They were, in those last years of their lives, on different orbits. So much so that, looking back from the time of their deaths, it would not be strange to wonder just what they once might have had in common. It would be false, certainly, to lift Larsen, even Cooper, to the same political plane as Du Bois. It might be true to say that Larsen's fiction struck a note in the last years of the Harlem Renaissance like the one with which *Souls of Black Folk* had rung in the new century. Yet, even the color line of which Du Bois wrote in 1903 had changed. From the 1920s on, the racial divide was drawn more to the

North, more to the cities, and far from the rural South. Du Bois and Larsen, both born in the North, were ultimately of the North, even though they had both been shaped by years spent in the feudal South. But Cooper, who had lived her adult life in urban Washington, D.C., and enjoyed worldly honor in Paris, was in the end still a daughter of North Carolina where she was buried. Du Bois and Larsen returned to the South only of necessity—Du Bois to Atlanta in 1934, after he quit the NAACP; Larsen in 1931 to confront her husband's infidelity. In the end, Du Bois and Larsen always rode the trains back North, to New York.

Nella Larsen, like Du Bois, was in Harlem in the 1920s. Cooper in those years was still in Washington, finishing her doctoral thesis, teaching high school. But Cooper's Washington was worlds apart from Harlem. The District of Columbia was still a dimly Southern city. Harlem was part of a global one. Cooper's world was passing away before the sweeping changes that altered the face of America, black and white, and the world in the 1920s. Harlem was not merely in the North. It too was of the North—and of the world. Harlem was the world capital of black culture, as New York itself was becoming the cultural capital of the World.[11]

Manhattan in the 1920s was, in many ways, *the* newest and most important global city, especially of the European Diaspora. The United States had been the decisive military power in the Great War. It had underwritten British and French war efforts. Europe suffered many times more severely. America lost fewer than 200,000 men. Each of the major European parties to the Great War had lost upwards of 2,000,000. Spared the devastation of war, and the turmoil of the revolution in Russia, America was left alone to become the global center of culture—even of the world politics its majority disdained. Woodrow Wilson's failure at Versailles in 1919 was the projected voice of American isolation. Turned inside out, isolation was the harbor for its cultural independence. Diplomatically, passive; economically, America was already, as she would be for much of the rest of the century, the world's first banker. The Great War had braced and transformed its culture as it had Europe's. The Gilded Age was over. Something less innocent, more honest, slightly less obscene, evidently more wild, took its place. And New York City was the focus, and more often than not, the source of this new culture.

"Terrible honesty" is Ann Douglas' phrase for it (though she drew the words from the culture itself). Manhattan below 125th Street was the center of that culture. More than any other, Freud was its figure of speech and thought. The honesty had two sides, as honesty always does. One dark; the other light, even breezy enough to thin the terror. The literature of the times expressed both. Sinclair Lewis' *Main Street* (1920), Willa Cather's *My Ántonia* (1918), Sherwood Anderson's *Winesburg, Ohio* (1919), and especially F. Scott Fitzgerald's *The Great Gatsby* (1924) were tales rooted in the small town, Midwest origins of their authors. They exposed the easy values of the small town or the great city against the despair and ruin of their characters.

Main Street is such a bitter denunciation of small-minded America because it plays the completely decent, if foolish, Dr. Kennicott against his cultured, urbane wife who struggles with the futile wish to better his little world. Carol Kennicott escaped to the big city in the East in one final search for freedom before being led back to Gopher Prairie, and the end of her life. From the porch of Sinclair Lewis' boyhood home in Sauk Center, Minnesota, you can still today look two blocks to the prairie he fled, for the East and New York where he found fame, and death in a bottle. Rural America casts its eyes away from the open countryside to listen longingly for the trains to the Northeast. To live on the plains is to listen—for the wind, for the train whistle, for the radio beacon. Willa Cather, too, and Sherwood Anderson. Willa Cather's *My Ántonia* is a tale told of the far Western plains, but told from the urban East by an impossible love who could not bear the undefined open spaces. Its uneasy, but gentle sexual tension embraces the land, just as sexual perversion lurks behind the shade-drawn rooms of *Winesburg, Ohio*. George Willard of Anderson's *Winesburg* is last seen aboard the train, escaping to the city. Anderson's story is dark, where Cather's is light. Sex and America are their ties.

Here was the reversal of America's nineteenth-century hostility to the city and the bracing recognition of that urban America, while not an answer to life's mysteries, was at the least more honest. The Jazz Age New York of Fitzgerald's *Great Gatsby* is set in *the* American city. Sex and drink are its veneer. It is never clear where, exactly, Gatsby is *from*—in any sense of the word. Fitzgerald puts his origin somewhere on the Western shores of Lake Superior (not far from Sinclair Lewis's Gopher Prairie). But the place means little. Gatsby's story is of a man who comes from nowhere to descend for a brief passage in the bright light of New York. It is clear from the first that Gatsby's West Egg parties are where and what they are meant to be—emptily fated for nothing more. Whatever its name, New York City was the city.

In the 1920s, white Manhattan, of which Gatsby's West Egg parties were but a reflection, ignored Prohibition. Life was high. The radio made it the world's new media center. Its skyscrapers made Manhattan the visual center of world modernism. They were built on credit against Manhattan's commercial success, which was broken in 1929, only to revive after the Second World War. Even so aggressive a critic of its modern ways as Sigmund Freud was appropriated as the resource for understanding the good life, for advertising the burgeoning consumption culture, and for the figurative symbol of the decade's honesty. Madison Avenue, then as now, is a probe to the unconscious desire for pleasure. Psychoanalysis, among much else, migrated from Europe to New York City in the 1920s. Psychoanalysis, with all its many contradictions, played out the honesty of the era. It exposed the darker nature of the Self, demonstrated its limits, and encouraged the idea that the most primitive of all natural instincts was real and powerful.

In the 1920s no primitive urge was more powerful than sex.[12] For the 1920s to have become what they were in Manhattan, it was necessary to slay

Mother Victoria. Victorian prudery, which Freud both attacked and embodied, was the hard hand of societal control over much of American culture. Sex was not so much excluded as put under the covers—the same moral covers that were meant to keep nature in its subordinate place. Freud and psychoanalysis did not themselves liberate the sexual drives. But psychoanalysis was the body of social thought that named and normalized the force of sex that ran freely on the select islands of the European Diaspora and on none more dramatically than black and white Manhattan.

The conventional line in early psychoanalytic thought was in its way as confused about sex and the sexualities as was the Victorian culture psychoanalysis unmasked. Freud himself notoriously relegated female sexuality to a derivative back seat. *Totem and Taboo* (1913) was Freud's first attempt to project his psychology of the unconscious into a sociology of the human. There he put the slaying of the primitive father at the original center of human society. Society arose not from the well-mannered social contract, nor even from fear of each other, but from the collective guilt over the hatred of father. Freud turned Hobbes's Leviathan around to take him from the rear.

Totem and Taboo was a sequel to his rendering of Sophocles in *The Interpretation of Dreams*. But Freud's Oedipus was even a regression from Shakespeare's *Hamlet*. Freud's son treats the mother as a pitiful object of desire in a tragic drama with the father—a drama in which the mother is but a passing object. Ever aware of his scientific responsibilities, Freud borrowed Electra from Aeschylus in a feeble effort to balance the ledger between the motherfucking desires of the boy and the father-envy of the girl.

But Ann Douglas, with the 1920s well in mind, argues for a reversal of the play of sex and aggression—a reversal that, I would add, is necessary to the reversal of play between the longing countryside and the terrible city. Why was it not possible for Freud to imagine the foundations of society as a matricide? Why not, in effect, treat the two basic, natural drives that became the centerpiece of his thinking in the 1920s as a primitive tension between sexual and murderous desire for the mother? Douglas answers:

> In the first section of *Totem and Taboo*, entitled "The Horror of Incest," Freud discussed the pervasiveness and tenacity of the taboo in primitive cultures on sexual interaction between mother and son, and, even, in some cases, on what one might think of as routine contact between them, but his culminating fable of origins illustrated that taboo rather than analyzing or breaching it; like the savage people he described, Freud could not place the mother because he literally could not face her. *Totem and Taboo* is a matricidal not a patricidal text in part because, in it, Freud denied, demoted and obscured, not the father but the mother. Yet like the vampire figure to whom he compares the father, she will not stay in the grave.[13]

Freud's own mother is often said to account for his own private prudishness. What Douglas says directly about Freud applies as well to Manhattan. For the boy, or the girl, to leave the country, he, or she, must break with mother. Yet, even amid the freedoms of urban pleasure, the mother's moral voice must be killed if the modern world is ever to heal the breach with its rural, more primitive past.

Manhattan culture of the 1920s was in open rebellion against Mother Victoria—against the same analytic moralism that led, on the one hand, to Prohibition and, on the other, to Women's Suffrage. The Eighteenth Amendment to the United States Constitution prohibiting the production and sale of liquor was ratified in 1919, one year before the Nineteenth gave women the vote. Victorian rule asserted itself in the one, as it liberated women in the other. Or did it truly liberate women—all women?

It is well known that the first great suffragist, Elizabeth Cady Stanton, began her work as an abolitionist in the 1840s. The nineteenth-century social movements against slavery and for the civil rights of women were united from the first. From the margins of society, race and sex were once one. By the end of the century, they were cut apart—and the cut was delivered in every instance by the white feminists. To the last day of his life, Fredrick Douglass worked to bring white feminists to the cause of blacks. But as early as 1868 Douglass protested their ignorance of the racial realities:

> The right of woman to vote is as sacred in my judgment as that of man, and I am quite willing at any time to hold up both hands in favor of this right. It does not however follow that I can come to Washington or go elsewhere to deliver lectures upon this special subject. I am now devoting myself to a cause [if] not more sacred, certainly more urgent, because it is one of life and death to the long enslaved people of this country, and that is: negro suffrage.[14]

Douglass was not alone in reminding the white feminists that black people, though disenfranchised, were also being lynched as a matter of course. But such pleadings fell on deaf, singleminded ears. All of the great turn of the century white feminists—Stanton, Susan B. Anthony, Charlotte Gilman, Jane Addams, Anna Shaw, Carrie Chapman Catt—eventually abandoned blacks and black women in their struggle for the vote.

This precisely is the condition between the races that Anna Julia Cooper understood so well in her eerily restrained rebuke in *A Voice From the South* (1892) of the White Woman of the South—and of Shaw and Anthony, most pointedly. Ann Douglas, writing more than a century later, was far less restrained in saying that the racism of the white suffragist movement was a direct consequence of its feminist essentialism.[15] To fight for "woman's" right to vote while excluding the black woman is to deliver the deepest racial cut of all. The exclusion of blacks in the name of womanhood was at least racist, certainly essentialist, and nastily analytic. And the cuts were ugly, as when Jane Addams, an early member of the NAACP, abandoned blacks in the name of women's rights because, in her view, black men were inclined to be rapists.[16]

During the Harlem Renaissance, black Manhattan was far less troubled by the terrible honesty syndrome than was white.[17] Scott Fitzgerald gave the decade its name, The Jazz Age. The truth of the name, needless to say, owed to Harlem where the New Negro broke the conventions of the rural South from which so many had come. Music, literature, dance, art, theater loosened the color lines in Manhattan. Whites traveled uptown, as black culture moved downtown. The races mixed, openly, as never before. The Jazz Age was a spontaneous assault on the sharp cultural and social divides between the races every bit as much as the musical form itself, once discovered by whites, surprised and tempted the appetites of the dominant culture. There was sex, to be sure. And plenty of it was openly, aggressively interacial. But the sex at play in the play between Harlem and white Manhattan in the 1920s resonated with global change in the broad sense that psychoanalysis had in mind. Fitzgerald meant just this: "The city seen from the Queensboro Bridge is always the city seen for the first time, in its first wild promise of all the mystery and beauty of the world." Sex is fucking, but it is much, much more.

The 1920s were the beginning of the consumption culture that would eventually panic social critics in the 1950s. In 1924 a new Ford could be had for $290. By the end of the Twenties one out of every five Americans owned a car. Ford, soon to become an "ism" all its own, had taken over the productive enterprise on the pledge of selling pleasure cars to everyone. Consumption, as opposed to productive labor, is about ease, and pleasure—not discipline and hard work. The first wave of eroticized consumption in the 1920s would end in 1929, only to revive after the Depression and the Second World War. But that was when, and New York was where, more than another time and place, the pleasure principle took hold in modern society.

The terrible honesty syndrome was an expression, as Douglas says, of both the bracing effects of the Great War and of the struggle interior to culture to come to terms with mother—with woman, with sex. Among the desires, mother fucking is always snug alongside mother killing. How else could they so readily collapse into insult? This was Freud's idea, which he nearly ruined by his perverse aversion to women, which caused him to turn the human desires for sexual union and for aggression into oddly generic drives or instincts. But psychoanalysis had the right idea.

Harlem, Manhattan, America, and the European Diaspora were many things in the 1920s. The Harlem Renaissance was hardly all fun and dancing. No neighborhood where W. E. B. Du Bois remained could possibly lack for seriousness—for honesty of its own kind. Harlem in the 1920s was the black capital of the world in part because there, at last, the barriers set up by those, like Jane Addams and Elizabeth Cady Stanton, of whom little was expected, did not seem to matter any more than the more overt Jim Crow racism prevalent in the South. These insults to human society did matter, of course. But what was different in that time was that the color line, still in force, was loosened. The mixing of the races brought out of the closet the other false cuts between people—those governing the assignment of women to the homes, those separating the classes as well as the races, and—above all—those of Mother Victoria that hid the truth of sex and sexualities.

This was the world into which Nella Larsen rose to her few years of fame. It was the world, and its global and cultural consequences, her two short novels told of.

Nella Larsen helped slay Mother Victoria. Well, if not this mother herself, then moralism's most perverse kin in nineteenth-century America. The ideal of True Womanhood, as Charlotte Gilman and many others understood, grew in the deep recesses of both agrarian and industrial capitalism. The economically necessary family form required the assignment of the bourgeois woman to domestic duties. Her most urgent duty was the enforcement of its moral code upon the new generations. She was necessarily a child bearer. Her goodness was her truth.

In the cultural imagination, the True Woman was, as a matter of course, white. But she imposed herself less with regard to race than to class. Black bourgeois women were held up to the same moral duty as were whites. Women like Anna Julia Cooper were able to resist, or at least to work around, its confinements. Cooper did because she kept her ties with the impoverished slave origins of her mother. Until she could work no more, Cooper devoted her life to service to the poor. Many lived, as she did, in the manners of bourgeois life. They worked alongside women, like Mary Church Terrell, who never knew poverty and were, perhaps as a consequence, the more true women.[18]

That women like Terrell and Copper were thrown together because of their race does not mean that they lived and thought in the same way. The difference is, however, not simply one of preferences, or choices. It is a difference fixed by the economic accidents of birth in the years after Emancipation in 1863. Though not always, those who kept themselves at the margin, or outside the sway, of the True Womanhood ideals were born, like Cooper, to poverty. Those who resisted less firmly, like Terrell, were born to the middle classes.

By the 1880s when Anna Julia Cooper and Mary Church were students at Oberlin, the class line between them and their hopelessly poor sisters in the South was still hard and fast. Cooper worked her way into the middle class life. Without diminishing Mary Church's accomplishments in the least, *she* required no admission. She was born to the urban middle class of Memphis. For the vast majority of black women of the South in years after the failure of Reconstruction, college and the bourgeois life were perhaps an ideal, but not a likely prospect. This is the class line that was unsettled, and redrawn, by the migrations North and the settlement of black and partly bourgeois neighborhoods, of which Harlem in the 1920s was the most important.

Nella Larsen was, along with Jessie Fauset (1882–1961), first among the Harlem writers who challenged and reset the analytic divisions affecting black women in America. She wrote, as did Fauset, from a different experience. More Northern, more urban, less impoverished, more culturally open to Harlem in the 1920s—and thus to sex and sexuality. Larsen wrote of black women as openly and actively sexual—as women, thereby, able to live outside the conventions of marriage.[19] But Nella Larsen's fictional women—Helga Crane in Quicksand and Clare Kendry in Passing—are not just sexual. They are complicated women—human in ways the True Woman, black or white, never could be. Ann duCille puts it this way:

> [They] cease to be singularly and uniformly heroic, good, pure, blameless— victims of patriarchal privilege and racial oppression who persevere against all odds; they become instead multidimensional figures, full of human (and, in some cases, monstrous) faults and foibles.[20]

Their humanity as black women came with their sexuality, which is particularly dangerous and potent when sex enjoys an open relation to race and gender.[21]

Quicksand opens with Helga Crane suffering under the oppressive bourgeois morality of Naxos, a southern black college. Naxos is Tuskegee, where Nella Larsen worked as a nurse. She arrived in 1915 just the day before Booker T. Washington died. The Principal himself lived on in the shadow of Larsen's story. She knew first hand Southern culture's oppressive moral smugness. "The South. Naxos. Negro education. Suddenly she hated them all. Strange, too, for this was the thing which she had ardently desired to share in, to be part of this monument to one man's genius."[22]

Helga Crane cannot stand it. She decides to quit the South and Naxos. She must first break off her engagement to James Vayle—appealing, wealthy, from one of Atlanta's finest bourgeois families; but righteous and dull. She must also break her contract with Naxos—the moral and cultural hope of the Black South. Its young and handsome president, Dr. Anderson, tries to seduce her, in both senses. He fails. But sex enters. The sexual tension between Dr. Anderson's unconsummated seductions and the bourgeois sterility of proper Mr. Vayle sustains the story from the first. Helga cannot escape. Both men revisit her. They are the dilemma of her life's migrations—and her fate.

Helga returns to Chicago to find what is left of her white mother's family. But the new wife of her dead mother's white brother refuses to have anything to do with his mulatto niece. Helga is banished from what family ties she has. She is alone. Poor, but resourceful. She deploys her education and cultured background to gain a position as personal assistant to a famous, good, but unappealing race-woman.

> Mrs. Hayes-Rore proved to be a plump lemon-colored woman with badly straightened hair and dirty fingernails. Her direct, penetrating gaze was somewhat formidable. Notebook in hand, she gave Helga the impression of having risen early

for consultation with other harassed authorities on the race problem, and having been in conference on the subject all day long.[23]

Mrs. Hayes-Rore, though lemon-colored, lives in another racial world from the light-skinned Helga. The one has settled into her race, the other not. Sex is the difference. But the singleminded race-woman is good. She sends Helga east on a mission and thus provides Helga her ticket from Chicago to Harlem. Helga Crane's cultural charm and physical beauty soon draw her into the "distracting interests" of the Harlem life. From there the story turns on the uncertain play of the races, sex and marriage, the city and the South.

Out of nowhere, a lost letter arrives. It had followed Helga's flight—Naxos, Chicago, Mrs. Hayes-Rore, then Harlem. Her white Uncle Peter regrets her expulsion from the family. His letter bears a check for $5,000—a small fortune in 1928. Another ticket—from Harlem to white but racially generous Copenhagen and the society of another remnant of her mother's family. Helga quits Harlem. She loved and hated its racial excitement. "While the continuously gorgeous panorama of Harlem fascinated her, thrilled her, the sober mad rush of white New York failed to stir her."[24] "Someday" she would marry one of its "brown or yellow men who danced attendance on her."

Copenhagen is a racial mix of another kind. She is accepted, again a social star—an object of delight. Alex Olson proposes marriage. For him, she is exotic; for her, he is not. Again she refuses a proper marriage. But this time, it is because white Copenhagen, while accepting, lacks the racial tension. Or, is it sexual? She was neither happy in Denmark, nor in her own skin. "This subconscious knowledge added to her growing restlessness a little mental insecurity."[25] Helga decides to return to Harlem. "*These* were her people." The Copenhagen life fades astern. "Tears rose in Helga Crane's eyes, fear in her heart." Nella Larsen is writing in the years just after Fitzgerald's *The Great Gatsby*. It is hard not to think of the small, surprising word after the truth of Gatsby's love for Daisy is out. They set off for home, and *death*.

Even before arriving home, Helga Crane knew that Dr. Anderson had married her Harlem friend, Anne. Still she returns to "the miraculous joyousness of Harlem." She returns to its social temptations. James Vayle, now assistant principal at Naxos, is in Harlem on school business. He again proposes marriage. Helga ignores him except to rebuff his Southern scorn for the Harlem life. "I'm a Negro too, you know."[26] She walks away. But she cannot walk away from Dr. Anderson. He takes her by surprise. She responds to his deep kiss, then breaks away. She is unsettled. Weeks pass. They arrange a rendezvous. This time Helga opens herself to Dr. Anderson's seduction. She is completely open to him. But he is not to her. His sex is, as always, allure without body.

Helga Crane cannot recover. She falls into despair, and onto the streets. Walking, soaked with rain, not in her right mind, she comes upon a mission. She is drawn into its religious ecstasy, and to the arms of Reverend Pleasant

Green—crude, uneducated, poor. "And so in the confusion of seductive repentance Helga Crane was married to the grandiloquent Reverend Pleasant Green"[27]—his world as absurd as his name. She returns with him to small town Alabama, where she falls under the minor privileges and heavy burdens of the preacher's wife. She bears his children. Her health declines. Her story ends: "And hardly had she left her bed and become able to walk again without pain, hardly had the children returned from the homes of the neighbors, when she began to have her fifth child."[28] Helga Crane had returned to the South where sex wore on her bones. She had lost herself in seductive repentance. Quicksand. The dark and righteous, rural South. Death.

Like Ann duCille, Hazel Carby notices the originality of Nella Larsen's complicated liberation of the black woman's sexuality.

> Larsen's representation of both race and class are structured through a prism of black female sexuality. Larsen recognized that the repression of the sensual in Afro-American fiction in response to the long history of the exploitation of black sexuality led to the repression of passion and the repression or denial of female sexuality and desire. But, of course, the representation of black female sexuality meant risking its definition as primitive and exotic within a racist society. Larsen attempted to embody but could not hope to resolve these contradictions in her representation of Helga as a sexual being, making Helga the first truly sexual black female protagonist in Afro-American fiction. Racist sexual ideologies proclaimed the black woman to be a rampant sexual being, and in response black women writers either focused on defending their morality or displaced sexuality onto another terrain.[29]

Hence, the analytic bind. Dr. Anderson is to James Vayle what the sexual exploitation of black woman is to her sexual repression. Faced with the extremes, she comes upon more subtly terrible prospects. Alex Olson, proper and wealthy, makes of her a primitive, exotic object. Reverend Pleasant Green brings her back to the primitive reality itself—and death. Between Copenhagen and Alabama, Harlem opens possibilities Helga cannot live with. Larsen, in Carby's view, represents the impossible options for the black woman—her inability to represent a single stable truth, an inability brought on by the coming out of her sexuality.

Of all the major critics of Larsen, even David Levering Lewis and Ann duCille, Carby is the most explicitly sociological. Helga Crane represents the unrepresentability of race, of black women. Helga's social position is in the unresolved tension between the folk culture of the South and the higher ways of the city. Her sexual value, more open in the city, becomes the unstable force that unsettles her race, her class, her social being. When Larsen was writing in the 1920s, the black woman in America was neither folk, nor urban. She was unable to stand up, or in, for either. She had no settled home for her being.[30]

Judith Butler takes a similar, but more radical, view of Larsen's inability to represent the sexual black woman. Carby's idea refers to the social and historical position of black women in the 1920s—the position Larsen herself occupied. Butler goes further. She poses the question asked incompletely four decades earlier by Anna Cooper. Does the sexual black woman represent the unrepresentability of *any and all* analytic categories? Is she the one who unsettles all instances of social segregation—race, gender, class, sex; all of them? After granting Carby's point, Butler turns to the queer nature of this woman. In Larsen's day, "queer" had not yet come to mean homosexual. But it did mean eccentric, obscure, perverse, out of sorts; hence the verb "to queer," meaning, "to quiz or ridicule, to puzzle," but also, "to swindle and to cheat."[31] Queering, Butler observes, is the correlate of passing.

Passing is always dangerous. The cover requires continuous maintenance. Any little thing can blow it away. Passing works against the near certainty that it will be queered. This is the subject of Nella Larsen's second novel, *Passing*.

Larsen tells her story of passing through the fictional Irene Redfield. Irene is happily married to Brian, a physician. They live comfortably in Harlem with their two children. They enjoy an active social life. Irene Redfield is light skinned. She could pass as white. She does not. Clare Kendry does—most dangerously to her nigger-hating white husband. Clare is the story's object of fascination. She toys with her racist husband, John Bellew; and with Irene, who cannot escape Clare's eerie power, which turns out to be sexual as well as racial.

The tale begins in Harlem. Irene is going through the morning's mail. She comes upon a seductive note from her childhood friend. Clare wants a meeting, a renewal of the friendship that, after being lost for many years, had been rekindled two years before in Chicago. They had met by accident on a hot day in the roof garden at the Drayton—one of Chicago's best hotels. Irene had to pass to find relief from the heat. Only a person of means, of whichever race, would know where to go. At a table, she rests, waits. Her eyes are met and held by another woman. "Did that woman, could that woman, somehow know that here before her very eyes on the roof of the Drayton sat a Negro?"[32] This was Clare, also passing. They rediscover each other. Irene is intrigued, excited, but cautious. She is unsure of an invitation to visit Clare at home. But she accepts. In the company of third friend of their youth, one also light-skinned, Irene comes for tea to meet the passed upon husband. Mr. John Bellew has no idea that he was in the presence of three Negroes. Clare's passing is a marvel. Bellew's nickname for his (to him) dark-skinned wife is "Nig." The tease is on.

Two years pass. The letter arrives. Clare is in New York. The seduction, under wraps in Chicago, is more in the open—though not explicitly sexual.[33] Clare writes to Irene:

> For I am lonely, so lonely . . . cannot help longing to be with you again, as I have never longed for anything before; and I have wanted many things in my life. . . . You can't know how in this pale life of mine I am all the time seeing the bright pictures of that other that I once thought I was glad to be free of. . . . It's like an ache, a pain that never ceases.[34]

From Clare's "pale" life, Irene is full of color. After they lost contact years before, Irene had heard rumors of Clare's passing. But she had put her out of mind. Clare lightly blames Irene. The note concludes: "It's your fault 'Rene dear, at least partly. For I wouldn't now, perhaps, have this terrible, this wild desire if I hadn't seen you in Chicago." Clare's desire is wild, but its object is unclear. Is it Irene's racial life in Harlem? Or her sexual appeal? What exactly does Irene represent? We never know. From the start the story is a tease.

Irene succumbs to Clare who enters her Harlem life in every way—an intimate at home, a companion to Dr. and Mrs. Redfield in their social life. The intimate details of Clare's society with Irene's family are unclear, but exciting. Clare's desire for Irene is, it seems, reciprocated. But never is the joining of their feelings more evident than at Irene's most anguished moment of uncertainty. Is Clare her husband's lover? The prospect dawns just when Irene finds Brian at some inexplicable limit in their life in Harlem. They argue. The apparent subject of their encounter is race, but Irene thinks that it may be more, and that Clare is at fault. She worries:

> For, to her, there had been something ominous in the scene she had just had with her husband. Over and over in her mind his last words: "Don't expect me to give up everything," repeated themselves. What had they meant? What could they mean? Clare Kendry?[35]

Irene's world is at risk. Is her husband's refusal to give up "everything" the projected reversal of Irene's sense of loss? And what is at risk? The family? Their racial world? An object of sexual desire? And, for whom? Brian? Clare?

Passing, like *Quicksand*, ends in death. Both stories move upon a danger signal known from the first. In *Quicksand*, Helga Crane escapes the opposing embraces of Dr. Anderson and James Vayle only to fall through their arms. She dies where the story begins, in Alabama. In *Passing*, Clare Kendry's fate is sealed by her husband's nickname, "Nig." The story ends at a party in Harlem. John Bellew comes upon the eroticized scene. His wife is close by Irene. Bellew spews out the meaning of his wife's comfortable association with blacks. "So, you're a nigger. A damned dirty nigger."[36] Clare's cover is blown. She passes away, falling from the window ledge where she and Irene had been so intimately seated.

"One moment Clare had been there, a vital glowing thing, like a flame of red and gold. The next she was gone." Did she fall? Or leap? Was she pushed? By Irene? Bellew's cut is joined. He becomes the beast he feared; "There was a gasp of horror, and above it a sound not quite human, like a beast in agony. 'Nig! My God. Nig!'" His agony is met by Irene's final confusion. "Irene struggled against the sob of thankfulness, it turned to a whimper, like a hurt child's."[37] In the end, as from the beginning, we never know whether Irene is drawn and repulsed—by Clare's racial life, or by her sexual appeal. As we cannot know how she died, we cannot *ever* know why she died, or who she truly was. Was she the "Nig," or the sexual "flame of red and gold"—or both at once?

To read *Passing* is to attempt to read any passing. Those who look or listen can feel the hints here and there. But one never knows for sure. That is the point. Larsen's fiction creates in the reader the feelings one has when left outside the cold comfort of analytic clarity. There are no certain categories. It is impossible even to determine which is the principal character. Is it Irene? Or Clare? If Irene, then is it her sexual interest in Clare, or her racial? If she kills Irene, is it for fear of losing (or giving up), something precious? If so, who? Brian? Clare? Family? Harlem? Does Clare leap? If so, because she is outed?—for her race?—for the sexuality racists project onto "nigs"? Or, is Clare the object of Irene's desires—the one who acts out what Irene, the more true woman and mother, cannot? In killing Clare, if Irene kills her, is she killing the sexual feeling inside as Helga did by her fatal marriage to Pleasant? Everything turns on the interpretation of the final scene which is beyond interpretation—queer in every sense.[38]

Is *always-beyond* and *always-uncertain* more than a literary effect? In the years just before the great eclipse of social things, analytic thinkers went on the defensive. They protested again and again that questions such as this one are a disastrous lapse into what they call "relativism." For them "relativism" is self-evidently a bad thing for which no explanation is required, and none is given. Against which, a good number of people, myself included, wonder, So what if the relations among the elemental forms of human association are just that: "relations"?

What if, after all, we should all be reorganized in one loose department of social relations? What if, in effect, analytic cutting kills the social body by segregating its skin and blood, its sex, its desires—and all of the other of its juices—from each other? What if, as Larsen (and those drawn to her writing) seemed to think, the sexual is the one, final unloosening of the body of social relations? And the one that reveals the *always-uncertain* of any attempt to think the bodily parts?

As Judith Butler says, "queer" did not become slang for homosexual until after Larsen wrote. Yet Larsen queers the easy distinctions of modern society by bringing sex and sexualities to the fore. *Passing* uses the word "queer" an astonishing number of times—and always with reference to sex—or to sex and race together.[39] From the first moment when Irene is drawn into Clare's passing before John Bellew, the racial danger is aggravated by sex. And at the end, the final leap is foretold by an accidental slip of the truth. Before the death party, Clare is walking arm-in-arm with Felise, an unpassably Negro friend. By chance, John runs upon them on the streets. His pleasure turns, uncertainly. "But the smile faded at once. Surprise, incredulity, and—was it understanding?—passed over his features."[40] He knew before the confrontation at the window ledge. After he had hurried on, "Felise drawled: Aha! Been 'passing,' have you? Well, I've queered that." Butler thinks that the queering operates as the inverse correlate of passing—as that which is done to queer, to disavow that which is falsely avowed in passing.[41] I agree.

One might even say that analytic relations in society turn on a double passing, and double disavowal of the truth. Even the best analysts know they are not speaking the truth of the things they cut apart. They want their good to cover the damage done. Whether the passing is done from the stronger or the weaker side of the Veil, it is done upon a disavowal. Passing is an act of avowing what I am not. Queering is the act of disavowing the avowal. It is a way of getting at the only truth there is—the true bodily nature of social intimacies. And sex may be the most bracing of these loose but undeniable facts of social life.

Both Ann duCille and Deborah McDowell see the disavowing power of sex in the lives of the black women writers of the Harlem Renaissance. And they see that these writers were part of the Jazz Age—their avowals of a black woman's sexuality akin to those of Harlem's Blues women, singers like Bessie Smith, Alberta Hunter, and "Ma" Rainey. Ann duCille:

> Jessie Fauset, Nella Larsen, and Zora Neale Hurston are only three of the many female voices and visions, politics and poetics which helped shape the literary life and cultural climate of the 1920s and 1930s. As with the other blues literature, the tenuous nature of male-female relationships lies at the core of their respective fictive inventions. But Jessie's blues and Nella's blues and Zora's blues confront, as well the roles that social values, patriarchal ideology, and racial oppression play in making erotic relationships tenuous. I read their "bourgeois blues" as subtle, frequently subversive responses to the oppressvie, materialist rhythms of their evolving black communities.[42]

Jazz Age Manhattan—downtown, or on Gatsby's Long Island, is one thing; uptown, it's another. But the two cross over, touch each other through the sexual notes of the Blues singers. But no such crossover is a giving over of the full nature of the separated experience. The Jazz Age meant one thing to Gatsby, another to Clare Kendry. Both died for loves lost, or not attained. But Gatsby's tragedy was an overreaching of wealth on the assumption he would win back Daisy. His tragedy was in not foreseeing the turns and twist of others outside. Clare, like Helga, died from the twists and turns of her inner experience. Her passing into the white world was always doomed because she could not relinquish her desires, which were driven by her black world.

In the European Diaspora, the Jazz Age was when the parts of social being began to come together. Not finally. Not permanently. But loosely. It was when the dream of modern progress, crushed by the Great War, pried open the closet door. The Jazz Age was also the Age of Freud. It was when, in select but powerful places like Harlem and Paris, even Berlin and Vienna, the underside of society was exposed. Not everyone wanted to talk about it. But most everyone knew. Sex was more in the open, bearing its truths that can only spill from an unconscious gland. The animals fuck in public, without embarrass-ment. Shame is human. To have no shame is to refuse to give in to the prevail-ing code of the street. To have no shame is to refuse the artifice of human order—the avowal of truths the falsity of which must not be told. Because it renders us naked to the skin and flesh of our disavowals, sex reminds us—and I mean us—of the closet in which we are expected to hide our shame.

The Jazz Age was not an age of miracles. Its honesty was, indeed, terrible. Men and women of all the classes and races died deaths tragic with the weight of their impossible lives. The 1920s in Manhattan may have been more cultur-ally honest than elsewhere, but they were far from the only islands on which people sought to escape in order to understand the horrors that lay just behind and ahead. The Jazz Age glittered. But it was not gilded. No amount of wealth or beauty could out-dance the truth of human society that had been outed by the Great War, and by the wars to come.

Between the two world wars of the twentieth century, the migrations and out-ings of the Jazz Age loosened the hard selfish thinking that rode the rails of early industrial progress. But the harder realities that followed in the 1930s soon tightened up the modern mind. There was however an important slip-page of the mind brought on by the modern age's attempt to recover from the Great War. This slippage was not always visible to the naked eye. But, on close inspection, it can be seen to have allowed both the new social and sexual reali-ties of the Jazz Age to soften somewhat the return of the analytic culture that sought, vainly, to order what remained after the second of the wars.

It is not, therefore, surprising that the finest analytic work of the social sci-ences was published on the eve of the Second World War. Parsons was but one of its better expressions. Analytic philosophy was another. Both sought to clar-ify the parts of a human truth, the progressive wholeness of which could no longer be considered self-evident. But the deeper analytic thinkers were no other than cousins to the technocratic urge that would attempt, after the sec-ond war, to put Humpty-Dumpty back together again. John Maynard Keynes came to be the devil of conservative thinkers not because he gave rise to the idea that the state must play a strong role in economic policy. He was hated by those nostalgic for the eighteenth-century free market because he said what Wittgenstein said. Analysis must go deeper. It may not trust the appearance of meanings. Meaning is not real in itself. Its value is in the analytic withdrawal— of social science, of philosophy, of fiscal policy, of language, of logic. These were the building blocks of thinking that led to an analytic renewal after the Second World War, when a mostly American faith in social technology would be turned to peacetime ends. The analysis of "social problems" issued from a perfection of the idea that the Strong-We need only break them into their parts. Poverty, the race "problem," the economic crisis in postwar Europe, the productivity "problem", the rebuilding problem in Japan, the communist men-ace—on and on went the litany. The new dogma only looked like the old. It was just as naive in its confidence that these analytic cuts would hurt only for a while before progress set in once again.

But the European Diaspora had learned from the Jazz Age. Its analytic efforts were, under the cover of liberal exuberance, more sober. This is why the postwar generation went berserk over the communists. They had learned, against every wish to the contrary, to look for themselves in the evil of others. Though the American gulag was not nearly so terrible as Stalin's, it was a gulag of consummate cruelty. Faith in progress was ever after cut against the certainty that the evil empire was as much within as without. This was the lesson of the 1920s and, though many taught it well, no one taught it better than Nella Larsen.

The Jazz Age collapsed with the market in 1929. Its effects endured in the sober blues of its writing and music, as in the sober self-doubt of its postwar exuberance. The truth was out. Because we are all sexual, we are all several parts at once, loosely organized. If even the Strong-We hid in the dark closet of modernity's dishonesty, then universal humanity could no longer be dreamt as handholding or color-blindness or liberal tolerance. The only universal fact of the human condition is that We are several, each with our own ways of hiding the truths.

What Would Jesus Have Done? 1965

In the weeks of late March 1965 white Northerners, many of them clergy, crept under the cover of night by bus and caravan into Selma, Alabama. One of their kind had been killed. For years to come many of them would tell of having been called to this dangerous mission by Martin himself. As literal fact, this vocation was statistically improbable. But as a spiritual reality its truth was certified by the courageous good works they achieved.

Few realized then that this would be, for all intents and purposes, the last time blacks and whites would join effective hands under the banner of a civil rights movement. In 1965 good white folk helped win the right to cross the Edmund Pettis Bridge out of Selma, then to walk the forty miles east to Montgomery, where the unrepentant George Wallace sat in power—where the movement had begun on a bus ten years before. Selma led to the passage of the Voting Rights Act in August of that year. But, after that, the limits of civil rights legislation having been reached, the name of the racial game changed. Obedient whites would thereafter stay home, sent away by the power they had encouraged without realizing how swiftly it would turn on them. Then the pall of black power would fall over white intentions. There would remain this one last movement of righteously integrated civil rights struggle.

No one who came to Selma that last March could forget the experience. They were sanctified by holy allegiance to those whose hearts were buried in sacred plots and dams of earth up and down the Mississippi. Before it would be over, yet another white was to join the grave of her black brothers and sisters. Still they came in fear and trembling by cover of night to seek relief in the company of others. Once they had crossed the barren stretches of rural Alabama, travelers were surprised by safety in the Selma community where the children of Brown's Chapel held off Sheriff Clark's now wary boys.

The greater danger was on the roads beyond the guardian reach of Selma's children. This is why so many stories of the comings and goings survived over the years to come. The one that recurred to me nearly forty Advents later is remembered if at all by the small group of those who shared the incongruent experience.

Six well-collared men from Boston packed into the old Chevy of a newly minted minister. In those days, pay for clergy was mostly in kind—a meager salary, free housing and other allowances, an occasional gift of food. None had a decent car. We wedged ourselves into this old clunker under the desperate optimism that our visibly religious company, borne by a car of rotten fenders, would be a hedge against violence were we stopped. We survived the trip down.

Our story turned on the return home. Somewhere in northern Alabama, or perhaps it was western Georgia, this little band came upon an overturned car, its wheels still spinning skyward. A white man was spilled on the roadside, his blood already soaking the gravel cushion. His wife begged for help. The driver of our car, with the uncertain support of others, meant to refuse her. They were all headed home to families and parishes that needed them more than this one man.

One alone among them protested. He threatened to "turn them in." To whom, for what, he did not say. Just the same, the car stopped, returned, and released this one to offer his help. In time, another of the company came out. Whether to join the ministry or hurry it along was never clear. The others remained, fixed by fear, in the car. A state trooper happened upon the scene just as the injured man died in the arms of the Samaritan. The trooper, torn between duty and rage at these intruders from the North, sent them on their way. There was nothing else to do.

All of these traveling men were good people. None lacked faith. All were courageous. All had flocks to tend which alone justified a greater prudence than that of the one who sought to comfort the man who died. To this day, I do not know what Jesus would have done, and never thought it was for me to judge.

The Race of Time: Deconstruction, Du Bois, and Reconstruction, 1935–1873

Presentism is the sin of holding persons native to an earlier time accountable to the standards of a present time. Those blamed in the first place are usually dead, or otherwise indisposed. They cannot defend themselves. Yet they are accused. There are many examples. One could say, for example, that by today's standards Charlotte Perkins Gilman was at best a feminist essentialist, at worst a racist. Or it is possible to blame Anna Julia Cooper, one of her generation's most brilliantly timeless thinkers, for her failure to touch upon sex. And even W. E. B. Du Bois, than whom none among those in his several time zones was more prescient, could be accused of insufficiency with regard to women. He was a feminist in his way, but by present standards he was not a good enough one.

The thing about presentism is that it turns complaint upon the complainer. The deficiency of the one held to standards not of their time is converted into a criticism of the critic for his own failure to keep historical time in order. Yet presentism is not an entirely silly complaint. People do have to watch out for mistakes made in respect to rules they could not possibly have understood.

Still presentism may not be either the only or the worst failure of this kind. Though seldom remarked upon, it is readily apparent that there is a sin similar in its confusion of times, but different in the direction of the confusion. If *presentism* is the fault of holding the long, recently, or soon-to-be dead responsible for the manners of present company; then X is the error of failing to grant the real or virtual dead credit for having understood present manners *better* than present company. Since *pastism* is more monstrous a term even than *presentism,* why not call it, simply, X? The difference between X and *presentism* turns on the distinction made ever so delicately by the *Book of Common Prayer*—that between sins of omission and those of commission. Presentism, thereby, is the sin of committing a faulty attribution of omission to the dead who, at the time they were living, could not have known the rules they failed to obey. By contrast, X would be an active neglect by the living of the achievements of the dead—a commission exercised upon the refusal to grant that others knew the rules before they did. Within full-bodied analytic culture one might expect the X to be filled with something like "culpably feasible ignorance of the present-promise of past deeds." Since this won't do, let us call it X.

As it turns out, X is a good term with a history of its own. It was the X in Jacques Derrida's early writings on erasure that may have started the argument in the first place. His idea was that all could never be said and done. This he derived from the erasing X that he drew through most of the sacred ideals of the modern West—the primacy of voice, the privileging of articulate consciousness, the presumption of present meaning, the moral authority of the Self, the principles of the Center, and so on. The most notorious of Derrida's X's was in an essay that appeared in *Théorie d'ensemble*, the 1968 collective manifesto of the then new French social theory. There he explained his very squirrelly concept, *différance*, with the following remarkable statement:

> Or si la différance ⬚ (je mets aussi le "⬚" sous rature) ce qui rend possible la présentation de l'étant-present, elle ne se présente jamais comme telle.[1]

To make a long story short, Derrida meant to say that when we come upon certain crucial words like "is" (perhaps the most crucial and duplicitous of all words), we must think twice. To say "is" is to suggest that some or another (material or immaterial) subject "is" in the present time of the statement uttered. "Derrida is still alive."/The man is present in the present time. Were "Derrida" to be a fictional character, as his detractors seem to suppose, the effect would be the same. The reader is asked to think of him, whoever he is, as present.

Whenever "is" is uttered, problems abound. The first of which is with "Being" itself—chief among those words about which Derrida (borrowing here with reservations from Heidegger) thinks we must think twice. When we utter "is," we are committing an ontology of sorts. It is impossible to utter the word "is" without implying a judgment about Being. Derrida was saying, in effect: Always and ever, put such words "under erasure" (*sous rature*) because nothing is ever present as such. This is a loose translation, but looseness is the famous point of the concept *différance*. Everything we say and think is loose— open to suspicion. Even, and especially, speaking itself is at best loosely related to one's *vouloir-dire*—to whatever one "means to say," to meaning itself. When some one or some thing "is said to exist"—that is: is meant to be thought of as "present"—Derrida means for us to draw the implication that such ones or things are, in fact, never truly present at the moment of the saying. There is, in effect, no "being present."[2]

As shocking as it may be to some, Derrida's experiments with X's as a way of managing the uncertainty of Being in human affairs is actually a Nietzschean commitment to writing philosophy with an eye to sociology. The famous "*La différance*" essay could not have appeared at a more poignant historical moment, 1968. This text was a short version of his earlier criticism of Husserl's philosophy of the voice as present meaning, *Speech and Phenomena*

(1967). That in turn followed Derrida's two influential essays of 1966, "Structure, Sign and Play in the Discourse of the Human Sciences" and "Freud and the Scene of Writing."[3] It was not by accident that the latter two turned on the problem of the unconscious in social life. "Structure, Sign and Play" attacked the unifying ideals of modern culture, including the human sciences. This famous essay, said to be the beginning of deconstruction in America, displaced the modern world's cultural Center by drawing an objection to Lévi-Strauss's structural anthropology. Structuralism, said Derrida, reclined too easily upon the hidden potency of the linguistic sign in order to fulfill the analytic ambitions of modern thought by reuniting nature and culture. "Freud and the Scene of Writing," with its astonishing recovery of Freud's metaphor of the child's magic writing pad, accounted for the absence of the unconscious itself in its tenuous presentations in dreams. Psychoanalysis deferred the meanings uncovered by the anthropological signifier.[4] Still, in both—the absence of nature in culture and of the unconscious in conscious life—Derrida called attention to the slips and tricks whereby the modern West meant to organize the world in its presence. Across and between the lines of these writings is the visual darkness of the colonial world from which he came and of which he refuses to speak.[5] The decentering of Western thought is the deferred effect of the political economy of the global decentering wrought by the decolonizing movements that were at their most acute in 1968. Hence, the irony: everything said in the de-mode is still meant to be a construction.

In short, deconstruction is reconstruction with a difference. It is not an analytic method so much as an attitude. It is a rewriting of the history of thought—and, by implication, of history itself—by the trick of using the language of thought to turn thinking—and history—on their sides, if not on their ears. Since, and before, those crucial essays and books around 1968, everything Derrida himself has done has been a relentless rewriting of Western thought from within its language. This is deconstruction, a word that has entered popular culture to odd, disturbing effect. I once heard a television announcer of an American football game say, "Let me deconstruct the New York Jets defense for you." What he was in fact saying when he used the word deconstruction was, "Let me tell you the meaning of what just happened on the field." That's what American football announcers do, accompanied by video playbacks. Hence, he was actually offering not a deconstruction but a garden-variety reconstruction—a vain attempt to bring events back into the present. (Only those who know American football will know just how vain the offer.) Deconstruction would have been, "Let us figure out what did not go on on the field and never could have and how this absence—these events that were not present, and never could have been—are the reason everything that did go on on the field was as it was."[6] Deconstruction is an aggression against any form of historical thinking, including all of History's selfish ontologizings—of its pretenses to make meanings present in order to organize the world in which they transpire. In the long course of modern culture, there are many versions of this deception, but the ideals of History, and of the progressive Subject, are as good as any for it.

Deconstruction, one might say, allows the meanings that would otherwise be said to remain in their naturally loose state of deferral—of being always at a remove from any attempt to capture and organize them, of being never present. Deconstruction thus acknowledges the race of time. The time of modern culture is historical time in which everything depends on the possibility of running the past through the present in order to promise a "better" future that could ever "be." Modern time is, thus, time out of place. It refuses to account for the possibility that the present is nothing at all because all of its meanings are always somewhere else—waiting to said, heard, written, acted upon.

The present races so fast as to be virtually always somewhere else. The question that could, therefore, be asked is, What does the race of time have to do with the time of race?

There could be no better source for an answer to such a question than W. E. B. Du Bois. In the present, early millennium, Du Bois is being brought into the present with a vengeance. Yet, many of those who attempt to make him present might be looking in the wrong place.[7]

Souls of Black Folk is, unquestionably, a fine work of literature, as it is an excellent source of social theories of the double consciousness, of the talented tenth, of the Veil and the color line, and of race theory in general. As great as it may be, *Souls* is not Du Bois's most important work. That distinction must fall either to his earliest important book, *The Philadelphia Negro* (1899), or to the much later *Black Reconstruction* (1935). Where *Souls* inspires and suggests new ways of thinking, *Philadelphia Negro* works through the factual account of the turn of the century urban Negro. Yet, to the same degree that *Souls* was instantaneously famous, *Philadelphia Negro* was largely ignored (as it still is) by the sociologists for whom it stands, by more than a decade, as the first important example of urban ethnography in America. The trouble with great ethnographies is that it is difficult to go back to them when they describe neighborhoods in the distant past.

Black Reconstruction—a work that offers both the literary pleasures of *Souls* and the scholarly detail of *Philadelphia Negro*—may well be Du Bois' greatest book. *Black Reconstruction* thinks race through in more enduringly substantial ways than does the famous essay at the beginning of *Souls*, which is oddly indefinite on the nature and upbeat on the prospects of the doubly conscious American Negro. Plus which, *Black Reconstruction*'s evidence is global (hence, relatively timeless) where *Philadelphia Negro*'s is local (hence, considerably time-bound). Still, it is not *Black Reconstruction*'s special literary and empirical effects that recommend it to readers in a new century. That distinction resolves upon its service as a meditation on the off-center time of race—of which Du Bois's book is surely the first and most important. Ever so cautiously, one might even describe *Black Reconstruction* as an early work in the prehistory of deconstruction. Between Nietzsche's *Genealogy of Morals* (1887) and Derrida's *Edmund Husserl's Origins of Geometry* (1962) and *Speech and Phenomena* (1967), few works come more quickly mind for their reworking of the displacement of power upon so terrible an absence of human possibility. In any case, *Black Reconstruction* deserves very high regard because it, at least, approximates the work of sociological deconstruction that both Nietzsche and Derrida implied but never executed.[8] *Black Reconstruction* moves the critique of modernity's double-edged presentism beyond philosophy (where it is has been well-served) into the empirical deferrals of social history—which itself has been struggling since Henry Adams to understand its own confusion with the present.[9]

By whatever name, *Black Reconstruction* is a study of the race of time founded upon an investigation of the time of race. To understand the book is to expose one's sense of historical time to the very uncertainty it is meant to overcome. Where the time of modern Progress is meant to order, the time of Du Bois's thinking—and of his subject—in *Black Reconstruction* is the time of suspense, if not disorder.

From the first, one must wonder why this book, and why then? On the surface, the answer seems simple. The origins of the book may have been as early as 1929 when the *Encyclopedia Britannica* rejected Du Bois's invited essay on the American Negro. The encyclopedia editor recognized the excellence of the essay, but objected to one, seemingly temperate, statement of fact with respect to Reconstruction:

> White historians have ascribed the faults and failures of Reconstruction to Negro ignorance and corruption. But the Negro insists that it was Negro loyalty and the Negro vote alone that restored the South to the Union; established the new democracy, both for white and black, and instituted the public schools.[10]

The refusal by the world's most prestigious encyclopedia to print even so deliberate a remark reveals the extent to which racist dark thoughts pervade liberal culture.

But the motivation for *Black Reconstruction* may have been the publication, also in 1929, of an overtly racist interpretation of Reconstruction. *The Tragic Era*, by Claude G. Bowers, was the book that prompted Anna Julia Cooper to urge Du Bois to an answer.[11] Du Bois hardly needed urging. He had already, and some time before, staked out his claims against the prevailing (and white) scholarly and popular opinion that the failure of Reconstruction was due to the cultural and political insufficiencies of the freedman, not of the American system itself. As early as 1909, at the meetings of the American Historical Association, Du Bois had presented "Reconstruction and Its Benefits" before the establishment of American historians. His audience on that occasion included the leader of the one school of thought he and other reasonable scholars had most reason to fear.

William Archibald Dunning of Columbia University had not only published (in 1907) the most influential of liberal but still anti-Negro interpretations of Reconstruction (*Reconstruction, Political and Economic: 1865–1877*),
but he was the leader of a school of historians who advanced the same old white
Southern thesis—that it was the Negro who had failed Reconstruction, not the
other way around.[12] The position of the Dunning school was, in short, that the
white South was prepared, after the Civil War, to enter the work of rebuilding
the South and its union with the North, but that the freed Negro's lack of education and general unreadiness and unwillingness to assume worldly responsibilities caused its failure.[13] The line between the Columbia position and overt
racism was as fine as the analytic scruple that caused the *Encyclopedia Britannica*
editor to refuse Du Bois's 1929 essay. But it was visible enough.

In 1910, in Du Bois's published version of the AHA paper, he chose to
emphasize just exactly those qualities the establishment felt were lacking
among freed Negroes—thirst for learning, civic duty, political responsibility.[14]
Some (notably David Levering Lewis) see this article as the "germinal essay for
what would become *Black Reconstruction*."[15] Certainly, the 1910 paper is written in the prodigiously documented style of the 1935 book. But the earlier
paper lacked the theoretical lift of the later book. It was too much Du Bois, the
social scientist, responding to an opposing thesis. It lacked just exactly what
made the book so distinctive—scholarship turned to propagandizing ends.

Between 1910 and 1935 Du Bois had spent a full quarter-century as editor
of *The Crisis*, the foremost (if contested) organ of public communications for
the National Association for the Advancement of Colored People (the
NAACP). In 1934, he left the organization he had helped found in 1910. He
was fed up with those in the NAACP (and especially Walter F. White) who
sought to trim his sails as the de facto spokesman for the movement and the
Association. Though Du Bois had returned to Atlanta University in 1934,
which gave him to time to work on *Black Reconstruction*, it is hardly likely that
Du Bois would have cast overboard the sustained political work of his mature
life. In 1935 he was 68 years old. He was, no doubt, glad to return to his scientific work. But, the record of his life's work, before and after 1934, is clear. He
would permit no silencing of his voice on behalf of the American Negro—at
least not until he did so voluntarily by giving up, at the very end, on America
herself.

If there was an early outline for *Black Reconstruction* it was not the 1909–10
paper but a still earlier work—the 1901 *Atlantic Monthly* essay "The
Freedmen's Bureau" (which appeared as "Of the Dawn of Freedom," in *Souls* in
1903). A more beautifully composed and succinctly stated history of
Reconstruction there could hardly be. Yet, its high literary values make no
exception to his already-then theoretical conviction that the failure of
Reconstruction turned on a systematic failure of the nation to extend civil and
economic justice to the Negro.[16] This essay, written at the turn of the century
when Du Bois was barely thirty, lacked the bracing sense of economic and

political reality of *Black Reconstruction*, written during the Great Depression when he was late in his sixties. Still, its broad conviction that cultural or moral failure is always also a fault of the political economy is already evident (as it was, to be sure, in the 1909–10 response to Dunning).

Du Bois' 1935 book, thus, confounds attempts to understand Du Bois in his own time. There is no question that *Black Reconstruction* deserves its reputation as the earliest of his major works most obviously influenced by Marxism. Du Bois, like most others, changed his mind as time went by. Yet, his basic ideas were evident from the beginning. Those who doubt that *Souls* (1903) was already a political-economy of race in the making might submit their doubts to *Philadelphia Negro* (1899). It is hard to say when and where he began to think as he thought in *Black Reconstruction*. It is not difficult at all to conclude that this was his most mature work—the coming out of ideas that were long a-brewing, the coming together of his scientific and political work, the coming to fruition of what turned out to be his last major book written under the already attenuating sway of the nationalism central to the double consciousness of the *American* Negro.[17]

Du Bois was well aware of his place in history. He was, in this and other ways, self-conscious. Yet, he seldom stood on ceremony. He was more than ready to take himself out of a present that ill-served his own, sometimes out of place, sense of historical progress. This, precisely, is what he did in 1934 when he quit the NAACP after so many years. He quit on principle. But which principle and, again, why then? Some may be surprised to learn that the principle was whether or not there were situations in which the NAACP would tolerate racial segregation. Du Bois took the position that there were. Walter White, then in the early years of his own twenty-five years service as Executive Secretary to the NAACP, claimed that the organization never did and never could condone it. White, an intellectual in his own right,[18] should not have taken up the debate with Du Bois, who surely knew the facts better. But Du Bois did not enjoy White's support by the majority of NAACP's Board. As from the beginning of the organization, those of more traditional values wanted Du Bois to toe the organizational line, whatever it was. The dispute over segregation philosophy in 1934 was pretext for White's move against the editor of *The Crisis*, which led to Du Bois' resignation. Judging from his statements at the time, Du Bois was not fooled. Still, he joined the argument, if only to demonstrate his superior adherence to principle.

The Board's position was that Du Bois was wrong to condone segregation even for strategic reasons. At issue was his May 1934 editorial in *Crisis*, "Segregation," which called for real politics.[19] He began, "The thinking color people of the United States must stop being stampeded by the word segregation." In effect, Du Bois' argument was the one that would reappear in *Black Reconstruction*. The American Negro must not allow an overdetermined race consciousness to blind him to the class consciousness necessary for "his economic emancipation through voluntary determined cooperative effort"—

including, importantly, cooperative effort with sympathetic whites of the working class even when they demanded social segregation. This was 1934 (but think of what satisfaction the argument would have given Booker T. Washington, dead since 1915). White, representing the Board's position, claimed that Du Bois had contradicted the NAACP's official position. They demanded his compliance. The Board sought to vet all such statements by Du Bois before they were printed in *The Crisis*. You can imagine! They knew of course what he would say. They were forcing his hand. The dispute continued heatedly through the early summer until Du Bois insisted upon his resignation, effective July 1. The outcome was never in doubt. Still, he relished the debate. Du Bois's initial reply came early that year, January 17, 1934.[20] He sneered that White hardly knew what he was talking about. The Board had in fact "advocated and strongly advocated a segregated Negro officer's camp after we found that we were not allowed to enter the regular officer's camp during the war." The subtext of the sneer must have been that during the war White was a young, recent graduate of Atlanta University where Du Bois had taught before joining the NAACP. (In later retorts, Du Bois gave other, later examples.) The January letter challenges White and the Board to prove him wrong. But the defiance is mostly part of the game. Du Bois knows he is right. He knows what moves are being made against him. He is ready for the fight; even more, he is clear on the principle.

Du Bois concludes the January 17th letter with a telling distinction of principle, which may have everything to do with different times along which he and the organization he helped found were traveling. Just after issuing the challenge that White prove him wrong (and knowing that it cannot be done), Du Bois addresses the issue of principle:

> Of course in my editorial and in your letter, it is manifest that we are not both speaking always of the same thing. I am using segregation in the broad sense of separate racial effort caused by outer social repulsions, whether those repulsions are a matter of law or custom or mere desire. You are using the word segregation simply as applying to compulsory separations.

Though it would seem to be at worst a fine theoretical distinction, or at best a choice of tactics (as it was), Du Bois's remark is also calling attention to a difference in the racial times that in 1934 segregated him from the organization to which he had devoted so much. In his final letter of resignation (June 26, 1934), he describes those differences—and they have everything to do with economic crisis then at hand:

> I firmly believe that the National Association for the Advancement of Colored People faces the most grueling of tests which come to an old organization: founded in a day when a negative program of protest was imperative and effective; it succeeded so well that the program seemed perfect and unlimited. Suddenly, by World War and chaos, we are called to formulate a positive program of construction and inspiration. We have been thus far unable to comply.

> Today this organization, which has been great and effective for nearly a quarter of a century, finds itself in a time of crisis and change, without a program, without effective organization, without executive officers who have either the ability or disposition to guide [it] in the right direction.
>
> These are harsh and arresting charges. I make them deliberately, and after long thought, earnest effort, and with infinite writhing of the spirit. To the very best of my ability, and every ounce of my strength, I have since the beginning of the Great Depression, tried to work inside the organization for its realignment and readjustment to new duties. I have been almost completely unsuccessful.

Du Bois means to say that his opponents in the NAACP are living in another time—and that the time the American Negro must live is the time of the Great Depression in which positive programs of economic development must come first, before all else—even before stands against segregation that could put Negroes out of work, income, or housing.[21] The new time required a political economy of racial history—not a theory so much as a practice and a program.

What was the time of *Black Reconstruction*? Was it the biographical time of its author who had come to the end of the line with NAACP integrationism? Or, more broadly, was it the time of the history of the American Negro who, having moved from country to city, and served in the Great War, then faced his own choice between racial and economic goals? Or, more broadly still, was it the global time of economic change and the political adjustments required by the rise of industrial capitalism?

In 1931 Du Bois received the first of the small grants that supported his research for *Black Reconstruction*. This was in the second year of the Great Depression. In 1932 he was at work on the book. His research began. This was the worst year of the Depression.[22] In the United States eleven million were unemployed—nearly twenty percent of the work force. Industrial production was half of what it had been in 1929. National income fell by thirty-eight percent in the same three years. The economic crisis was global. Shipbuilding, coal production, steel manufacture declined sickeningly. Farm prices collapsed. Industrial and farm workers alike were out of work, and income. Among industrial powers, the United States and Germany were the hardest hit. In 1933, Franklin D. Roosevelt became president of the United States, just weeks after Adolf Hitler became chancellor of the German Republic. The die was cast. A second world war would follow upon the economic crisis which in turn followed, in part, the economic and political uncertainties unresolved by the Great War. In 1934 Du Bois broke with the NAACP. He was in Atlanta, working primarily on the book. By the time of its publication in 1935, nothing anyone did or thought, anywhere, was done out of the time of the Great Depression. The Twenties were long gone. No more parties—not at Gatsby's at West Egg, nor at the Redfields' in Harlem.[23]

Still, why a book on Reconstruction in the American South, a story which had come to an end six decades before, in 1877, when Du Bois was still a schoolboy in Massachusetts? Why at such a remove in time did Du Bois turn his attention to what became, by any measure, the most sustained, and demanding, scholarly work of his life[24]—but on a topic seemingly so out of time with the Great Depression that had crystallized his stern coming to odds with official NAACP principles?

The answer is clearer than meets the eye. Anyone thinking deeply about Black America during the Great Depression could hardly not have been led back, sooner or later, to the Long Depression that began in 1873. In Du Bois's case, it was sooner—and for good reason. The Long Depression began with the panic of 1873 and continued episodically for a quarter century until the recovery of 1896 that lent so much hope to the turn of the century.

For whites, the Long Depression meant, in E. J. Hobsbawm's phrase, the bust of the boom that had driven the Age of Capital, the end of the longest period of economic expansion in the early history of industrial capitalism.[25] Between the run on the banks in 1873 and 1878 when ten thousand business failed, half the nation's iron producers also failed, as did half of its railroads, leading in turn to the collapse of industries and business that had risen with these heavy industrial enterprises.[26] It meant also an interruption of the migration of white labor from Europe that would not recover until the 1880s. Everyone was caught up in the crisis. But blacks suffered differently.

For blacks freed after Emancipation in 1863, the Long Depression meant the end of Reconstruction. Though the end did not come until the compromise of 1877, it was foretold by the collapse of the Freedmen's Savings and Trust in 1874, brought on by the panic of the previous year. The ultimate collapse of Reconstruction as an effort to support the economic, political, and educational development of freed blacks came as a direct political result of the economic crisis. Though the Republicans had wavered in their support of Reconstruction since Lincoln's assassination in 1865, they remained the party most friendly to Southern blacks. But the economic crisis diverted the attentions of the Northern whites, and led to the rise of the Southern Democrats. By a quirk of American electoral laws, in 1877 a Republican, Rutherford B. Hayes, eventually won the presidency after losing the popular vote. This famous compromise was the exchange of votes in the U.S. Congress required for certification of Hayes as president for the abandonment of Reconstruction in key Southern states. At that point, Reconstruction came to an end, to be replaced by the restoration of white dominance throughout the South.

The Civil War and Reconstruction have been called, by some, the Second American Revolution. Du Bois called Reconstruction the Second Civil War. North and South, blacks and whites, suffered through the Long Depression—but the crisis and its consequences returned them to their separate historical times. Freed men and women in the South were thrown back to feudal conditions made more severe by the crippling effects of war upon an agrarian system that had lost its most valuable commodity—enslaved labor. The white South was itself divided between the poor whites forced to compete with freedmen in an unstable labor market, and the propertied class that rose from the ashes to reassert its domination. Hence the arrangement—described first by Du Bois, and recently by David Roediger—of the racial wage. Poor whites were granted the racial privilege of their whiteness in compensation for their misery in the economic system.[27] The Reconstruction, so-called, of the American republic, and of its war-ravaged South always meant something different to whites than to blacks. With the collapse of Reconstruction as a national goal, the principals in the Southern drama were returned, if not to the exact structural positions that prevailed before the War, at least to their respective historical times. It would be another full century until late in the 1970s before the American South would significantly shed the vestiges of its feudal past. For the long duration of that century, the South remained more or less bound to the feudal conditions from which the planters profited, the white worker survived with the modest privilege of his racial status, and the black worker suffered unspeakable human and economic misery.

Here was the reason necessary and sufficient to *Black Reconstruction*. The Long Depression of 1873 darkened the prospects of the first and second generation of freedpeople in the United States, just as the Great Depression of 1929 crushed the hopes of the third and fourth generations.[28] For Du Bois, the social historian of the American Negro, the reversion of times was utterly apparent—1929 brought back 1873, which in turn brought forward the burdens of the feudal past. For him it must also have brought up the bond in memory between his childhood among the first and second generations of post-Emancipation blacks and his "new duties" (as he put it in the 1934 letter of resignation) to the third and fourth generations. For a man of his political and scientific sensibilities, writing in 1934, there could have been no more obvious way to reason.

Du Bois was, in effect, writing out of his time back into the displaced time of the Reconstruction in American history that was, for the American Negro, a deferral of black hopes that turned out to be a deferral of national hopes, even global ones. No event in American history, and few in global history, more starkly uncovered the dark thoughts veiled by the bright promises of modernity, of capitalism, and of democracy. Slavery is evil. Reversion to its time, however displaced, is the darkest thought imaginable. By 1934, the darkness loomed again—a darkness familiar to blacks, surprising but still familiar to poor whites, and terrifying to white propertied class. And this, precisely, is the point Du Bois makes at the beginning of *Black Reconstruction*.

> Here is the real modern labor problem. Here is the kernel of the problem of Religion and Democracy, of Humanity. Words and futile gestures avail nothing. Out of the exploitation of the dark proletariat comes the Surplus Value filched from human beasts which, cultured lands, the Machine and harnessed Power veil and conceal. The emancipation of man is the emancipation of labor and the emancipation of labor is the freeing of that majority of workers who are yellow, brown and black.[29]

The labor problem is inseparably a racial problem—and both are a global problem.

The disjointed times of colored peoples and white ones always had curved uncertainly toward each other—coming together in times of economic crisis, coming apart in better times. The crisis of the Great Depression was world-wide. Du Bois meant to address it by reverting to the crisis of the Long Depression of the previous century where the times, once again, stood still, reverted, and took up their segregated paths. *Black Reconstruction* both was and was not a book on a specific period in American history. It was every bit as much a working out of the loose uncertainties of modernity. Behind the page upon page of thick description in the book, this principle breathes life into the sad truth of historical fact.

Black Reconstruction is the story of three characters of the Old South. They can neither abide nor escape each other. In the end, they survive—each broken or otherwise cut off from his desires. Evil invites sympathy. Good stirs the higher spirits. None, however, can outrun his times. The tale cuts quickly to its tragic chase. No elaborate prologue or introduction. It begins with the story's lead character, the Black worker who, though local to the American South, stands at the heart of world civilization. "Easily the most dramatic episode in American history was the sudden move to free four million black slaves in an effort to stop a great civil war, to end forty years of bitter controversy, and to appease the moral sense of civilization"[30] (3). The slave is introduced with dignity for what he was, a worker. Du Bois does not waste words on sentiment for the victim. The black worker is the soul of the South, the energy of progress, and the soul of civilization. Du Bois does not waver on this. It is his answer to Bowers and the Dunning School, to all of ignorant hostility. But he holds back his theory across some seven hundred pages until the final chapter, an epilogue on "The Propaganda of History" (711–29). The writer keeps to the story.

The second most sympathetic character is introduced next (chapter 2). The White Worker is in the middle. He is offered the privilege of racial status which proves, in the end, utterly devoid of fungibility. Against the greed of the Southern aristocrats, the planters who eventually restore themselves to power, white power runs downward only, against the black worker. The white worker has little but his hatred to soften the economic deprivations.

Were this a local story of one nation's backward region, the third actor (chapter 3) would be evil incarnate—the Simon Legree of the tale. But the time of this story is closer to Faulkner than to Stowe. The planter seeks to restore his position lost in the war. But "with the Civil War, the planters died as class" (54). Still the aristocracy returned to political, if not economic, power after the Northern armies and Freedmen's Bureau left the south. Then they engaged their sordid compromise with the white worker to use race hatred and violence to gain the upper hand. "It is this that explains so many characteristics of the post-war South: its lynching and mob law, its murders and cruelty, its insensibility to the finer things of civilization" (54).

The book's first three chapters are detailed play notes, describing the tale's dramatic characters—of which the black worker is written into the role of the Greek figure of Nemesis (237). Then the tale begins in earnest with the Civil War. One of the book's finer literary qualities is that, just as it holds back on heavy-handed theory, it resists phony sentiment. This quality may be one of the reasons *Black Reconstruction* has not been read, as it should be. It is designed to stir without pandering but not to pander to the easy feeling or thought. Thus, neither the North, nor Father Abraham, is portrayed as the saving hero. This is plain in the book's controversial fourth chapter, "The General Strike." Du Bois uses the language of labor, which encourages the facile idea that the book is an exercise in Marxist theory. It is anything but that, even in this chapter. The general strike is the slow dawning realization by both the Southern aristocrats and the Northerners, including Lincoln, that neither understood the black worker. During the War, the Southerners counted on him not to rebel. The Northerners, not withstanding their many liberal Abolitionists, thought little of him, very often sharing the white South's loathing without any direct knowledge of the Negro's labor power. He was to them "a curiosity, a subhuman minstrel" (56). This is one of the book's minor, but powerful, themes. Even Abraham Lincoln had to be drawn toward the Emancipation Prolamation. It is of course well known that Lincoln resisted the move as long as he could. But Du Bois makes him out to be more passive and dawdling than even his heroic image allows. When it came to the black worker, the majority of the leaders of the North were in their way as naïve as the Southern planters.

> When Northern armies entered the South they became armies of emancipation. It was the last thing they planned to be. The North did not propose to attack property. It did not propose to free slaves. This was to be a white man's war to preserve the Union, and the Union must be preserved. (55)

They had to face reality, and the reality was the 4,000,000 slaves and 250,000 free blacks in the South. They were a formidable force. And they would, and did, rebel once war began.

Not only did Lincoln himself come to realize that he could not win the war without Negro troops, but Northerners generally came to realize what the South had always known. The black worker, especially in such numbers, was "a valuable asset" (66) and the "key" to the war (63). Thus the North and Lincoln had little choice. Whatever humanity they possessed, it was the general strike, as Du Bois chose to call it, of the black worker that was basic. When the war began, the plantation system stalled. Black workers readily gave their labor power to the North, even before the Emancipation Proclamation on January 1, 1863. Not only that, the North came to realize that its lofty ideal of preserving the Union meant nothing before the disgust of Europeans for American slavery. Europe was more than ready (in Great Britain even eager)[31] to recognize the Confederacy as a sovereign nation, which would have reopened its ports to international trade and provided the Southern armies with an industrial life-line. Only Emancipation could forestall a diplomatic turn that might have cost the war. Du Bois, trained in Berlin and at Harvard as an economic historian, was nothing if not a political realist—and a very sober one at that. But not so sober as to leave his story's dramatic tension unrealized.

The story itself comes to an early climax in the four chapters following chapter 4 on the general strike. At first, these chapters (5 through 8) seem strangely out of kilter. They are, it turns out, central to the unfolding drama of Reconstruction. "The Coming of the Lord" (chapter 5) is not what it would seem. It does indeed play on the popular sentiment of Abe Lincoln as Father Abraham, the sacred force of Emancipation. But it plays with a bare, almost sar-castic, truth. Though Lincoln spoke principally of saving the Union, he admit-ted four months before he acted, that Emancipation "would help in Europe," that "slavery was the root of the rebellion," and that loss of black labor would "weaken" the South (85). But Father Abraham had no particular faith in blacks, fearing that "if we were to arm them within a few weeks the arms would be in the hands of the rebels."[32] Though he would soften over the fewer than three years that remained of his life, Lincoln's confidence in the black worker's polit-ical capabilities, as distinct from his labor power, was virtually nil. As late as early April 1865, just before he was shot, Lincoln said: "I can hardly believe that the North and South can live in peace unless we get rid of the Negroes" (149). "The Coming of the Lord" tells the truth about Lincoln in order, it seems, to suit the terms of Du Bois's now well-described drama. The are no saviors in the story, yet there is salvation. Emancipation is a miracle of God.

> To the four million black folk emancipated by the civil war, God was real. They knew him. They had met Him personally in many a wild orgy of religious frenzy, or in the black stillness of night. His plan for them was clear; they were to suffer and be degraded, and then afterwards by Divine edict, raised to manhood and power; and so on January 1, 1863, He made them free. (124)

Here Du Bois suspends, for a moment, his sometimes harsh attitude toward Negro religion in order to affirm the larger ideal. He grants the ordinary folk their due, and even tips his hat, but with a sneer (125), to Father Abraham.

The final few pages of "The Coming of the Lord" achieve the same high lyrical quality of the best passages in Souls.[33] Du Bois in a sense gives himself over, not so much to crude feeling, as to the higher truth of Emancipation as, at long last, a justification for democracy. "And yet emancipation came not just to black folk in 1863; to white Americans came slowly a new vision and new uplift, a sudden freeing of hateful mental shadows" (124).

Though Du Bois's story turns on historical figures—the black and white workers, the planters, Father Abraham—no individual character is given the stage, not even Lincoln. Each plays within limitations of character and circum-stance. The alert reader begins to sense that Du Bois' retort to Bowers and Dunning, ever understated, rests on the refusal to overstate any one historical actor in the drama. He refuses to glorify either the black worker or the good Northerner against the evil Southern white. All of Du Bois's characters are—in the phrase of Max Weber, of whom he first learned in the Berlin years—ideal types; that is, historical individuals who are not really individuals. *Black Reconstruction*, as I say, is not a book about Reconstruction, but about the perverse nature of historical time and its effects on the democratic ideal and the future of civilization.

Du Bois's restraint—his refusal to vilify—is most striking in the book's longest chapter (and longest by far), "Transubstantiation of a Poor White" (chapter 8). The apparent subject of this chapter, like the apparent subject of "The Coming of the Lord," is an individual. Andrew Johnson, who assumed the presidency upon Lincoln's assassination, plays the historical individual in this chapter as Lincoln had in the earlier one. Du Bois understands Johnson, and to some extent sympathizes with him. Andrew Johnson had been born to poverty. He earned a modest living as tailor. By hard work, he rose from local political local office in Tennessee, to the United States Senate, to the nation's penultimate office. Lincoln had selected Johnson as his running mate in the 1864 election for some of the same reasons John F. Kennedy selected Lyndon Johnson nearly a century later, in 1960. Though from Tennessee, Andrew Johnson's hatred of the Southern aristocrats was strong among the reasons he opposed the Confederacy. As a poor white, he had feared Negroes. Still, Lincoln respected Johnson's service on behalf of the Union and saw his politi-cal value in the election, and beyond the War when his administration would have to deal with the South.

Thus on April 15, 1865 the poor white workingman who hated the planters more even than he feared the black worker became President of the United States. Andrew Johnson came to power by the accident of war politics. He was driven by forces he could not control. Du Bois means to say that the white worker, though no hero, was powerless—even in the deflated prestige derived from race hatred. The white worker, typified by Johnson, was more the pawn than the black worker who had moral right on his side. And he was less free of blame than the white planter who after the war did his evil in a vain attempt to restore a once glorious way of life—the long deferred end of which was already sealed by defeat at the hands of Northern industrial power. The feudal way, with all of its nasty entanglements and impossible dreams, was, thus, at the heart of Reconstruction every bit as much as it had been the reason for the War itself.

"The Transubstantiation of a Poor White" sets the earlier "The Coming of the Lord" chapter in the analogue of Johnson to Lincoln. For Du Bois, Lincoln's virtues come clearer by the contrast to Johnson. "Lincoln came to know Negroes personally. He came to recognize their manhood. He praised them generously as soldiers, and suggested that they be admitted to the ballot. Johnson, on the contrary, could never regard Negroes as men" (248).

Thus it happened that the Reconstruction of the feudal South, and of the Negro freedpeople to full union, fell to a man of the weakest possible position in the drama. Johnson's hatred of the white aristocrats led to his position of power. His ignorance of the black worker led to his failure to use it well. Johnson's impeachment in 1868, his final year in office, was the result of a belligerence bred of these impossibilities. He tried to evade the requirements of constitutional amendments, of congressional legislation, of the will of the majority. The bill of impeachment came upon his defiance of the Congress's Reconstruction Acts of 1867. The Congress had ordered a reorganization of the military administration of Reconstruction in the South that expressly allowed for voting rights for all adult males. Johnson could not abide the Negro vote. He responded by removing military officers sympathetic to the congressional order, replacing them with those who would frustrate Reconstruction. He was, therefore, ruined by a well-structured incapacity to embrace the Negro's full freedom. Hence, the ironic fate of the poor white man who hated the planter aristocracy.

> The transubstantiation of Andrew Johnson was complete. He had begun as the champion of the poor laborer, demanding that the land monopoly of the Southern oligarchy be broken up, so as to give access to the soil, South and West, to the free laborer. He had demanded the punishment of those Southerners who by slavery and war had made such an economic program impossible. Suddenly thrust into the Presidency, he had retreated from this attitude. He had not only given up extravagant ideas of punishment, but he dropped his demand for dividing up the plantations when he realized that Negroes would largely be beneficiaries. Because he could not conceive of Negroes as men, he refused to advocate universal democracy, of which, in his young manhood, he had been the fiercest advocate, and made strong alliance with whose who would restore slavery under another name. (322)

But the story of this poor white man—this emblem of a drama spun out of control—plays out on a much larger and global stage. And this is where the time of Reconstruction loops back to the time of the Great Depression to justify its own displacement.

Black Reconstruction is a book of near perfect narrative balance set amid such a wealth of facts and sources that its surface order tends to bury the story. After telling of the moral limitations upon the poor white man, the book comes to the summary point in "The Price of Disaster" (chapter 9). Reconstruction was doomed by forces superior to its better intentions. The white worker, powerless before these forces, nonetheless was the one who promoted, almost unwittingly, Reconstruction's failure and the second civil war of racial-based hatred that ensued. Again, the action is driven, not directed. After the War the planter needed the black worker more desperately than before. The freed people needed the work, land, and opportunity that, even under the Northern military administrators, were still mostly in the hands of the planters. This "rekindled" the "old enmity and jealously of the poor whites against any combination of the white employer and the black laborer which would again exclude the poor white." (351) The planter, caught by his need of labor, nonetheless had to withhold "sympathy and cooperation with the black laborer." (351) The War had weakened both his social and his economic position, forcing him back into the unholy alliance with the white worker. Thus the black worker, even while he had the support of the Freedman's Bureau and the North, was left in the Southern lurch—his labor bound over in due course to a new system of economic slavery.

Here is where the plot thickens. Not even the poor white who applies the violence on behalf of the new masters of economic oppression in the South acts on his own. Andrew Johnson was thus the perfect emblem of the poor whites from whom he sprang, on whom he turned. He was the dark spot—the abiding lack—at the core of the American system:

> Johnson thus illustrated the Blindspot of American political and social development and made logical argument almost impossible. The only power to curtail the rising empire of finance in the United States was industrial democracy—votes and intelligence in the hands of the laboring class, black and white, North and South. (377)

Here, then, is the temporal shifter that structures and unsettles *Black Reconstruction*. The industrial worker who was most threatened by the Great Depression was projected back into the Long Depression as the hope for American democracy—as the unifier of the races, of the nation, of the classes.

An earlier chapter—one of two Du Bois lodged disconcertingly between "The Coming of the Lord" (chapter 5) and "The Transubstantiation of a Poor White" (chapter 8)—begins with a touching allusion to the social affinities that linked poor laborers of both races and regions:

> A printer and a carpenter, a rail-splitter, and a tailor—Garrison, Christ, Lincoln and Johnson, were the tools of the greatest moral awakening America ever knew, chosen to challenge capital invested in the bodies of men and annul the private profit of slavery. (182)

Lincoln *and* Johnson—and both in the company of Christ and the radical abolitionist, William Lloyd Garrison. The moral deferrals of Lincoln, and the deficits of Johnson, are washed away before the moral awakening of industrial democracy, of the working people. The passage begins "Looking Forward," the chapter that comes just before the long agony of the poor white man, and stands with another that reverses its orientation in time.

Is it by some coincidence of language that Du Bois chose to give these two intervening chapters matched but reversed titles referring to Reconstruction as a great temporal divide?—"Looking Backward" (chapter 6) and "Looking Forward" (chapter 7)? The question occurs upon the interruption of the time of the story. Du Bois's story unfolds easily up to the point of these two chapters: the black worker (chapter 1), the white worker (chapter 2), the planter (chapter 3);—the black worker strikes, his labor power is recognized as key to the War (chapter 4);—the coming of the Lord: the War ends; the black worker is freed (chapter 5). Then, one would expect either "Looking Forward" (the story of progress, perhaps) or "The Transubstantiation of the Poor Man" (the story of the poor white who yields to the planter aristocrat) to follow. Neither does. There is a pause—or, again, a deferral. On what level Du Bois understood what he was doing here probably will never be known. What is known is that he always thought against expectations. He had begun the work on this book at odds with the times of the NAACP, as he had long been at variance with the varieties of white progress. He understood very well the time of the American Negro in which the Civil War, even Emancipation, was anything but a second American Revolution—and he understood it particularly well writing in the depths of the Great Depression.

He had framed this story as the story of labor power, black and white, but not because of some sudden discovery of Marxist theory. Du Bois was a superior and subtle thinker. But his theory usually served his politics. A political view of history required that the story tell the facts, indeed; but it must also tell the truth of history. That truth of Black Reconstruction in the United States in the 1860s was bitter. No matter how wonderful the Lord who comes to set you free, freedom is always deferred for those who seek it the most. What Du Bois understood is precisely what the white historians of his day, and a good number in ours as well, could never understand. He knew what no one who had not lived the time of those who seek emancipation could fully know.

A story told by one engaged with the time of the world's colored people, and told from the time of the Great Depression, is a story of the failures of the time of liberal progress and its promises. The good liberal, in the broad Euro-American sense of liberal, looks about at History for its next good step. Those who for right reason are suspicious of promises, and cautious about Progress, look at history differently. They would never, figuratively or literally, capitalize its H. Du Bois knew this time and lived it. Hence the interruption of the developing line of *Black Reconstruction*, which turns out to be not a mistake in literary judgment, any more that it is a confusion of historical fact. Du Bois understood that the story of *Black Reconstruction* was the story of emancipation and progress to be sure. He was no fool. But, even deeper, it was the story of a time out of place. It was the story of progress deferred to such an extent that the concept progress, if used at all, had to be used with caution. One might even say that the odd, interrupting chapter, "Looking Backward," is the erasure put upon liberal ideals of historical progress.

"Looking Backward" is the other side of the emancipation epiphany. The coming of freedom for the black worker spelled trouble. "The very joy in the shout of emancipated Negroes was a threat" (132). In the face of a labor system in disarray in 1865 (134), the "planters, having lost the war for slavery, sought to begin again where they left off in 1860, merely substituting for the individual ownership of slaves, a new state of serfdom of black folks." (128) This may not surprise. But the story of the "Lord" incarnate, Abraham Lincoln, might. The chapter is also about the North's, and Lincoln's, deferral of responsibility in the early years of Reconstruction (which began not with the end of War but as early as 1861 with the Port Royal experiment and in 1862 in Louisiana).[34] Lincoln's first Reconstruction plan (late 1863) was exceptionally lenient (perhaps because victory was far from assured). He required the expressed loyalty of a mere ten percent of voters for readmission to the Union. And, even as time went by, he was unwilling to impose the franchise for blacks. In his letter congratulating the first appointed governor of freed Louisiana (March 13, 1864), Lincoln said:

> Now that you are about to have a convention, which, among other things, will probably define the elective franchise, I barely suggest, for your private consideration, whether some of the colored people may not be let in, as, for instance, the very intelligent, and especially whose who have fought gallantly in our ranks. (157)

"Barely suggest," indeed. Lincoln bore impossible burdens as leader of a nation at war with itself. In so many things, including the Emancipation Proclamation, his judgment was sure and pure. But as regards the Negro he was a white man. His bare suggestion in 1864 for the enfranchisement of blacks meant, in effect, that it would be another full century before the Civil Rights Act of 1964 and the Voting Rights Act of 1965 would begin to secure that franchise. Even when the Congress sought to correct him, Lincoln deferred—notably in his pocket veto of the 1864 Wade-Davis Bill, which would have greatly strengthened the rights of Negroes and the requirements for readmission to the Union. It was not that Abraham Lincoln was a racist of any particular kind, but that he could not find the way to full, unqualified social justice. Lincoln's generosity of spirit worked with his white caution to play into the hands of the planters.

In effect, Lincoln reverted to the vexed uncertainty of Washington and Jefferson (131–132), Southern planters among the founding fathers. "Looking Backward" tells the story of the restoration of planters to power, led not by the vexed but by the crass. Hence the rise of violence, the Black Codes, the Ku Klux Klan, Jim Crow and all the rest that arose from hatred bred of fear born of economic greed:

> The white planter endeavored to keep the Negro at work for his profit on terms that amounted to slavery and which were hardly distinguishable from it. This was the plain voice of the slave codes. On the other hand, the only conceivable ambition of a poor white was to become a planter. Meantime the poor white did not want the Negro put to profitable work. He wanted the Negro beneath the feet of the white worker. (130–31)

In the time of white history, Reconstruction was an interregnum of rule by ignorant, undisciplined blacks who destroyed their own chances. This was the view Du Bois was countering. But he countered it not so much by the sort of direct challenge he had put to Walter White in 1934 but by telling the story as it was. That story was not one of an interregnum so much as of a continuation of civil war in the South that began upon the deferrals of the good North and began almost as soon as the first had ended. In the story he is telling, the black worker must face continued abuse at the hands of the white worker and the planter who, in the short run of the next full century, won out over the confused generosities of even the better white folk of the North.

The time of Reconstruction was not forward, but backward. Even so, Du Bois was not without hope, as he wrote in the depths of the Great Depression, looking back. "Looking Forward" (chapter 7) is the part of the story that comes visible only by looking backward from the time of Great Depression when the crisis of labor was more at the heart of world democracy than at any time before, or since. The difference in the end between Lincoln and the planters—even Washington and Jefferson—was that he was not a planter. Hence, "Looking Forward" begins with line linking Lincoln with Christ, and Garrison, and even Johnson (182). These were all working men. Du Bois surely understood that the white worker, even the white worker of the industrial North, saw the time of progress differently from the black worker. In many ways that is his point. Johnson, the white worker who became the lackey of the planters he hated, was different, but not utterly different, from Lincoln, the white worker become moral leader who could not put an end to planter greed. Du Bois did not forgive them, but he understood them sympathetically. And because he did, he was able even when writing backward to the failures of Reconstruction to draw from its story what threads of hope there were. What is so astonishing about Du Bois, the often arrogant and ultimately disdainful critic of American ways, is that had held out such determined hope, even as the innocence of the time of *Souls* gave way to the realities of the time of the 1930s, and after.

"Looking Forward," like "Looking Backward," is written in black time. Just as the "backward" was the constant time of violence and slavery, the "forward" time was not the defeat of progress. Black time is the reverse of white time. What progress there was—and there was progress—was displaced not upon near promise but upon things to come that were already growing. And this is where Du Bois's book comes full bloom as a story in global history.

The 1860s were the high water mark of early industrial capitalism. In the United States, as in Europe, the capital benefits of the world colonial system were sunk deep into heavy industry. Coal, steel, and railroads were the foundations of the factory system of which Marx wrote in *Capital*, the first edition of which appeared in 1867 just as the American Reconstruction was beginning its downward slide into economic greed. Coal, steel, and the railroads were also precisely those industries that, along with the banks and small business, had begun their sickening long decline in 1873. Still, Du Bois understood that the future of the black and white worker lay with industrial democracy—as he was to put it later in his final word on Johnson and the Blindspot in America: "The only power to curtail the rising empire of finance in the United States was industrial democracy-votes and intelligence in the hands of the laboring class, black and white, North and South" (377).

So it is that "Looking Forward" is the chapter that unites the underlying themes of Du Bois's story. *Black Reconstruction* is told from 1934 back to 1873; hence, from the time of full-blown industrial crisis back to the first great crisis of industrial capitalism. Another reason one might even dare to think of Du Bois as Derridian before the fact is that he realized that industrial democracy had no precise origin. He realized that its beginnings in the 1860s were really a play upon the structuring work of the nearly four centuries of world building of the European Diaspora and its foundational colonial system. And he realized that this system, in turn, was a displacement of the West's dark pretenses of progress out of the primitive and colored past. How could he not have? But Du Bois also understood, most clearly in *Black Reconstruction*, that this color line was ever and always a long attenuated line through the laboring class as between the labor class and the propertied. The racial wage that bought off the white worker was not just another exchange *within* the capitalist system of surplus values. It was *the* exchange upon which everything else depended.

Put starkly, for Du Bois the race of progressive time was the time of race. There was, in his mind, no being-present when it comes to a system based on capital and exploitation. But there was exploitation—whether that of capital applied directly to human laborers in the feudal slave system, or the more analytic capital affixed to abstract human labor power in the factory system. Du Bois used Marx's ideas to be sure, as in *Souls* he used William James, perhaps, to reinvent the double consciousness. But he always *used* the thoughts of others to his own unique—arrogant, if you prefer—intellectual and political purposes. *Black Reconstruction* may be Marxist, in the sense that anyone writing in the 1930s with a genuine interest in industrial democracy would have written with Marx in mind. But Du Bois's book is not Marxism. Marx framed the continuities between the modes of production along the historical line of ownership of production's means. Hence, the transubstantiation of the feudal serf, or slave, was for Marx a change in the structure of ownership, from which came the transformation in the mode of production. Ownership, however, even when Marx discussed it in the early manuscripts like *German Ideology* and those of 1844, is an analytic concept borrowed from the political economists, from the ideology of modern, liberal thought. Du Bois borrows too, and surely his borrowing includes from Marx among other liberals; but Du Bois comes to very different conclusions, conclusions that in their way are those for which Marx was striving but never quite achieved.

Du Bois made no effort to iron out the history of labor's exploitation onto the flat plane of purposive history. He was the historian who disavowed

History. The path between the backward and forward of the story in *Black Reconstruction* was not of a common, or even parallel, relation of ownership to labor. It was that, true; but more. The path was rather that through the worker himself—the black and white workers, upon whose backs *both* the system of feudal agriculture and modern industry depended. Marx valued the worker, for whom everything that matters mattered. But Marx's worker was, from the first of his explicit writings on the elementary labor process, never truly in history. His disavowal of the early modern method of projecting history back to an origin prior to history was more a rhetorical move than an accomplishment. For Marx, History was the history of the fall of free labor before the varieties of ownership. For which the proof was in the dream of the classless society as the redemption of History.

Du Bois thought about History and history in very different terms. He dreamt of no final utopia. He never gave the least thought to History with an Origin in Paradise. For Du Bois there was no History. Only histories—narrative accounts of hopes wrought against the record of oppression of the worker. Hope was founded, therefore, on the prospects of industrial democracy. In 1934, near the worst of the Great Depression, he could not have held this hope too firmly. But he held it—and not as matter of principle (his principles led to action)—but as a matter of hard-won experience with the reality of work that was always racial. Marx, we might say, never more fully revealed his debt to the very liberal culture he claimed to abjure than in his famous inability to see the darkness of labor. Both the black and the white worker were bound in the subaltern system that industrial capitalism had, in the 1860s, perfected to its own ends. Neither truly saw the vision of paradise regained, because both in their segregated ways understood that the working class will forever be pushed, to the extent workers permit, back into the darkness. Liberal History claims there is only progressively more light. Du Bois's history, with its tenacious readiness to see the reversals—the forwards and backwards—of historical time, was always a story of the play of darkness upon the light.

This is the story of *Black Reconstruction*—clear and compelling; yet remarkably ignored save by specialists in the field of American history. When a great book is so avidly not read by those who need it most, this must be because it tells a truth they do not want to hear, least of all understand. This was the kind of truth Du Bois told near the end of his story (but just one-third through the book itself) when he wrote "Looking Forward." The forward of the new class of working men, white and black, was the forward of the struggle that was so salient in the 1930s, but already dawning as the Civil War ended—and as the Long Depression put a global pinch in industrial capitalism itself. It was the struggle between the possible decency of industrial democracy and the "American Assumption," which was the assumption of industrial capitalism that "wealth is mainly the result of its owner's effort and that any average worker can by thrift become a capitalist" (183).

   The three tragic characters of Reconstruction were trapped in futility of massive proportions. The Civil War, though a dramatic event in the American republic, was ultimately but a salient variation on a global struggle. Though in the 1860s the European Diaspora would hold its exploitative grip on the colored people of its colonies from whom it stole its resources and labor power, by the time of the 1930s that grip would begin to slip—in part because of the Great War, in part because of economic distractions, and in part because of the uncertain rise of labor as a fellow sufferer in what progress there was to be had.[35] Still, Du Bois realized that the key to what reconstruction there might have been was the same as the key to the Civil War—the black and white worker. Not the planter. Not the great Liberator himself. Not the liberal North. But the worker. The tragedy fell upon them all because, even as early as 1864, when Reconstruction was first taking its fatal shape, and certainly by the crisis of 1873, it was plain for all who *could* see its history that the action would never be solely in the hands of the worker—black or white, Southern or Northern, African and Asian or those in the European Diaspora of the global North.

   "Looking Forward," thus, is the story of dying old men of the North who were better, in their ways, than even Lincoln. Thaddeus Stevens of Vermont in the Congress and Charles Sumner of Massachusetts in the Senate carried forth the radical Republican vision of Reconstruction. But neither lived to see even the first fruits of their righteous demands. Stevens died in 1868, just before Sumner fell out of favor (he died in 1874). The vision they inspired won some gains of no minor importance. The Thirteenth, Fourteenth, and Fifteenth Amendments to the Constitution established basic rights and protections for the freedpeople of the South. Even though the South, with its Black Codes, and political leverage on the North, managed to outrun the rule of law, these protections eventually caught up with justice itself. It took a full century for even these fundamentals of justice to become the true law of the land. None of the best Northerners saw this day. Lincoln could not even imagine it. Stevens and Sumner died long before—their gains wiped out by Andrew Johnson and the others who sided with the planters for one final century more. Du Bois saw this history clearly, which is why he vested what hope he had—then as in the 1930s—in the worker.

Black Reconstruction tells its story in less than half its heft. If Du Bois erred in composition, he erred as a man late in his seventh decade might. (Not even he could foresee the three full decades left to him.) He wrote the book quickly, revising to the end. Under such deadlines as he imposed on himself, he probably could not step back to see that *Black Reconstruction* was really two books at once, if not three. After Chapter 9, "The Price of Disaster," which ends on page 381 of a book of 737 pages (just shy of one-half), Du Bois offers five detailed chapters on the nature of the successes and failures of Reconstruction in the various regions of the South and the Border. These are, in themselves, brilliant for their historical nuance. He analyzes the different times and fates of

Reconstruction according to the social and economic differences of the states. The black majority in South Carolina suffered a different outcome from the black majorities in Mississippi and Louisiana, than did the black minorities in the rest of the South and the Border States. These accounts are worth reading in themselves. They extend by fine detail the narrative of the first nine chapters. But they could have stood on their own—at least for those whose primary interest is the question with which I began. Why this book—and why then?

Similarly the final four chapters (14 through 17) could very well have been a second, smaller book. These are the crux of Du Bois's response to Dunning and all the others. His revision of Reconstruction history is the work of the first half of the book. These concluding chapters are the ones that bring the point home in so many words. "Founding the Public School" (chapter 15) documents, for example, the deep commitment of the freedpeople to learning and how they learned in spite of the limitations of their schools which were the model for public education nationwide. This was his reply to those who wanted to throw the freed blacks into the mystified stew of scalawags and carpetbaggers—thus to displace the greed from the planters and the capitalists. *Black Reconstruction* concludes, straightforwardly enough, with "Back Toward Slavery" (chapter 16)—his summary account of the renewal of civil war upon the doom of Reconstruction—and "The Propaganda of History" (chapter 17)— his direct reply to the establishment of Reconstruction historians.

The problem in reading *Black Reconstruction* is not its length and heft, nor its varieties of parts, but its defiance of our usual ideals of History—hence of our orientations in time. The time of race is, as Du Bois thought, the time of truths that are never present, even though they, in their absence, are always there. It is possible that the most widely known line ever written by Du Bois is his remark at the beginning of *Souls*. "The problem of the twentieth century is the problem of the color line." The appeal of the figure of the color line rests on its defiance of progress. As years, or decades, in the century now over passed on their way, the color line remained as it was at century's start, giving the figure an ever growing force. As the century ended, the color line remained in fact, if not in form, as it was in 1903. The reason for this cannot be found in *Souls*, but it can be teased from *Black Reconstruction*.

Even at the dawn of the twentyfirst century—when the industrial system has fallen away, when work itself is transformed, when labor is put more on the margins of economic life—the twisted logic of racial time remains. The passing over into a new millennium, the passing away of an older economic system, the passing into public view of new (including racial) assertions of what were once Weak-We peoples—these are the marks of the new time in which the question ought be asked: Can the world be understood under the intoxicating sign of History's Progress? Or must we think of it, and live in it, under the sober sign of time that races by only to revert, reverse, and revise itself?

Dreaming in the Dark, November 26, 1997

More often than not, dreaming is done in the dark. If the psychoanalysts and other sages of the human tribe are to be believed, dreams also come from a dark place—the unconscious, perhaps; or the spirit world of dead ancestors. But what is one to make of dark—racially dark—dreams?

Early in the morning of November 26, 1997, I had such a dream. Here it is, with slight revision, as I recorded what I could remember of it soon after waking:

Joyce Mueller! She still looked young as when she taught me to jitterbug, if that is what it was, in the early summer of 1952. I can feel her breasts through the cashmere as if it were yesterday. In the dream she was two years younger. A reversal! That one time, she made me feel like a little, little boy. The dream had us in a group. We were going out. I was in heaven. We came to a palace. It was Minister Farrakhan's. But it was in Harlem, not Chicago. It was a second floor dance hall, not the landscaped and guarded palace in South Side Chicago.

We climbed the stairs. I was invited to enter. Then I noticed that Joyce and her group were gone. The dance floor was empty, but the large hall was filled with feeling. The Fruit of Islam, always ready, kept themselves at a discreet distance. I saw Minister Farrakhan across the room, surrounded by followers. His own head was on the body of Martin. People came and went. I looked for the bathroom. I saw a sign that read "White Women." I was appalled. I left in indignation, but loitered about on the street below on a public square from which I could see the well-lit palace ballroom through floor-to-ceiling windows. Veiled women, under command, threw my belongings out the window to the street below. I immediately regretted that I had left. I wanted to go back up and protest by using the "Colored Men's" bathroom. And so I did. But the bathroom was merely a closet from which I could see the women's bathroom. Both were unadorned, plain, but clean. Once inside, it was clear to me that they were not segregated as I had thought.

I left again. I stood around on the street again, looking up. I saw the Minister's guards at the windows. They were dressed, not in their usual black suits and white shirts, but in outfits like those worn by gymnasts. One leaped feet first from the window above to the street. He landed a perfect 10. Feet planted, arms raised. Once again my belongings were being thrown from the window. He caught them as they fell. I felt rejected. But when they landed I saw that the things tossed out were religious objects. One was a candelabrum—perhaps a menorah.

> *The Minister himself then came down to join the crowd that had gathered on the street. He and I walked together, arm in arm. We talked intimately. We liked each other. We knew we did. But we said nothing of this. He hinted even less than I. But I knew. I wanted to tell him that I had once visited his place in Chicago and had taken a picture of it after one of the Fruit of Islam gave me permission. I really had wanted to tell him this, but there was no time. We were talking too much about important things. The dream ended just as I began to imagine myself replacing Ben Chavis as his advisor for the next Million Man March. I had begun to scheme how I would get him to drop from his speech all that ridiculous stuff about "the number 19."*

Where does such a dream come from?

One idea about dreams is that they are the wishes and desires of the dreamer, and thus have little to do with the people who appear in them. Yet, the people who come into our dreams are real in their way. Joyce Mueller was. Minister Farrakhan is. So too is Ben Chavis. In our dreams they tend to get all mixed up with each other. Joyce Mueller became Minister Farrakhan who, in turn, was occupying Malcolm X's mosque while living in Martin Luther King's body. Who was the pure object of desire? Was it Joyce Mueller, or other white women whose bathroom repelled me? Or black men whose plumbing turned out to be just as plain as that of the white women? Was the desire sexual? Or racial? Or what? Or was it the desire to beat out other men for the affections of the real Man? Ben Chavis, before he became Chavis Muhammad and a Muslim minister, had been an ordained Christian minister in the same denomination to which I am ordained. Was he the one who did what I never could?

The questions never end. But dreams do, usually just when they have done the work of expressing the wishes one cannot bear in conscious life—often when they come to the point of expressing what one cannot bear to imagine in either life. How close did I really want to be to Minister Farrakhan, who may have had a hand in killing Malcolm X, yet whose speech in 1995 at the Million Man March was, I thought, wonderful—except for all that business about the number 19, which I feared was not good for the cause. *Whose We?*

The thing about dreams is that, for their brief duration, they can eliminate altogether any and all *Whose We?* problems. There is no We in a dream, at least not in its latent contents. In them we are walking arm-in-arm with ourselves—or, rather, with our innermost, momentarily unrestrained, wishes to join a We for which we are neither qualified nor prepared. This is the power behind all "I Have a Dream" speeches. When uttered in public, at the right moment, by the right person, they draw all those willing to march back down deep into their dreams in the dark.

There is a catch, however. Just as some few can call others back into their dreams beyond the *Whose We?*—so others can do the opposite. Malcolm X was so terrifying in his day, as Minister Farrakhan has been since, because they speak, in their better moments, of the American nightmare that there is not, and ought not be, any such thing as a societal We. Such a nightmare is the American white man's darkest thought. It may well be as dark for all white colonizers in the European Diaspora. In fact, there is no We in America, any more than there is in the world. And of all the ways by which the human We is divided, drawn and quartered, the analytic cut upon the skin—the racial cut—is the most visible.

One dreamer draws us back into the dark before there was any cut, to when there is only one undivided We of our most primitive wishes to be at one with the breasts at hand. Yet, the risk of that good, primitive dreaming in the dark is that the censoring self will not wake us up in time. Then along comes a Malcolm or Louis, or whoever, to bring on the nightmares. Number 19!—whatever that might mean.

Most of my dreams are about houses that are not quite homes. I grew up in houses like that. In my dreams these houses are always off—just like my darkest feelings about myself. They are unsettled at their foundation. They may have long winding corridors that go nowhere. They may be perched unevenly beside a river, ready to fall.

But there is one house dream that was different. I had it many years ago—before the habit of writing my dreams down. Yet, I can remember its crucial details just as well as I remember that night in 1952 when I felt Joyce Mueller's blossoming breasts touch my heart forever. It is unusual that anyone remembers a dream so well, and can repeat it from memory:

> *I was in the basement of the house my father built in 1941 before he went to war. It was, I should say, the house in which Florence had lived with us before she bought her own at 54 York Street, downtown. In the dream I was looking around in the basement for something or someone. The space was clean but barren, lighted just enough to see my way around. Otherwise, the basement was dark as basements can be. I was looking for something. The light came from a room.*
>
> *I was drawn to that room. I felt the pull. Its door was ajar. I went to it. I felt guilt, but I could not stop. Inside, I found a most beautiful scene. A fine wooden table, Victorian and well polished, was covered with a lace cloth—perhaps even a veil. On the table was a burning lamp. The scene made me feel warm, welcome, alive. I was the only person in that dream.*

Now I ask, which kind of dark dream was this?

In real life, my biological mother, whom I think of as the birth mother, always set a hurricane lamp at the window on a table where she would sit to drink her last cups of coffee. Its glass shade was a deep, dark red. It was usually on when I came home as a kid. It must have been burning when I came back from that dance with Joyce Mueller. When my mother died I took that lamp. It sits beside me now. It is the first light seen when anyone comes up the hill to our home.

Dreams, whether those of a shaman or a psychoanalyst, are always condensations, displacements, and reversals of the stories we wish to tell ourselves in the dark. Was this dream of the lamp a dream of my wishes that my birth mother could be—could have been—what my other mother was in fact? And was it empty of any human form because the lit lamp was the reversal of those affections—the ones I had wanted so much in the upper floors of the house and could only find in the basement? The room in which the lamp on the table was dreamed was the room in which Florence had slept when she lived with us. I do not recall ever going into it wide awake. But I was able to dream it more than a half century later.

How many little boys and girls have dreams of their other mothers whose affection fills in for the ones withheld by the mothers other to the other mothers? And how many of those other mothers are colored people? Do we dream of them always in code—condensed, displaced, reversed? If we do, is it not then that dreaming in the dark is the vain attempt to calm the soul's aching for the ones whom one was never permitted to love as they loved us? If so—if only a tiny bit so—then it must be that these dreams we create by ourselves are always filled with the social imagination of those upon whom we trusted for our very lives.

Is it possible that white people everywhere dream in and of the darkness that holds steady the uneven foundations of their wobbly houses and uncertain selves?

Justice in the Colonizer's Nightmare: Muhammad, Malcolm, and Necessary Drag, 1965–2020

The goal of social ethics is to encourage those goods likely to be good for some societal whole. The practice of social ethics is, therefore, plastic if not quite elastic. It hardly makes much difference whether the society for which the good is encouraged is a community, a nation, or the global society of all beings.[1]

Social ethics, however, is a kind a bastard child of both philosophical and religious ethics, which are the more familiar and traditional sources of ethical ideas and decisions. Social ethics will therefore occasionally appeal to philosophical or religious principles. Karl Marx, for one example, founded his early ideas of human alienation on Hegel, just as (after 1848) his idea of the classless society was a crypto-Christian ideal of paradise regained. Just the same, even from the earliest, Marx and Marxism make no sense except as a social ethics. Much the same can be said of nearly every other variety of social ethic, except perhaps those arising outside the sway of Western metaphysics.[2] Social ethics is a practice of its own kind—and one that cannot help but worry about the nature of existing social worlds such as they are. The worse they are, the more social ethics worries. This is why such a practice should be of interest to people facing a new time with old ideas. At times like these there is a lot to worry about.

One of the differences between social ethics and the other kinds of ethics is that a social ethic tends to be a closet sociology. Likewise, sociology is usually a closet social ethic. In practice, however, both tend to pass as less than they each must be. Still, each is both at once. If they do the same things in different proportions, they do for the simplest (if seldom admitted) reasons. When all is said and done, it is impossible in such worlds as the ones we live in to begin to say what a good society *ought* to be if nothing is said, first, about the actually existing worlds. By the same token, it makes very little sense to go to the trouble of figuring out what *is* going on in a world at hand if one does not want to make that particular society better—that is, more good—than it is.

Thus it happens that among the greatest sociologists you will find several who are also among the greatest social ethicists—Max Weber and Emile Durkheim, as well as Marx who was the first important social ethicist of the industrial era. Sociology began as social ethics. Unfortunately, as the twentieth century went on, sociology fell into its disappointing analytic habits. When cutting things up became more important than making messy worlds better, professional sociologists paid less attention to their *oughts* and stopped thinking of their work as social ethics. One might even say that the most serious, if least apparent, analytic cut was the foundational one whereby the study of human and social things was turned into a professional, academic discipline. Much good has come from the so-called social *sciences*, but not enough, I think, to heal the originating wound. The effect of that wound is to give reason to the ludicrous idea that professional social ethics and sociologies are, and ought to be, different from the practical ones. Sociologies are social ethics because, like social ethics, sociologies are concerned with encouraging the Good Society, which is exactly what any sensible member of a society is concerned to do. Both trade on practical matters.

The problem of course is that most societies, whether small or large, are seldom very good. A social ethicist will call this the inevitable difference between the *ought* and the *is*, from which she will take an obligation to deter-mine which good *ought* to be—that is, which one *ought* to become the prevail-ing *is*. A sociologist, by inconsequential contrast, may suppress the explicitness of his *oughts* in order to study the *is*, from which he may or may not take an obligation to recommend a few applicable *oughts*. The social ethicist may over-state her *ought* and the sociologist may overstate his *is*. But anyone who pokes around in either field will sooner or later come upon both.

So, when a sociologist tries to pretend he is not also a social ethicist with an *ought* for those he studies, he will get caught. This happened, famously, in 1965 when Daniel Patrick Moynihan thought he was being "just" a good sociol-ogist, while many who read his report on the Negro family felt the sting of his social ethics. This was just one of many cases at the time when people of all kinds started to call out the social ethics of good sociologies by asking, not always quietly, *Whose We?*

In the years just after 1965, a good number of subjects of various objective reports began to take stock of the social things that were not working very well. By about 1968, over much of the globe, most things weren't working very well, or so it seemed. This was when sociologies began to look like the worlds they were studying. Curiously, just then, rebels of all kinds insisted, in effect, on the social ethics of any public sociology. When they did, the already fine line between professional and scientific sociologies and the practical ones by which people get by on the streets began to leak or collapse. What appeared to be revolutions of various degrees of seriousness were actually reversions to old habits, long forgotten. After about 1965, more and more sociologists, including professional ones, gave up the analytic discipline in which they had been reared to rediscover the social ethics of their great-grandparents. Social ethics underwent a bit of a transformation about the same time.[3] But its reversal of form was less necessary because social ethicists—though not very good sociologists—have always been less inclined to the kind of analysis that cuts people into their disciplinary cells—at least they grew less inclined after the days of St. Thomas, initially, and then John Calvin and those who cut and classified in his name.

After 1965, the sociologists had to rethink their ethics in part because they had become quite terrible philosophers, as well as studiously hostile to religion. Having thus cut themselves off from the traditional resources, they relied all the more, for much of the twentieth century, on an empty analytic culture. Many of them actually thought of values as interesting objects of analysis that had to be kept out of the analytic work itself. As a result, they were, in many instances, totally at a loss when it came to dealing with lovers, students, fast-food workers, waiters, domestics, car wash men, maintenance people, and others who suddenly lacked all respect for the values of the professor. Social ethicists, one might add, embraced this low-key refusal of regard perhaps because so many of them were ministers and clergy of various kinds—a vocation devoted to the embrace of humility.[4]

Though social ethics and the social sciences had grown ignorant of each other's ways and methods, somewhere around 1965—just when time headed in all seriousness down the slope toward eclipse—some old light went on. Thereafter, and still today, the younger people who had the bigger stake in the future grew impatient with the idea that facts should be free of values—that an *is* could make sense without an *ought*. As I say, this was because the world had begun to change in urgent ways. It should not surprise that chief among the changes had become the urgency of dark, even racial, thoughts.

The early spring of 1965 was an odd time for those of advanced social rank. It was not so much a bad time as one impossible to figure. It would be another three years after 1965 before they would begin to see what they already feared.[5]

In 1965, the United States was then, as it had been for some time, the world's leading colonizer. The U.S. was uncertainly engaged in a dishonest relation with the corrupt government of South Vietnam, which in turn was pursuing its civil war with the North. The Americans presented themselves as military "advisors" of which there were some 20,000. On February 5, 1965, the American base at Pleiku was attacked by the Vietcong, forces friendly to the North. A few Americans were killed. American President Lyndon B. Johnson had already been considering an increase in the United States military presence. The days just following the raid on Pleiku, McGeorge Bundy, one of Johnson's most trusted and brilliant advisors, was returning from a visit to South Vietnam. He had found the situation already bad. Pleiku was at least a public relations disaster. Bundy recommended a "sustained reprisal."[6] The President, who actually had convinced himself that his grandfather had fought at the Alamo, took up the challenge. He ordered bombing raids to the North. Thus began the American phase of the Vietnam War. By year's end the 20,000 military "advisors" would become a ground force of 200,000. In that year alone, the United States sent forth 55,000 bombing missions against the North and its allies. By 1968 there would be a half-million U.S. troops in the South.

It would take these three years after 1965 before the failure of this colonizing adventure would be evident to those who dared to know. By 1975 the last Americans would flee Saigon in disgrace. The last great American colonial invasion was over. But in 1965, very few would have guessed it. Vietnam was only part of the unforeseen mystery that dawned early that year.

At home that year a struggle of another kind was underway in the U.S. It too was entering, unforeseeably, into a final stage. The Civil Rights Movement had been stalled since the previous August when the courageous work of the Mississippi Freedom Democratic Party was essentially brought to naught. The summer of 1964 in Mississippi, a most viciously racist state, had come to be known as Freedom Summer. Workers faced assaults on all sides. In June three young men were murdered. Yet, whites and blacks joined together the rest of that summer to prepare and register people to vote.[7] The Mississippi Freedom Democratic Party was one of the most revolutionary results of that work. The MFDP presented itself in August to the nominating convention of the Democratic Party. It sought to replace the all-white delegation. In the end, President Johnson, seeking nomination for his own full term as president, was unwilling to risk the alienation of white voters throughout the South. He ordered the seating of the all-white and segregationist delegation. The MFDP was enraged by the rejection, as were young blacks everywhere. This one event, more than any other, led the young and impatient away from civil rights to a more aggressive rebellion. Slowly, thereafter, the trouble grew in earnest. The integrationist promise of Martin Luther King's "I Have a Dream Speech" of the previous August of 1963 was fading, especially among the young.

Still, in the early spring of 1965, the movement in Selma, Alabama, breathed fresh life into the Civil Rights Movement. Selma would be the last dramatically successful action in the American Civil Rights Movement. It succeeded just enough in drawing national attention to racial injustice as to create a political climate that would secure passage of the 1965 Voting Rights Act that August. President Johnson, unwilling to stand up for the black delegation from Mississippi in 1964, had been safely reelected. By the spring of 1965 he was willing, and able, to push through the Voting Rights Act of 1965 that at long last completed the Reconstruction begun a century before in 1863.

On the American surface, in the spring and summer of 1965, things seemed to be on the upward slope of Progress. What most white people called a "riot" in the Watts district of Los Angeles that summer was, in fact, an eruption of the same political lava that, several months before, had spilled out in the Vietcong "riot" at Pleiku. People thought to be natives were growing ever more heated in their protest. Those in the liberal position worldwide were not yet able to see the implications of their moves. Though the blindness was global, in no other place was the gathering darkness less visible than in the United States. The liberal establishment in government and business was marching in line with President Johnson's War on Poverty. In 1965 alone, Johnson sent down to Congress more progressive social legislation than had been proposed in any other year in the nation's history. Not even Franklin Roosevelt ever had such a legislatively focused vision of the Good Society.[8]

Even in Europe itself, recovering at last from the effects of war, the liberal eye was cast on the bright future. Those with a stake in the future could not see the trouble working itself out in Vietnam and the other remaining colonies of the European Diaspora. Nor could they see the gathering storms at home in the cities and other meeting places of young men and women without allegiance to the European Diaspora. But three years remained of the long enduring liberal innocence. For that short while, war abroad and turmoil at home were still naively thought to be mere technical obstacles to the Good Society. But already in 1965 some were surprised by the fury that came in the face of their best intended proposals.

No one was caught more unawares than a brilliant young social scientist employed by the U.S. Department of Labor in 1965. And what made the embarrassment all the more acute—thus pertinent to questions of the play between values and facts—is that that he was very much a social ethicist as well as a social scientist. The one caught unawares was, again, Daniel Patrick Moynihan, who in 1965 had already been in government work since the early days of the Kennedy administration. He was, as they say, a very good man—and among the best and brightest who brought their science to politics in order make society better. Like others enlisted from the early days of the War on Poverty, Moynihan believed that good social analysis applied to the most unyielding of social problems would produce good results. His famous analytic report was transmitted to the office of the President of the United States in March of 1965, just when the President was heating up two wars at once—against poverty at home, against colonial rebellion in Vietnam.

"The Negro Family: The Case for National Action" has entered history as "The Moynihan Report."[9] Though Moynihan himself went on to a distinguished career as a liberal U.S. Senator from New York, his report endures as one of American history's most striking instances of good liberal intentions gone bad. The President embraced the Moynihan report in a public announcement of policy at Howard University on June 6, 1965.[10] In "The Negro Family" Moynihan did little more than provide the evidence for what many people had been thinking for a long time. Here is Moynihan's conclusion:

> What then is the problem? We feel the answer is clear enough. Three centuries of injustice have brought about deep-seated structural distortions in the life of the Negro American. At this point, the present tangle of pathology is capable of perpetuating itself without assistance from the white world. The cycle can be broken only if these distortions are set right.

> In a word, a national effort towards the problems of Negro Americans must be directed towards the question of family structure. The object should be to strengthen the Negro family so as to enable it to raise and support its members, as do other families. After that, how this group of Americans chooses to run its affairs, take advantage of its opportunities, or fail to do so, is none of the nation's business.[11]

These lines are as good an instance as one can find of the dark thoughts of those who think from the other side of Du Bois's Veil. They see little. What they see dimly is, in Moynihan's word, "distorted." The not so thinly veiled idea was: *The Negro family is pathological. "They" do not live "as do other families." They have problems they cannot solve on their own. The nation must help "them." After that, they are "none of the nation's business."* One wonders what Moynihan would have thought if someone had said this about, say, the drinking problems of the Irish.

But Moynihan's purposes were good. He wanted the nation to help. The problem was caused by "three centuries of injustice." This report was, in effect, a rigorously documented social ethical statement of which the subtext was: *Negroes are not, in fact, like other Americans. More than others, they are victims of an ancient injustice. As a result, they are caught in a "tangle of pathology." They ought to be like the rest of us. We ought to help them.* From the *is* of the matriarchal family, abundantly documented with evidence of the devastating, ongoing effect of the absence of fathers from the Negro family, Moynihan drew his *ought* a little too quickly. This was the good man's *ought: Let's all get to work to help them so we can leave them to their own devices.* Or, put in the language of justice: *Give them help to give them a chance, so they can be left equally alone to their own ways.*

In President Johnson's Howard University Address in early June, he concluded with his own social ethical principle:

> For what is justice? It is to fulfill the fair expectations of man. . . . American justice is a very special thing. For, from the first this has been a land of towering expectations. . . . And all—all of every station and origin—would be touched equally in obligation and in liberty.
>
> Beyond the law lay the land. . . . And beyond this was the dignity of man. Each would become whatever his qualities of mind and spirit would permit. . . .
>
> This is American justice. We have pursued it faithfully to the edge of our imperfections. And we have failed to find it for the American Negro.[12]

To his credit, Johnson followed with the important acknowledgement that to right "the one huge wrong of the American nation" would be to effect a good for all. Johnson's speech, written by Moynihan and Richard Goodwin, was indeed a concise summary of the American ethic of justice: *Americans join together, when they do, to provide equal opportunity. Once provided, they go their separate ways.* In other words, rights to freedom are basic; justice is the assurance of access to these rights. Other nations in the European Diaspora would put just access to social goods more to the fore (as others would nearly neglect justice in favor of individual rights).

But the American idea of justice, if extreme in its rejection of social obligation to assure the good life, is well within the analytic culture of the European Diaspora. The modern world system's social ethic of justice is, in effect, predicated on the dogma that, over History's time, human beings in society deserve at least an equal right to some things, if not all good social things. In Moynihan's social ethic: *Get the family straight, then let them find their way.* This is not bad or evil thinking. It is perfectly consistent social ethics. The question to ask of it is what kind of good does it do? And for whom?

Moynihan's report and President Johnson's speech were napalm. The fires began in many, sometimes surprising, places. But none was more confusing to the business-as-usual crowd than the religious coming out of a professional prizefighter.

Just a year before, in late winter 1964, Cassius Clay had shocked the world of prizefighting by handily beating the Heavyweight Champion of the world, Sonny Liston. Clay had won an Olympic gold medal in boxing in 1960. He was young, brash, and outrageous. Few took him seriously. Certainly not against Liston, who had punished previous opponents. In the public eye, Liston was thought of as the evil black man. Clay was the minstrel clown.[13] But Clay's victory over the evil one was not to be his biggest surprise.

Soon after becoming the World Champion of Boxing on February 25, 1964, Clay announced his commitment to the Nation of Islam. He was soon thereafter to be known as Muhammad Ali, a name change many among his confused and outraged public would refuse to honor. As early as the previous September there were reports of Clay's interest in the Nation. But the young boxer's interest in Islam began before that in 1962 when he met Malcolm X for the first time. Malcolm was, at the time, the most respected and best-known minister of the Nation of Islam. Even so, Malcolm's eloquence and force of leadership had begun to provoke the Nation's leader, Elijah Muhammad. Still, Clay and Malcolm became friends. "Malcolm X and Ali were like very close brothers. It was almost like they were in love with each other. Malcolm thought Ali was the greatest guy he'd ever met and Ali thought this was the smartest black man on the face of the earth, because everything he said made sense."[14] As late as the months before the fight with Liston in February 1964, Clay and Malcolm were visiting back and forth in Miami and New York.

Ali's friendship was important to him, but it was doomed by the growing differences between Malcolm and Elijah Muhammad. As word got out of Clay's relations with Malcolm and the Nation of Islam, promoters began to worry about bad publicity for the Liston fight. The American public already feared the Islamic brand of black radicalism, about which almost nothing was known but for Malcolm's fiery speech. This was enough to alarm a public already uneasily aware that once docile blacks were changing their tune.

Whites could barely get with "We Shall Overcome." They could hardly imagine what tune they might have to sing if the music came from anything Islamic.

One of Malcolm X's more often noted (and to whites terrifying) public statements was made just after the assassination of John F. Kennedy on November 22, 1963. Though Malcolm had been ordered by Elijah Muhammad to refrain from comment, he nonetheless uttered his notorious remark on the spread of violence in American society. "The chickens have come home to roost." A few years later, a presidential commission on violence would in effect say much the same thing about violence and racial trouble in the United States.[15] But in 1963 it was unthinkable for a powerful black man, of such foreign associations, to say so starkly that the beloved white President was the victim of white society's own inherent violence. Malcolm X was nothing if not consistent in his stern principles of racial differences. He was even too strict and outspoken for the Nation of Islam. Elijah Muhammad used Malcolm's breach of discipline as pretext to censure and silence him. Clay (in fact already "Ali" in every respect but public announcement) was forced to choose. He chose the Islamic religion he has followed ever since, which required a break with Malcolm X. Shortly after beating Liston late in February, Clay announced his allegiance to the Nation of Islam and his change of name.

In March 1964, Malcolm broke his ties with the Nation of Islam. He had but months to live. In that short time he changed much of his thinking, in large part because his pilgrimage to Mecca had convinced him that the true Islamic way did not exclude relations with whites. Malcolm X was murdered on February 21, 1965—just when Lyndon Johnson was firing up his wars against poverty and the Vietcong. The murder of Malcolm X, like that of Martin Luther King three years later, took from the scene a leader who, though aggressive in speech, was already moving away from racial confrontation toward a position that would have been, at least, easier for whites to bear, if not to accept.

As tempests go, this episode was small beside the larger issues of colonial wars, poverty, and racial conflict. But it turned out to be one of the more dramatic of the colonizer's confounding nightmares. The protest against Moynihan's Negro family report was largely the preoccupation of those outside the internecine struggle of Nation of Islam. But the failure of good liberals in their search for the facts to comprehend black experience was soon joined to their equal and distant failure to understand the deadly course they had taken in Vietnam. Oddly, just as the dawning cloud of the hostility of the world's people of color to white rule was curving around the world in one direction from Mecca, it was coming from the other shores, over the Pacific, from Hanoi. And both met in the convictions of one elegantly simple, apolitical man. Muhammad Ali, while not anything close to being a front line player in the complex racial politics of the mid-1960s, was the one who most poignantly joined the global and the local for all to see. This he did almost by accident.

Ali's victory over Liston started him on the remarkable path that led to his being for much of the rest of the century the most recognized and famous man on earth. Yet, at home, in 1964 after the fight, Ali was to many still the clown, a role he understood and played to the hilt. He was despised for his new name and religion. But it was less the name than the religion, which this narrow-minded "Christian" society, considered anathema—at least, in those early years of anti-Muslim prejudice. In 1965 what most of those who paid even passing attention to sports understood about Islam was, before Ali, taken from sound bites of the speeches of Malcolm X. After the eclipse they would be forced to know what in 1965 they ignored with impunity. Malcolm was for the many in those days their first experience of terrors unjustly attribution to Islam.

Malcolm X was, indeed, a terror with words. So much so that he threatened the leadership of the Nation of Islam every bit as much, or more, as he disturbed those whites who had never before heard themselves called blue-eyed devils by a black man. If there is one speech, more than any other, that struck terror in the hearts of white folk, it was "The Ballot or the Bullet"[16]—delivered on April 3, 1964, before a still then mainstream civil rights organization, the Congress of Racial Equality. That speech was, in effect Malcolm's inaugural address after the final break with Elijah Muhammad. He had been waging war on two fronts: against the Nation of Islam, which had sent him into exile; against, the integrationist Civil Rights Movement. He was attempting to build his own movement between what had become the extremes of racial difference for the white world. The jealous and corrupt Elijah Muhammad posed a threat to Malcolm's success, not to mention his life. Martin Luther King, on the other hand, was still a rival for the heart and soul of young black men in the cities, and an icon, to Malcolm, of appeasement to the blue-eyed devils. "The Ballot or the Bullet" is finely crafted, fiery, and merciless rhetoric. The speech begins unflinchingly, presenting the logic of its title:

> The question tonight, as I understand it, is "The Negro Revolt, and Where Do We Go From Here?" or "What Next?" In my little humble way of understanding it, it points toward either the ballot or the bullet.
>
> I'm not a politician, not even a student of politics; in fact, I'm not a student of much of anything. I'm not a Democrat, I'm not a Republican, and I don't even consider myself an American. If you and I were Americans, there'd be no problem. Those Honkies that just got off the boat, they're already Americans; Polacks are already Americans; the Italian refugees are already Americans. Everything that came out of Europe, every blue-eyed thing, is already an American. And as long as you and I have been here, we aren't Americans.
>
> Well, I am one who doesn't believe in deluding myself. I'm not going to sit at your table and watch you eat, with nothing on my plate, and call myself a diner. Sitting at the table doesn't make you a diner, unless you eat some of what's on that plate. Being here in America doesn't make you an American. . . . They don't have to pass civil rights legislation to make a Polack an American.[17]

Then came the line of direct confrontation with King and with the liberal Americans who shared his dream.

> No, I am not an American. I'm one of the 22 million black people who are the victims of Americanism. . . . I'm speaking as a victim of this American dream system. And I see America through the eyes of a victim. I don't see any American dream; I see an American nightmare.

By the simple fact of saying these words for all to hear, Malcolm X made himself the American nightmare in the minds of whites. Though he did not advocate violent initiatives, he did reject nonviolence as either an absolute or an end in itself—and, most terrifying of all, he asserted the Negro's right and responsibility to take up arms when attacked.

Moynihan would agree early the following year that American Negroes were victims. But he and his president would trust the combined force of good social science and decent government to solve the problem. Martin Luther King later than same year would accept the Nobel Peace Prize in Oslo. Though his speech was a defense of nonviolence, King took pains to define his movement as a global one. He thus began the journey of his few remaining years. Thereafter, his program shifted slowly but evidently from civil rights to economic and social justice; from a domestic struggle to a global one that would soon appear in his opposition to the war in Vietnam.[18] Later that year, his last, Malcolm would return from Mecca to begin his short journey back from hatred of the white devils. Hence the irony of those times, that at the time of his death Malcolm had begun a new trajectory toward some vanishing point after King's own death—when, had they both survived the bullets, they would very likely have joined hands as leaders of global struggle for justice for black people.

In the meantime, Muhammad Ali was enjoying his triumph in sport and finding his way in his new religion. Within two years, in 1967, he would lose his title because of his faith. He had twice failed the intelligence test for military service. It is at least possible that the government recalibrated its own minimal standards in order to draft Ali. Whatever the official spin, no one who knew the darkness of racial punishment was fooled. Ali's case was nothing different from the punishment white America imposed on any who could and would denounce its values. Where Malcolm had been the condemning preacher, and Elijah the coy manipulator, Ali had been the completely simple and honest truthteller. His clown act was sincere, in its way. But it was also taken, as it was simply intended—as the jester signifying on the very system that his religious beliefs sternly condemned. When Ali was asked why he refused to step forward to be inducted into the United States Army, he did not say what legend claims, "No Vietcong ever called me nigger." He did say, when he knew he would be drafted, "Man, I ain't got no quarrel with them Vietcong." It was a defining moment. The reporter to whom he said those words missed their significance altogether and much later observed: "For the rest of his life he would be loved or hated for what seemed like a declarative statement but was, at the time, a moment of blurted improvisation."[19]

Ali was no more a clown than he was a political strategist. His refusal to serve in Vietnam came from the heart of his newfound religion. His most famous and serious line was, thus, off the cuff of deeper matters. After Malcolm was killed, Ali regretted breaking off their friendship. As the years went by there was never a sign that Ali was a man of hatred. He bore his racial separatism with grace. But that one remark welling up from his already deep religious faith assured Ali's place as the King of the World—as a cultural hero and visible sign for the black peoples of the world. Eventually, he won in the courts and regained his boxing title. By the end of the century, he was recognized on some lists as the century's outstanding athlete. Even if, after the events in his life in the years around 1965, he was ever after known, where he was loved, for his religious and moral courage. Where he was hated, he was hated for this too.

At century's end, Muhammad Ali, ravaged by illness brought on by too many years at his trade, remained one of the world's most admired men. He was never an intellectual, and never cared about politics. Just the same, he was one of the first to dramatize, from within the body politic of the European Diaspora, that Vietnam and racial politics were one and the same. The metaphoric marriage of decolonization and domestic racial policy brought home the inextricable harmony of the global struggle of colored people. Ali was neither the first to know it—nor the first to say it. And when he said it, he may have said it by accident. But, because of who he was, and would become, Ali brought home the deeper meanings that were dawning in different ways on Malcolm X and Martin Luther King, even on Daniel Moynihan and surely on Lyndon Johnson.

Whether one event or several, the cumulative effect of 1965 was that it become the moment when, in the race of time, everything after would be different from nearly everything before. In the few years from 1965 to the year of the revolutions, 1968, the time of liberal progress halted, paused, and reversed itself. The chaos of 1968 led to political counter-insurrection that led America and the West to Reagan and Thatcher in the 1980s, to the cowardly politics of the third way, enunciated with such deceptive brilliance by Clinton, Bush junior, and Tony Blair. Ever since the moment of black rebellion in 1965, until and after the eclipse, the liberal ideas of social and economic justice were up for uncertain grab. Government sponsored social programs for the poor, legislative actions for civil rights, and the social will for social progress itself would fall harshly on the hard ground of the greedy gated community of the well-off few.

As the new century began, it had become uncertain what justice meant in such a world. Few were quite aware just to what extent the liberal ideal of justice fell apart because it was unable to sustain its promise before the bitter snarl of Malcolm X's nightmare, or even to save face before the terrible swift jokes of Ali's religious assault on white power and American global privilege.

The events that began to haunt[20] various corners of the world in 1965 spread rapidly. By the dramatic year of the revolution, 1968, they were out in the global open. By then, even those who had never heard of Malcolm X's announcement of the American nightmare, had surely heard of other, similar reversals of the worldly dream of liberal Progress. The writings of Frantz Fanon had outlived his early death (in 1961). *The Wretched of the Earth* had become a handbook of the revolution issuing from the decolonizing movements that by then were already two bracing decades along.

> The naked truth of decolonization evokes for us the searing bullets and the blood-stained knives which emanate from it. For if the last shall be first, this will only come to pass after a murderous and decisive struggle between the two protagonists. That affirmed intention to place the last at the head of things, and to make them climb at a pace (too quickly, some say) the well-known steps which characterize an organized society, can only triumph if we use all means to turn the scale, including of course, that of violence.[21]

By the time these words had echoed across the European Disapora, the best liberals were beginning to see that Gandhi, like the younger Martin Luther King, dealt them the better hand in a losing game.

The ghosts of the colonized, then and thereafter, began to haunt the colonizers whose power, therefore, was deployed randomly, even passively. The world's most powerful could still rule the skies and the seas, but not the caves and back alleys. Obsequious proclamations of liberal justice did nothing to disguise for long the hesitations and deferrals that brought the white world's worst nightmare to the light of day. The colonizers began to see the bed they had made for themselves. They hated Malcolm X for his wake-up call, and in the first years they hated Muhammad Ali all the more because he *was* the nightmare—undisputed champion of the world and a trickster who worked the media to perfection.

Fanon was, then, a relative unknown, but he was not alone. The wake-up calls of Third-World intellectuals were impossible to dismiss as tomfoolery. Aimé Césaire was just another among many:

> Unless, in Africa, in the South Sea islands, in Madagascar (that is, at the gates of South Africa), in the West Indies (that is, at the gates of America), Western Europe undertakes on its own initiative a policy of *nationalities*, a new policy founded on respect for peoples and cultures—nay, more—unless Europe galvanizes the dying cultures or raises up new ones, unless it becomes the awakener of countries and civilizations—this being said without taking into account the admirable resistance of colonial peoples primarily symbolized at present by Vietnam, but also by the Africa of the *Rassemblement Démocratique Africain*, Europe

will have deprived itself of its last chance and, with its own hands, drawn up over itself the pall of mortal darkness.[22]

In the dawning of the years between 1965 and 1968, it was widely understood, even while being denied, that the dark thoughts were the portents of this mortal darkness.

It is true, of course, that the terror of the late 1960s inspired the counter-revolutionary movement that prevailed through the end of the century. First, the law and order enforcers—Nixon and Reagan in the U.S., Thatcher and Giscard in the European centers; then, the gentle brutalities of the third way as Bill Clinton and Tony Blair sought to revise the analytic culture from within, only to abandon the economically weak in the rhetoric of compassion and globalization. Sometime in these last years from 1968 to the end of the century, a new year of terror slowly arose to replace the Orwellian 1984.

The year when it is said that the nightmare will come into its final, material reality is 2020. It is then—according to all projections, from the more conservative to the more extreme[23]—that world population will begin its crossover toward unsustainable rates of growth. In the United States that same year, 2020, is thought to be the year when the combined nationwide population of colored peoples will decisively exceed the number of white people—a global crossover that may well pass in the belly of the human to the foundations of the earth. The world, already dark, was then to become darker in fact at the very core. As 1965 was the year when the decolonizing forces began to strike home, 2020 has become the phantom year of the certainty of reversal in the time of the races. Already by 2001 (another phantom year in the culture) it would be known that the vast numbers of other-than-white people of the European Diaspora had no good reason to share any of the finer points of its analytic manners. They were, already, too overwhelmed with the burden of disease, poverty, exposure to the worst effects of environmental deterioration, and all the rest.

That year, 2020, might be said to be the as yet indefinite, but certain to become, moment when liberal culture will arrive at its true limit—not necessarily the end of the world, but the end when it will no longer be possible to avoid Césaire's dictum that the end of the colonial demands a rethinking of the order of global things. Then the culture of the analytic divide will have no inherent value. The idea of Progress will not mean what it once did. And, most certainly, the social ethics of practical life will turn of necessity away from the easier thoughts of rights and freedoms to the challenge of rethinking justice and equality in terms as yet unthought.

As the new millennium began, as soon after the eclipse found its tragic signifying even, the old categories—and most of all the old ways of thinking about justice—were already exhausted. It was a time when, as often happens in times of social and economic crisis,[24] that thinking turned to the beyond of this world—to, in effect, religion, that is: to the acceptance of the human as the always and forever limited, whose dreams of progress were contrived to avoid the dark.

In the meantime, the best of liberal thinking—of the very thinking that inspired Daniel Moynihan and so many others at an earlier time—attempted to revise or recover analytic culture's most fundamental values. The result was thinking deeper and darker than ever before. The strange coincidence was that so much of it turned, as did the worldly turns in 1965, on the coming together of religion and justice.

At the beginning of the twenty-first century, there were few better examples of a public philosopher devoted to a reconsideration of the liberal foundations than Richard Rorty. Among the others, Charles Taylor and John Rawls,[25] differently, shared many of the same purposes. Surely, Juergen Habermas and Jacques Derrida, again differently, do too. But Rorty is exceptional, if only because of his ambition to straddle the fences of irony and liberal hope.

There may be no better case to be made for the value of an honest and robust social justice than that of what becomes of philosophical ethics when they try to become sociological. It goes without saying that when sociology tries to become ethical it is just as clumsy. But since the empirical social sciences usually (if unwisely) cede the high ground to philosophies of various purposes, one would expect them to do their social theory at last half well. They seldom do. Philosophical ethicists, whether implicit or explicit, generally start with a compelling *ought*, well defined and often alluringly introduced. Yet, when they turn to the social realities, whichever ones they may be, their *oughts* fall on the face of *ises* more complex than they imagine. John Rawls is without question the one against whom all attempts to revise the liberal ideal of justice must be measured. His daring ambition to revise the classic seventeenth-century method of people in the original position was, in its way, implicitly sociological from the start. But even his later, more rigorously social, restatement of the *fairness* principle as the *law of peoples* is offered to a world peopled by contentious differences.[26] Those who followed Rawls along ever more openly sociological lines, enjoyed not much more success in the face of social differences. Charles Taylor's ideal of the *undamaged human personhood* fails, as I say, at just the same concrete point as does Habermas' variants of the *ideal speech situation*.[27] Though both are astutely critical of the distorting evils of liberal societies, both nonetheless assume the functional equivalent of a context-sensitive democratic essence capable of transcending the varieties of social differences and injustices. Derrida, by contrast, assumes nothing whatsoever about the vestiges of liberal modern culture. He trips at the other side of the equation. By stipulating social differences as the *ironic deferral* of what Taylor would perhaps call *fully present personhood*, he allows very little room for the contrived and imposed silences by which those most unfairly deferred suffer or defend their Weak-We positions.[28] Between the extremes of innocence and irony one finds Richard Rorty, who grants the irony that Derrida insists on and the hope Taylor and Habermas cling to. But in so granting, he sets himself up in an impossible nether space between methodological irony and ethical hope.

What makes Rorty so special and interesting is that, in contrast to those, like Nancy Fraser, who want to have their cake and eat it without anyone noticing,[29] he struggles with the sociological realities his ironic method cannot quite contain. At no point is this more painfully evident than in his attempt to deal with an actually existing societal *is*—America the beautiful, which subject he treats respectfully. If even this kind of intellectual venture could fail, then one might conclude that the problem is not so much Rorty's as one that goes with the terrain—the impossibility of thinking one's way out of the liberal dilemma when social reality demands an ethic so far beyond irony as to be, in a Malthusian word, dark.

In *Achieving Our Country*, as in previous books, Rorty attempts to derive a liberal principle of hope from pragmatisms—in this case those of Walt Whitman and John Dewey. The book makes frequent and intriguing references to religion, including civil religion. Religion, including religious ethics, is a likely and surprisingly useful resort when a philosophy faces the uncertainty of social differences. If for no other reason, post-fundamentalist religious ethics have, since Kant at least, tended to the ethics of ends or of contexts—thus, in the former case, a kind of high utilitarianism and, in the latter, implicitly more interested in the social—but in both cases decidedly cautious as to universals.

But the religion Rorty has in mind is not so much a religious social ethic, much less even a civil religion, as a cartoon American religion at its Cotton Mather or Elmer Gantry worst than anything having to do with a serious philosophical or sociological idea of religion. For example:

> Both Dewey and Whitman viewed the United States as an opportunity to see ultimate significance in a finite, human, historical project, rather than in something eternal and nonhuman. They both hoped that America would be the place where a religion of love would finally replace a religion of fear. They dreamed that Americans would break the traditional link between the religious impulse, the impulse to stand in awe of something greater than oneself, and the infantile need for security, the childish hope of escaping from time and change. They wanted to preserve the former and discard the latter. They wanted to put hope for a casteless and classless America in the place traditionally occupied by knowledge of the will of God. They wanted that utopian America to replace God as the unconditional object of desire. They wanted the struggle for social justice to be the country's animating principle, the nation's soul.[30]

What is so unsettling about this passage, as about *Achieving Our Country* as a whole, is that Rorty—now faced with a social ethical question, with that is a real, live *is*—abandons the very irony he had done so much to call attention to in earlier writings.[31]

The confusion at the heart of Rorty's philosophy is a commanding illustration of the complications that descend upon any attempt to use liberal faith, including a religious one, to compose a global theory of justice. While Rorty himself has been anything but preoccupied with religion, he has devoted himself to reworking the very idea of social and philosophical thought with due and comparable consideration to the necessity of irony and the possibility of liberal hope. It is possible that he has not succeeded because his political philosophy lacks an essential ironic principle of the human condition that religion may best supply.

While not all religions as practiced are ironic, religion itself is. When religion is conceived, as it must be, as the state of being bound with all other human beings to something greater than the human,[32] then religion is, by its very nature, ironic. Religion, at its best, and notwithstanding its many varieties, compels attention to the irony that human hope is bound to human finitude. The fundamental religious impulse is not simply awe before the holy but, in Rudolph Otto's[33] classic expression, *fascination* with it, and fascination is most decidedly not the attitude of infantile fear and childish escape in Rorty's caricature. Even western Christianity, the fundamentalist versions of which are as little ironic as it is possible to be, turns upon the ironic notion that the way to life is through death—that finitude is the first fact of human life. At their best, some Western theologies have been supremely ironic, most memorably Paul Tillich's summary of his ethical theory: "The courage to be is rooted in the God who appears when God has disappeared in the anxiety of doubt."[34] But Christianity is far from alone in this.

Harold Bloom, in his attempt to reconstruct the Gnostic foundations of millenarian religion, quotes the Jewish Kabbalah: "What makes us free is the Gnosis [inner, spiritual knowledge] of wherein we have been thrown." Then he adds in his own words:

> "Thrown" is the most important verb in the Gnostic vocabulary, for it describes, now as well as two thousand years ago, our condition: we *have been thrown* into this world, this emptiness. Cast out, at once from God and from our true selves, or sparks, we live and die our sense of having been thrown, daily. Let us grant that there is an exhilarating dynamism in our condition, but this does not prevail, and it is not the norm of our existence.[35]

Though Bloom cites a Jewish source, his reference is to the universal principle of religion. It would be hard to imagine what the appeal of religion could have possibly been over so many centuries and across so many cultural differences were it not that which adds to social life some compelling solution to its most disturbing riddle, *How can it be that life is lived, whether alone or in company, against the end of life?*

Typically, but in this case curiously, Rorty puts greater stock in Dewey's pragmatic progressivism, while casting aside without so much as a comment the religiously derived political realism of writers like Reinhold Niebuhr, Jean Bethke Elshtain, even of Augustine.[36] What has become of Richard Rorty, the realist of *Philosophy and the Mirror of Nature* and of *Contingency, Irony, and*

Solidarity? It was he who, in the latter book, defined an ironist as one who has "radical and continuing doubts about the final vocabulary she uses." It is true, of course, that the entailment of Rorty's earlier idea of irony was that, as he went on to say, the ironist does not think her vocabulary is "in touch with a power not herself."[37] He meant of course to present a strong theory of epistemological contingency, on the one hand, while holding out for a politics consistent with a progressive ideal of social hope.[38] His rejection of ontological realism is, of course, the perfectly reasonable requirement of his rejection of foundationalism, of epistemological realism. But is not political realism still another matter?

Is it possible, in real and complex societies, to have realistic hope if one is not a political realist? The problem with liberal hope, apart from its failure to delivery the goods equitably, has been its frequent lapses into a rhetoric of hope so broad as to be, in the fine expression Habermas revived, quasi-transcendent.[39] But rhetoric, even if it is the high-minded rhetoric of Rorty's philosophy as textual criticism, is seldom, if ever, of precise value in shaping local political action. Whatever may have been true in the early days of modern philosophy, when philosophical work was done by courtly hangers-on and, later, by bourgeois gentlemen, philosophy in the form Rorty proclaimed in his earlier writings must be philosophy in and among social differences. This, surely, is why the literary ironist must take over for the philosopher of essences. Whether explicit or not, the present state of complex societies is the social condition for Rorty's critique of philosophy as a mirror of nature, just as it is for social theory. If this is so, then social theory must contend with the political reality that politics today is neither the art of courtly diplomacy nor the well-intended manners of the bourgeois gentleman. Politics today is the work of men and women, and very often of their children, who must contend with a social world in which, quite apart from the lack of a final vocabulary, there is no transcending power. It is a social world in which competing interests must come together over differences.

Even so, any reach for transcendence, however quasi, and whether philosophical or sociological, sooner or later runs aground the facts of complex, late modern societies in which the artifice of normative consensus comes apart in the face of protests founded on real, not imagined, social differences. Sociological quasi-transcendentalists from Todd Gitlin to Alan Wolfe want to argue that these differences are not politically or sociologically real, that they are epiphenomena of what is so tiresomely called, usually with a sneer, identity politics.[40] Social theorists who accept a responsibility for the empirical may be less inclined to worry about transcendental categories of being or understanding. But they cannot neglect the primary social fact of late-modern times that social differences are no longer merely disputes over values and manners, as the privileged had for a long time presumed. Whatever ordinary human foolishness may be done under the banner of identity politics (which is certainly not, on average, more foolish than the record of the earlier old and new lefts), the politics of social differences pose a challenge to the highest hopes of liberal social and political theory.[41] We need not go back even as far as Talcott Parsons' failed, but serious, attempt to contend with social differences in his own social ethic of the power of cultural values to maintain the patterns that, he hoped, would adjudicate competing interests.

Richard Rorty's later approach is just as decent, and perhaps more sensible, a liberal quest for transcending political values. The question he, and others who strive as he does, must answer is not so much philosophical or social-theoretical as historical, hence empirical. *Are not the contradictions of the liberal ethic unavoidable, hence symptomatic of the crisis of social and political thought provoked by the now avoidable fact of unsettling social differences?* It seems entirely possible that what has happened in Rorty's case is that his two-decade-long project of reestablishing liberal hope on the weak foundation of the textual criticism of vocabularies with no final word is that hope wanes when it is unable to consider the political realism of incommensurable struggles over interests and needs. It is one thing not to be able to *convince* the other. Quite another not to be able to feed one's baby. Political realism has to do with the latter. In this respect, reversion to the already implicated nineteenth-century dismissals of religion as child's play leaves Rorty exposed to the trouble in the project itself. It also raises the question of the value of religion, which then brings us back to the matter of human finitude.

Rorty's epistemological doctrine of contingency is no substitute for a political realism able to generate real, bread-winning liberal hope. I think it can be shown that the *might have been* of a more adequate political realism than Rorty's requires a more adequate theory of religion. The possibility that Rorty, surely one of the most important public philosophers at work today, might have tripped on the entailments of his own theoretical contingencies invites religion back in; at least to the extent that the leading social theoretical controversy of the day is itself fraught with questions of irony—so fraught as to pose the question of what lies beyond the terrible ironies of the social theoretical dark thoughts.

When social differences are taken for what they are—as, that is, the *given* of the human condition, as opposed to the *surpassable* of animal passions—then social thought must recalibrate its measures. It is one thing to believe that social conflict arising from differences is the short-run frustration for which a transcending principle must be sought. It is quite another to consider that social contestations are both the beginning and the end of social life. The former may have been the founding principle of social thought, beginning at least with Marx, if not Hegel. The latter, though always lurking in the modern unconscious, has yet to be fully thought—that is, thought as though it were more than a fad or an experiment; thought as though it were the most urgent of all questions.

It is not, of course, that no one has thought the Unthought of social things—only that we, for the most part, with our irrational fear of irony, think it half-heartedly. Even as social theory tries to avoid that which will surely one day come to pass—long after the crashing towers have been absorbed into whatever reserve of historical understanding it finds (or causes to be invented), it struggles with the uncertainties of the realities already upon us. The struggle is everywhere—in the resistances and the experiments. It goes by any number of names and possibilities—but none more haunting than its appearance at the heart of liberal good intentions.

Chief among the examples of social theory's struggle to deny its own resistance to the impossibility of a universal, transcending truth of the social, is the argument over the presumed incommensurability of a politics of recognition and a politics of distribution. Though the question is posed by many, from the serious to the half-serious, its most disciplined, and focused, presentation is in the arguments among Judith Butler, Seyla Benhabib, and Nancy Fraser.[42] Their exchanges in a number of places over the past years provide excellent documentation of the issues because, though they themselves would resist easy classification, they represent more or less the three important attitudes in the debate—the allegedly postmodernist (Butler), the frankly quasi-transcendentalist (Benhabib), and the vexed post-socialist (Fraser). Though their numerous exchanges are set at a very high level of theoretical abstraction, the argument is at bottom over politics. There may well be clearer, more down-to-earth political formulations of the issues they consider, but it would be hard to find a more succinct presentation of issues that any and all social theories must, one way or another, confront.

It is not by accident that, in the last two decades of the twentieth century, the debate over the fate of universal values in the face of multicultural politics has been carried forth by writers who, however they may think of themselves, are generally thought of as feminists. Though academic feminism's relationship to women of color is still, for the most part, uncertain and confused, it would be hard to deny that, more than any other concerted movement in the universities, feminism has well posed the question of universal values in politics and social thought. It has because of its own uncertain relation to the subjugations visited upon the oppressed by modernity's liberal ideals of subjecthood. This is why, though it is often repeated, Nancy Hartsock's complaint against Foucault still serves to illustrate feminism's interest in the debate over differences: "Why is it that just at the moment when so many of us who have been silenced begin to demand the right to name ourselves, to act as subjects rather than objects of history, that just then the concept of subjecthood becomes problematic?"[43] Though Hartsock herself wishes to dismiss what she takes to be Foucault's all too radical view of social differences, her identification with those previously silenced, in all their many differences, fixes the horns of the dilemma.

Nancy Fraser, for important example, has pursued her calling as the *tertium quid* of these debates by presenting an especially clear summary of the differences and possible points of communication between the politics of recognition and the politics of redistribution.[44] What appears to be an elegantly obvious distinction turns out, upon inspection, to be a grab bag of theoretical and political confusions. This is why, of course, Fraser has set about to organize them as best they can be. The politics of recognition refer, as one would suspect, to the new cultural politics which, in the rhetoric of debate, are commonly characterized as identity politics. Theorists of the lefts, old and new, consider cultural things lesser than economic ones. They, thereby, dismiss identity politics as misguided—first, by misplacing values; and, ultimately, by emphasizing local interests in recognition at the expense of universal principles of social and economic justice.

Using a form reminiscent of no one more than Talcott Parsons, Fraser attempts to display the political possibilities that may arise in the differences between the two politics. "Imagine a four-celled matrix," she says.[45] Imagine, indeed, that the two supposedly incommensurable politics are analytically decomposed against two no less different axes of political possibility, affirmation and transformation. These latter represent of course the strategic choice between liberal reform (affirmation) and social revolution (transformation). By cross tabulating (if I may) the four against each other, Fraser generates what she considers the four properly leftish political choices in the present situation: 1) *the liberal welfare state* (redistributive affirmation), 2) *mainstream multiculturalism* (affirmative recognition), 3) *socialism* (redistributive transformation) 4) *deconstruction* (transformative recognition). Without, for the present, attempting further to account for what she means by the four ensuing political choices, one begins to see where this is headed. A very well-intended effort produces categorical options as little likely to console the rivals in the original debate as they are to feed hungry babies.

Fraser proposes that the recognition-redistribution problem may be overcome by rejecting the first two of the four options (they being both weakly affirmative) and combining the latter two, transformative options. Why these two? Among other reasons (most especially the need to maintain a post-socialist radical politics), Fraser claims that "socialist economics combined with deconstructive cultural politics works best to finesse the dilemma for the bivalent collectivities of gender and 'race'—at least when they are considered separately."[46] Why gender and 'race' (race being marked to signal the analytic instability of the term)? Because these two among the boundary terms of the politics of difference (as distinct, that is, from class and sexuality) are those spheres of political and social encounters that demand, at one and the same time, *both* recognition and redistribution, both cultural and economic justice.

The degree to which Fraser's third-force attempt to reconcile reputed opposites fails is evident in the responses of her rivals. Seyla Benhabib and Drucilla Cornell, the quasi-transcendentalists among the disputants in *Feminist*

Contentions,[47] simply ignore Fraser altogether. This partly, one supposes, because they detest her fourth cell, "deconstruction," or, more likely, because, as Benhabib puts it (after the Hartsock line), "we as women, have much to lose by giving up the utopian hope in the other."[48] Deconstruction and postmodernism (those who detest these things tend to consider them the same) can at best teach some lessons in short-run skepticism. At their worst, they weaken the will for social utopia which alone can emancipate us from oppression which *au fond* is always class-specific and, thus, a matter of economic injustice.[49] *En fin*, the assumption is that emancipation requires a universal principle of justice. So much for Fraser's attempt to reconcile the quasi-transcendental, post-socialists with those she considers the cultural politics people.

Regarding Fraser's view that gender and race—and neither class nor sexuality—are the pivotal "bivalent collectivities," you can imagine how Fraser's view goes down with Judith Butler. Butler, in her exchanges with Fraser in both *Social Text* and *New Left Review*,[50] attacks the redistributive left's crude characterization of queer politics: "Queer politics is regularly prefigured by the orthodoxy as the cultural extreme of politicization."[51] Butler then, in effect, attacks Fraser's scheme as typical of the cultural politics of the left orthodox, who in seeing everything as economic think of everything else as "merely cultural." Butler then attempts to demonstrate (not always convincingly) that sexualities are as much material and economic things as cultural, hence as eligible for orthodox attentions.[52] Where she is completely persuasive, I think, is in her insistence on the political necessity of difference and conflict and, thus, the impossibility of political equanimity among the various lefts. Politics, far from being the art of the possible, is struggle at the limit of the impossible—or, of the Unthought.

New political formations do not stand in an analogical relation with one another, as if they were discrete and differentiated entities. They are overlapping, mutually determining, and convergent fields of politicization. In fact, most promising are those moments in which one social movement comes to find its condition of possibility in another. Here difference is not simply the *external* differences between movements, understood as that which differentiates them from one another but, rather, *the self-difference of movement itself*, a constitutive rupture that makes movements possible on non-identarian grounds, that installs a certain mobilizing conflict as the basis of politicization. Factionalization, understood as the process whereby one identity excludes another in order to fortify its own unity and coherence, makes the mistake of locating the problem of difference as that which emerges *between* one identity and another; but difference is the condition of possibility of identity or, rather, its constitutive limit: what makes its articulation possible at the same time makes any final or closed articulation possible.[53]

If Butler is right, and I for one think she is, the argument between, as Fraser calls them, the cultural recognitionists and the socioeconomic redistributionists is grossly misplaced. Cultural politics, in any of its forms, including identity politics, when viewed historically, is more the "constitutive rupture" of political change than the beginning of another wave of excluding factions. It is far too early to tell what these new movements will become in the wider scheme of things.

Given the sad history of new and old left factionalization, it is not surprising that those with legitimate interests in renewing left politics want to avoid the kind of excluding differences with which they are so familiar. Nor is there any reason to doubt that already in its short history cultural politics have served, in some instances, to factionalize the political whole. The proper issue, however, as Butler begins to suggest, is the conditions under which new political formations arise. Little gain is made when the short-run failures of any of the lefts is allowed to confuse thinking aimed at long-run political change.

The issue, therefore, is not, How does one choose between or reconcile the cultural and economic? The question with which social and political theory must contend is, rather, *How is justice to be understood in the moral space created by the collapse of the welfare programs of the liberal-left and the appearance, almost at the same moment, of the new cultural politics of difference?*[54] It is surely at least possible that these new cultural politics are, in Butler's word, the source of "mobilizing conflict" appropriate to the present situation. If possible, then why the preemptive strike by the older new left against the cultural left?[55] No answers will come from such aggressions any more than they will come from projects like Fraser's recategorization strategy. "The redistribution-recognition dilemma is real," she says.[56] Real, yes. But in what sense?

What is the underlying reality between the need for universally distributed socio-economic justice and the need for social and cultural recognition? Charles Taylor has proposed an answer. In his essay on the politics of recognition, Taylor begins by challenging the notion that these are a frivolous politics:

> Misrecognition shows not just a lack of due respect. It can inflict a grievous wound, saddling its victims with a crippling self-hatred. Due recognition is not just a courtesy we owe people. It is a vital human need.[57]

But, Taylor goes on (in keeping with the general themes of *The Sources of the Self*) to show how cultural recognition is embedded in the history of modern ideas about the moral self that emerged in the eighteenth century (adding importantly what is usually ignored: that the moral self was always a dialogic self). The charm of Taylor's philosophy for sociologists is that he aims, implicitly, to be sociologically responsible. He, thus, locates the modern self in its modernizing social conditions beginning with the Enlightenment; as he situates today's politics of difference in their own social and moral framework.[58]

In the end, and apropos of the recognition-redistribution dilemma, Taylor offers an almost out of the closet nod toward religion[59] from which he draws the conclusion to his essay:

> There is perhaps after all a moral issue here. We only need a sense of our own limited part in the whole human story to accept the presumption. It is only arrogance, or some analogous moral failing, that can deprive us of this. . . . What it requires above all is an admission that we are very far away from the ultimate horizon from which the relative worth of different cultures might be evident. This would mean breaking with an illusion that still holds many "multiculturalists"—as well as their most bitter opponents—in its grip.[60]

Taylor, here, is as far short of developing the idea of religion he proposes as he is ahead of those who cannot but see the dilemma in all too limited, and theoretically unstable, terms. Not even Fraser's well-intended but impossible attempt to reconcile by the grace of her categories leads where Taylor's comment might.

In one sense, the question of justice in a multicultural age is relatively simple: *Are we able to recognize the humanity in others who, being different from us in nontrivial ways, demand their fair share of "our" goods?* Like all such summary statements, the query is loaded. What is humanity? What is a nontrivial social difference? What is a fair share? What is fair? Who owns the goods? Who has a right to the goods? Yet, however charged, this is the practical question that gives rise, equally, to the mobilizing conflicts of new politics as it does to any coherent, transcending commitment to social and economic justice. The full answer is not so easily arrived at, to be sure. But it is the answer that must be sought if ever there is to be a way out of the dilemma social and political theory is now in—that is, a way out that issues in well distributed bread.

Taylor, like Rorty, is to be admired. Though he suffers the limitations of too much liberal hope, he, again like Rorty, knows where to look when this-worldly hope is not enough. If, as Taylor says, the current dilemma has to do with an arrogant unwillingness to accept "our own limited part in the whole human story," then must we not be political realists about the limitations of the human story itself? This recognition is why he (and Rorty in his way) turn for resource to the religious. Whatever else a religion, or a religious ethics, may entail it must lead to the most profound of all sociological *and* social ethical principles. We in all of our collective comings together and goings apart are finite, and death is the first and final arbiter of social things—hence of justice. Whatever we choose to call it, religion or something like it has always been in the recorded history of social gatherings less that which holds things together (as Durkheim believed) as that which reminds those gathered that beyond all their differences there is death—and that therein lies what common humanity there may be.

Sociologies without social ethics, like philosophies without a more bracing religious ethics than those to which Rorty appeals, are bound to ignore the one basic fact of social life—that human beings in society are *doubly* finite. As *individuals*, we cannot transcend the social relations that form us. As *members with all others*, we cannot escape the limitations of our humanity. Both are necessary recognitions for there to be any truly and deeply honest recognition of the social differences. And without the affirmation of those differences how, indeed, can there be anything but a partial idea of justice—that is, a justice-in-fact as well as in-promise; and a justice thoroughly social in its nature? Can there be a *justice* that is not real *and* social?

Though the answers to all questions of recognition and redistribution may well be a long way off, any realistic hope of their attainment lies in distinguishing between the humanity of our hope and the finitude of our efforts. Those so wedded to various versions of the left or liberal hope (*that by their own efforts they will produce the transcending principle of social justice*) might well be chastened by the daunting reality of just how much bread must be grown, baked, and fed before the utopia comes. Utopias are different from heavens, being the liberal dreams of human aspiration. Heaven, by contrast, is the metaphoric expression of the human ideal that, being commonly limited, we are bound to all others, even to those different in social kind. Human justice will come, perhaps, when we recognize that we, among all others, have no greater or lesser need for recognition or for our daily bread.

In the end, the colonizer's nightmare has always been the bread line—the prospect that the *ought* of a permanently deferred pay off would be called out by those living the *is* of social finitude—those, that is, nearer to the universal end of human finitude by virtue of having been deprived by the left-handed wickedness of the liberal ethic.

There is nothing beyond good and evil. The wickedness of the liberal ideal of civilization was that it encouraged a good half-millennium of colonizing, of attempting to settle the global mind as though it were One. The claims and plot markers of its massive analytic work were present for all to see as something "merely cultural"—as the means of proper administration and decent civilization. Those subjected to Europe's administrative ministries knew all along that these colonizers went for their minds as the most efficient route to control their bodies, without which there would be insufficient labor power to extract colonial wealth.

In the months, and years, after the eclipse, it had become clear to everyone in the colonizing worlds that, whatever else was true, the world despised the colonizer. The Taliban would be rooted out of the caves, but the hatred would not soon quit the hearts of those subjected to the colonizer's injustice. Insofar as Islam had come to stand for this hatred bred of an evil masquerading as the good, it has slowly begun to dawn in the West that there is no universal mind in which the liberal ideal has only to grow with proper civilizing care. When and where the Islamic world despises the West, it does because it remembers the indignity of the defeat of its Ottoman armies. The West came to be an analytic culture in the nineteenth century by expropriating Rome and Greece as the sources of the civilization. But Europe would not have had access to Greece, perhaps not even Rome, had it not secured its borders to the East, beginning with Turkey. The Ottoman Empire was a warrior culture, whose first defeats at the hands of those who would become "the West" were in the sixteenth century, just when Europe was consolidating its empires in the new westward worlds and beyond. Warrior cultures do not forget defeat, and especially not when the wound inflicted gives rise to a successor empire even more powerful and global than the Ottoman had been.[61]

Whether local or global, injustice is always, and unavoidably, a question of how what goods there are ought to be distributed. At no other point is the social ethical *ought* so starkly exposed to the demands of the sociological *is*. Justice is about measurement. Who gets what always comes down to how many bags of rice or wheat are meted out, in what quantities to whom? In the West, the why of the measurements was always an afterthought. Liberal justice was, thereby, the very essence of the "merely cultural"—of the justification of the deaths of those measured unworthy by the standards of good business. "Merely cultural" is the slogan of European social ethics—from the trickle-down heirs of Adam Smith to the aging new-left children of Karl Marx.

The psychological wounds inflicted upon the world's left-out are the only essences there are. To be human is to die, hence to return to the comfort of the dark. All ideals that begin in liberal hope, as most of the European ones do, entail a blindness to the very dark where human comfort begins. The colonizer knows—everyone knows—that those left out in the distribution of the goods of daily life suffer and die. Yet the colonizer's nightmare has always been that the truth everyone knows might one be truly known in the light of day. Left-liberal compassion is nothing more than the unsettled suspicion that there is a limit beyond which those measured insufficient will not go—nothing to lose but the chains!

The poor are not merely culture—not, that is, merely bad copies of the grand European Man. As in sex, drag is not simply a way of copying the one true way of doing and being. Drag, as Butler reminded before anyone else, is the necessary condition of the human.[62] We are all, she says, in drag. We dress up to present an outside as similar or different to this or that crowd, all of whom are dressed up for the very same reasons. If there is a ubiquitous, if not essential, human fact of life, it is that whatever We there may be is the Weak-We of reluctance to accept the reality of social differences as all there is.

If only we could believe that we are all dying, the differences might not be measured so harshly. Dying is the return to the dark that the rulers fear, their subjects must live with, and the colonizer pretends will go away with the progress of his righteous time. Meanwhile, the one We there may be affirms its common lot by dressing ourselves each morning in costumes that reveal just how similar we are in our differences.

Ten

A Call in the Night, February 11, 2000

On this Friday night, as on others, we had a drink. Met some friends. Saw a movie. Drove home. But on this night, we drove into a darkness that would not end.

All the house lights were lit. There was a United States Government car parked in the driveway. I knew in an instant that this was the call the parent of a Marine prays will not come. In our darkest dreams, we who love fighting men and women of all kinds prepare for this worst for which there is no preparation. And this one was, in its way, worse than most.

Matthew had been found dead earlier that day. He was twenty-nine, an officer in the Corps, a beautiful and brilliant man, strong of body, a shining light—and my firstborn. He died in service at the Marine Corps Flight School in Corpus Christi, Texas. He was doing what he loved. He would have "gone up," as they say, in a matter of days.

Still, he hanged himself. He was last seen early in the morning on Tuesday, when he locked himself in his smartly furnished apartment. He may have died some time on Wednesday or early Thursday, which means two terrible things at once. He chose death. He died alone—hanging above time eternal.

Only now, months later, can I correct myself. These are not two different things; and they may not be as terrible as they feel to the grieving. We all die alone. Those who kill themselves are different only for having composed the time and place of it. Our lives in this world hang at the edge of the same eternal.

Two Marines came to stand with us, as others were standing watch over my boy's body in faraway Texas. I moaned deeper than ever before, or ever I will again. Matt's mother and his brother, Noah, who had known for some hours, were close behind. Their faces were already washed hollow with the pain slowly flooding into my bones.

Captain James Ready and Sergeant Roberto Arenas steadied Geri and me. We who love Marines know the feel and tone of their bodies. These good men held us at a tender distance not ten feet from the spot where, just six weeks before, I had last held and kissed my boy. Even now I can revive the feel of his strength in the touch of the remembered bodies of these young men. In life,

Matthew *always* said good-bye with a bear hug and, "I love you Dad"— *always*. That was to be the hug that would have to last for the always until whatever.

Why did he choose this time and place to enter into the pit that awaits us all? We who have been left by suicides want to know the answer more than anything. But, in this world, we will never know it. Here, more darkly than the theoretical mind can imagine, is the final, unbridgeable line that defines this side of the veil of finitude. It is the most personal of unknowables and the most precious surd of human life. Between the unknown and the absurd, suicide is a harsh tug on the fragile threads that bind human beings to each other.

I cannot say why, but among the first images to flood my mind as I tried to erase the one of him hanging alone was of a generic mother in far Sudan moaning the death of her babies. Through her I found my brothers and sisters along the way—those in all the far corners of the globe who were crying into the abyss as I was. In any given moment thousands upon thousands of babies die, most of them from starvation. Their sobbing mothers and fathers are a company of mourners more alone than I, less able to cover the burial costs, even to accept the generous handouts of food and comfort I would receive.

They—this imagined community of those who never read a newspaper—braced me in the days that followed. When we were not planning the services, or getting ourselves ready for the sad flight to his remains in Corpus Christi, I wandered about the place moaning, only: "Oh, make him warm. I want him to be warm." It was, I suppose, my wish to have held him secure as he fell into the eternal—at least that, if there was nothing I could have done to prevent the fall.

One of the lessons to be learned from suicide is actually very simple, yet it is a lesson almost no one learns while there is time. It is that we all take that fall—all of us; no exceptions; none. This is the one true We, neither strong nor weak, that binds all breathing creatures. By choosing to fall when and where they do, suicides give in to the fundamental truth of human life. Whatever their despair at the moment—however overwhelming their pain—suicides take this fall with a certain expectation. Even if it is only the expectation that their suffering will be gone when they hit bottom—and, even if they are out of their "right" minds—it is their decision. A dear friend whose oldest son also saw to the when and where of his death reminds me that there is something noble in a suicide. This is the nobility of those who accept the lesson that the monks have taught for centuries. We are all suffering the fear of this fall. Those who plan their own fall, as Matthew did, step into it, knowing better than the rest that this suffering has an end.

When you lose someone in such a way, you look for a sign. Perhaps a note, or letter, to come in the mails; even, against all odds, one final phone call ending as always, "I love you, Dad." Though not the one we looked for, we got such a sign.

Early the week after that Friday night, just before we were to leave for Corpus Christi to be with what remained of Matt and to accept the loving embrace of his Marine Corps companions, we heard little Annie shouting with unusual force. "BOIDIES! BOIDIES." We rushed to the windows to see.

Our house is in the trees, and near a nature preserve, so it is not unusual to be visited by birds. But never birds like these. They floated on vast wings, with grace and peace. Three of them fell gently on the air between the main house and my study. We rushed outside with a noise that would normally scare away such creatures. But they held the sky in their unperturbed arms. Between the tears, I cried, "Oh thank you, Matt. God bless you."

They rose to a high branch. Two held themselves aloft, wings spread-eagle on either side of the one who perched himself at righteous attention. Then the two flew off, leaving him alone to say, "I'm flying at last. I'm okay. I love you." And then he went up and away to follow the others.

We have a photograph of the scene. Some will say we were fooling ourselves, hoping against hope that this was the eagle of our beloved. In his last years, Matthew wanted nothing more than to fly, to have his Marine Corps wings. This was the last and best, if not quite achieved, of his wishes to live against death. From the earliest days, he always took the hardest path, even when he knew it might lead to failure. He climbed dangerous mountains, as he also defied the odds in his social life. He meant to thrill us, and indeed he did. He meant also to ward off the pit, to show he could live with it. It was, perhaps. . . . (We who are left by suicides are always saying "perhaps" or "I suppose.") It was, perhaps, the way those who cannot sit still practice life with death.

The day these Marine-like eagles visited us was the first warm day in February. The sun shone brilliantly. I felt for the first time that he was warm, and that, perhaps, one day I would be too.

The Gospel According to Matt:
Suicide and the Good of Society, 2000

Is it perverse that, in the weeks after my son committed suicide, I began to rethink the sociology of Emile Durkheim? I could not help myself—in part because I knew that Durkheim lost his own beloved son, André; not to suicide, but to war. Soon after he learned that André had perished, Emile gave up on life. He suffered a stroke and died the next year.

Grief does terrifying things to those who remain. The mind races at random, at frightful speeds, searching for whatever may be out there. Some find a shred of meaning to hang on to. Others do not. At the mortal moment, Durkheim's sociology lent him little of the solace he thought it should. As it happened, I first learned my Durkheim from two sociologists who survived the loss of children to suicide. From all appearances both found something to cling to where Durkheim could not quite hold on. We shall see what becomes of me.

Whatever that might be, right now it still seems natural, if not normal, for the mind to seek relief in the familiar. Stranger still would it be for a sociologist faced with the suicide of a child not to give some thought to Durkheim's famous book on suicide.

Though published more than a century ago, in 1897, Durkheim's *Suicide* is still respected and not just by sociologists. Even today you will find its unusual theory of the causes of suicide cited in the clinical literature. Still, also, for a practicing sociologist of the predominantly professional kind, Durkheim's *Suicide* enjoys an enduring value because it was *the* classical work that began the field's now century-long flirtation with analytic science.

Durkheim's main idea was that suicide, apparently the most private of acts, has its origins not in the psychology but in the sociology of the one who kills himself. Suicide, Durkheim argued, is a thoroughly social thing. For example, he found unusually high rates of suicide among widowed men. This he attributed to their loss of the moral guidance provided by conjugal society—by married life, that is.[1] Durkheim amassed fact upon fact to describe a series of similar social causes—economic or political crises, religious groups unable to build social cohesion, loss of important group leaders, and the like.

All were situations in the collective life wherein the rate of suicide increased as people faced a sudden loss of good and helpful society. Durkheim was still a relatively young man of not quite forty years when he studied suicide.

In 1897, when he published *Suicide*, Durkheim had no way to foretell his own fatal grief twenty years ahead. He wrote, thus, about suicide for reasons having less to do with suicide itself than with the founding of the analytic science dear to his heart. Sociology, he reasoned, could only gain the respect of the public if it could demonstrate that such an analytic science solved problems not normally thought to be sociological. Hence, if he could show that suicide—the supreme act of individual psychology—was in fact caused by social forces, then the case for sociology would be made.

By this line of reasoning, Durkheim set himself up as the Houdini of the analytic social sciences. His claim that the apparently psychological is actually sociological was a most unnatural stunt—one performed upside down and, in effect, under scientifically very hot water. Durkheim, like the great escape artist, meant to dazzle his audience by untying the tightest of all knots under extreme duress. If the riddle of suicide could be solved in the tank of social things, then sociology, the science Durkheim meant to conjure up, would be forever cut off from psychology. This was his analytic wish, based on an appreciation for psychology's popular appeal as the most fundamental and only necessary of the analytic sciences of human behavior.

Durkheim was a shrewd tactician. He knew just how strong the appeal to psychology was to the general public, not to mention among academics. Once, a very long time ago, a man younger than I used just such a popular logic to ridicule me. He was at the time intent upon stealing away a lover. Since I had no business being in the involvement to begin with, I was already vulnerable to his clever assault. On the one occasion he and I and the woman of our respective attractions were together—a moment just before she would fly away to him—this wise guy, under the guise of conversation, asked me point blank: "Well, just what is sociology anyway?" Before I could reply (in itself a mistake), he interrupted: "Isn't it little more than the psychology of two or more people?"

This precisely is the attitude Durkheim meant to counter. If he hadn't tried, it is entirely possible that professional sociology would not have come to be. The bias against the very idea of sociology as a proper analytic science is so powerful that extreme measures were required. Hence, Durkheim's trick was to execute the magic of taking the *very most* psychological of acts—one that could *only* be executed by a solitary individual—and turning it into an act of the societal whole. By all accounts, Durkheim was a most sober man, serious beyond all reason. Still, this trick by which he more or less singlehandedly invented sociology as an analytic science was impertinent.

"Impertinent" may seem to be the wrong word. But what, we might ask, could possibly be more invasive, presumptuous, insolent, absurd, *and* improper than toying so with the reasons for which people suffering the unbearable kill themselves? I am still, and will be for time to come, an expert (if that is the word) on the utter seriousness of suicide. Believe me when I say that suicide is the most serious of matters for those who commit it, as it is for those who survive the loss to relive it again and again for the rest of their days. It is not exactly a subject that invites insolence, impropriety, or other of the nuances of impertinence. How could anyone ever think that so deeply lonely an act could be social in nature?

Psychologists, undaunted by Durkheim's insolence, still take suicide as a subject of their understanding. In the clinical literature, one of the most compelling psychological interpretations of suicide is Kay Redfield Jamison's *Night Falls Fast*. Redfield is a clinical professor of psychiatry at the Johns Hopkins University School of Medicine. She specializes in the treatment of manic-depressive disorders—of which she herself suffers to the point of having failed in a suicide attempt made at about the same age my son succeeded at his. She knows of what she speaks when she writes:

> Each way to suicide is its own: intensely private, unknowable, and terrible. Suicide will have seemed to its perpetrator the last and best of bad possibilities, and any attempt by the living to chart this final terrain can be only a sketch, maddeningly incomplete.[2]

Not even those who have been on the verge of it, nor those closer than breath itself to those who commit it, can enter fully into the private psychology of killing oneself—of an aloneness so severe, a tunnel so dark, that even the gods will not go there.

In *Night Falls Fast* (a stunningly apt title), Jamison quotes a good many notes left by suicides. One of them was oddly comforting:

> I have had a wonderful life but it is over and my nerves get worse and I am afraid they will have to take me away. So please forgive me, all those I love and may God forgive me too, but I cannot bear the agony and it [is] best for everyone this way. . . . No one is to blame—I have wonderful friends and they do all they can for me. . . . I've tried very hard all I know for a year and its gets worse inside, so please take comfort in knowing I will not suffer anymore.

Matt left no such note. But this one sounds like him. He suffered deeply. He was very ill in ways and degrees he hid from us. He could not write because he loved us so. Somehow, he may have thought, if he was thinking at all during his last moments, that the note itself would add to our grief. The boy could write. It was just that, in the end, he *could not*. The pain had closed too much in on him. And so he locked himself alone for two whole days, then and there to face the remains of his life—finally, to fall into the sweet comfort of death. Whatever else it is—even the thought, and certainly the action—suicide is so vastly the work of the individual all alone that it truly is impertinent for someone to build an analytic world on the idea that it is nothing more than a social fact.

Durkheim's impertinence was doubly audacious. It was, in effect, an insult to those who suffer unto their own self-destruction. Durkheim's insolence was to steal from the individual any and all responsibility for the most acutely urgent fact of a life. Those who kill themselves seek more than relief from the unbearable. This they seek on the best of what few terms they can imagine. They very often kill themselves for high moral purposes.[3] Whatever went through my boy's mind at the last moment, what I know of him was that he was a very moral character—too much so for his own good at times. He way well have thought of himself as doing the honorable thing. From the point of view of a sociology of such a death, that may seem odd. From, even, a clinical psychology of suicide, it may seem pathological. But, from the point of view of an officer and a gentleman of the Marine Corps it may mean something else. We who remain have no idea what that meaning might have been. Those who suffer unto their own deaths may well have only two things to hang on to—an urgent need for relief, and one last hope for honor. The facts of this most final matter must have something to do with these two things— whether they are social, psychological, or simply moral.

What, then, you might ask, is a fact? The whole of analytic science turns on the claim that facts can be had if, and only if, one is clear as to the way the complex reality is cut into its discrete shreds.

There is no fact of life more real than the death of a loved one. There is no darker thought beyond which all analytic cuts are meaningless. Once dead, the dead enter some nether space of which the living know only what the poets dream. Their bodies remain, for a while, fodder for the sciences. From some, organs may be harvested. Others may become cadavers cut apart by medical examiners or medical students. In most cases, in most social groups, the cold, stiff bodily remains are the physical planes upon which are projected any number of analytic studies. Into the cavities and tissues probes dig at the once lively to determine the causes of this death and all others—each set against or with other causes to secure some or another theory of Life. When all is done, in many societies, the bodies are then pumped with alien fluids, sewn together, and dressed for viewing, then for burning or burying. I chose not to look at my son's dead body. His brother and mother did and assure me he looked like a dead person—still, made up, not quite real, nothing like the memories. What they saw had already been cut, parts taken for the medical examiners who reported in the end that he died of asphyxiation. This we knew already. The Marines, ever faithful, conducted a long post mortem, which included a psychological autopsy that concluded he may have suffered from a severe mood disorder. This, to our dismay, we had not considered. No one will ever know.

But where, in the cutting and draining—in all the interviews, and reports—are the true remains of this dear and once very alive boy? I surprised myself by my lack of interest in all these analytic considerations.

The facts of his material remains, of the cause of his death—facts which can only be arrived at by cutting and analyzing to a most uncertain effect—these facts are what facts always are. They are interesting to some, up to a point. They are, no doubt, necessary for many important purposes, including the sciences of life and death. But they are utterly, completely, inescapably beside the point of the living boy—of life itself, which most definitely goes on in spite of his, as they say, passing to god knows where.

Passing? Could it be that this all-too-common euphemism for the dying into which every single one of us enters is more loaded that we suppose? Is not this "passing" the only true analytic embrace by which all who were and are and will be become the We without differences or distinctions? If so, is it possible that the dead pass for the living—in the sense of presenting a false face? Are not what we call ghosts actually the real presences of death—of, that is, the dead who matter still to those who have yet to pass over the truest line of all? If so, then is it not so that we who think of ourselves as alive are, in fact (and merely for the time being), the ghosts of the dead and dying? Is this not the one analytic line that passes in both directions without causal privilege? Why do we suppose that the reality of life is only on one side of this most ubiquitous and universal of all possible social identities? If, as is surely the case, the living can understand themselves best as the universal clan of those who are currently dying, then why can we not say that living itself is the passing-at-hand? We who live—or, I should say, we who live under the sway of the European Diaspora's euphemistic culture of undying human Progress—are in fact joined by this one, and only, true human fact: that we will die one day, sooner or later; for some sooner than we expect.

This is the fact—and the only uncontested fact there is—that puts all other facts in their place. It is not that nothing else is true. Just that everything true is surely overcome by the beyond of its claims upon the factual. Is it not astonishing, in some final sense, that the one, uncontestable analytic distinction— that between the living and the dead—is in the end nothing at all?

Like Helga Crane and Clare Kendry we all pass over one or another—typically, several—of the analytic lines that would put us in the place society requires of us. The factual basis of our social existence—as distinct from, say, our biology or physiology or biochemistry or, if one can say it this way, our physics—lies not so much in what we are, or in what we present ourselves to be, as in how we contend with the several or many lines that would cut us into bits. Of these, none is more impertinent than the passing we attempt to pass over by referring to our dying as a "passing."

What is so terrible about not knowing where we are going in our dying? What, even, is so terrible about our going nowhere at all if that is where the to-what-of-dying turns out to be? Again, it is only, or perhaps mostly, we Europeans of the Near West who fear the possibility that we may be going nowhere at all, or nowhere we can describe. We fear it because, were such the case—as it surely is—then we could not hold to our learned faith in the pilgrim's Progress—in the forward, unending movement of social things from which we derive our pretense of the Good Society as that which will come to pass in the last days.

Hence the irony of it all. Liberal culture is, in truth, its own kind of soft eschatology in that it looks to the future that could not be with a prior confidence in the ongoingness of human life. The Calvinists of whom Weber taught us were right and wrong. They were right to say that we can never know what lies ahead; and wrong in their rational calculation that we could wager against the odds. The truth of modernity, of this liberal culture of the European Diaspora, is the truth that all facts in this world are, at most, a good bet. They can be a very good bet, which is different however from their being very Good in the sense of being the final resting place we are building for our children and dreaming of for ourselves.

There is no reason to be too harsh with Durkheim. He was, if not a Calvinist (which he surely was not), at the very least a courageous gambler. His wager was that no one would notice if he told them that the price of the Good and Moral Society, of the Society able to protect us all from the worst sort of death, was the loss of this other life that even sociologists know is there. Still, everyone who feels must surely have noticed that his Good Society—the one capable of keeping us from killing ourselves—was, truth be told, a society without individuals. The solitary are those who must die outside the pale. And so it happened that ever since the disciplinary sociologists and social philosophers accepted this uniquely French social contract: The general will is everything there is and the only true source of collective goods. Either this or the Anglo-Scottish alternative: that the Good is the accident of an invisible hand over the inexplicable commonwealth of what few enlightened individuals there may be.

Ever since the disciplinary social sciences were founded at the end of the previous and the beginning of the last century the analysts of the social struggled, as they do still today, with the alternatives posed on either side of the Channel. As the last century of that previous millennium just ended, the more sophisticated of positions came to be no more than the farce that passes over the tragedy Durkheim tried to analyze away. Many say today that it can be both at once—that the solitary individual lives with or in the structured societal just as the structured social somehow resides with or in the solitary one. This is the final, unresolved sociological riddle. What exactly is the where and what of the between of the individual and the societal—of the between of the one who acts on the ground and the structures against and because of which he acts as best he can? The sociologists are only the latest of the lineage of those, since at least Luther and Calvin, perhaps Descartes, to wonder about the analytic divide between the individual who lives and the wider world of things unseen that cannot be thought of, in any factual sense, as living. But under the sway of Durkheim—or of the need to contradict him—sociologists, more than others, have become the ones who fixed the dilemma in stone. They are not alone in this of course. Others, many others, sustain the dilemma. But it is the sociologists who are culpable because they are the ones who, having taken up the vocation of explaining the social in relation to the real, should, thereby, know better. Where is the properly honest sociologist who, meditating upon his subjects or the data they give birth to, is not struck by the riddle that, analytically speaking, the only real observables are the on-the-ground behaviors of more or less solitary individuals in some kind of local and temporary concert? Against whom, structures (whatever they are) are by any reasonable calculus, dead to those living individuals who, by just as reasonable a calculation, cannot live without them—however evil they may be.

There is only one way out of this riddle of social life. It is to accept the intolerable lesson taught most perfectly by the suicide. We who outlive, so to speak, those who kill themselves must ever after meditate, not on the analytic truth of their passings, but on the nether region into which they enter at the time of their decision to pass away. My boy's decision to pass away from suffering surely had both an inside and an outside. The enduring pain within was somehow aggravated by the false idea of a failure or shortcoming of his membership in his many social outsides—the Marines, his many friends from all over the world, his companions on various mountain tops, his parents and brother and sister who held him against many of the depths of his years. Yet, we who held him, as I did that last time in the very spot where I was told by good men of his death, were the basic observable realities of the social-withouts upon the individual-withins. This is the unbridgeable space of a between, the truth of which infuriates all sciences of the social. All attempts to bridge it by the finest of categorical assertions—such as those that seek to define these nether regions according to their object or subject statuses, their macro or micro volumes, their exterior or interior gravities—all such cuts are doomed to fail the best tests of their significance.

A suicide is not to be desired, or recommended. But it is that sort of final moment in respect to which the frailities of any and all analytic solutions to the dilemma of the social are there to be observed, darkly, for what they are. Those who kill themselves do so for their own reasons, among which, surely, are to be found both social and private ones. Those who survive to live their days as other living ones do, live their days in much the same way—for their own reasons, such as they are, among which are to be found social and private ones. Only the disciplinary professionals seek, as they must, to cut apart the reasons themselves for assignment to some or another analytic region. Often these professionals do very good work. It is necessary in its way, and wrong or false only when the regions they invent are taken with ultimate seriousness. The good news of it all is that, in the end, whatever our professional or disciplinary allegiances, we are all members of the We who must pass, for the time being, as if we were alive. The good news, in effect, is that we need not put all the eggs in the basket of scientific analysis, which is different from not putting any eggs in such a basket. The social thinker is, in his way, among the more pitiable of human creatures. He must deny what he knows to be true in order to gain recognition for the analytic truths he knows to be, at best, not nearly as true as he would wish. The good news is that we need not pass, in the end.

A gospel is any rumor of good news. Though the English-language word "gospel" seems to have come into play as the familiar religious term, among its variants is the word "gossip"—as in, a religious gossip who spreads the word. It might be said, that a gospel is any rumor of good news, especially it if bears some life-saving promise. Though his background was Jewish, and deeply so, Durkheim's sociology was intended as a gospel of good news for those suffering the evil effects of early industrial democracies. He believed that modern societies could overcome their divisions. Durkheim believed in the good secular society, and he believed in it nearly as deeply as his rabbinical forefathers believed in the value of religious society. While the line of rabbis in his native village in eastern France trusted that the ancient covenants of their faith were the source of the good society, Durkheim, having left them and their ways behind, came to the secular faith that facts of a certain kind are the foundation of a possible good society for moderns.

In the simplest possible terms, Durkheim was a truly modern man. Though he was anything but an optimist, he believed in the modern formula that knowledge applied to social problems could produce moral progress. For him, the knowledge in question was analytic sociology. For modern society, in his view, the paramount social problem was the loss of moral guidance—or, in his famous term, *anomie*. The more people were left to their individualistic impulses, the more they were at risk of self-destruction. The good news, for him, was that sociology could be that very science able to produce the knowledge necessary for progress toward a good—that is to say, morally safe—society.

The idea that knowledge can lead to moral progress is one of the foundational principles of modern culture. From Descartes in the seventeenth century to Rousseau and Kant in the eighteenth to Hegel and Marx in the nineteenth, social thinkers believed that knowledge could liberate those who suffer. Durkheim, however, was one of the first to recommend a specifically scientific knowledge—the analytic knowledge of the sociology he was trying to invent. Though he was himself a rather sober and cautious man, his ideas were among the most important precursors to the golden age of liberal ideology that came after World War II.

The high cultural version of this later Durkheim doctrine was Daniel Bell's classic work, *The End of Ideology*. Bell meant, to be sure, to announce the end

of socialist politics in the name of the then new, post-war American exuberance for its own military, economic, and social success. Bell's discussion,
which came to pass as an early version of his much more conservative views,
was in effect a sociologically refined expression of the liberal ideas then prevailing in American politics and culture. These ideas, more simply put, were
that the twentieth was to be the American Century because America's economic and military prowess—undeniably superior at the end of World
War II—had demonstrated for all to see what the Good Society could be.[4]

More importantly, this liberal ideology of the attainable Good Society was
thought to have transcended the early modern political ideologies, including
those inspired by Marx. Modernity's strong hope for final, conclusive social
progress was based on nothing less than the power of sociology and the social
sciences to do for the Good Society what the nuclear physicists had done for
warfare and the administrative scientists had done for the war mobilization
effort. From the sciences applied to industrial and military problems it had
been a short step to the administrative sciences applied to the militarized state.
In the 1950s, many, including Daniel Bell, trusted that it was but one more
step to a social science able to solve the most obdurate of social problems. The
golden age of American sociology in the 1950s was an age of widespread social
exuberance. The vanquishing of Hitler, the victory on two different global
fronts, and the war mobilization effort itself which led the United States out of
the Depression of the 1930s—all of these astonishing achievements were
widely, and not unwisely, taken as proof that America now possessed the sociological know-how required to produce the Good Society.

The short-lived golden age achieved its zenith in 1965 after the election of
Lyndon Baines Johnson to his own term as President of the United States. The
centerpiece of his Great Society politics was of course the War on Poverty—a
war that was to be fought with sociological facts applied by human good will to
the hitherto intractable social evil, of which none was more basic than the
poverty that wrecked the social lives of American blacks. Though the War on
Poverty would endure in various, incrementally lesser, forms down through
the end of the twentieth century, the golden age of liberal ideology fell on bad
times almost from the first.[5]

Not only was 1965 the birth year of the War of Poverty, it was simultaneously the beginning of America's significant involvement in the War in
Vietnam. It would take but three short years for Johnson to be driven from
office by the growing outrage over the deaths and terror in Southeast Asia. But
one of the more hapless victims of that war was the war at home against the
death and terror of urban and rural poverty, notably among blacks. Such programs as Head Start, model cities, and school nutrition problems would continue in the face of political opposition after the election of Richard Nixon in
1968. But the wide-eyed liberal faith that the Good Society could and would

be perfect here and now was dead from the moment in February 1965, when Johnson sent the first sorties of Rolling Thunder north to escalate a futile war against Vietnamese peasants.

Faith in facts—a belief that Durkheim first announced in the 1890s—died, or began to die, in the 1960s—and there is no better symbol of that death that the ill-fated 1965 report of Daniel Patrick Moynihan on the Negro family in America. In American society, at least, there is no darker thought than the inexorable sociological mysteries of the Negro family. From Moynihan's codification of the "facts" of this matter through the end of the American Century the poor, urban black underclass remained—more than any other social riddle—the unknown and unknowable. As has been said since the days of Alexis de Tocqueville in the nineteenth century, race has always been the American obsession.

But what, when all is said and done, is the object of that obsession? It is very well known by those who care to know it that the direct results of America's convoluted feelings toward racial differences are lives of pain and misery for those on the wrong side of the color line. The color line, far from being a turn of phrase, is in reality a hard-edged veil—one that tears every bit as much as it cloaks, and tears as much at the body as the heart. Just as medical examiners cut the bodies of sufferers like my boy to determine the truth of his death, so the analytic sociologies cut upon the body of racial differences to determine the truth of *race* itself.

Race, the concept, was itself cut out of the whole cloth of modernity. It was there from the beginning in the first world explorations—in the search for colored gold in the East Indies; in the accidental discovery of the West Indies; in the fast rising slave trade triangle that brought spices to Europe for slaves from Africa for labor in the Americas; in the settling of the West's world capitalist system into the convenience of colonizing greed; in the iron grip of the white European Disaspora upon all the colored peoples of the globe; in the liberal outlawing of slavery that made way for the legal sanctioning of economic dependencies in the American South, the Caribbean, the rest of the Americas, the far North, in Asia, in the Middle East, in Africa; in, today, the rapid-fire web of information around the globe sending capital to search out the last remains of colored labor power. What began in the Americas was nothing more than the first famous disembarkation of the European culture's darkest thought that the color line between the white and dark was an illusion, of which the acceptance of the American exotics in Paris or London or Copenhagen—Louis Armstrong, James Baldwin, Josephine Baker, Nella Larsen's Helga Crane—were thought to be the factual evidences.

The European Diaspora held the concept *race* in high disregard in order that it might serve its purposes under the surface of social things. The racial segregation of the world, under and within which we still live in the new century, was the foundational necessity of world capitalism. The proposition

strikes even the most liberal as absurd. It *is* absurd, as are all superficially innocent analytic cuts. But none is more certifiably absurd than the cut of *race*—a
concept taken over from an earlier, quaint usage as simply "people" in order to
divide the peoples of the globe into their lesser and greater moieties.

From the first, nearly every human clan seems to have organized itself in
more or less neatly defined totemic parts, each separately organized more or
less equally into a half of the whole. It was not, however, until the modern era,
and late in modernity at that, that members of the human "race" took up the
places once reserved for natural beings, which generally are not thought to be
susceptible to self-organization into *a* race, or even *several* of them. In the strict
totemic system, upon which Durkheim, again, was one of the first and most
compelling commentators, creatures of the sea and air and forest served as collective representations of the natural human urge to divide its whole into two
parts, each with its respective greater or lesser members. The Wotjobaluk, a
race of people original to New South Wales, divide their social universe
between the sun moiety, and the not-the-sun peoples. To the former belong
the sub-clans of hot wind, the *white* crestless cockatoo, and other things
belonging to the sun; to the latter belong the deaf adder, the *black* cockatoo,
and the pelican.[6] Each has its place in the scheme of things which are themselves organized by races defined by the sun and its absence—in effect, by the
light and the dark. On the one side live the people of the white and crestless
cockatoo; to the sunless side live those of the black cockatoo. People were, as
it is sometimes said, "raced" from the beginning. But only in modern times did
the racial groupings of people became an analytic cut that wounded, or killed,
some while saving the others.

Modernity's dream of the Good Society is now, as it always was, just that—a
dream. Dreams, to be sure, are the first and most important source of the
imagination—in this case of the social imaginary. If we are to take the wisdom
of psychoanalysis seriously, dreams must be accepted as their own kind of systematic language, a discourse of a special sort. Inverted, displaced, and condensed—these were the qualities of dream talk assigned by Freud.[7] To interpret a dream the analytic patient must be willing to consider its manifest story
contents as always, and necessarily, opposite, distant, and symbolically packed
representations of some unconscious wish.

To dream, as I have, of a bright, beautiful Victorian lamp on a sparkling
white, lace-covered table in a room in the basement of my childhood home
was, for me, to dream the dark thought society taught me to deny. The white
light was my dark, forbidden desire for my dark other mother—for Florence
Lyons, the mother who gently wiped my bottom, spoon fed my hungers, and
held me to her breast. She was the mother who did what my bio-mom, Helen,
wanted to do but, for whatever reasons, could not. This dream of mine is no
different in symbolic kind from those of the Wotjobaluk who live under the

sign of the black cockatoo, there to take for themselves the lesser place on the trail of the setting of sun. Their wish, to be sure, is to be the clan whose place is fixed, not by some human unworthiness, but by movement of the heavenly bodies over the natural wonders of the animate world about. The white light, like the black cockatoo, are the dreamlike stories of inverted, displaced, and condensed possibilities for which persons as strange to each other as could be dream of the good society they cannot ever have.

Though we think of dreams, when we think about them at all, as utterly private, as indeed they are, they are, just the same, the subterranean tunnels through which we join our private wishes to those of others in the so-called conscious world. Thus dreaming is, in effect, the energy behind whatever social imagination we have. When, in the days after the news of my son's death, I had this vision of the three strong-winged birds, one settling to stand at attention on a high limb, the other two aloft at either wing, I saw my dead boy alive in that moment. Beyond all the analytic reasons, that majestic bird, standing as he stood in this life, strong and upright, was Matthew. It was, of course, my wish to have some final word from him. Of course, in this analytically real world he was not a bird of any kind. Or was he? He was one who flew—through the joys and pains of his days toward the highest mountains, toward what turned out to be the impossible dream of his Marine Corps pilot wings.

When I spoke at services held before the gathered corps of Marine pilots at his final base in Corpus Christi, I told the story of his appearance as a bird. I told these strong and alive men and women how much he would have loved to have had his wings, to have flown with them. I asked them, if they could, occasionally to tip their wing to him as they flew. They knew what I meant. When they all flew up and out, after receiving their wings, they sent me the flight jacket that would have been Matt's. Did they think that bird was real? It all depends what you mean by real. It was a wish that, in those moments, joined me to my dead boy, and in the telling of his story, him to the Marine Corps family in whose arms he quit this life. His story was just one of the hundreds they had already heard, or will hear as the years go by. But it was, I am sure, just as real and necessary to their flying as their precise technical knowledge of vectors and velocities. One can hardly go up and away on analytic knowledge alone. It takes a certain courage, for which the social imagination is required. This, it seems to me, is how and why people in whichever circumstances bind themselves to each other when and for however long they do.

This, no less, is the sort of dreaming white people of the European Diaspora have dreamed for some centuries now. They dream of alabaster cities, of snow-capped mountains rising above fruited plains, of the westward march of the sun. Always, it turns out, westward with the light. Their dream of progress was, thus, an inverted, displaced, and condensed expression of their wish not to be in the place of the black cockatoo—not to be what their knew they were. Their darkest thought was that they had cut the world into twos. Their race for progress required them to *race* the whole of human things—of society. Hence, they cut out "society" for the analytic purpose of defining, organizing, classifying, and assigning themselves as the other to those they wished they were not.

In this sense, whatever our phenotype, to be human is to live in, for, or in spite of the dark. The irony of the modern world is that the white people hold the darkest thoughts—the fear that they are, as they know they are, forever just as dark as those against whom they set themselves. In spite of what they say, race is never ultimately about skin and blood. These are merely the surfaces upon which whites project their upside-down distortions of what they fear the most.

Matt's skin was as visibly white as mine. Yet, he was the only white person I've ever met who took my feelings of blackness at face value. Though he had hardly known Florence, he understood who she was to me, and I to her— and he knew it without reservation. When Annie was born, he walked about the town handing out cigars, saying: "My sister's a sistah!" Was he clowning? Was he signifying on my pretenses to a certain interior blackness? Were we, together, being all too familiar with those who, in spite of our being a bit wise, might not claim us as their own? Of course we were. How else does one live with the differences by which social life is constituted, unless it is through a necessary foolishness? How else does one imagine the social whole of things—with all its goods and evils, its joys and pains, its light sides and dark ones? How else, if not by the dreamlike play of truths inverted, displaced, and packed tightly?

Clinically, it is almost certain that Matt defied death by his risk-taking because he feared it. Abreaction is normal at the extremes of human suffering. Then, too, what are dreams, if they are not the abreactive to the analytically true? Are not dreams of all kinds—including those that compose the social imaginary of a civilization—projections of possible ideals against the dark backdrop of the realities that may dawn again as one wakes, soaked with sweat, to a cold house in the middle of the night? Do we not all commit a kind of suicide when we give in to the private dreams behind the official public ones? When we allow ourselves, under the cover of night, to see what we truly, deeply feel and fear? The reasons dreams must always be in a complexly distorted code is that we could not bear them otherwise. Because he suffered in silence for so long, Mattie must have been entirely familiar with the death he chose to visit. It is entirely possible that the dark thoughts of depression and death that visited him every day were what allowed him not to fear his own blackness, or mine. I do not mean to say he was not afraid, or that his dying was somehow an unqualified act of human transcendence. What it was—what he was, I think—was in its way an act arising from his having already been all-too-familiar with the darker realities.

When, socially, we consign people to the darker moiety of the human race, we who do this are protecting ourselves. We white people know very well that our skin and blood gives us no diplomatic immunity from the dark thoughts of death that visit, limit, and, funnily, enliven all men and women. Race is the deepest analytic cut of all because it cuts to the quick of human fear. Suicides, in their way, are beyond that fear. They enter into the utter, complete aloneness—into the dark tunnel of which Kay Redfield Jameson speaks—because they despair of this life. For them it is a last and only resort. But however, and whenever, they take the step off into the sweet mercies of death they no doubt take it honorably. It is a way for some at least to rejoin the living by entering unqualifiedly into their darkest thoughts.

Is suicide a good? No, of course not. It is surely beyond good and evil. But then so is the analytic society cut out to define the good of certain clans of men. Modernity's lovely wish to make all things better in due course is not foolish; neither is it good any more than it is evil—which is not to deny that it has made fools of the many who have chosen to do evil or tried to do good in its name. The good news of suicide is that there are those—among them my dead boy—who went where we all will go. If we are separated from suicides by the small difference of their agency in the matter, then we are joined to them—not just by sentiment—but by the reminder that they bring home the gospel of the beyond of good and evil. If there is no taboo against our feeling our darkness, then there are no taboos of any final salience. James Baldwin, who hated analytic sociology with a passion, once said that the race problem will be solved only when everyone screws everyone else. That may well be true, but how will we ever get to that degree of social intimacy if it is not by, first, allowing ourselves to relax into the arms of the one true nakedness—the dreamlike presence of death in the pleasures of life?

"Dark thoughts" is a figure of speech that tells the gospel as it is. We whites make some darker than they are in order to survive the fall. We dream of them through the night. They are, sometimes, our own. They are us. Before there was ever any sort of analytic cut—before there was analysis of any kind—one supposes, according to the modernist method of dreaming the first peoples, we were all of one clan. The black cockatoos must dream of the white crestless cockatoos, as the white ones dream of the dark. Whatever social thought and social living are about, they must be—that is, they ought to be—about overcoming the fear of social intermingling that led to the analytic divisions that cut the good from the bad. Whatever truth there is—and however necessary it may be in some circumstances to make some cuts of this kind—the larger social truths are the truths we dream at night, or in the day when we see a great bird high above us and reach to him, there to find our humanity.

Acknowledgments

More even than most, a book like this—so much of it intimate—owes to a considerable company, living and dead, with whom I have had relations of various and varying kinds. I could not possibly thank them all—if only because to begin such a list would be to end it too soon. This book has been around, in one or another version, for years. Why it took so long to come right is hard to say. Over the years, I made every effort to thank those who helped. They, in any case, should know how I feel about them and what they have done for me. And so I limit my acknowledgments to a few and ask the larger host to trust the mysteries whereby all things work together for good.

Years ago, Ann duCille set me straight on the Nella Larsen chapter. Patricia Clough, in the old days, kept me honest when it comes to Freud and Derrida. Lauren Craniotes lent me her copy of *Passing*, which I still have. Norman Denzin gave good advice on tone and contents. Elaine Markson put an earlier version out for sale and thus helped me learn that the book needed to be completely rewritten, as it has been. Ilene Kalish edits with such grace and humor that I never minded being told what to do. Phyllis Meadow taught me much of what I know about dreams. Dena Reed has long been my guide to the dark within. Kate Rushin is the source of the line on Elvis's black back-ups. Steve Seidman warmly supported the original idea. Had he not, I might not have stayed with it. Audrey Sprenger is that most special of intellectual companions who often understands what I am doing before I do.

In a somewhat different category, I am beset by an irrepressible urge to thank members of my childhood family—this, perhaps, because the writing refreshed my experiences and altered my standpoint. Among those dead, I thank: Charles C. Lemert, M.D. (I'm trying), Edwin Lemert (you were the first to help me understand), Gertrude M. Lemert (I'm sorry I couldn't sing "Amazing Grace" for you), Helen R. Lemert (I know you tried your best), and Florence Lyons (again, always). In the very last days of writing this book, my brother Mike, still very much alive, let me know that he saw what I saw—which means more to me than he might suppose.

More formally, some parts, here and there, are previously published and reprinted here by permission of the publishers or by prior agreement. Traces of chapter two appeared as "Dark Thoughts About the Self," *Social Theory and the Politics of Identity*, Craig Calhoun, ed., (1994), pp. 100–138. The latter part of chapter three is based on "Multiculturalism," *Handbook of Social Theory*, George Ritzer and Barry Smart, eds., (2001), pp. 297–308. Chapter four is essentially the introduction to *The Voice of Anna Julia Cooper*, Charles Lemert and Esme Bahn, eds., (1998). Chapters five and six, in somewhat different forms, were my "Charlotte Perkins Gilman" and "W. E. B. Du Bois" entries in *The Blackwell Companion to Major Social Theorists*, George Ritzer, ed., (2000). And a good bit of chapter eight appeared in *Sociology Hesitant: Thinking With W. E. B. Du Bois* (Ronald A.T. Judy, ed.), a special issue of *boundary 2*, Volume 27, number 3 (fall, 2000): 215–249. Traces, but not much more, of chapter nine are from "The Might Have Been and Could Be of Religion in Social Theory," *Sociological Theory* Volume 17, No. 3 (November 1999): 240–265. All this I have taken from myself. I have tried, without overdoing it, to note everything I took from others. I never quote from notes, so everything is direct from the sources. All dictionary definitions and word histories are from the *Oxford English Dictionary* (second edition).

Finally, Geri, Annie, and Noah are the ones with whom I live most intimately. Together we invent the mix of touches and tears, shouts and hugs, jokes and dances that make life together complex but a hell of a lot of fun. The picture on the dedication page of Matthew with Annie and Noah shows him as he was his last Christmas. He embraced those he loved with humor, strength, and a deep familiarity with the dark as well as the light. You can see, if you look closely, the haunting spirit that made him so real, even when it hurt a lot. You can also see Noah, taking the distance of the one who holds social things as they are, one day at a time. Between, Anna Julia delights in the mix like the old soul she is. What you don't see is Geri and me taking it all in—just as we did the days following, just as we will the days to come.

—Charles Lemert
Killingworth, Connecticut

Endnotes

Chapter One

1. The *Oxford English Dictionary*, from which this definition (like others in this book) is taken, is itself an analytic work. Often the OED analyzes with a sense of humor; in this case, with a remarkable grasp of the philosophical issues. The entry quoted above unites two analytic subsections: "of things material" and "of things immaterial." It then follows with the entry: "to analyze away"—the limiting threat of analysis.

2. See Walter Benjamin, "The Work of Art in an Age of Mechanical Reproduction," in *Illuminations* (New York: Harcourt Brace & Co, 1968). The others to whom I refer are, of course, those associated, as was Benjamin, with the original Frankfurt School in Germany in the 1930s.

3. Václav Havel, "The End of the Modern Era," *The New York Times* (March 1, 1992); reprinted in Charles Lemert, ed., *Social Theory* (New York: Westview Press, 1998), pp. 594–596.

4. Toni Morrison, *Toni Morrison/Nobel Prize Acceptance Speech* (New York: Knopf, 1994), p. 19.

5. George Kennan, "The Long Telegram," *Memoirs 1925–1950* (New York: Pantheon/Little, Brown, & Co., 1967), p. 549.

6. One of the most remarkable connections between the Russian and the American people was their shared nineteenth-century dream of settling barren open spaces. For the Americans it was, of course, the Great Plains. For the Russians it was the rich Amur River basin in oriental Russia, which Russians once thought of as their Mississippi and Ohio valleys. See Mark Bassin, *Imperial Visions: Nationalist Imagination and Geographical Expansion in the Russian Far East, 1840–1865* (Cambridge, UK: Cambridge University Press, 1999), especially chapter 5. [Thanks to Andy Day for the reference.] Relatedly, for a brilliant, recent discussion of just how American imperial visions continue into the new millennium as an entanglement of Asian and East Asian geopolitics, see Bruce Cummings, *Parallax Visions: Making Sense of American–East Asian Relations at the End of the Century* (Durham, NC: Duke University Press, 1999).

7. One the best of these is David Held et al., *Global Transformations* (Stanford, CA: Stanford University Press, 1999). Though, in many ways, the most thorough study of globalization, the argument is that global change is not a true structural change so much as a transformation of world order that leaves the nation state in a different but still central place in the world system.

8. Immanuel Wallerstein has done more than anyone to establish the idea of modernity as world system. Yet, even he occasionally reveals that the new global order may have undercut the modern world structure, most especially in the eclipse of the liberal nation state. See *Utopistics: Or, Historical Choices of the Twenty-first Century* (New York: The New Press, 1998); *Geopolitics and Geoculture: Essays on the Changing World System* (Cambridge, UK: Cambridge University Press, 1991) and, among others, *After Liberalism* (New York: The New Press, 1995).

9. Ferdinand Toennies, *Community and Society: Gemeinschaft und Gesellschaft*, translated by Charles Loomis (New York: Harper & Row, 1957), p. 33.

10. Charles Lemert, *Social Things* (Lanham, MD: Rowman & Littlefield, 2002), chapter 3.

11. Alan Sokal is the character in question. For one introduction among thousands available see Charles Lemert, *Postmodernism Is Not What You Think* (Oxford, UK: Basil Blackwell, 1997), pp. 11–15.

12. For one striking example, see James Coleman, *Foundations of Social Theory* (Cambridge, MA: Harvard University Press, 1990).

13. See Charles Lemert, *Sociology After the Crisis* (New York: Westview Press, 1995), chapters 2 and 3 for a full discussion of Durkheim.
14. The most succinct summary of the three Enlightenment principles is in Isaiah Berlin, *The Roots of Romanticism* (Princeton, NJ: Princeton University Press, 1999), pp. 21–23. Berlin's are, in effect: There are questions, to be sure. All questions have an answer (if not, they are irrelevant). Still, there are unsolved puzzles.
15. The numbers change from year to year, but the ones mentioned here are trends of long duration. See Lester Brown, Michael Renner, Brian Halweil, *Vital Signs* 1999 (New York: W. W. Norton/Worldwatch Institute, 1999).
16. Frantz Fanon, *The Wretched of the Earth* (New York, Grove Press, 1968), p. 36; quote following, p. 37.
17. *Ibid.*, p. 37.
18. Again, see Berlin, *Roots of Romanticism.*
19. Goffman makes the distinction between dark and strategic secrets in *Presentation of Self in Everyday Life* (New York: Anchor/Doubleday Books, 1959), chapter 4. But the idea is just as basic to *Stigma* (New York: Simon & Schuster, 1963). Goffman is also the source for the loose analytic use of the word "face"; see "Face-Work," in *Interaction Ritual* (New York: Random House, 1967), chapter 1.
20. See, for a striking example, Margo Jefferson, "Authentic American," *The New York Times Book Review*, February 18, 2001, p. 35.

Chaper Two
1. Joseph Ellis, "A Note on the Sally Hemings Scandal," *American Sphinx: The Character of Thomas Jefferson* (New York: Knopf, 1997), pp. 303–307. The facts about and interpretations of Jefferson in this section are based on Ellis, *American Sphinx*. It should be said, however, that Ellis, probably the most astute interpreter of the American founding fathers, takes a dark view of Jefferson, darker than of the others, like Adams, Madison, and Monroe, even of Hamilton. See, more recently, Ellis, *The Founding Brothers: The Revolutionary Generation* (New York: Knopf, 2000).
2. One of the most striking events on the first months of the new century is that so shortly after Jefferson's blood was found under the skin of other than white children, there began a major revision in the pantheon of founding fathers. Both Ellis's *Founding Brothers* and David McCullough's *John Adams* (New York: Simon & Schuster, 2001) were atop the best-seller lists through 2001.
3. Among the many stories of people coming upon racial surprises and crossings over: see Shirlee Taylor Haizlip, *The Sweeter the Juice: A Family Memoir in Black and White* (New York: Simon & Schuster, 1994) and James McBride, *The Color of Water* (New York: Riverhead, 1996). For an account of one white man's attempt to travel on the other side of the color line, see Walt Harrington, *Crossings: A White Man's Journey into Black America* (New York: HarperCollins, 1992). On the biracial life, see Lise Funderburg, *Black, White, Other* (New York: William Morrow, 1994). And for a brilliant discussion of the whiteness of famous blacks (Frederick Douglass, Ralph Ellison, Bob Marley), see Gregory Stephens, *On Racial Frontiers* (New York: Cambridge University Press, 1999).
4. Though originally "Creole" referred to blacks born in the New World, it soon took on the meaning of all those, whether of African or European descent, born in a New World or other colony. As in many other things, the best discussion is Benedict Anderson's in "Creole Pioneers," *Imagined Communities* (London: Verso, 1983).
5. *Jefferson/Autobiography Notes on the State of Virginia, Public and Private Papers, Addresses, Letters* (New York: The Library of America, 1984), pp. 1–102. The autobiography was written in 1790.
6. *Ibid.*, 22.
7. Gary Wills, *Inventing America: Jefferson's Declaration of Independence* (New York: Doubleday, 1978), pp. 66–8.
8. Ellis, *American Sphinx*, chapter 1.
9. Among other important sources, see Alberto Melucci, *Challenging Codes* (New York: Cambridge University Press, 1996) on the importance of the marginal in the new social movements.
10. H. B. Cavalcanti of the University of Richmond in Virginia transmitted the data following on November 18, 1999. His version is attributed to Phillip M. Harter of Stanford University. I

have previously seen copies of the same numbers distributed by the Commission on Racial Justice of the United Church of Christ (US).

11. Chief Red Jacket, "We Also Have Religion," in *Our Nation's Archive*, edited by Erik Bruun and Jay Crosby (New York: Black Dog & Leventhal Publishers, 1999), p. 208. One of the more remarkable reversals found among the Weak-We is their sense of the reversals of space and loss brought on by the Strong-We colonizers. Another notable example is the telling line in a speech given by a Stockbridge Indian before a congress of whites in 1775: "I was great and you were little" (*ibid.*, p. 123).

12. *Narrative of Sojourner Truth*, edited by Margaret Washington (New York: Random House, 1993), p. 118. These are the concluding words of Sojourner Truth's famous 1851 "Ar'n't I a Woman?" speech which is the subject of considerable controversy. For the history of the conditions and distortions of this famous speech see Nell Irwin Painter, *Sojourner Truth: A Life, A Symbol* (New York: W.W. Norton, 1996). And for an insightful discussion, see Donna Haraway, "Ecce Homo, Ain't (Ar'n't) I a Woman, and Inappropriate/d Others: The Human in a Post-humanist Landscape," *Feminists Theorize the Political*, edited by Judith Butler and Joan W. Scott (New York: Routledge, 1992), pp. 86–100.

13. Gloria Anzaldúa, *Borderlands/La Frontera: The New Mestiza* (San Francisco: Spinsters/Aunt Lutte Press, 1987), p. 20.

14. See, Gloria Anzaldua, "The Homeland, Aztlan" in *Borderlands*, chapter 1, for her history of the borderland.

15. Lisa Lowe, *Immigrant Acts: On Asian American Cultural Politics* (Durham, NC: Duke University Press, 1998), p. 21.

16. A sociological bonus of Benedict's *Rule* is that, though his birth and death dates are established, the exact authorship of the *Rule* can only be estimated. The principal biographical source on Benedict is Gregory I the Great (540–604), who as pope the last fourteen years of his life can be credited with recognition of the revolutionary sociology of Benedict, who was admired by Gregory more for the monastic movement that followed the *Rule* than for the text itself.

17. Also, according to Ellis, *American Sphinx*, pp. 56–59, Jefferson seems to have read Locke's psychology more closely than his politics.

18. Immanuel Kant, *Metaphysical Foundations of Morals*, from *The Philosophy of Kant* (New York: The Modern Library/Random House, 1993), p. 187.

19. For whatever it may be worth, the OED entry for "psyche" prints out to a mere four pages, while that for "self" is twenty-four.

20. Jean Laplanche, "The Unfinished Copernican Revolution," *Essays on Otherness* (New York: Routledge, 1999), chapter 1.

21. William James, *Principles of Psychology* (1890; reprint, Cambridge, MA: Harvard University Press, 1981), p. 15.

22. *Ibid.*, p. 212.

23. *Ibid.*, p. 279. All quotes immediately following, *ibid.*, pp. 279–288.

24. *Ibid.*, p. 316.

25. William James, *Varieties of Religious Experience* (1902; reprint, New York: Fontana Library, 1960), p. 176.

26. Norbert Wiley, *The Semiotic Self* (Chicago: University of Chicago, 1994); Karl Scheibe, *Self Studies* (Westport, CT: Praeger, 1995).

27. George Herbert Mead, *Mind, Self & Society* (1934; reprint, Chicago: University of Chicago Press, 1962), p. 136.

28. Erving Goffman, *Stigma: Notes on the Management of a Spoiled Identity* (New York: Simon and Schuster, 1963), p. 128.

29. *Ibid.*, p. 130.

30. *Ibid.*, p. 57.

31. *Ibid.*, p. 123.

32. For a discussion of the historical setting of Goffman's basic ideas, and their value even today, see Charles Lemert, "*Goffman*," in Lemert and Ann Branaman, eds., *The Goffman Reader* (Oxford, UK: Basil Blackwell, 1997),pp. ix–xliii.

33. Charles Taylor, *Sources of the Self: The Making of Modern Identity* (Cambridge, MA: Harvard University Press, 1989), p. 197; see chapters 10 and 11 especially on Descartes and Locke.

34. *Ibid.*, p. 27.

35. *Ibid.*, p. 35.

36. *Ibid.*, pp. 51–2.

37. Craig Calhoun, "Morality, Identity, and Historical Explanation: Charles Taylor on the Sources of the Self," *Sociological Theory*, 10:2 (1991): p. 260. Quote below same page.
38. Patricia Hill Collins, *Fighting Words: Black Women & the Search for Justice* (Minneapolis: University of Minnesota Press, 1998), p. 188.
39. *Ibid.*, p. 187.
40. For an exposé of the way in which analytic social scientists use citations and other formalities to keep the secrets of their guild, see Ben Agger, *Public Sociology* (Boulder, CO: Rowman & Littlefield, 2000).

Chapter Three

1. See, for more detail: Charles Lemert, *Postmodernism Is Not What You Think* (Oxford, UK: Basil Blackwell, 1997), chapters 1–3.
2. A fool is one who fools himself. For my view of Sokal, see: *ibid.* pp. 7–11.
3. For a particularly bizarre example, see: Andrew Abbott, "Engaging Exemplars or Touting the Top Ten?" *Perspectives: American Sociological Association Theory Section Newsletter* 20:4 (1998): pp. 4–8. Fortunately, those who abuse the language in such ways occasionally have friends who encourage them to do better; for example, in reference at least to the last three terms mentioned. For a hilarious reply to Abbott, see: Alan Sica, "Mr. Abbott's Miss Bennet: So Much Not to Read; So Little Time in Which Not to Read it," *ibid.* 21. 1999 (1): pp. 1–8.
4. Stanley Fish, "Boutique Multiculturalism, or Why Liberals Are Incapable of Thinking About Hate Speech," pp. 31–54 in Philip Lopate, ed., *The Anchor Essay Annual: Best of 1998* (New York: Anchor/Doubleday 1998).
5. Samuel Huntington, *Clash of Civilizations and the Remaking of World Order* (New York: Simon and Schuster, 1996); Nathan Glazer, *We Are All Multiculturalists Now* (Cambridge, MA: Harvard University Press, 1996). For a discussion of the "apparent" victory of "multiculturalism" in the culture wars begun in 1987 by Allan Bloom's *The Closing of the American Mind*, see Frederick Buell, "Nationalist Postnationalism: Globalist Discourse in Contemporary American Culture," *American Quarterly* 50:3 (1998): pp. 548–591.
6. For the example of the monoculturalist view, see Francis Fukuyama, *The End of History and the Last Man* (New York: Free Press, 1992); and for the end of the West, see: Huntington, *Clash of Civilizations*.
7. Richard Rorty, *Philosophy and the Mirror of Nature* (Princeton, NJ: Princeton University Press, 1979).
8. See, for example: Stratos Constantinidis, "Greek Drama and Multiculturalism," *Journal of Modern Greek Studies* 14; 1 (1996): pp. 1–30.
9. Isaiah Berlin, *The Roots of Romanticism* (Princeton, NJ: Princeton University Press, 1999).
10. Ralph Waldo Emerson, "Nature," in Brooks Atkinson, ed., *The Complete Essays and Other Writings of Ralph Waldo Emerson* (New York: Random House, 1940).
11. Arthur Schlesinger, Jr., *Disuniting of America* (Knoxville, TN: Whittle Direct Books, 1991), p. 76.
12. Abdule R. JanMohamed and David Lloyd, *Nature and Context of Minority Discourse* (New York: Oxford University Press, 1990).
13. Lisa Lowe, *Immigrant Acts: On Asian American Cultural Politics* (Durham, NC: Duke University Press,1996).
14. Jean Bethke Elshtain, *Democracy on Trial* (New York: Basic Books, 1995), chapter 2.
15. Gloria Anzaldúa, *Borderlands/La Frontera* (San Francisco: Aunt Lutte Books, 1987).
16. Juergen Habermas, "Struggles for Recognition in the Democratic Constitutional state," pp. 120–148 in Charles Taylor et al., *Multiculturalism: Examining the Politics of Recognition* (Princeton, NJ: Princeton University Press, 1994).
17. Immanuel Wallerstein, *After Liberalism* (New York: The New Press, 1995), especially chapter 12. Also: Wallerstein, *Utopistics* (New York: The New Press, 1998). And: Arjun Appadurai, *Modernity at Large: Cultural Dimensions of Globalization* (Minneapolis: University of Minnesota Press, 1996).
18. Schlesinger, *The Disuniting of America*.
19. For a summary of the issues in relation to multiculturalism, see: Charles Taylor, "The Politics of Recognition," pp. 12–74 in Charles Taylor et al. *Multiculturalism: Examining the Politics of Recognition* (Princeton, NJ: Princeton University Press, 1994).
20. John Rawls, *Theory of Justice* (Cambridge, MA: Harvard University Press, 1971).
21. Immanuel Wallerstein, *After Liberalism*; also: Wallerstein, *Utopistics*, pp. 21–25.

22. Erving Goffman, *Stigma* (New York: Simon and Schuster, 1963), pp. 123–25.
23. Todd Gitlin, *Twilight of Common Dreams* (New York: Metropolitan Books, 1995).
24. Elshtain, *Democracy on Trial*, p. 58.
25. Goffman, *Stigma*.
26. Charles Taylor, *Sources of the Self* (Cambridge, MA: Harvard University Press, 1989); also Taylor, "The Politics of Recognition," in *Multiculturalism*.
27. For a summary, see: Michael Walzer, *On Toleration* (New Haven: Yale University Press, 1997), chapter 2.
28. Elshtain, *Democracy on Trial*; and Wallerstein, *Utopistics*.
29. Robert Hughes, *The Culture of Complaint* (New York: Warner Books, 1993).
30. Roberto Unger, and Cornel West, *The Future of American Progressivism* (Boston: Beacon Press, 1998), p. 25.
31. Anthony Giddens, *Beyond Left and Right: The Future of Radical Politics* (Stanford, CA: Stanford University Press, 1994), pp. 11–21.
32. Wallerstein, *Utopistics*.
33. Isaiah Berlin, *The Roots of Romanticism*.
34. Charles Taylor, *Sources of the Self*, pp. 25–44; 63.
35. For example, Nancy Fraser, *Justice Interruptus: Critical Reflections on the "Postsocialist" Condition* (New York: Routledge, 1997). Also Iris Marion Young, *Justice and the Politics of Difference* (Princeton, NJ: Princeton University Press, 1990).

Chapter Four
1. Darlene Clark Hine, with Elsa Barkley Brown and Rosalyn Terborg-Penn, eds., *Black Women of America* (Brooklyn: Carlson, 1993). The same photo appears on the covers of two important biographical studies of Cooper: Louise Daniel Hutchinson, *Anna Julia Cooper: A Voice from the South* (Washington, DC: Anacostia Neighborhood Museum/Smithsonian Press, 1981) and Leona C. Gabel, *From Slavery to the Sorbonne and Beyond: The Life and Writings of Anna J. Cooper* (Northampton, MA: Smith College Studies in History, 1982).

 In the same vein, the most important history of black women in America takes its title from one of Cooper's most famous lines: Paula Giddings, *When and Where I Enter: The Impact of Black Women on Race and Sex in America* (New York: William Morrow, 1984).
2. Anna Julia Cooper, *A Voice From the South*, in *The Voice of Anna Julia Cooper*, Charles C. Lemert and Esme Bhan, eds. (Lanham, MD: Rowman & Littlefield Publishers, Inc., 1998), p. 145.

 Please note: Hereafter *A Voice* refers to the original book by Cooper *A Voice From the South*, which appears in its entirety as chapters 1–10 of the book edited by Lemert and Bhan, *The Voice of Anna Julia Cooper*. The later, edited work will be cited as *The Voice*. In short *A Voice* is but one of many writings by Cooper in *The Voice*.
3. Cooper, *A Voice*, in *The Voice*, see note 101 for her disdain for the expression.
4. Cooper, "Status of Women in America", in *The Voice*, p. 117.
5. Cooper, "Womanhood: A Vital Element in the Regeneration and Progress of a Race," in *A Voice*, in *The Voice*, chapter 3, p. 54.
6. The most prominent scholarly discussion of the idea of the cult of true womanhood is Barbara Welter, *Dimity Convictions: The American Woman in the Nineteenth Century* (Athens, OH: Ohio University Press, 1976). A famous recent use of the idea is Ann duCille, "The Occult of True Black Womanhood: Critical Demeanor and Black Feminist Studies," *Signs*, 19, no. 3 (1994), pp. 591–629, (reprinted in duCille, *Skin Trade* (Cambridge, MA: Harvard University Press, 1996).

 It should be said that, since Barbara Welter's original presentation of the true womanhood ideal in 1976, subsequent scholarship has shown that among white Southern women, especially in the antebellum period and during the Civil War, responsibility for moral and domestic culture was always painfully bound up with the economics and politics of the plantation system. See, for example, Drew Gilpin Faust, *Mothers of Invention: Women of the Slaveholding South in the American Civil War* (Chapel Hill, NC: University of North Carolina Press, 1996). Just the same, the concept as Welter described it remains a central issue in interpretations of Cooper, and rightly so.

 Most prominent among those who consider Cooper too indulgent of true womanhood doctrines is Mary Helen Washington, "Introduction" to the Oxford edition of Cooper's *A Voice From the South* (New York: Oxford University Press, 1988), p. xlvi. Most notable among others who question Cooper on this score is Karen Baker-Fletcher, *A "Singing Something": The Literature of Anna Julia Cooper as a Resource for a Theological Anthropology of Voice* (Harvard University doctoral thesis, 1991), chapter 5. Baker-Fletcher's thesis has been published in substantially revised form as *A Singing Something: Womanist Reflections on Anna Julia Cooper* (New York: Crossroad, 1994). References to Baker-Fletcher's work will be to the thesis unless otherwise indicated. Somewhat less persuasive is Jesse Michael Lang's discussion of this theme in Cooper's writings: *Anticipations of the Booker T. Washington–W. E. B. Du Bois Dialectic in the Writings of Frances E. W. Harper, Ida B. Wells, and Anna Julia Cooper* (Georgetown University master's thesis, 1992). The most demanding argument on the other side is Hazel Carby's in *Reconstructing Womanhood: The Emergence of the Afro-American Woman Novelist* (New York: Oxford University Press, 1987), chapter 5.

7. Cooper, "The Early Years in Washington: Reminiscences of Life With the Grimkés," *The Voice*, p. 310.

8. Nella Larson (1891–1964) published two important novels (*Quicksand* in 1928, and *Passing* in 1929), both involving the theme of passing. See *Quicksand and Passing*, ed. Deborah McDowell (Trenton, NJ: Rutgers University Press, 1988).

9. Mary Eliza Church Terrell (1863–1954) was Cooper's classmate at Oberlin in the 1880s and her colleague at the M Street School. Ida Bell Wells-Barnett (1862–1931), the anti-lynching campaigner and black women's suffragette, was not personally close to Cooper, though they shared many causes, including opposition to Booker T. Washington. Fanny Jackson Coppin (1837–1913), of an earlier generation, preceded Cooper and Mary Church at Oberlin by twenty years. Yet, in 1893, Cooper and Coppin shared the platform at the women's congress of the Chicago World's Fair. There is a photograph of Cooper, Terrell, and Ida Wells-Barnett (their classmate at Oberlin) in their later years in Louise Hutchinson, *Anna Julia Cooper: A Voice from the South* (Washington, D.C.: Anacostia Neighborhood Museum Smithsonian Press, 1981), p. 187.

10. Cooper, "The Third Step: Cooper's Memoir of the Sorbonne Doctorate," in *The Voice*, pp. 320–330. Charlotte Forten Grimké (1837–1914), more the contemporary of Fanny Jackson Coppin, was Cooper's closest friend among the politically active black women of her day.

11. When still a child she assisted in the instruction of mathematics at St. Augustine's College in Raleigh, North Carolina, from which she eventually graduated. Many of the much older students, especially those in the seminary, were from rural areas with no benefit of prior education. Cooper's service as a teacher of mathematics was, in effect, a kind of work-study arrangement.

The date of her teaching experience at this early age is entered in her report in Charles Johnson's 1930 "Occupational History" survey in the Moorland-Spingarn Research Center archive at Howard University.

At the other end of her life, after retiring from public school teaching in 1930, when she was seventy-two, Cooper assumed the presidency of Frelinghuysen University, where she continued to teach well into her eighties.

12. See Cooper, "Legislative Measures Concerning Slavery in the United States: 1787–1850," in *The Voice*, p. 327, for Cooper's response to Bouglé.

13. Cooper, "Womanhood: A Vital Element in the Regeneration and Progress of a Race", in *A Voice* in *The Voice*, chapter 3, p. 63.

14. Cooper, "The Ethics of the Negro Question," in *A Voice*, in *The Voice*, chapter 12.

15. For examples, see *The Voice of Anna Julia Cooper*, chapters 11, 12, 17, and 20. Karen Baker-Fletcher's *A Singing Something* (New York: Crossroad, 1994), is the most thorough, if occasionally unconvincing, interpretation of the religious and moral aspects of, in Baker-Fletcher's words, "theological voice."

16. After 1916, she built the home of her later years at 201 T St., N.W. in the District of Columbia.

17. Cooper, "The Third Step: Cooper's Memoir of the Sorbonne Doctorate," in *The Voice*, chapter 27. Paula Giddings offers a particularly balanced discussion of the personal politics of women like Cooper in *When and Where I Enter*, especially pp. 108–117.

18. Cooper, "Souvenir," Xi Omega Chapter, Alpha Kappa Alpha Sorority, (December 29, 1924), in *The Voice*, chapter 28.

19. Since it is probable that she did not have her remarks printed until the mid-1940s, the added note may have been written quite late in Cooper's life. The note is on the file copy of the "Souvenir" in Box 23–4, folder 28, Moorland-Spingarn Manuscript Collection.

20. The most thorough report on the controversy, as in many other matters, is in Hutchinson, *Anna Julia Cooper: A Voice from the South*, chapter 4.
21. Du Bois's first shot was "The Evolution of Negro Leadership," *The Dial* (1901) and revised as "Of Mr. Booker T. Washington and Others," *The Souls of Black Folk* (1903), chapter 3.
22. The most complete and reliable discussion of the 1900 incident is found in David Levering Lewis, *W. E. B. Du Bois: Biography of a Race* (New York: Henry Holt, 1993), chapter 10.
23. Cooper, "Selected Letters and Other Writings," for their letters, and "The Early Years . . . ," for reminiscences, in *The Voice*, pp. 345–347, and 310–320.
24. Mary Church Terrell, *A Colored Woman in a White World*, ed. Nellie McKay (1940; reprint New York: G.K. Hall, 1996).
25. Cooper Letter to Du Bois, in "Selected Letters and Other Writings," in *The Voice*, p. 336.
26. Cooper, "The Status of Woman in America", in *The Voice*, chapter 6, p. 112.
27. bell hooks, *Ain't I A Woman: Black Women and Feminism* (South End Press, 1981), p. 167.
28. Cooper, "The Status of Woman in America," in *The Voice*, p. 167.
29. There are indications that her foster child, John Love, when he was an adult, may have proposed marriage to Cooper and that she promptly declined.
30. Among Mrs. Cooper's papers in the Moorland-Spingarn Collection at Howard University there is a bulky file of greeting cards from friends and family, which she kept until the end of her life.
31. From Cooper's response to Charles Johnson (1930).
32. Cooper. *The Voice*, p. 114
33. The lines quoted are found in Nell Irvin Painter, "Sojourner Truth," in *Black Women in America*, Darlene Hine, ed., p. 1173. In her biography of Truth, Painter shows that the "Ar'n't I a Woman" line may well have been a later invention of Frances Dana Gage, who also is likely to have composed the dialect on the lines quoted.
34. bell hooks, *Ain't I A Woman*, p. 166, cites this passage at the crucial place. Collins, *Black Feminist Thought* (Boston: Unwin Hyman, 1990), p. 37, cites a related passage from Cooper's 1893 speech to the Congress of Representative Women (see *The Voice*, chapter 11). But neither works out the implications of Cooper's idea.
35. Ann duCille, referring to a talk by Louise Newman, seems to share the conclusion that Cooper's Christian "ethnocentrism" (Newman's word) "led her to marginalize Asian and non-Christian women," duCille's words, in T*he Coupling Convention* (New York: Oxford University Press, 1993), p. 53. On the other hand, Hazel Carby stops just short of declaring Cooper a forerunner of postcolonial thinking—"a perspective which gave insight into the plight of all oppressed peoples." See Carby, *Reconstructing Womanhood*, p. 103.
36. Cooper, "Woman Versus the 'Indian,'" in *The Voice*, chapter 5.
37. Susan Bordo, "Feminism, Postmodernism, and Gender-Skepticism," in *Feminism/Postmodernism*, Linda Nicholson, ed., (New York: Routledge, 1990), chapter 6; Donna Haraway, "A Cyborg Manifesto," *Simians, Cyborgs, and Women: The Reinvention of Nature* (New York: Routledge, 1991), chapter 8; Sandra Harding, "The Instability of Analytic Categories," *Signs* Vol. 11, no. 4 (summer, 1986); Judith Butler, *Gender Trouble: Feminism and the Subversion of Identity* (New York: Routledge, 1990). For a particularly interesting discussion of the Sojourner Truth line, see Donna Haraway, "Ecce Homo, Ain't (Arn't) I a Woman, and Inappropriate/d Others: The Human in a Posthumanist Landscape," in *Feminists Theorize the Political*, Judith Butler and Joan W. Scott eds., (New York: Routledge, 1991), chapter 5. See also Sandra Harding, *The Science Question in Feminism* (Ithaca, NY: Cornell University Press, 1986)—the *locus classicus* of this debate.
38. Paula Giddings, *When and Where I Enter*, and Carby, *Reconstructing Womanhood*, chapter 5.
39. Mossell, *Work of the Afro-American Woman* (New York: Oxford University Press, 1988), p. 61.
40. Claudia Tate, *Domestic Allegories of Political Desire: The Black Heroine's Text at the Turn of the Century* (New York: Oxford University Press, 1992), p. 128.
41. Jones, Labor of Love, *Labor of Sorrow: Black Women, Work and the Family, from Slavery to the Present* (New York: Random House, 1986), p. 104.
42. Ann duCille, *The Coupling Convention*, p. 53. DuCille errs, however, when she includes Mary Church Terrell as the daughter of a slave. Terrell was born in 1863 to parents of the black elite in Memphis. Cooper and Wells-Barnett were born to slaves. Still, in its broader meaning, the point is well taken.
43. Mary Helen Washington, "Introduction" to *A Voice From the South* (Oxford University Press, 1988). Karen Baker-Fletcher, in *Singing Something*, similarly has reservations about the true

womanhood issue but is just as affirming of Cooper's importance in black womanist thought (as she puts it). Another, recent affirmation of Cooper's importance is Elizabeth Alexander, "'We Must Be about Our Father's Business': Anna Julia Cooper and the In-Corporation of the Nineteenth-Century African-American Woman Intellectual," *Signs*, 20, no. 2 (1995), pp. 336–356.

44. Hutchinson, *Anna Julia Cooper: A Voice from the South*, and Gabel, *From Slavery to the Sorbonne* are for the moment the two leading biographies. Hutchinson's is the more complete, though Gabel's includes some interesting details omitted by Hutchinson. Many of the subsequent biographical commentaries (including those in *The Voice*, and Karen Baker-Fletcher's) rely on Hutchinson along with the archival sources.

45. Even Carby, the most important of these sources, tends to present Cooper more as a socio-logical theorist of post-slavery America than as a feminist. Ann duCille and Claudia Tate tend to understate the complexities of Cooper's feminism. Though these somewhat incom-plete examinations of Cooper's feminist social theory are perfectly understandable when the subject is the literary tradition (as it is in all three), it is somewhat more surprising when the subject is black feminist thought as such. In this respect, the most important systematic work on the subject recognizes Cooper but does not analyze her theory in spite of its convergence with the author's own theoretical scheme—see Patricia Hill Collins, *Black Feminist Thought*; compare Collins, *Fighting Words* (Minneapolis: University of Minnesota Press, 1998).

46. Baker-Fletcher—in *Singing Something*, p. 136—understands the division of *A Voice From the South* as a self-conscious use of the voice metaphor in its musical sense—the first part a solo performance, the second more as a chorus of the black community. Somewhat in the same view, though a little more convincing, is Alexander's interpretation of the voice-theme (in "'Father's Business'") as an expression of Cooper's voice as a political as well as cultural rep-resentative of the Black Woman's social position. Still, Baker-Fletcher's idea of the second part as a chorus is not without merit.

47. They threatened to fire her in 1924 if she did not return from a research trip to Paris, tried to block her trip in 1925 to defend the thesis, and actually dared to fail her on the teacher's examination that would have allowed a pay raise (see Cooper, "The Third Step," in *The Voice*, chapter 27, and the Wilkinson letter in chapter 28). She defied them at every turn.

48. A poignant illustration of this belief is found in one of her friendly disputes with her friend, the Reverend Francis Grimké. Grimké, a strict fundamentalist as to Biblical interpretation, objected to the license Cooper took in her poem on the theme of Simon of Cyrene, the black man who is said to have borne Christ's cross. Cooper had it that Simon had chosen this call-ing. Grimké, the more puritanical as well as fundamentalist, insisted that the duty had been imposed because that is what the Bible says. See *The Voice*, chapter 26, for the poem and her account of it.

49. Cooper began her studies at Oberlin at age 23, then as now, older than average. Her class-mate Mary Church, for example, was five years younger than Cooper.

50. Barbara Welter, *Dimity Convictions*, p. 21.

51. Mary Church Terrell, *A Colored Woman in a White World*.

52. The Atlanta Compromise was the speech in which Washington proposed the hand and fin-gers analogy for racial cooperation. To paraphrase, he proposed that, in all things economic, the races should be one as the hand, but in all things social, they should be as separate as the fingers. See Cooper's "Humor of Teaching," in *The Voice*, chapter 16, for her views on this.

53. Mary Helen Washington, "Introduction," p. xlvi.

54. Baker-Fletcher, *A "Singing Something": The Literature of Anna Julia Cooper as a Resource for Theological Anthropology* (unpublished Harvard thesis, 1991), p. 247; compare chapter 6 of the thesis, especially p. 214. See also Baker-Fletcher's book, *A Singing Something*, chapter 6.

55. Cooper, "Womanhood: A Vital Element in the Regeneration and Progress of a Race", in *The Voice*, chapter 3.

56. hooks, *Ain't I a Woman*, p. 157.

57. For example, in the striking passage in which she replies to a white woman's assumption that, in her experience, men of "your" [Cooper's] race "outstrip" women, Cooper refrains from contradicting the beliefs behind the intrusive question (see *The Voice*, p. 85).

58. Cooper, "Status of Woman in America", in *The Voice*, chapter 6.

59. Mary Helen Washington, "Introduction," p. xlvi.

60. DuCille, *The Coupling Convention*, p. 52, where her view on the Cooper's contradictions is also found.

61. *Ibid.*, p. 144.
62. *Ibid.*, p. 53.
63. Tate, *Domestic Allegories*, pp. 156–157. The issue here is the value of higher education. Tate is calling attention to Cooper's ability to appreciate, and use, learning, both to maintain domestic values and to criticize some black men's patriarchal attitudes.
64. *Ibid.*, p. 132; compare p. 152.
65. Carby, *Reconstructing Womanhood*, p. 101. See pp. 98–101 for Carby's general discussion.
66. *Ibid.*, p. 104.
67. The following section will document this point with respect to Cooper's literary methods, but for an illustration of it at work in her practical politics see her 1926 letter to Wilkinson, in *The Voice*, chapter 28.
68. Cooper, "Woman Versus the 'Indian'," in *The Voice*, chapter 5.
69. Cooper, *The Voice*, chapter 28. See "Wimodaughsis," that is: *wi*ves, *mo*thers, *daugh*ters, *sis*ters. It is hard to imagine that Cooper is not joking here, either by making up the ridiculous acronym or, if it was indeed the name of a club, by using it without comment. In either case, it would harder still to invent a better target at which to aim a criticism of the true womanhood values.
70. Cooper, "Woman Versus the 'Indian'," *The Voice*, p. 88.
71. *Ibid.*, p. 89.
72. Hutchinson, *Anna Julia Cooper*, p. 93. See also Hutchinson's discussion of Cooper's growing commitments to the Black Women's Club Movement. For example, Cooper's "Higher Education of Women" in *The Voice*, chapter 4, was originally a speech at Howard University before a precursor meeting of the Colored Women's League.
73. Cooper, "My Racial Philosophy" in *The Voice*, chapter 17.
74. Cooper, "Woman Versus the 'Indian'," in *The Voice*, p. 89.
75. Mary Helen Washington, "Introduction," p. xlix. Note also that, in her complaint about Cooper's use of benign descriptors for the black woman, Washington marks "cream-colored" as if it belonged to the same series as "pleasing," "sweet," "gentle" in reference to real black heroines. In the text, however, Cooper is clearly setting "cream-colored" against, one might say, the sugar-coated manners of the Kentucky secretary.
76. Cooper, "Woman Versus the 'Indian'," *The Voice*, pp. 89–90.
77. This, if I understand her correctly, is the implication of Claudia Tate's interpretation of Cooper.
78. Cooper, "Woman Versus the 'Indian'," *The Voice*, p. 91.
79. In Baker-Fletcher's 1991 thesis, the theological anthropology theme is more pronounced, while in its revision in the 1994 book, Cooper's feminism is more at issue.
80. And, in spite of (or because of) Baker-Fletcher's shift in themes in the book (see previous note), she fails, in my opinion, to stress that Cooper's voice is in fact a strategic (hence, political) voice.
81. The "Singing Something" is most explicitly developed by Cooper at the time of her 1925 thesis defense; see *The Voice*, chapter 24. Though Alexander does not refer to the phrase, her excellent essay is on the same idea. In the key passage (*The Voice*, pp. 293–294), Cooper is defending her thesis against Celestin Bouglé's idea that the democratic principle is restricted to the Northern regions. Cooper argues that it is universal because it is, in effect, the divine spark in all human beings—thus leaving open the question as to whether it is the divine or the human that sings (hence the point of Baker-Fletcher's theological interpretation).
82. Though she did on occasion. Also, her 1893 speech at the Chicago World's Fair is often cited as evidence that she did in fact, even in the early years, have the poor very clearly in mind. See *The Voice*, chapter 11.
83. Cooper, "Sketches from a Teacher's Notebook: Loss of Speech through Isolation," in *The Voice*, chapter 14.
84. *Ibid.*, p. 227.
85. *Ibid.*, p. 229.
86. Cooper, "The Negro's Dialect," in *The Voice*, chapter 18.
87. And, this too is a point Hazel Carby makes so well.
88. Cooper develops this idea in the essay "Has America a Race Problem?" in *The Voice*, chapter 7.
89. Cooper, "Woman Versus the 'Indian'," in *The Voice*, p. 95.
90. *Ibid.*, p. 96.
91. *Ibid.*, p. 100.

92. *Ibid.*, p. 101.
93. See *ibid.*, pp. 102–103, for Cooper's views on "forced association." Though its purposes are different, Cooper's idea is not entirely free of the implications of Booker T. Washington's yet to be pronounced Atlanta Compromise.
94. *Ibid.*, p. 104.
95. *Ibid.*, p. 105.
96. *Ibid.*, p. 105.
97. In language, by the way, which, not incidentally, does communicate to great numbers of the poor, like the congregants of the Reverend Pleasant Green of Nella Larsen's *Quicksand*.
98. Cooper, "Woman Versus the 'Indian'," *The Voice*, p. 105.
99. *Ibid.*, p. 108. Here, importantly, she returns to the judicial motif that appeared first in her preface "Our *Raison d'Être*," in *The Voice*, chapter 2. *The Preface* also uses "Black Woman," capitalized. That both usages appear in the preface suggests that Cooper herself thought of "'Woman Versus the 'Indian'" as the most important in the book.
100. Cooper, "Woman Versus the 'Indian'," *The Voice*, p. 95.
101. Cooper, "The Status of Woman in America," *The Voice*, p. 117.
102. *Ibid.*

Chapter Five

1. Charlotte Perkins Gilman, *Women and Economics: A Study of the Economic Relations Between Men and Women as a Factor in Social Evolution* (Boston: Small, Maynard and Co. 1898; reprinted New York: Source Book Press, 1970).
2. Charlotte Perkins Gilman, *The Home: Its Work and Influence* (1903; reprinted, Urbana, IL: University of Illinois Press, 1972).
3. Charlotte Perkins Gilman, "The Yellow Wallpaper" (1892; reprinted, in *The Yellow Wallpaper and Other Writings*, ed. Lynne Sharon Schwartz. (New York: Bantam Books, 1989).
4. Charlotte Perkins Gilman, *Herland* (1915; reprinted, in *Herland and Selected Stories by Charlotte Perkins Gilman*, ed. Barbara Solomon, (New York: Signet, 1992).
5. Betty Friedan, *The Feminine Mystique* (New York: W. W. Norton, 1963).
6. Charlotte Perkins Gilman, *Diaries of Charlotte Perkins Gilman*, 2 vols., ed. Denise Knight, (Charlottesville: University of Virginia Press, 1994), p. 520.
7. Charlotte Perkins Gilman, *The Living of Charlotte Perkins Gilman* (1935; reprinted, Madison: The University of Wisconsin Press 1990).
8. Edward Bellamy, *Looking Backward* (1888; reprinted, New York: Penguin 1960).
9. W. E. B. Du Bois, *The Souls of Black Folk* (1903; reprinted, New York: Bantam 1989).
10. Charlotte Perkins Gilman, *The Living*, p. 381.
11. Mary A. Hill, ed., *A Journey Within: The Love Letters of Charlotte Perkins Gilman, 1897–1900* (Lewisburg, PA: Bucknell University Press, 1995).
12. Mary A. Hill, *The Making of a Radical Feminist: 1860–1896* (Philadelphia: Temple University Press, 1990), p. 74.
13. Gilman, *Diaries*, p. 86.
14. *Ibid.*, p. 87–88.
15. Gilman, *The Living*, p. 78.
16. *Ibid.*, p. 141. Here she names Dora as the last.
17. Steven, Seidman, *Romantic Longings: Love in America, 1830–1980* (New York: Routledge, 1991).
18. Adrienne Rich, "Compulsory Heterosexuality and Lesbian Experience" (1980; reprinted in *The Lesbian and Gay Studies Reader*, eds. Henry Abelove, Michele Aina Barale, David M. Halperin. New York: Routledge, 1993), pp. 227–254.
19. *Ibid.*, p. 239.
20. Arlie Hochschild, *Second Shift* (New York: Avon Books, 1989).
21. Judith Stacey, *Brave New Families* (New York: Basic Books, 1990).
22. Gilman, *Living*, p.331.
23. Du Bois, *Souls*, p. 3.
24. Anna Julia Cooper, *A Voice From the South* (1892; reprinted in *The Voice of Anna Julia Cooper*, Charles Lemert and Esme Bhan, eds. (Lanham, MD: Rowman & Littlefield Publishers, Inc., 1998), p. 117.
25. Gilman, *Women and Economics*, p. 340.

26. *Ibid.*, p. 8.
27. *Ibid.*, p. 7.
28. *Ibid.*, p. 14.
29. *Ibid.*, p. 338.
30. *Ibid.*, p. 339.
31. Gilman, *The Yellow Wallpaper*, p. 1.
32. *Ibid.*, p. 2.
33. *Ibid.*, p. 4.
34. *Ibid.*, p. 3.
35. *Ibid.*, p. 10.
36. *Ibid.*, p. 15.
37. *Ibid.*, p. 20.
38. Denise D. Knight, "The Reincarnation of Jane: 'Through This'—Gilman's Companion to *The Yellow Wallpaper*," *Feminist Studies* 20. 1992: pp. 87–88.
39. Gilman, *Women and Economics*, p.331–332.
40. Gilman, *The Home*, pp. 124–125.
41. *Ibid.*, pp. 38–40.
42. Nancy Chodorow, *Reproduction of Mothering: Psychoanalysis and Socialization of Gender* (Berkeley: University of California Press, 1978).
43. Gillman, *The Home*, p. 273.
44. Charlotte Perkins Gillman, *The Man-Made World or, Our Androcentric Culture* (1911; reprinted by the Johnson Reprint Corporation, 1971), p. 260.
45. Gillman, *Herland*, p. 56.
46. Nancy Cott, *The Grounding of Modern Feminism* (New Haven, CT: Yale University Press 1987), p. 41.
47. Carl N. Degler, "Charlotte Perkins Gilman and the Theory and Practice of Feminism", *American Quarterly* 8 (1956; reprinted in *Charlotte Perkins Gilman: The Woman and Her Work*, ed. Sheryl L. Meyering, Ann Arbor, MI: UMI Research Press, 1989), p. 11.
48. Mari Jo Buhle, "Charlotte Perkins Gilman," *Encyclopedia of the American Left*, Mari Jo Buhle, Paule Buhle, and Dan Georgakas, eds (Urbana, IL: University of Illinois Press 1992), p. 270.
49. Susan S Lanser, "Feminist Criticism, *The Yellow Wallpaper*, and the Politics of Color In America," *Feminist Studies* 15 (1989): pp. 415–441.

Chapter Six

1. W. E. B. Du Bois, *The Souls of Black Folk* (1903; reprint, New York: Bantam, 1989), p. xxxi.
2. *Ibid.*, p. xxxi.
3. *Ibid.*, p. xxxi.
4. W. E. B. Du Bois, *The Philadelphia Negro* (1899; reprinted, New York: Schocken, 1967).
5. *The New York Times*, February 28, 1998, p. A1.
6. W. E. B. Du Bois, *Dusk of Dawn: An Essay Toward an Autobiography of a Race Concept* (1940; reprint, New Brunswick, NJ: Transaction, 1984).
7. See Adolph L. Reed, Jr., *W. E. B. Du Bois and American Political Thought* (New York: Oxford University Press, 1997), and Hazel Carby, *Race Men* (Cambridge, MA: Harvard University Press, 1993), for notable examples.
8. W. E. B. Du Bois, *Black Reconstruction in America, 1860–1880* (1935; reprinted, New York: Antheneum, 1992).
9. Du Bois, *Souls.*, pp. 2–3.
10. Du Bois, *Dusk of Dawn*, p. 139.
11. Erich Maria Remarque, *All Quiet on the Western Front* (1928; reprint, New York: Fawcett Press, 1982).
12. David Levering Lewis, *W. E. B. Du Bois: Biography of a Race, 1868–1919* (New York: Henry Holt, 1993), p. 513.
13. Du Bois, *Souls*, p. 31.
14. *Ibid.*, p. 137.
15. W. E. B. Du Bois, *Darkwater: Voices Within the Veil* (1920; reprinted, New York: AMS Press, 1969), p. 14.
16. W. E. B. Du Bois, *The Autobiography of W.E.B. Du Bois* (New York: International Publishers, 1968), p. 108.

17. *Ibid.*, p. 120.
18. Du Bois, *Souls*, p. 48.
19. Carby, *Race Men*, chapter 1.
20. *Souls*, p. 45. The Josie story, including quotes, is in *Souls*, pp. 45–50.
21. *Race Men*, p. 20.
22. *Souls*, p. 52; emphasis added.
23. Du Bois, *Dusk of Dawn*, p. xxix.
24. David Levering Lewis, *When Harlem was in Vogue* (New York: Oxford University Press, 1979), p. 21.
25. Weber to Du Bois, *The Correspondence of W. E. B. Du Bois/Selections, 1877–1934*, Vol. 1, ed. Herbert Aptheker (Amherst, MA: Universtiy of Massachusetts Press, 1973), pp. 106–07.
26. Lewis, *W. E. B. Du Bois: Biography of a Race*, p. 190.
27. W. E. B. Du Bois, *Black Reconstruction in America, 1869–1880* (1935; reprint, New York: Antheneum, 1992).
28. David Roediger, *The Wages of Whiteness* (London: Verso, 1991), pp. 11–13.
29. See, among others: Arnold Rampersad, *The Art and Imagination of W. E. B. Du Bois* (New York: Schocken, 1976), pp. 74–75; Lewis, *W. E. B. Du Bois: Biography of a Race, 1868–1919*, pp. 282–83; Gerald Early, *Lure and Loathing* (New York: Penguin, 1993), pp. xvii–xxii; Henry Lous Gates, "*Darkly, As through a Veil*," Introduction, *Souls of Black Folk* (1989), pp. xviii–xxii; Shamoon Zamir, *Dark Voices: W. E. B. Du Bois and American Thought, 1888–1903* (Chicago: University of Chicago Press, 1995); Charles Lemert, "A Classic From the Other Side of the Veil: Du Bois's *Souls of Black Folk*," Sociological Quarterly, 35 (1994), p. 389.
30. Paul Gilroy, *Black Atlantic* (Cambridge, MA: Harvard University Press, 1993), p. 127.
31. W. E. B. Du Bois, *The Suppression of the African Slave Trade to the United States of America, 1638–1870* (1898; reprinted, New York: Russell & Russell, 1965).
32. W. E. B. Du Bois, *W. E. B. Du Bois Speaks: Speeches and Addresses, 1920–1963*, Philip S. Foner, ed. (New York: Pathfinder, 1970), p. 327.
33. Lewis, *W. E. B. Du Bois: Biography of a Race Concept*, p. 474.
34. *Souls*, p. 3.
35. *Dusk of Dawn*, p. xxiv.
36. *Darkwater*, p. 49; emphasis original.
37. *Dusk of Dawn*, p. 268.
38. David Levering Lewis, *W. E. B. Du Bois: The Fight for Equality and the American Century, 1919–1963* (New York: Henry Holt, 2000), pp. 335–348. See also Manning Marable, *W. E. B. Du Bois: Black /Radical Democrat* (Boston: G.K. Hall, 1986), chapters 6–7.
39. *Dusk of Dawn*, pp. 117–118.
40. *Ibid.*, p. 289.
41. *Ibid.*, 129.
42. Gilroy, *Black Atlantic*, pp. 126–127.
43. Roedigger, *Wages*, pp. 111–13.
44. *Dusk*, p. 171.
45. *Souls*, p. 3.
46. *Autobiography*, p. 404.
47. Aimé Césaire, *Discourse of Colonialism* (1955; reprint, New York: Monthly Review Press, 1972). Albert Memmi, *The Colonizer and the Colonized* (1957; reprint, Boston: Beacon Press, 1967). Immanuel Wallerstein, *The Modern World System*, I (New York: Academic Press, 1974).
48. Frantz Fanon, *Black Skin, White Masks*, (1952, reprint; New York: Grove Press, 1982); *The Wretched of The Earth* (1961; reprint, New York: Grove Press, 1968).
49. *Racial Formation* (New York: Routledge, 1994).
50. William Julius Wilson, *The Declining Significance of Race* (Chicago: University of Chicago Press, 1980).
51. *Race Men*, p. 30.
52. *Ibid.*, p. 38–9.
53. Lewis, *W. E. B. Du Bois*, p. 71.

Chapter Seven

1. David Leeming, *James Baldwin: A Biography* (New York: Knopf, 1994), p. 247. The David mentioned by name in the passage was in fact Baldwin's brother. David Leeming was present at the time as Baldwin's personal secretary and friend.

2. Talcott Parsons, *The Structure of Social Action* (New York: Free Press, 1937), p. 730. In a manner that Parsons himself did not intend, analytic culture in the social sciences turned to analytic technique, while neglecting his sensitive respect for the interplay between theory and fact. Still today, in the new century, many sociologists would protest that their technologies are so well advanced that even in quasi-experimental applications it is possible to maintain sensitive control over inappropriate excesses, or insufficiencies, of attention to one or more categorized variables. Still, even those with high confidence in these analytic technologies use them with a wonderful fatalism as to the prospects that they may indelicately damage the data themselves. I cite one notable comment, by a contemporary master of analytic thinking: "Multivariate data analyses are especially hurt when researchers or theorists are unaware of this distinction [between symmetrical and asymmetrical causes]. If a model employs a variety of independent variables to account for a dependent variable, some of the linkages might quite easily be reversible and others irreversible. Attempts, under those circumstances, to talk about the relative importance of one as opposed to another independent variable are even more foolhardy than they would otherwise be." See Stanley Lieberson, *Making It Count* (Berkeley, CA: University of California Press, 1985), pp. 70–71.

3. I refer to the Social Relations experiment at Harvard for which the textbook (in Merton's sense of a scientific network's textbook) was Talcott Parsons, Edward Shils, Kaspar D. Naegele, Jesse R. Pitts, *Theories of Society*, 2 vols (New York: Free Press, 1961). To this day, though many (myself included) have tried, no one has come so close to compiling the basic resources for a unified analytic science of social systems.

4. Talcott Parsons, "The Kinship System of the Contemporary United States," *Essays in Sociological Theory* (New York: Free Press, 1954), pp. 189–194.

5. The most important documentation of the pain experienced by women in the decade prior to Betty Friedan's *The Feminine Mystique* (1963) is Elaine Tyler May, *Homeward Bound* (New York: Basic Books, 1988). For the best general discussion of the problem, see Winifred Breines, *Young, White, and Miserable: Growing Up Female in the Fifties* (Boston: Beacon Press, 1992); and see especially chapter 5, on the life and death of Talcott Parsons's daughter, "Alone in the Fifties: Anne Parsons and the Feminine Mystique."

6. Judith Butler, *Bodies That Matter* (New York: Routledge, 1993), p. 168. Emphasis added.

7. Judith Butler, "A 'Bad Writer' Bites Back," *The New York Times* (Saturday, March 20, 1999), Section A 15.

8. Butler's work over many writings can be construed as a sustained attack on the analytic refinements in modern thought. Beginning with her earliest work on Hegel, she has carefully rethought the basic works of social thought in critical terms. The now classic beginning of this effort is *Gender Trouble* (London: Routledge, 1989). But see also, among works too numerous to list: *The Psychic Life of Power: Theories of Subjection* (Stanford, CA: Stanford University Press, 1997); *Excitable Speech: A Politics of the Performative* (London: Routledge, 1997); and, for the earlier work on Hegel, *Subjects of Desire: Hegelian Reflections in Twentieth Century France* (New York: Columbia University Press, 1987).

9. Letter to Francis Grimké (31 January 1935), in *The Voice of Anna Julia Cooper*, edited by Charles Lemert and Esme Bhan (Lanham, MD: Rowman & Littlefield, 1997), p. 338; and Letter to W. E. B. Du Bois (31 December 1929), *Voice of Anna Julia Cooper*, p. 336.

10. See Thadious M. Davis, *Nella Larsen: Novelist of the Harlem Renaissance, A Woman's Life Unveiled* (Baton Rouge, LA: Louisiana State University Press, 1994), for the various instances of the mystery of Larsen's life referred to in the following section. Note Davis' subtitle, "A Woman's Life Unveiled," which is a double-play on the mystery of her life but on the mystery of race as well. See also the same theme in Charles Larson's introduction to his collection of Larsen's fiction: Larson, ed., *An Intimation of Things Distant: The Collected Fiction of Nella Larsen* (New York: Anchor Books, 1992), pp. xi–xxi.

11. Here, and the following, my discussions of Manhattan in the 1920s including the Harlem Renaissance are based principally on Ann Douglas, *Terrible Honesty: Mongrel Manhattan in the 1920s* (New York: Farrar, Straus and Giroux, 1995). On Harlem, of many sources, I found, as do most others, David Levering Lewis, *When Harlem Was in Vogue* (New York: Oxford University Press, 1981) the most valuable; but also, especially on the "capital of Black world," see Nathan Irvin Huggins, *Harlem Renaissance* (New York: Oxford University Press, 1976). On New York as a global city in the 1920s, see Janet L. Abu-Lughood, *New York, Chicago, Los Angeles: America's Global Cities* (Minneapolis: University of Minnesota Press, 1999), chapter 4. For another, and wonderfully brilliant, view of New York, modernism,

and sex in the 1920s, see Christine Stansell, *American Moderns: Bohemian New York and the Creation of a New Century* (New York: Henry Holt, 2000).

12. This paragraph is directly based on Ann Douglas' ingenious rereading of Freud's oedipal theory in *Terrible Honesty*, chapters 6–7. Compare Stansell, *American Moderns*, chapters 7–8.
13. Douglas, *Terrible Honesty*, p. 232.
14. The passage is from Douglass's letter of refusal to attend a woman's suffrage meeting in Washington in the fall of 1868, quoted in William S. McFeely, *Frederick Douglass* (New York: Simon & Schuster, 1991), p. 268. The reference just above to the day of his death is to February 20, 1895. Douglass died at home that evening after having addressed a women's rights rally in Washington.
15. Douglas, *Terrible Honesty*, pp. 254–299.
16. *Ibid.*, p. 256.
17. To the extent that they were it expressed itself in the biblically based themes of the Blues. See Douglas, *Terrible Honesty*, chapter 10.
18. That Mary Church Terrell was more true to the True Womanhood ideal does not mean that she did not understand the experience of all black women. Terrell begins her memoir: "This is the story of a woman living in a white world. It cannot possibly be like a story written by a white woman. A white woman has only one handicap to overcome—that of sex. I have two—both sex and race. I belong to the only group in this country which has two such huge obstacles to surmount. Colored men have only one—that of race." Terrell, *A Colored Woman in a White World* (Washington, DC: Ransdell Inc., 1940), p. vii.
19. See Ann duCille, *The Coupling Convention: Sex, Text, and Tradition in Black Women's Fiction* (New York: Oxford University Press, 1993), especially chapter 5 on Larsen and Fausset.
20. *Ibid.*, p. 87.
21. Outside the literary study of Larsen, the complicated relationship between race, sex, and gender is increasingly well understood, mostly because of the intellectual honesty of black feminists. For a notable example in the social sciences, see Patricia Hill Collins, *Black Feminist Thought* (Boston: Unwin Hyman, 1990) and *Fighting Words: Black Women and the Search for Justice* (Minneapolis, MN: University of Minnesota Press, 1998).
22. Nella Larsen, *Quicksand*; reprinted in Charles Larson, ed., *An Intimation of Things Distant: The Collected Fiction of Nella Larsen* (New York: Anchor Books, 1992), p. 38. All references to Nella Larsen's fiction are from this collection.
23. Larsen, *Quicksand*, p.68.
24. *Ibid.*, p. 77; quote following, same place.
25. *Ibid.*, p. 111; quotes following, pp. 125 and 123.
26. *Ibid.*, p. 130.
27. *Ibid.*, p. 145.
28. *Ibid.*, p. 162.
29. Hazel Carby, *Reconstructing Womanhood* (New York: Oxford University Press, 1987), p. 174. Important to note that Judith Butler quotes this paragraph in *Bodies That Matter*, p. 175. See also Ann duCille's excellent analytic summary of the elements of the new black woman's sexuality, *Coupling Convention*, p. 87.
30. For Carby's view of the crises of representation in Larsen see *Reconstructing Womanhood*, chapter 8, especially pp. 164–169.
31. Butler, *Bodies*, p. 176. Butler's interpretation of Nella Larsen is "Passing, Queering: Nella Larsen's Psychoanalytic Challenge," *Bodies*, chapter 6.
32. Larsen, *Passing*, p. 178. All references to this novel are from *Intimation of Things Distant*.
33. On the sexual nature of the relationship, see Deborah McDowell, "Introduction," *Quicksand and Passing* (New Brunswick, NJ: Rutgers University Press, 1986).
34. Larsen, *Passing*, p. 174.
35. *Ibid.*, p. 264.
36. *Ibid.*, p. 271. Quotes following, next paragraph, same place.
37. *Ibid.*, p. 174.
38. A sampling of the best critical work includes, in addition to those already mentioned: Hortense Spillers, "Cross-Currents, Discontinuities: Black Women's Fiction," in Marjorie Pryse and Hortense Spillers, eds., *Conjuring: Black Women, Fiction, and Literary Tradition* (Bloomington, IN: Indiana University Press, 1985), pp. 249–261; Claudia Tate, "Nella Larsen's *Passing*: A Probem in Interpretation," *Black American Literature Forum* 14 (1980): pp.

142–46; Cheryl A. Wall, "Passing for What? Aspects of Identity in Nella Larsen's Novels," *Black American Literature Forum* 20 (1986): pp. 97–112; Mary Helen Washington, *Invented Lives* (New York: Anchor 1987); Robert Bone, *The Negro Novel in America* (New Haven, CT: Yale University Press, 1958); W. E. B. Du Bois, Review of *Passing* in *Book Reviews* by W. E. B. Du Bois, ed. Herbert Aptheker (Millwood, NY: Krauss-Thompson, 1977), p. 137.

Ann duCille puts Irene in the stronger role. Butler, McDowell, Claudia Tate, and Hortense Spillers focus on Clare. Ann duCille sees Irene as the ambivalent protector of domestic order. Butler and McDowell, though for different reasons, make Clare the projective expression of the true woman's desires. Then there is the question of Larsen's craft—apart from, and in addition to, her thinking. Tate is "unable to determine" the cause of Clare's fall, thus raising the question of the book's literary indeterminacy. McDowell, however, views the indeterminacy as a literary means for conveying the ambiguity of Larsen's idea of the black woman herself—a view that circles around to duCille's. Butler, who tends to agree with McDowell on this, raises the ante by distinguishing the sociological level of the story (presented by Carby and Mary Helen Washington) from the psychological (Tate, Wall, McDowell).

And to complicate the picture, men who have commented on *Passing* tend to be put off by the ambiguity of the plot: "perfunctory and entirely unsatisfactory" (Huggins, *Harlem Renaissance*, p. 160); "artificial" (Lewis, *When Harlem*, p. 235); "false and shoddy" (Bone, *Negro Novel*, p. 102). But, by contrast, Du Bois considered *Passing* "one of the finest novels of the year." Curiously, one chooses to ignore *Passing* altogether in favor of *Quicksand*, thus in a way to finesse the issue; see J. Martin Favor, "A Class of Birthrights: Nella Larsen, the Feminine, and African American Identity," *Authentic Blackness* (Durham, NC: Duke University Press, 1999), pp. 81–110.

39. Butler, *Bodies*, pp.176–185. The observation on Larsen's use of "queering," and much of my interpretation here, are directly from or heavily influenced by Butler.
40. Larsen, *Passing*, p. 259. Quote following, same place.
41. Butler, *Bodies*, pp. 176–178; in particular the following passage, page 176: "Conversations in *Passing* appear to constitute the painful, if not repressive, surface of social relations. It is what Clare withholds in conversation that permits her to 'pass'; and when Irene's conversation falters, the narrator refers to the sudden gap in the surface of the language as 'queer' or as 'queering.' At the time, it seems, 'queer' did not yet mean homosexual, but it did encompass an array of meanings associated with the deviation from normalcy which might well include the sexual."
42. Ann duCille, *Coupling Convention*, p. 84. McDowell (Introduction, p. xiii) takes a similar view, though she tends to be less affirming of the "daring" of Larsen and the others.

Chapter Eight

1. Derrida, *"La Différence,"* *Théorie d'ensemble* (Paris: Editions de Seuil/Collection Tel Quel, 1968); reprinted in *Marges de la Philosophie* (Paris: Editions de Minuit, 1972), p. 6.
2. Hence, to say "Derrida is still alive." is to mean to say what truly cannot be said: that he is "present" in the current time. This, of course, is a foolish saying because the "being-present" to me of anyone, including Derrida (in whose presence I have never knowingly been, not once), is always at a distance. However thin or thick that distancing space is—whether passable in an instant or in the duration necessary to cross an ocean or more—the alleged presence of another is always, and necessarily, deferred. Hence, *différance*. It is impossible, thus, to speak of "being-present" without meaning to discuss the simultaneity of time's space. Even if "Derrida" is a fictional character, meant to be thought of as currently alive in the time of my reading about him, he cannot be, at any negotiable present, here with me. Hence, further, the irony that fictional characters stand a better, but still futile, chance of being-present.

Even if a nonfictional Derrida were, at the moment, "here" in the sense of "in my vicinity," he would not likely be present to or with me. Imagine, if you will, that he were "here" in the sense of being in my vicinity, perhaps "at" my home. Were he, he would not be here, where I "am." I am in my study, writing. He might be elsewhere in my vicinity, perhaps chatting with my twenty-month-old daughter, who, at present, is in her room. They would have some important things to discuss. Both are exiles of a sort. Plus which, at her not quite verbal stage, Anna speaks somewhat in the loose manner that Derrida would respect. She is capable of uttering open-ended phrases without verbs. "Dad-dy, I . . . uhn . . . up." This can mean any number of things. Its precise meaning is determined by accompanying gestures of various kinds (pointings, arm wavings, hand takings, and the like). She may mean, "I want to be up on your lap" (+arm waving). Or, "I want to be upstairs listening to music" (+hand-tak-ing). Or, "I want my tricycle to be up in the family room" (+pointing). "Dad-dy, I . . . uhn . . . up." (Or, sometimes: "I . . . uhn . . . Dad-dy . . . up." Pronounced: "Aah..uhn.. Daay-dee..uup.") You see how the omission of variants of the verb "to be" reflects a late pri-mary process suspicion of the fixedness of things in Being. She is putting an "X" through her "Is"-es.

Anyhow, were Derrida "here," he might be chatting with Anna since I am writing at the moment. He would be "here" only in a loose, even metaphoric sense. But suppose a friend (say, Patricia Clough) were to call. I, speaking loosely, would likely say: "Patricia, you won't believe it, but Derrida is here." This would not be accurate since he would actually be only in the vicinity, not immediately here. Patricia might say, however, "If he is, let me speak to him." Since he is reputed to be a very obliging man, Derrida would surely come to the phone if told that Patricia wants to speak—that is, to "be"—with him. Still, she would have to wait some few minutes for him to come to the phone. (Anna does not readily allow people she likes to leave her presence.) When and if, in due time, Derrida came to my study to pick up the phone, he would still not be "present" to Patricia as they spoke. He would not even be literally present to me were he to hang up the phone and say, perhaps, "*Alors, Charles, com-ment-ça va?*" Even that question, which is intended to have the effect of putting the two of us in the same presence, does not achieve its purpose. No saying, no writing, no utterance can put us where we are meant to "be" when the intention is that of "being present." Even in speech between two currently living face-to-face characters, there is always a pause, even when the respondent has a reply at the ready.

I know. This is tedious. One must wait too long for its "meaning."

But what are we to do, if we are to talk about that which can never truly be spoken about in so many words? We must, in short, put an X through words we are forced to use. (If not, "must," then at least we "ought" in the loose ethical sense of the word.) We ought, that is, to speak as if we were writing. Writing (including, one supposes, Anna's context-bound gestures) is the only form of utterance in which we can see the X's,—or the silent "*a*" in *différance*,—or, the deferrals across space of the desire to be present with all those others, close and remote, with whom we can never be present.

3. "Structure, Sign and Play in the Discourse of the Human Sciences," *Writing and Difference*, translated by Alan Bass (Chicago: University of Chicago Press, 1978), pp. 278–294, was originally a lecture delivered on October 21, 1966, at the International Colloquium on Critical Languages and the Sciences of Man at Johns Hopkins University in Baltimore. "Freud and the Scene of Writing," *Writing and Difference*, pp. 196–231, was originally a lec-ture at the Institut de Psychanalyse, Paris; whereafter it appeared first in France in *Tel Quel*, no. 26, 1966. Also, Derrida, *Speech and Phenomena*, translated by David Allison (1967; reprinted, Evanston, IL: Northwestern University Press, 1973). Also from these two years, *Of Grammatology*, translated by Gayatri Chakravorty Spivak (1967, reprinted: Baltimore, MD: Johns Hopkins University Press, 1974).

4. Derrida was not the only one to contemplate the odd, if different, juxtaposition of psycho-analysis. Foucault took a similar liberty in his concluding comments to *Les mots et les choses* (Paris: Editions Gallimard), 1966.

5. See Christopher Norris, *Derrida* (Cambridge, MA: Harvard University Press, 1987), pp. 11–17.

6. In a strange footnote of reality upon text, the principal architect of the New York Jets' foot-ball team defense, Bill Belichick, resigned on January 4, 2000, the day after his mentor Bill Parcells resigned as head coach in order, it seems, to give Belichick the head coach job. Parcells wanted, perhaps, to prevent Belichick from taking a job with another team whose owner tried, three years before, to prevent Parcells from leaving his team to coach the Jets. No one knows why Belichick resigned on his first day on the job. Some think it was so that he could get out from under the pressure of his mentor, Parcells. Others think it was to take the job Parcells had left with the other team. In any case, whatever it was, in fact, going on on that particular field of dreams was never, and never could be, completely present and can only be supposed—which, it turns out, is the principal purpose of sports talk radio in the U.S.

7. With rare exceptions, writings on Du Bois refer narrowly to *Souls*. For example: Hazel Carby, *Race Men* (Cambridge, MA: Harvard University Press, 1998), pp. 9–44; Paul Gilroy,

The Black Atlantic: Modernity and the Double Consciousness (Cambridge, MA: Harvard University Press, 1993), pp. 111–145. Even the sweeping commentary on Du Bois's politics by Adolph Reed, *W. E. B. Du Bois and American Political Thought* (New York: Oxford University Press, 1997) makes no reference to *Black Reconstruction*, while offering a detailed exposition of *Souls*.

8. I realize the extreme nature of this claim. Still, it bears consideration if only because Derrida's relation to Nietzsche turns importantly (if not exclusively) on the idea that the only positive science of social things is one that issues from a study of absences. Derrida's contribution to social thought thus turns on his discovery of a middle passage between Saussure and Freud that makes Nietzsche's sociology of morals thinkable as a social theory—that allows language to serve at once as the medium and object of social studies. Curiously, save for Gilles Deleuze and of course Michel Foucault, few others attempted anything like an explicitly sociological investigation. When they did, as in the famous case of Roland Barthes's early semiological researches, they took an aggressively structuralist line, making them vulnerable to the criticism Derrida directed at Lévi-Strauss. Even Foucault suffered an odd sort of structuralist lapse in works like *Les mots et les choses* (1966) which in a fashion broke the developing line from *Naissance de la clinque* (1963) to *Surveillir et punir* (1975). In any case, the test of the claim lies not in the avowal of a philosophical affinity (Foucault was famous for his disavowals), but in the disavowal of a positive metaphysics, which certainly is what Du Bois did.

9. Henry Adams was himself repulsed by what was present at the end of the nineteenth century, which did not keep him from writing about the new industrial order with respect to what it was bringing into history in relation to what it was destroying. See, especially, Adams, "The Dynamo and the Virgin," *The Education of Henry Adams* (1906/1918; reprinted: New York: Modern Library, 1931), pp. 379–390. Adams's memoir was, in fact, a medium for his final, general social theory of history, which is stated explicitly in the book's concluding chapters.

10. W. E. B. Du Bois, *Black Reconstruction in America, 1860–1880* (1934; reprint: New York: Atheneum, 1992), 713. On background to the writing of this book, see David Levering Lewis's "Introduction," Du Bois, *Black Reconstruction*, pp. vii–xvii.

11. Ann Julia Cooper, Letter of 12/31/29 to Du Bois, in *The Voice of Anna Julia Cooper*, edited by Charles Lemert and Esme Bhan (Lanham, MD: Rowman & Littlefield, 1997), p. 336. Lewis, "Introduction," p. ix, reminds that Cooper was one among many (notably, James Weldon Johnson) who urged Du Bois to respond.

12. On the 1909 AHA paper, see Lewis, "Introduction," p. vii.

13. For a summary of the Dunning position, see Eric Foner, *Reconstruction: America's Unfinished Revolution: 1863–1877* (New York: Harper & Row, 1988), pp. xix–xx.

14. "Reconstruction and Its Benefits," in *Writings by W. E. B. Du Bois in Periodicals Edited by Others*, Vol. II, edited by Herbert Aptheker (Millwood, NY: Kraus-Thomson Limited, 1982), pp. 6–22.

15. Lewis, "Introduction," p. vii.

16. W. E. B. Du Bois, *Souls of Black Folk* (1903; reprint: New York: Bantam Books, 1989), pp. 10–29 (especially 28–29).

17. I discuss this more thoroughly in chapter 6.

18. Walter F. White (1893–1955) graduated from Atlanta University in 1916. Two years later he served as assistant to James Weldon Johnson, Executive Secretary to the NAACP. During the 1920s he published two novels and won a Guggenheim in 1926, which supported research for a major study of lynching. He succeeded Johnson in 1931.

19. "Segregation," *The Crisis* 41 (January, 1934); reprinted in *Writings in Periodicals Edited by W. E. B. Du Bois: Selections from The Crisis*, Vol. 2, edited by Herbert Aptheker (Millwood, NY: Krauss-Thomson Limited, 1983), p. 727. Compare the editorial written in the midst of the crisis with the Board, "Segregation," *ibid.*, p. 755.

20. Du Bois to Walter White, January 17, 1934, *The Correspondence of W. E. B. Du Bois, Vol. 1, Selections, 1877–1934*, edited by Herbert Aptheker (Amherst, MA: University of Massachusetts Press, 1973), pp. 475–75. For the following see also the Du Bois to Board of Directors of the NAACP, May 21, 1934, and to the Board, June 26, 1934, *ibid.*, pp. 478–80.

21. The reprise of the January "Segregation" editorial in the May issue of *The Crisis* refers specifically to his support of a government funded but segregated housing project that would provide homes for 5,000 Negroes.

22. Facts following are from: J. M. Roberts, *Twentieth Century: The History of the World, 1901–2000* (New York: Viking, 1999), pp. 339–345; and Martin Gilbert, *A History of the Twentieth Century, 1900–1933*, Vol. I (New York: William Morrow, 1997), pp. 808–828.

23. References are to two of the greatest novels of the 1920s, F. Scott Fitzgerald's *The Great Gatsby* and Nella Larsen's *Passing*.

24. The book is twice as long as *Philadelphia Negro* (1899; reprinted, New York: Schocken Books, 1967) which, in spite of massive detail, was completed in half the time. The fourth of Du Bois' major scholarly works (as distinct from general histories, essays, collections, fictions, and memoirs) was the doctoral dissertation, *The Suppression of the African Slave-Trade to the United States of America, 1638–1870* (1898; reprinted, New York: Russell & Russell, 1965), which was broader in temporal scope but narrower in historical focus (and, still, shorter by a factor of three).

25. E. J. Hobsbawm, *The Age of Capital, 1848–1875* (New York: Mentor Books, 1979), pp. 27–47. See also: Foner, *Reconstruction*, pp. 512–563.

26. Foner, *ibid.*, p. 512.

27. David Roediger, *The Wages of Whiteness: Race and the Making of the American Working Class* (London: Verso, 1991); and Du Bois, *Black Reconstruction*, p. 700.

28. The connection is drawn with wonderful precision by Jeffrey Kerr-Ritchie, *Freedpeople in the Tobacco South: Virginia, 1860–1990* (Chapel Hill, NC: The University of North Carolina Press, 1999), p. 248.

29. *Black Reconstruction*, p. 16.

30. *Black Reconstruction*, p. 3. Hereafter, in the discussion of *Black Reconstruction*, the page references will be given in the text as here.

31. *Education of Henry Adams*, pp. 110–179; compare *Black Reconstruction*, p. 88.

32. Du Bois is quoting remarks Lincoln made in September, 1862—just one of many instances of this book's largely unappreciated value as a source of primary materials from the drama. Quote: *Black Reconstruction*, p. 85.

33. From *Souls* he also replicates the device of juxtaposing text (or, in this case, statements of his own) from the circumstances of "Black folk" to a high literary text from European civilization. "Coming of the Lord,' for example, ends with Schiller's own hymn of joy, "*Freude, schöner Götterfunken*," left in the German.

34. With superior naval power, the North won the islands off South Carolina early in the War. The land left by the fleeing plantation owners was turned over to the ten thousand freed slaves under loose administration of the occupying Union military. In 1862, when the Union won back Louisiana, even more concerted experiments with reconstruction were begun.

35. On the slip, if not decline, of Empire in the 1930s, see Eric Hobsbawm, *The Age of Extremes: A History of the World, 1914–1991* (New York: Vintage Books, 1994), pp. 194–222; compare Roberts, *Twentieth Century*, pp. 271–338.

Chapter Nine

1. For prominent example, see: Gary Snyder, "A Village Council of All Beings," in *A Place in Space: Ethics, Aesthetics, and Watersheds* (New York: Counterpoint Press, 1995), pp. 74–84. Compare Henry David Thoreau, "Walking," in *Walden and Other Writings of Henry David Thoreau* (New York: The Modern Library: 1992), pp. 625–663.

2. For example, The Dalai Lama, *Ethics for a New Millennium* (New York: Riverhead, 1999).

3. The odd thing about social ethics in the 1960s is the extent to which it took one of two turns, both of which had the effect of preparing the field for new thinking that only began some time later, in the 1970s. In the West, religious social ethics lapsed into a radical contextualism, which was a revival of the softer implications of Kant's categorical imperative. Philosophical ethics more rigorously pursued the reconsideration of Kant, of which the most famous example is John Rawls's *A Theory of Justice* (published in 1971 but already influential through his lectures and essays in the 1960s). It would not, however, be too far wrong to say that in the U.S., Martin Luther King's surprising amalgam of the ethics of Reinhold Niebuhr and Gandhi was the most widely important revision of social ethics. In turn, King's ideas were just one instance of new social ethical ideas that drew surprisingly from non-Western sources—notably Islamic and Buddhist. Yet, the truly radical turn in social ethics came in the 1970s when, in particular, feminist ethics began to make a difference in social thinking. See for example the essays in Allison Jagger, *Living With Contradictions: Controversies in Feminist*

Social Ethics (New York: Westview Press, 1994). (Though the essays in this collection are all much later, they all show the influence of the feminist thinking of the earlier period, of which Simone de Beauvoir's *The Second Sex* (1949) is the pioneer work of philosophical rethinking of woman's ethical place in society.) Quite apart from today's astonishing revival of ethical reasoning, the most striking, if gentle, transformation brought about by the 1960s is the revitalization of practical or applied ethics. The various works of Peter Singer are the most notorious, but see the essays in two of his edited works: *Ethics* (Oxford, UK: Oxford University Press, 1994), where he uniquely juxtaposes the classic works with selections in applied social ethics; and *A Companion to Ethics* (Oxford, UK: Blackwell, 1991), parts V & VII.

4. It would not be far wrong to say that the two greatest social ethical texts by sociologists in this period were C. Wright Mills, *The Sociological Imagination* (1959) and Alvin W. Gouldner, *The Coming Crisis of Western Sociology* (1970). Coming, as they did, at either end of the 1960s, these books served to inspire the ethical revolution in sociology. Yet, each was quite astonishingly naïve, ethically speaking. For a discussion, see Charles Lemert, *Sociology After the Crisis* (New York: Westview Press, 1995), pp. 1–11.

5. For an account of the global situation in 1968, see David Caute, *The Year of the Barricades: A Journey through 1968* (New York: HarperCollins, 1988).

6. For a discussion of the duplicitous meanings of the expression see Charles Lemert, *Postmodernism is Not What You Think* (Oxford, UK: Basil Blackwell, 1997), pp. 115–120.

7. The preparation involved both tactical and practical knowledge of the obstacles thrown down to blacks seeking to register. The freedom schools of that summer served a number of purposes, including encouraging people accustomed to years of verbal, physical, even mortal, intimidation. For the very best narrative account, see Taylor Branch, *Pillar of Fire: America in the King Years, 1963–65* (New York: Simon & Schuster, 1998), pp. 341–510. Also, among countless others, Doug McAdam, *Freedom Summer* (New York: Oxford University Press, 1988).

8. For a particularly telling account, from the inside, of Franklin Roosevelt's cautious approach to social progress, see Blanche Wiesen Cook, *Eleanor Roosevelt: 1933–1938*, Volume 2 (New York: Viking, 1999).

9. "The Negro Family: The Case for National Action" can be found in Lee Rainwater and William Yancey, eds., *The Moynihan Report and the Politics of Controversy* (Cambridge, MA: The MIT Press, 1967), pp. 39–124. This book also contains a comprehensive selection of documents on both sides of the controversy.

10. Moynihan was a coauthor of that speech. See "The Howard University Address," *ibid.*, pp. 125–132. Howard University in Washington, DC is one of the most prestigious, traditionally black comprehensive universities in the world.

11. Moynihan, "The Negro Family," *ibid.*, pp. 47–48.

12. Johnson, "Howard Address," *ibid.*, pp. 131–32.

13. David Remnick, *King of the World* (New York: Vintage, 1998). See also, Nick Tosches, *The Devil and Sonny Liston* (Boston: Little, Brown, 2000); and Gerald Early, ed., *The Muhammad Ali Reader* (New York: Weisbach/William Morrow, 1998). These are among the many, many sources for the discussion following.

14. Observation of Ferdi Pachecho, a trusted member of Ali's entourage at the time. Quoted in Remnick, *King of the World*, p. 165. On Ali's relations with Malcolm and the Nation of Islam, *ibid.*, chapter 9. Compare Alex Haley, *The Autobiography of Malcolm X* (New York: Ballantine, 1965), pp. 332–337.

15. United States Congress, Joint Economic Committee, *Unemployment and Manpower Problems: Implications of the Report of The National Advisory Commission on Civil Disorders* (Washington: Govt. Printing Office, 1968) The Commission was chaired by Governor Otto Kerner of Illinois.

16. Malcolm X, "Ballot or the Bullet," in George Breitman, ed., *Malcolm X Speaks* (New York: Pathfinder Press, 1965), pp. 25–44.

17. *Ibid.*, pp. 25–6.

18. On the transformation of King's thinking, see his later writings, notably: Martin Luther King, Jr., *Where Do We Go From Here? Chaos or Community* (Boston: Beacon Press, 1967), which includes his response to Malcolm and the Black Power movement in SNCC (chapter 2). See also Michael Eric Dyson, *I May Not Get There with You: The True Martin Luther King, Jr.* (New York: Touchstone Books, 2001).

19. Robert Lipsyte, quoted in Remnick, *King of the World*, p. 287. Compare Lipsyte, "'I Don't Have to Be What You Want Me to Be' Says Muhammad Ali," *Muhammad Ali Reader*, pp. 90–100.

20. Since its publication, Avery Gordon's *Ghostly Matters* (Minneapolis: Univeristy of Minnesota Press, 1997) has become the *locus classicus* of, in the words of its subtitle, *Haunting and the Sociological Imagination*.

21. Fanon, *The Wretched of the Earth* (1963; reprinted: New York: Grove Press, 1968), p. 37.

22. Aimé Césaire, *Discourse on Colonialism* (1955; reprinted: New York: Monthly Review Press, 1972), p. 61. The key word, of course, is "nationalities"—plural! It would be a good many years before the term "multiculturalism" would come into play. But this, clearly, is what Césaire meant.

23. The year 2020 is somewhat, but only somewhat, arbitrary. That is the year when world population growth either will or will not level off. If it does not, the *worst* case scenario is one in which within the century following, the world's population could grow to as much as 700 billion, of which only 1.6 billion would live in the so-called developed areas. (This astonishing number is based on 1990 fertility rates, which have declined since.) See Joel Cohen, *How Many People Can the Earth Support?* (New York: W.W. Norton, 1995), p. 139. Even in the next to *best* case scenario allowed by United Nation's predications, world population would settle at a level slightly above the current approximately 6 billion (*ibid.*, p. 141). At current levels, by all measures, the mal-distribution of societal goods between the world's well off and the poor is at subhuman standards for the vast majority. See Christopher Flavin, "Rich Planet, Poor Planet," *State of the World 2001*, Lester R. Brown *et al.*, eds. (New York: Worldwatch/W. W. Norton, 2001), pp. 3–20. The racial crossover year, when traditionally white societies of the European Diaspora become predominantly non-white, is now likely to be well before 2020. In the U.S. this may be achieved by 2005 by some estimates.

24. Dreams, including dreams of revising the social world at hand, have long been known for their association with times of social crisis among the most poor. See Norman Cohn, *Pursuit of the Millennium* (New York: Oxford University Press, 1970).

25. For Rawls' reconsideration after *Theory of Justice*, see *The Law of Peoples* (Cambridge, MA: Harvard University Press, 1999) and *Justice as Fairness* (Harvard University Press, 2001).

26. See, in particular, *The Law of Peoples*.

27. On Taylor, see chapter 2, above; on Habermas, see chapter 3, above.

28. My discussion of Derrida in Chapter 8 is admittedly too playful for the present point. Hence the value of Du Bois to such an interpretation—he having been, I try to show, Derridean before the fact by the necessity of having to live in and interpret the race of time.

29. I come to Nancy Fraser later in this chapter.

30. Rorty, *Achieving Our Country* (Cambridge, MA: Harvard University Press, 1998), pp. 17–18.

31. Notably, *Philosophy and the Mirror of Nature* (Princeton, NJ: Princeton University Press, 1979) and *Contingency, Irony, and Solidarity* (Cambridge, UK: Cambridge University Press, 1989).

32. This argument about religion is developed more fully in Charles Lemert, "The Might Have Been and Could Be of Religion in Social Theory," *Sociological Theory* 17/3 (November 1999): 240–264.

33. Rudolph Otto, *The Idea of the Holy* (New York: Oxford University Press, 1957), especially chapter 6 in which Otto describes the fifth element of the *mysterium tremendum*.

34. Tillich, *The Courage to Be* (New Haven, CT: Yale University Press, 1952), p. 190. See also his famous definition of ethical courage: "The courage to be is the ethical act in which man affirms his own being in spite of those elements of his existence which conflict with his essential self affirmation" (*ibid.*, p. 3). Tillich, by the way, is the only theologian who, so far as I know, has been published by a major sociological journal: Tillich, "Protestantism in the Present World-Situation," *American Journal of Sociology* 43 (1937), which is reprinted in Tillich, *The Protestant Era* (Chicago: University of Chicago Press, 1948), chapter 14.

35. Harold Bloom, *Omens of Millennium: The Gnosis of Angels, Dreams, and Resurrection* (New York: Riverhead Books, 1996), pp. 241–42.

36. *Achieving Our Country*, p. 33. See Jean Bethke Elshtain, *Augustine and the Limits of Politics* (South Bend, IN: University of Notre Dame Press, 1995); and Reinhold Niebuhr, *Moral Man and Immoral Society* (New York: Scribner's, 1932). On Niebuhr, see Robin W. Lovin,

Reinhold Niebuhr and Christian Realism (Cambridge, UK: Cambridge University Press, 1995). And for a far more persuasive attempt to rescue left-liberal values, one that does take religion into account, see Ira Katznelson, *Liberalism's Crooked Circle* (Princeton, NJ: Princeton University Press, 1996).

37. *Contingency*, pp. 73–74.
38. For a recent statement of particular interest to social theorists, see Rorty, "Habermas, Derrida, and the Functions of Philosophy," *Truth and Progress* (Cambridge, UK: Cambridge University Press, 1998).
39. See Rorty on this issue: "Derrida and the Philosophical Tradition," *Truth and Progress* (Cambridge, UK: Cambridge University Press, 1998).
40. Todd Gitlin, *The Twilight of Common Dreams* (New York: Henry Holt, 1994) and Alan Wolfe, *One Nation After All* (New York: Viking, 1998), which latter is to be distinguished from Wolfe, *Whose Keeper* (Berkeley, CA: University of California Press, 1989). For an example of a quasi-transcendental sociology that does take social differences seriously, see Craig Calhoun, *Critical Social Theory* (Oxford, UK: Blackwell, 1995); compare Charles Lemert, *Sociology After the Crisis* (New York: Westview, 1995).
41. I attempt to defend this line more completely in Lemert, *Postmodernism is Not What You Think* (Oxford, UK: Blackwell, 1997).
42. Of which the most important single source (apart from those mentioned below) is Seyla Benhabib et al., *Feminist Contentions* (New York: Routledge, 1995). The book is organized around four previously presented essays by the four disputants. Drucilla Cornell is the fourth, along with Fraser, Butler, and Benhabib. The book concludes with commentaries by each on the other three essays.
43. Hartsock, "Foucault on Power: A Theory for Women?" in Linda Nicholson, ed., *Feminism/Postmodernism* (New York: Routledge, 1990), p. 163.
44. Fraser, *Justice Interruptus* (New York: Routledge, 1997), especially the lead essay, "From Redistribution to Recognition? Dilemmas of a 'Postsocialist' Age." See also, Charles Taylor, "The Politics of Recognition," in Charles Taylor, ed., *Multiculturalism* (Princeton University Press, 1994); and Iris Marion Young, *Justice and the Politics of Difference* (Princeton University Press, 1990).
45. "From Redistribution to Recognition," *op. cit.*, p. 27, and discussion following.
46. *Ibid.*, p. 31.
47. *Op.cit.*
48. Benhabib, ed., *Feminist Contentions*, p. 30.
49. Benhabib's position is so grave that she is willing in its name to say the most astonishing things, as: "The fact that the views of Gilligan or Chodorow or Sarah Ruddick (or for that matter Kristeva) articulate only the sensitivities of white, middle-class, affluent, first-world, heterosexual woman may be true (although I even have empirical doubts about this). Yet, what are we ready to offer in their place?" (p. 30). What's with the doubt in the parenthesis? If true, then true. The lack of an alternative is no justification for the failure. For an alternative, see Patricia Hill Collins, *Fighting Words* (Minneapolis: University of Minnesota Press, 1998).
50. Butler, "Merely Cultural" and Fraser, "Heterosexism, Misrecognition and Capitalism," both previously cited in their *New Left Review* versions. Both of which advance points against each made in *Feminist Contentions*.
51. Butler, "Merely Cultural," p. 38.
52. In this respect, Butler's attempt to take the ground from under the socialists is as little convincing as is Fraser's attempt to reconcile all comers. Fraser, in her reply ("Heterosexism," *op. cit.*) has little difficulty dismissing Butler. One of the most striking features of this exchange is how aggression is so thinly disguised behind polite expressions of mutual respect. Butler comes just short of accusing Fraser of participation in the kind of high-minded homophobia whereby queer politics are dismissed as "merely cultural". Conversely, Fraser is obviously pissed off that Butler, in making her the only disputant mentioned by name, makes her responsible for the sins of others, like the orthodox socialists.
53. *Ibid.*, p. 37.
54. The phrase is from Cornel West, "The New Cultural Politics of Difference," in Russell Ferguson et al., *Out There: Marginalization and Contemporary Cultures* (Cambridge, MA: MIT Press, 1990).

55. And how the new left opponents of the new cultural left forget. See Todd Gitlin, *The Sixties: Years of Hope, Days of Rage* (Doubleday, 1987); for example, *inter alia*: "We strain to foresee, but history refuses to purify the results of our efforts in advance" (p. 438).
56. Fraser, *Justice Interruptus*, p. 31.
57. Taylor, "The Politics of Recognition," *op cit.*, p. 26.
58. For example: "The politics of difference grows organically out of the politics of universal dignity through one of those shifts with which we are long familiar, where a new understanding of the human social condition imparts a radically new meaning to an old principle" (*ibid*, p. 39).
59. *Ibid.*, p. 72. Notice also that *Sources of the Self* ends similarly: "There is a large element of hope. It is a hope that I see implicit in the Judaeo-Christian theism (however terrible the record of its adherents in history), and in its central promise of a divine affirmation of the human, more total than humans can ever attain unaided" (*Sources*, p. 521).
60. *Ibid.*, p. 73.
61. "Military reversals inflicted psychological wounds." See Anthony Black, *The History of Islamic Political Thought* (New York: Routledge, 2001), p. 255. On the indignity of the defeats, see Bernard Lewis, "Annals of Religion: The Revolt of Islam," *The New Yorker* (November 19, 2001), p. 50–63.
62. On necessary drag, see Butler, "Imitation and Gender Insubordination," in Diane Fuss, ed., *Inside/Out* (New York: Routledge, 1991), pp. 13–31. Butler is also, as I said, the source of "merely cultural."

Chapter Ten

1. Durkheim argued that there were four types of suicide, each corresponding to what he thought was a different social circumstance. Of the four, two preoccupied his attention: *egoistic* and *anomic*. In brief, the former was, in Durkheim's mind, the type of suicide arising when individuals are too far separated from a social group. The latter, *anomic*, arose, he thought, when the social group failed to give individuals sufficient moral guidance—hence, left them literally "without norms." The other two types—*altruistic* and *fatalistic*—were not well developed in Durkheim's book. They are, roughly the two logical remainders of the major types: when individuals obey the group norms too much (*altruistic*) and when the group demands too much obedience (*fatalistic*). I take the view that the Durkheim's attempt to isolate four distinct types was a consequence of his analytic logic. The four types are, in fact, little more than variations of the central moral dilemma of the individual in complicated social groups—when does the individual give up when the group is unable to help? See Charles Lemert, *Sociology After the Crisis* (New York: Westview Press/Perseus, 1995), chapters 2 and 3.
2. Kay Redfield Jamison, *Night Falls Fast: Understanding Suicide* (New York: Knopf, 1999), p. 73; letter quoted below, p. 83.
3. At first it would seem that either of Durkheim's two marginal types of suicide, altruistic and fatalistic, would be those more purely induced by high moral purpose. For example, as an illustration of altruism, Durkheim cites those who kill themselves upon the death of a strong moral leader or figure; and of fatalism, where he could not imagine clear examples, one thinks of soldiers who kill themselves for the sake of too demanding a mission, order, or patriotic ideal. Yet, when all is said and done, it is clear that Durkheim was a moralist through and through. He held such a high moral expectation of the social group that all of the types entail a failure of society's moral function in the life of the individual.
4. It would be a mistake to characterize Daniel Bell's *The End of Ideology* (New York: Free Press, 1960) as typical of the innocence of postwar American culture. As Godfrey Hodgson makes clear with elegant simplicity, that culture was shaped by two powerful forces: the Cold War and the Red Scare which largely swept the slate clean of what remained in the U.S. of Old Left Marxism; and the powerful evidence of American technical genius represented by the very short time it took for the U.S. war mobilization to turn the economy from depression to the world's supreme military and economic leader. See Hodgson, *America in Our Time* (New York: Random House, 1978), which remains the most succinct summary of the ideology of liberal consensus I know of. For a somewhat more nuanced interpretation, see Walter Russell Mead, *Mortal Splendor* (New York: Houghton Mifflin,

1987). For other details, see John Patrick Diggins, *The Proud Decades* (New York: W. W. Norton, 1988) and David Halberstam, *The Fifties* (New York: Ballantine, 1993).

Apart from its devastating influence on global affairs, one of the more interesting effects of the liberal innocence of American culture at mid century is the extent to which radicals and liberals alike were caught up by it. Alvin Gouldner, a deeply and ingenuously left-Marxist critical theorist, came just short of praising the technical reason of the new class of corporate and engineering leaders as the best critical hand dealt us in the postwar era. See Gouldner, *The Future of Intellectuals and the Rise of the New Class* (New York: Seabury Press, 1979). For a mildly vexed liberal statement by a prominent sociologist of the enduring American naiveté with respect to the good society, see Robert Bellah et al., *The Good Society* (New York: Knopt, 1991). By contrast, Daniel Bell's position is far less sanguine, especially in his *Cultural Contradictions of Capitalism* (New York: Basic Books, 1976). By the mid-1990s the entire discussion began to seem quaintly out of date, which it was from the first.

5. The final nail in the coffin of the War on Poverty was President Bill Clinton's irresponsible signing in 1996 Welfare Reform Act the title of which told the truth of its conservative, anti-welfare intents, "Personal Responsibility and Economic Relief." But the War of Poverty was stillborn in that President Lyndon Johnson's folly in Vietnam, begun in the same year as the assault on poverty, led to his leaving the presidency, which in turn ushered in a series of conservative Republican and flawed liberal Democratic administrations through the end of the twentieth century.

6. Emile Durkheim and Marcel Mauss, *Primitive Classifications* (Chicago: The University of Chicago Press, 1963), p. 21; compare p. 61.

7. In addition to Freud's, and still the greatest, sustained work on dreams, *The Interpretation of Dreams*, the most succinct summary of the elements of dream language is his short primer on psychoanalysis, *An Outline of Psychoanalysis* (1940; reprint, New York: W. W. Norton, 1949), especially chapter 5.

Index

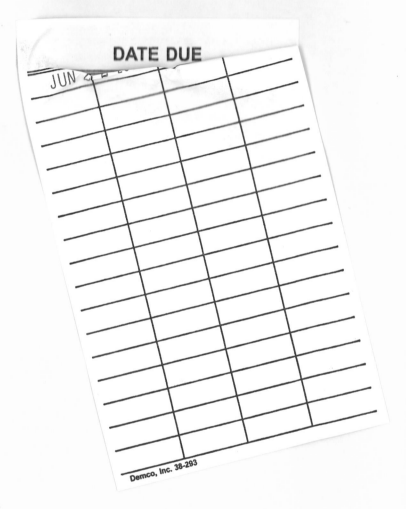

DATE DUE

JUN 2 7

Demco, Inc. 38-293